PHOENIX

PHOENIX

A FATHER, A SON,
AND THE RISE OF ATHENS

DAVID STUTTARD

Harvard University Press

CAMBRIDGE, MASSACHUSETTS

LONDON, ENGLAND

2021

Library of Congress Cataloging-in-Publication Data

Names: Stuttard, David, author.
Title: Phoenix : a father, a son, and the rise of Athens / David Stuttard.
Description: Cambridge, Massachusetts : Harvard University Press, 2021. |
Includes bibliographical references and index.
Identifiers: LCCN 2020042727 | ISBN 9780674988279 (cloth)
Subjects: LCSH: Miltiades, approximately 550–489 B.C. | Cimon,
approximately 450 B.C. | Marathon, Battle of, Greece, 490 B.C. |
Salamis, Battle of, Greece, 480 B.C. | Greece—History—Persian Wars,
500–449 B.C. | Greece—History—Athenian supremacy, 479–431 B.C. |
Athens (Greece)—History.
Classification: LCC DF226.M5 S78 2021 | DDC 938/.5030922—dc23
LC record available at https://lccn.loc.gov/2020042727

To my wife, Emily-Jane, and my mother, Kate;
and in memory of my father, Philip, in whose company
I first encountered Cimon and Miltiades.

CONTENTS

Maps ix

The Philaid Family xv

Introduction: Out of the Ashes 1

I INHERITANCE

1 Ancestors 13

2 When the Persians Came 40

3 Trials of Strength 64

II ATHENA'S BRIDLE

4 Between Two Wars 93

5 Dedication 120

6 Firestorm 145

III STRENGTHS OF MEN

7 Hegemon 173

8 Securing Athens 196

9 'I Am Eurymedon' 219

IV PERIPATEIA

10 Earthquake 245

11 Aftershock 266

12 At the Right Hand of Zeus 289

Timeline 315

Glossary 321

Notes 323

Acknowledgements 371

Map and Illustration Credits 373

Index 375

MAPS

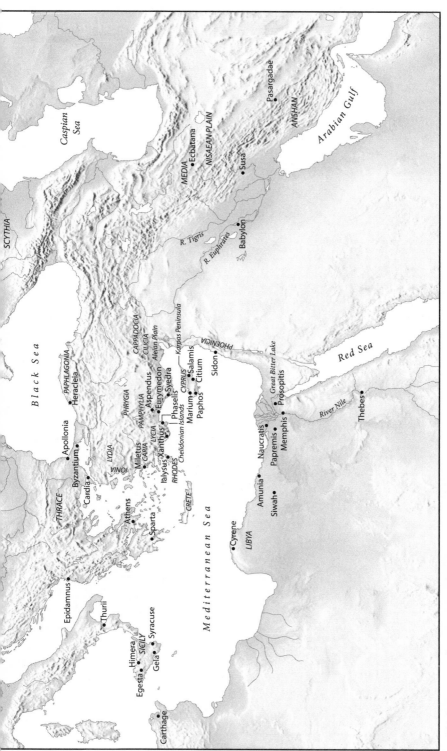

The Eastern Mediterranean and Western Persian Empire

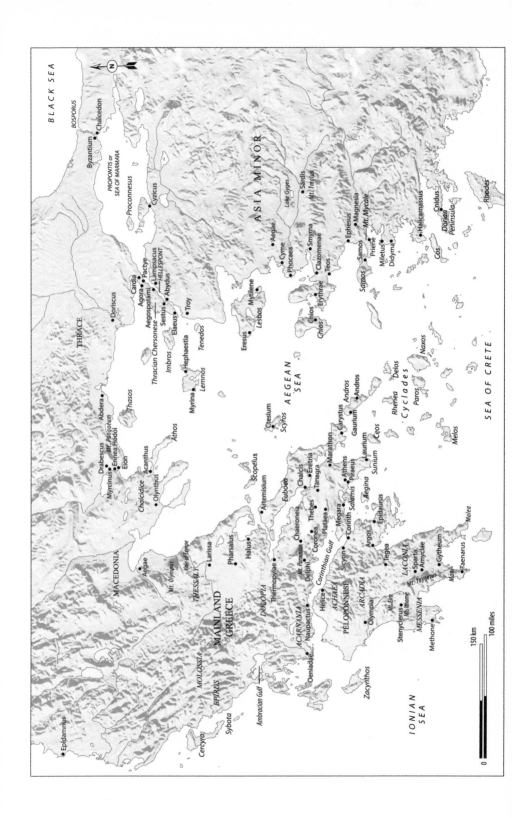

Greece: Eastern Central Mainland and North-east Peloponnese

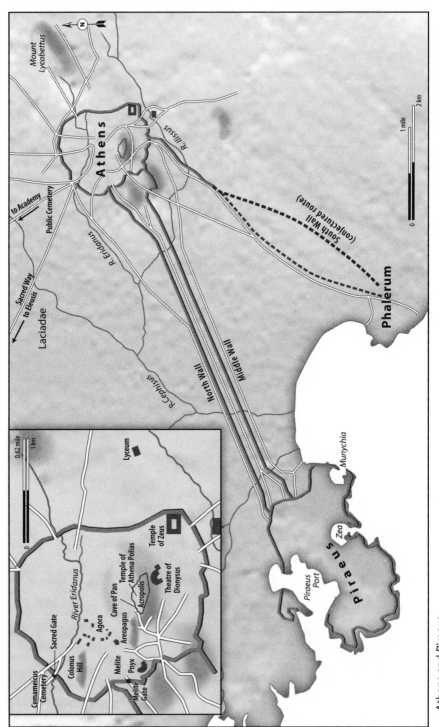

Athens and Piraeus

The Philaid Family

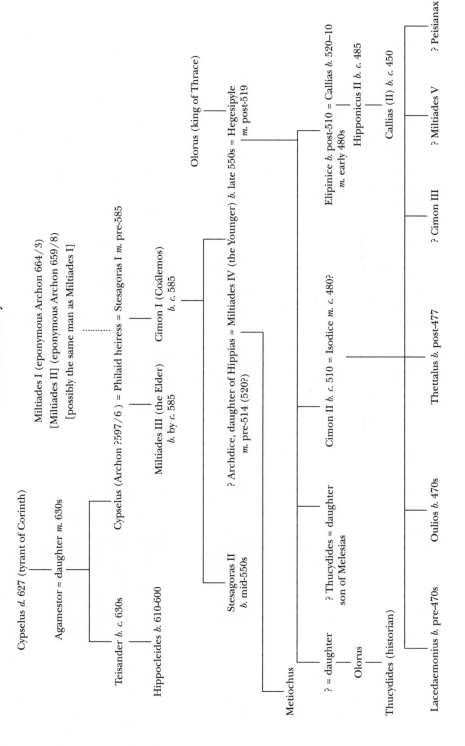

PHOENIX

INTRODUCTION

Out of the Ashes

phoenix: 1. a legendary bird that rose from the ashes
of its own immolation
2. a person of outstanding qualities

ATHENS, 480 B.C.

With every day that passes, tensions ratchet higher. For months the news
has been apocalyptic: a vast army, rumoured to be a million men strong,
assembling across the sea, drawn from every nation of the Persian Empire; troops on the march, so many they drink rivers dry; a fleet of warships, synchronised to shadow them at sea, gliding like sharks up past
the coast of Asia, hugging Thracian shores, turning their prows south-
wards for the kill.

A delegation of Athenians has recently returned with news from
Apollo's oracle at Delphi that is both chilling and perplexing: Ares,
god of war will shatter many high-towered citadels and torch the sanctuaries of gods, who even now 'stand sweating, trembling in fear as over
rooftops black blood surges'. Athens will fall, yet hope remains: her
people have been granted one 'inviolable stronghold', their 'wooden
wall'; trust this and Athens will be saved.[1]

But which wall does Apollo mean? Opinion is divided. Some—older
men, the more conservative—maintain it is the stockade built around
the heights of the Acropolis, Athena's sacred rock, the stony heart of
Athens. But others propose a radically different view. For them the
wooden wall is Athens' fleet, 200 state-of-the-art triremes newly built,
the latest thing in naval technology, their rowing benches manned by
no fewer than 34,000 poorer citizens. There are many rich aristocrats

who view this navy with distrust, who fear the People's power, who might prefer to take their chances with the Persians rather than see themselves indebted to the urban poor.

As arguments rage, tempers flare; and with fear comes paralysis. The Persian hordes are pressing ever closer. Yet Athens remains divided. No-one can galvanise her citizens to act—until one morning in the dusty sun-baked Agora, the city square, the usually loud, jostling crowds part and a hush descends as all eyes turn to watch an unexpected, curious procession: a handful of the richest young Athenians dressed in their finest robes, their curling hair glistening with oil, expressions solemn and determined, following the sacred route of annual processions in Athena's honour; and at their head the son of one of their most famous former generals.

Their interest piqued, some onlookers follow them, then more, until a crowd is filing up the slope, up past the Hill of Ares, then up the ramp that leads to the Acropolis. As they emerge onto the rock they see ahead the scaffolding around the half-built temple, conceived as a thank-offering to Athena for her help a decade earlier, when they defeated the last wave of Persian invaders in their famous victory at Marathon. But it is to another temple that the young men are now heading: the Temple of Athena Polias, Athena who Protects the City, home to the most sacred icon in all Athens, a less-than-life-size statue of the goddess hewn from olive wood, which centuries before fell from the skies.

With great solemnity, the young men near the temple's massive doors, beside which in the portico an old priestess is drowsing in the shade. Then, her permission granted, they enter the dark, incense-laden sanctum. And it is here, as crowds watch mesmerised beyond the marble threshold, that their leader makes his offering. A brilliant young caval-ryman, he has been carrying his horse's bridle in his hands. Now, in-toning prayers, he first presents it to the statue's gaze then lays it at its feet, so that it lies, its metal fittings gleaming in the lamplight, beside the hem of the well-pleated dress in which Athena's body has been swathed, its fabric woven with a scene of gods and giants in battle.

His offering made, his gesture seen, the young man turns and strides outside—back down from the Acropolis towards the city gates, and on down to the sea, where the newbuilt trireme fleet lies drawn up at Piraeus harbour. And the people follow him. Racing against time, women, children and the very old are ferried across the Saronic Gulf to safety, while men of fighting age complete final training exercises at the oars. For suddenly the mood has swung. The decision has been made. They will put their faith in the wooden walls—of their triremes. They will abandon Athens if they must and fight the Persians at sea. And they will defeat them.

Athens' evacuation and the determination of her citizens to fight the Persians at sea, one of the most significant decisions in Greek (and, possibly, world) history, were prompted perhaps more than anything by this dedication of a bridle to Athena. The young man who made it, and so showed that he, an aristocrat, a member of the horse-owning elite, was prepared to trust the democratic navy, would emerge as one of the most important figures in the growth of Athens' power: Cimon, son of Miltiades, the general who ten years earlier had led his men to victory at Marathon. While the city was indeed overrun, and her sanctuaries—including the great Temple of Athena Polias—destroyed, within days the Greeks had smashed the Persian fleet at Salamis; within a year they had driven the invaders from their soil; and two years later Cimon himself was leading a new Greek alliance in a string of dazzling victories that culminated at the Battle of Eurymedon, when his troops routed both the Persian army and its navy, to claim the Aegean Sea, its islands and its eastern coast for Athens and so lay the foundations of the Athenian Empire.

Today, however, although many know Miltiades as the hero of Marathon, his wider role in Athenian history remains for the most part obscure, while, despite his crucial role in saving Athens and establishing her empire, outside the world of classicists and ancient historians Cimon has been largely forgotten. Although his name invariably appears in books about the rise of Athens or the city's so-called Golden Age, for many non-specialists he remains an obscure figure, his reputation eclipsed by that of Pericles, his nemesis, or other generals and politicians, such as Themistocles and Aristides, with whom his life overlapped. Even when Cimon *is* mentioned, it is invariably as the epitome of conservatism, the representative of the reactionary elite, against whom Pericles and Ephialtes had to fight to hone their glorious democracy, as if it was only with his ostracism or death that the Athenian enlightenment could truly shine.

The fault lies partly in the paucity and partiality of our ancient literary sources, none of which were written in Miltiades' or Cimon's lifetimes, and all of which (for reasons sketched below) viewed Athenian and Greek history through the prism of the Periclean Age. For history, it is said, belongs to the victors, and the prime political victor in the peace following the Persian Wars was Pericles, whose father was a bitter rival of Miltiades, and whose own policies and outlook were radically opposed to Cimon's. Yet, fully to understand classical Athens and appreciate the lessons it holds for us today, we cannot overlook Miltiades and Cimon—especially, perhaps, Cimon, whose vision of a Greek world in which Athens and Sparta enjoyed an equal, joint hegemony, had it been allowed to flourish, might well have prevented the costly, catastrophic Peloponnesian War, a conflict precipitated not least by Pericles' jingoistic manifesto that saw him resort to trade embargoes, dangerous brinksmanship and international conflict in his determination to put Athens first.

If much of the history of fifth-century-B.C. Athens, then, is focussed through the lens of Pericles and his admirers (to such an extent that many still glowingly describe the years from roughly 461 to 429 as the 'Age of Pericles'), this book seeks to reposition his and his family's rivals, Miltiades and Cimon, centre stage, and consider the part they played not just in beating off the Persian threat but in ensuring Athens' freedom to experience an extraordinary cultural and economic, artistic, scientific and philosophical renaissance.

That said, the book does not pretend to present biographies of the two men—at least not in the sense of fully-rounded characters, whose ambitions and neuroses we can claim to understand. There is simply insufficient evidence to let us do so. Rather we shall use them as guides to help us navigate the greater story, scrupulously sifting what evidence we have both for their lives and for the world they lived in, and returning to them when the sources let us.

So, what then of those sources? The most immediately compelling are perhaps the literary histories, not least those of Herodotus. It is to him that we owe much of our knowledge of the Persian Wars, but while he writes irresistibly, his approach to historiography is different from our own. One of the apparent aims of his account, written two generations after the Wars and peppered with myths, tall stories and beguiling anecdotes, was to demonstrate the superiority of Greek steely independence (and especially Athenian democracy) over Persians living lives of subservience and enfeebled luxury within a wealthy empire. Moreover, his account depends less on forensic fact than on oral tradition and, while he may have interviewed eyewitnesses to many of the events that he recounts, by the time he wrote, it is likely that (human nature being what it is) some memories had become distorted by time while others had been warped by hearsay and rumour. No wonder, then, that many of Herodotus' details are so frustratingly vague—not least concerning Miltiades' motivations at the Danube Bridge and his later movements in the Thracian Chersonese—or that attempts at a coherent chronology are sometimes non-existent. Given that he ends his *Histories* in 478, it is perhaps small wonder, either, that Cimon plays only a minor role in them (he appears just twice).[2]

Miltiades and Cimon are largely absent, too, from the history of Herodotus' contemporary, Thucydides, who covers the period between the Persian and Peloponnesian Wars—the so-called *pentecontaetia*, or 'fifty years'—in a mere twenty-eight chapters of his first book, archiving events and telescoping time in such a way that it is difficult (if not impossible) to reconstruct a conclusive account of what happened in these years or even a confident chronology. Despite being probably related to Cimon (who died when the historian was a child), Thucydides was an admirer of Cimon's arch-rival Pericles, whose father Xanthippus had been Miltiades' chief political opponent. In addition (like Herodotus), Thucydides, notwithstanding protestations to the contrary, was far from impartial. He, too, had his own agenda—to trace Athens' moral decline from its heyday in his youth under Pericles to the infighting between radical politicians that in part led to her defeat by Sparta—and even his magisterial account, with its artfully constructed speeches and set pieces, and its moral of how pride leads to a fall, owes as much to contemporary ideas of drama as it does to solid fact. His misty-eyed memories of the halcyon days of his boyhood can be dangerously misleading.[3]

Even more unreliable are the historians, biographers, philosophers and orators who were to follow, each recalling an ever-receding age that, as Athenian and wider Greek power waned, appeared increasingly heroic. Despite the growth in literature, many still got their knowledge of the past (in common with Herodotus and Thucydides) through oral transmission, not least the progressively formulaic overview of history contained in the annual 'epitaphios logos', a speech delivered by a leading politician at the public grave of those Athenians who had died in battle during the previous campaigning season. Here, safe in the knowledge that no-one would contradict them or ask to see their evidence, orators would spin yarns of derring-do, blithely conflating episodes from the Persian Wars with myths of Athenian battles against legendary Amazons to create a heroic continuum linking valiant forefathers with present generations, buoying rapt audiences with a sense of inherent greatness.

No wonder, then, that other orators, men such as Andocides citing history as evidence in courts of law, would get away with being equally cavalier with historical fact. Meanwhile those with a more scholarly bent such as the author of the tract on the 'Athenian Constitution' (wrongly ascribed to Aristotle) or the historian Ephorus (both active in the mid-fourth century) found attempts to sift fact from fiction rendered more difficult by the interpolation into state and local archives of documents purporting to be copies of decrees and oaths that dated from the period of the Persian Wars, but were perhaps contemporary fakes.[4]

At least these works survive. Scholars lament the loss of histories by the fourth-century Ephorus of Cyme, Theopompus of Chios and Callisthenes of Olynthus. However, there is no reason to believe that they were any more trustworthy than those whose writings we do have, not least the first-century Sicilian, Diodorus, who used Ephorus as one of the main sources for his *Bibliotheke* (Library) to trace the history of Greece and Rome from the creation of the universe until 60 B.C. While Diodorus does include events and details of which we might otherwise be ignorant, his narrative should be approached with care, especially since his technique appears to have involved simply rewriting chunks from earlier historians in his own words sometimes in a desperately muddled way. It is especially unfortunate that his account is one of our few sources for the Battle of Eurymedon.

Contemporary with Diodorus was the Roman historian and biographer, Cornelius Nepos, whose little tracts on Miltiades and Cimon, sketchy and unreliable though they may be, are at least evidence for the interest that the nascent Roman Empire showed in them. Fuller (yet perhaps no more reliable) is the Greek intellectual, Plutarch, who, writing at the end of the first century A.D. and the beginning of the second, draws on a wide range of sources (many now lost) for his biography of Cimon, one of a series of 'Parallel Lives' that compared famous men from Greek and Roman history. Cimon's companion life was that of Rome's general, Lucullus, who likewise triumphed over an eastern enemy. Comparing the two, Plutarch wrote:

> Both were men of war, and of brilliant exploits against bar-
> barians, and yet they were mild and beneficent statesmen, in
> that they gave their countries unusual respite from civil strife,
> though each one of them set up martial trophies and won fa-
> mous victories. No Greek before Cimon and no Roman be-
> fore Lucullus carried his wars into such remote lands . . .
> Common also to their careers was the incompleteness of their
> campaigns. Each crushed, but neither gave the death blow to
> his antagonist. But more than all else, the lavish ease which
> marked their entertainments and hospitalities, as well as the
> ardour and laxity of their way of living, was conspicuous alike
> in both.[5]

For Plutarch biography was a way of exploring moral 'types', so it is un-surprising that he chose many anecdotes to suit his preconceived idea of Cimon's character. Plutarch's *Life of Cimon* is comparatively short (six-teen chapters, if we exclude the quirky and essentially unrelated intro-duction). At least as interesting and useful are episodes involving Miltiades and Cimon in his 'Lives' of other fifth-century figures, The-mistocles, Aristides and Pericles; however, historians should be constantly aware that Plutarch was not above reshaping his narrative to suit his present moral purpose. We must handle his writings with care.[6]

At least we do have these Greek and Roman authors. From the Per-sians, whose presence is felt constantly throughout this book, we have no written histories at all.

How then should we proceed to reconstruct the life and times of Mil-tiades and Cimon? There is, of course, a considerable body of other ma-terial both literary (stray lines of poetry; chance remarks in other later authors that shine an unexpected light on rituals, customs and beliefs) and physical—Miltiades' helmet, dedicated at Olympia in the aftermath of Marathon; sherds of pottery (some bearing Cimon's name and those of his contemporaries used for ostracism votes); vase paintings showing Persians and Greeks; inscriptions (Greek and Persian); and the remains of buildings (also Greek and Persian). While all can contribute to our understanding, each must be approached with care—for example, the true significance or 'meaning' of the so-called Eurymedon Vase, apparently depicting a sexually aggressive Greek and a defeated, passive Persian continues to be much debated.[7]

Because of the often scrappy, fractured nature of our evidence, it is, of course, impossible ever to create a complete and perfect reconstruction. Like a conservator in a museum reconstituting an amphora from broken fragments, we are forced to fill in empty spaces using what remains to indicate what might be lost and drawing on our wider knowledge to determine missing shapes and patterns. If the reconstructed vase is figurative, there still remains the challenge of interpreting its subject matter. Even if the image is complete, this is not always easy. When it is fragmentary, it is considerably harder.

Such is the case with the lives and times of Miltiades and Cimon. Occasionally our evidence lets us imagine the two men spotlit in sharp focus—Miltiades at the Persian bridge over the Danube or leading the hoplite charge at Marathon; Cimon reeling from his father's fine; or orchestrating sieges at Eion and Thasos; discovering the bones of Theseus; rallying Ionian allies against Persia; helping Sparta crush a rebellion of her helot serfs; or pleading to fight alongside his companions at the Battle of Tanagra—but much remains shadowy. To give examples: we do not know if or for how long Scythian incursions forced Miltiades to flee his fiefdom in the Thracian Chersonese; we are not certain of the identity of his first wife; we know little about Cimon's childhood and early adulthood or where he spent ten years of exile; and we do not even know the date of his most famous victory, the Battle of Eurymedon.

At the same time, it is not just possible but likely that at least some of the 'facts' recorded in our literary sources are invention—a forensic scholarly approach to Nepos' *Life of Miltiades* or Plutarch's *Life of Cimon* can leave us wondering whether they contain much of any value whatsoever. Equally, we should not embrace the opposite approach and blindly accept everything we read. Instead, we have to sift and weigh the evidence, measuring it against what else we know. Inevitably, in writing what we hope will be coherent narrative history for a general readership as much as for the classical enthusiast or expert, we are occasionally obliged to resort to imagination and conjecture (and when we do, the reasoning should be noted). Because of our lack of hard data, we must also employ a degree of deliberate imprecision not least when it comes to dates (though once more salient arguments should be noted). Inevi-

tably some will question the approach, but unless our subject is to lan-
guish on the shelves of academe, it is difficult to see how else it might
be done.[8]

For there is much in the lives and times of Miltiades and Cimon that
resonates through history and speaks to all humanity, and that should
be of interest to us all: the clash of cultures; refugees fleeing from atrocities; precarious democracy; politicians seemingly out only for themselves; states, nominally partners, always at each others' throats, constantly afraid that so-called allies will betray them. For what we often
call the 'Greek world' was deeply fractured. Poleis (or city-states) of
which there were about a thousand were constantly in disagreement or
at war with neighbours; even the existential threat of Persian invasion
was not sufficient stimulus for many to put rivalries behind them and
unite. To commemorate their ultimate victory, those poleis that did
manage to ally had their names inscribed at Delphi: out of perhaps a
thousand (scattered between south-east Spain and the eastern shore of
the Black Sea) there were only (around) thirty-one. The Persian Wars
were thus fought not by 'Greece' but by a ragged handful of Greek poleis and peoples. Many more such as Thebes capitulated on request,
while others such as Argos remained neutral.

But individual Greek cities were not internally united either. Athens,
since 507 a developing democracy, was riven by political faction. While
policy must be decided in the popular Assembly, politicians were often
representatives of ancient aristocratic families that had feuded for centuries. Within the city, too, there were not a few wealthy conservatives,
used to doing business with eastern potentates, who would rather throw
in their lot with Persia's Great King than pander to the People, and even
when the war turned out in Athens' favour, there were many who suspected politicians' motives—who knew what message Themistocles had
really passed to Xerxes on the eve of Salamis? Because the battle was a
victory for Greece, he claimed convincingly that he had tricked the Persians; but had it gone the other way, he would no doubt have assured
the Great King that it was his advice alone that won it.

However, while some such as Themistocles and Miltiades were victims
of faction and infighting, others seemed to rise above it. One was Aristides, later known even to detractors as 'the Just'; another was his friend
and protégé, Cimon. Yet even they were not immune. Both men were
ostracized, and, while their reputations remained undiminished by their

deaths, their role in bolstering their city was downplayed by those who came after them. The memory of both Miltiades and Cimon suffered especially from the hostile rivalry of Pericles, who after Cimon's death presided over Athens as 'first citizen' for twenty years and did not think it in his interest to promote the reputation of any but himself. To this period may already be assigned the start of Cimon's slide to relative obscurity. Yet the role he and his father played in both Athenian and wider history was pivotal, as this book aims to show. Now, two and a half millennia since he made his crucial dedication in the Temple of Athena Polias, the memory of Cimon—charismatic and incisive, handsome and personable, far-sighted, energetic, generous yet capable when need be of strategic ruthlessness—and of Miltiades, his father, deserves to rise again, like a phoenix soaring, shaking off the ashes from its outstretched wings.

I

INHERITANCE

1

===

ANCESTORS

My heart bids me teach this to the Athenians:
bad governance does much to harm the city
but good governance sets everything in proper order.

Solon fr. 4, 31–33 (West)

Mid-ocean, and the chase was on, as five Greek triremes, long oars dipping, rising rhythmically like beating wings, strained to escape to freedom. But still the sleek Phoenician warships of the Persian fleet were gaining on them, silhouettes becoming ever sharper in the golden midday haze. Weighed down with bullion and possessions and their cargoes of civilians, the Greek triremes were sluggish, unresponsive, struggling to maintain the six-knot speed that should have come so easily. Not that the captains needed to urge on their oarsmen. All on board had heard how Persians treated captives, and, as the enemy nosed closer, rumours of handsome boys castrated, turned into eunuchs while their sisters were dragged off to be sex slaves in harems, seemed set to turn into a nightmarish reality.[1]

Yet it had begun so optimistically: an orderly evacuation of the palace complex at Cardia, the Greek coastal town at the fertile head of the Black Gulf, from where for nearly twenty years Miltiades had ruled the Chersonese with local non-Greek Thracians' consent; the embarkation before dawn, Metiochus, the elder son, entrusted with commanding his own trireme, while his sisters and his younger brother, Cimon, took their places on the other ships beside their mother and Miltiades; the thirty-five-mile voyage south-west, sails and masts stowed, rowing to ensure good speed, the landmass on the port side so familiar, the coast receding to the south, before a straight course took them out to sea towards Greek Imbros, an island over which Miltiades still held control, just fifteen miles away.[2]

But as they left the cover of the Thracian Chersonese—disaster. The Persian fleet was on patrol. Lookouts saw them, captains gave the word, helmsmen turned ships, and the pursuit began. A well-trained crew could reach a speed of eight knots, and the Phoenicians were exceedingly well trained. Skimming the waters, they raced to catch the overburdened triremes, buoyed by the prospect of delighting their Great King.

With the distance between them closing by the minute, the Greeks could now make out the Persian cutwaters like long snouts tipped with lethal bronze, their bows adorned with two unblinking marble eyes, their glistening oars churning the sea white, and the low spit of the Chersonese receding like a dream on the horizon. But look the other way, and there ahead, and ever nearer, rose the jagged peaks of friendly Imbros. Only achieve landfall and they must surely escape danger. With luck and the gods' goodwill they might just make it. Perhaps Poseidon would protect them—for did not Homer tell how the sea god had once stabled his swift horses in a cave beneath these very waves while he stalked off to Troy? Perhaps he would respond to promises of offerings if they came safe ashore, perhaps if they made sacrifice?[3]

By now the Persians were dangerously close, a hundred yards or so behind the Greek ships, which were scattered in a ragged line, no care for any order—it was speed that counted, not formation. But Imbros with its cliffs and rugged coastline was so much nearer, too, luring, tantalizing, almost within reach. At last escape seemed possible. And then one of the triremes seemed to stall. As those standing on the decks of the remaining four looked back, they saw it for a moment on its own, becalmed, exposed, before the Persian fleet caught up with it and circled like a shoal of hungry sharks, before Metiochus, its captain, surrendered.

But what was happening, and why, was hard to tell, for already the distance was expanding, the Persians and their captives fading in the haze. Already the Greeks were coming in to shore on Imbros, rowers slumped, exhausted and elated, across shipped oars, the family stunned by Metiochus' capture. For the moment at least they were safe, but all knew that everything had changed. If, before, there had been any doubt about the Persians' intentions, now there was none. So, while Imbros might offer haven, it could be only for the briefest time. Very soon the refugees must sail on—to the only country with which they had close ties, now that the Chersonese and Thrace were falling to the Persians; to the only city that could offer freedom, although it, too, was under threat; to a society that to most (if not all) of the family would seem so alien and strange; to the land of their forefathers; to Athens.

Of all of them, only Miltiades had ever lived for any time in Athens, and while Metiochus, his lost son, had been born to an Athenian debutante, not only had that marriage been dissolved, her family had become so generally hated that it had been stripped of all its power, and driven into exile. As for the seventeen-year-old Cimon and his three sisters, they had been born and raised in Thrace, children of a local princess, their unashamedly patrician outlook and experience poor preparation for life in increasingly egalitarian Athens. Even Miltiades could not really know what to expect. Since he had sailed north twenty-two years earlier, his city had experienced such seismic social and political upheavals that by now much must be unrecognisable. His connections with the family of his former wife would certainly not play in his favour. So, as they sailed on south, breezes bellying the sails, it would have been no more than natural if Miltiades, until so lately ruler of the Chersonese, and Cimon, his son (and with Metiochus' capture now his only heir), were contemplating their position in the land of their asylum, weighing what assets they might still possess, considering how best to use them.[4]

Apart from the bullion they were transporting, their prime physical resources lay in their estates at Laciadae, a little west of Athens, beside the Sacred Way that led across the saddle of Mount Aegaleus towards Eleusis. With neat, fenced fields and honeyed orchards it was far enough removed from the city's hubbub to be relatively peaceful, but close enough for easy access to the centre of political life. During his master's years of absence, a trusted land manager had continued to run Laciadae with teams of agricultural slave workers, who tilled the soil and pruned the trees, looked after livestock and maintained the property, while female house slaves spun and wove and swept and cleaned, all under the watchful eye of dedicated members of Miltiades' close family. Such care was crucial—as the poet Hesiod first sang two centuries or more before,

A Roman replica of a fifth- or fourth-century-B.C. Greek bust of
Miltiades shows him as a heroic, helmeted warrior.

man's care must be 'to order his work properly, to catch the seasons carefully to fill the barns and store rooms. It is through work that men increase their flocks and wealth; through work they become dearer to the
gods.' Not that Laciadae was his only property. Miltiades also owned a
town house on Pnyx Hill west of the Acropolis in the city's Melite district near the Eurysaceion, a shrine sacred to the hero, whom the family
claimed as ancestor—Eurysaces, son of mighty Ajax.[5]

This ancestry was another major asset. In a society where every leading family claimed descent from heroes of mythology (or, better still, from gods), Cimon and Miltiades could trump most rivals—for Ajax was one of the most outstanding Greeks to serve at Asiatic Troy. His exploits blazed through Homer's *Iliad:* how he fought in single combat with the Trojan champion, Hector; how he battled waves of Trojans as they tried to torch the ships; how from the swirling melée of carnage he rescued the body of his cousin, great Achilles. And, though Ajax later turned his sword upon himself, his suicide (after a fit of madness), memorialized in art and sculpture across the breadth of the Greek world, was proof that he preferred death to dishonour—'a good and noble man', poets would proclaim, 'for there has never been in all the world a better man than Ajax'.[6]

Trace the line still further back, and glory shone there, too. Ajax's father, Telamon, ruler of Salamis, an island in the Saronic Gulf near Athens, had also fought at Troy, standing side by side with Heracles, in an earlier war to exact justice from the duplicitous Trojan king. But even he was not the first in this distinguished family to toil at Troy. Telamon's father, Aeacus, king of Aegina, another island close to Athens, helped Apollo and Poseidon—a mortal helping gods—to build Troy's walls, and, when the Trojan king refused to give them the agreed reward, it was simply more evidence of how little Asiatics could be trusted. How different was Aeacus! The son of Zeus himself (by a Corinthian river nymph), he was 'the best of men in thoughts and deeds', a paragon of justice, to whom people came from far and wide to have him arbitrate their lawsuits. Even after death he was said to pass judgement in the Underworld, one of a board of three who delivered sentence on the souls of the departed. Indeed, so potent were Aeacus and his family that on Aegina they were worshipped as divine protectors, their images revered, with sacrifices offered at their shrine.[7]

At Athens, Ajax's family was venerated, too: not just Eurysaces, but his son Philaeus. It was perhaps in the mid-sixth century that Philaeus (now dead by any reckoning for at least 500 years) granted his greatest bounty to Athenians. For a long time they had been locked in combat with the polis (or city-state) of Megara, their immediate western neighbour. Key to their struggle for security and the control of trade routes was possession of Salamis and the waters round it. But, though victory in battle went to Athens, Megara refused to concede; the war dragged on until, with no prospect of an end in sight, both sides agreed to bring the case for arbitration to the polis which at that time was universally acknowledged to be the strongest in all Greece: Sparta. A board of five deliberated long and hard, debating texts of oracles, pondering passages from Homer in which Athenians and Salaminians had beached warships side by side at Troy, and reflecting on the story of Philaeus. For he—as Athenians conveniently reminded them—had ceded Salamis to Athens and settled with Eurysaces in Attica, the one at Melite, the other south of Marathon at Brauron. It was enough to sway the Spartans, and Megara was forced through gritted teeth to concede that henceforth Salamis belonged to Athens. It was the city's first overseas territory, won by a compelling combination of argument and piety, force and guile, a powerful precedent for conquests still to come. But for Philaeus' descendants, the Philaid dynasty to which Miltiades and Cimon belonged, it was so much more: enhancing their ancestor's kudos, it endorsed their own importance in Athenian political life.[8]

It endorsed, too, Athens' general, the glittering young Peisistratus, a man of boundless confidence and dazzling ambition, who, riding the wave of victory, shouldered aside all opposition, surrounded himself with armed bodyguards, and proclaimed himself sole ruler, tyrannos, tyrant (a term which at the time possessed few if any of the pejorative associations it was later to acquire). Although in the following decade and a half he was twice ousted by aristocratic enemies, he returned on each occasion stronger and more confident—the first time thanks to diplomacy, the second when, buttressed by foreign friends, he defeated his Athenian opponents near his estates at Marathon—eclipsing every other politician of his day, thanks to the high regard in which the common people held him. For he unashamedly courted popular acclaim with charm and open-handedness, wowing his power base with festivals and games, and wooing them with fine new buildings, treating many of his patrician rivals with icy ruthlessness, while making others offers they could not refuse. Among those rivals were the Philaids, not least Miltiades the Elder (Miltiades the Younger's uncle), son of a doughty landowner and veteran politician, Cypselus, himself the grandson of the first tyrant of Corinth.[9]

In his early thirties this Miltiades embraced aristocratic life. His family estates at Laciadae boasted a fine stud of sleek horses, trained to the yoke to run as teams in chariot races at sacred games now held not only at Olympia but recently inaugurated, too, at Delphi, Corinth and Nemea for competitors from the entire Greek world. While anonymous professionals risked their lives to drive the teams, owners of victorious chariots could win stratospheric fame, since to cross the line before all others was to be favoured by the gods, to be touched by the divine, acclaimed in the hippodrome and lionized at home by fellow citizens. And at the Olympic Games of 560, Miltiades did just that, his team's victory confirming him as one of the international elite, and increasing Athens' growing fame—which cannot but have piqued and pleased Peisistratus in equal measure, as (so recently installed as tyrant) he basked in his city's glory, while sizing up Miltiades as a potential challenger. For neither was a fool, and although they found a means of peaceful coexistence, each viewed the other with well-placed suspicion. So it was perhaps fortuitous that only five years later (so the story went), in 555, when Peisistratus' enemies were planning trouble, events conspired to remove Miltiades peacefully from Athens.[10]

He was relaxing on his porch and looking out across his fields to the packed-earth road that led to Athens when he saw an unexpected sight—a band of riders, men with pointed beards, their fair hair tied in topknots, their skin tattooed, their clothing brightly coloured and exotic (tunics and cloaks in vibrant patterns, fox-skin hats and baggy pantaloons), spears in their hands and well-worn saddlebags. Intrigued, Miltiades waved them over and invited them to dine with him and spend the night. Then, as wine flowed and the time came when convention said a host might question guests, he asked them who they were, where they were from, and what their business was in Attica. Nothing could have prepared him for their response.[11]

They were ambassadors from Thrace, vast territories unknown to most Greeks at the time, that stretched far from the North Aegean coast east to the Black Sea's western shores and north to the Balkan Mountains and the Danube. But like the Greeks the Thracians were not united. Instead, they were plagued by inter-tribal wars, which was why these envoys were in Athens. They were members of the Dolonci tribe, whose home was in the Chersonese, the fertile promontory that stretches southwest from the European mainland to form the northern coastline of the Hellespont, the narrow channel linking the Propontis with the Aegean. Harried by eastern neighbours, the Apsinthians, and in need of powerful allies, they had taken what for non-Greeks was a strange and unexpected step: they had sought advice from the oracle at Delphi.[12]

Delphi was a place of mystery and power. Sited on the slopes of Mount Parnassus, ringed by cliffs and overlooking the Corinthian Gulf, for centuries it had been a centre of prophecy, where gods—most recently Apollo—spoke through a human agent, a local woman hand-picked for the task, who, crouching in a tripod in a secret room atop a covered cauldron poised above a chasm in the earth, perhaps intoxicated by the vapours rising from the rock or smoke from burning leaves and clouds of incense, babbled words that only priests could understand, and that, translated, they conveyed to anxious suppliants outside. By now Delphi's reputation was becoming international. Even Lydia's King Croesus, whose wealth appeared to know no bounds, was sending diplomatic gifts—huge gold and silver bowls and silver storage jars, a golden statue of a woman, another of a lion—in the hope of gaining high-value divine advice. For he had once set a test for a select group of oracles not just in mainland Greece but in Egypt, too, a test that Delphi was the only major shrine to pass with flying colours. The sanctuary was well and truly on the map.[13]

But as Croesus would discover, what made Delphi's oracle successful— apart from the fact that the sheer number and geographical diversity of those seeking its counsel provided its officials with unique insights into international affairs—was the riddling ambiguity of its responses. Not only did this let priests deny responsibility when those acting on the oracle's advice discovered that the outcome was the opposite of what they had expected, it encouraged those interpreting the utterances to examine their situation more objectively, and perhaps to question their ambitions. No wonder that above the temple doors would soon be carved the maxims, 'Know Yourself' and 'Nothing in Excess'.[14]

So the Dolonci must have been favourably surprised when, instead of an enigmatic answer, the oracle told them to take home with them the first man who, after they had left the temple, offered hospitality, for he would cause the Chersonese to prosper. Across the mountains they travelled on their wiry ponies, and across the flat Boeotian plain, where far-off Lake Copais shimmered in the sun, but nowhere did anyone invite them to his home. It was only as they came near Athens with the sheer Acropolis already clearly in view that they were welcomed; only at Laciadae with its neatly planted fields; only by Miltiades. Miltiades must be the man of whom the oracle had spoken. Although he enjoyed considerable prestige at Athens, to live constantly in Peisistratus' shadow cannot but have rankled. Besides, Miltiades was a man of action who thrived on challenges. Yet he was not impetuous. So he, too, made the pilgrimage to Delphi, offered sacrifices, purified himself in the sacred waters of Castalia's stream, paid priests their due and posed a question: Should he accept the Dolonci's invitation? The answer was emphatic: yes. So, returning to Athens, Miltiades assembled as many as were willing to join in his new adventure, boarded a ship and sailed out for the Chersonese, where the grateful Dolonci made him their ruler.[15]

The story as it stands was recorded by Herodotus more than a century later, but, despite the folksy nature of his tale, some kernels of hard history can be perceived. The chance meeting of Miltiades and the Dolonci is probably a fabrication, as is Miltiades' apparently nonchalant decision to accept the Thracians' proposal. More likely this was a calculated move by Peisistratus and his inner circle, of which Miltiades was probably a trusted member. To Athens the Chersonese was strategically important. As the city's population grew, so Attica's ability to feed it dwindled. There was simply not enough good agricultural land. Already, forty years earlier, measures had been put in place to curb the export of staple foodstuffs. Only olive oil, the produce of the 5 to 10 million olive trees that thrived in Attica's poor soil, could be exported—the revenue from tariffs formed a useful part of Athenian economy. But Athens was relying increasingly on grain imports, and control of the Chersonese could be invaluable. Not only was it prime farming land, its location was strategically important. Command the Chersonese, and Athens could command the Hellespont as well, that crucial channel through which grain ships must pass from the northern shore of the Black Sea. Moreover, good relations with local tribesmen offered other tantalizing opportunities. West of the Chersonese lay Mount Pangaeum, where Thracians mined for gold, and there were profitable gold mines, too, on nearby Thasos. To a man such as Peisistratus with an eye for opportunity, the chance to intervene to his advantage in a local dispute must have seemed a godsend. So, while the Dolonci probably did seek Athenian assistance, it was undoubtedly Peisistratus who, basking in this evidence of his city's growing status, ordered (or sanctioned) Miltiades' mission, and while he may have reckoned that in doing so he would remove a rival, he must have trusted him sufficiently to be confident that he would not abuse potentially so powerful a position. To Herodotus' readers, familiar with Philaid generosity, the story of Miltiades' hospitality simply added a layer of credibility.[16]

Greeks were used to setting out in ships to annex far-flung places. For well over two centuries many mainland and island city-states, faced with overpopulation, or seeking trading opportunities, had sent out boat-loads of determined young men to stake their claim on fertile coastal land from Sicily and South Italy, southern France and south-east Spain in the west to Cyrene in North Africa and far-flung Phasis on the east coast of the Black Sea. Normally they sought sanction from Delphi be-fore sailing, and usually they were headed by a leading politician, who might impose a constitution on his new foundation that mirrored ar-rangements back home, but seldom were they invited with such fervour as the Dolonci had displayed. While in part, then, this expedition was simply a repeat of many that had gone before, in other ways—not least the size and strategic value of the land concerned—it was entirely un-conventional. So, when Miltiades and his men were welcomed ashore by Thracian chieftains, splendid in vibrant cloaks and golden jewellery, who addressed Miltiades as their ruler (in Thracian terms their king, in Athe-nian their tyrant), he would have been excused for thinking that it was all too good to be true.[17]

Yet there was urgent work to do on behalf both of his new subjects and of Athens. Threatened by neighbouring Apsinthians, Miltiades first built a wall across the flat neck of the Chersonese, a distance of just over four miles. This done, he Hellenized his kingdom. Thracians tradition-ally lived in villages without major conurbations. Even rulers had no per-manent capital, preferring to progress through their realm, demanding hospitality wherever they might choose to spend the night. Greeks, on the other hand, were already people of the polis, the city-state, a tract of land whose hamlets and villages, fields and harbours were adminis-tered ultimately from a municipal urban centre. Indeed, so natural did this seem that later Aristotle defined humankind in general as 'the crea-ture of the city-state'. Little wonder, then, that Miltiades ordered the construction of a number of new towns, including not only Cardia at the north end of the wall and Pactye at the south but, between them, the market town of Agora, with further strategic settlements on the Hellespontine coast.[18]

Of course, fully to dominate the Hellespont would mean controlling its southern shores as well, which was why, early in his energetic rule, Miltiades turned his sights on Lampsacus, a thriving port at the northern entrance to the Hellespont, a colony of Athens' bête noire and close neighbour, Megara. But news of the attack leached out. The enemy was forewarned. As he attacked the city, Miltiades was ambushed, seized and taken back, a prisoner, to Lampsacus, where he might have languished had it not been for the timely intervention of a local friend and ally, the formidable King Croesus. From his capital at Sardis, Croesus' sprawling empire stretched from the River Halys in the east, south to the Taurus Mountains, west to the Aegean coast (where it subsumed a string of Greek poleis) and north to the Black Sea, the Propontis and the Hellespont—which, of course, included Lampsacus. Fortunately for Miltiades, Croesus had for many years been fostering good relations not just with Greek institutions such as Delphi's oracle, but with Athenians. Stories told how leading men from Athens found their way to Sardis, a city rich from both its empire and the River Pactolus, whose waters swirled with gold dust, and whose banks were busy with refineries. Here in his palace in the foothills of Mount Tmolus, above his bustling city with its venerable sanctuary of the nature goddess Cybele, Croesus was rumoured to have entertained the great Athenian lawgiver, Solon, not to mention Alcmaeon, the head of Athens' scandal-ridden family, the Alcmaeonids. This young tyro had so endeared himself to Croesus (it was said), that the king promised him whatever he could carry from the treasury; when Alcmaeon emerged, his clothing (the most voluminous he could find) stuffed to capacity with gold dust, the Lydian, delighted, doubled the amount and sent him home to be the wealthiest man in Athens. Now Croesus extended his largesse to Alcmaeon's fellow citizen, Miltiades, threatening the Lampsacenes that, if they did not free the Athenian immediately, they would find themselves cut down like a pine tree. It took the Lampsacenes some time to discover that, once felled, the pine alone of trees will not send forth new shoots, and so to grasp the full menace of Croesus' threat. When they did, they lost no time in returning Miltiades in safety to the Chersonese, where he settled down to a long, successful reign, grateful (like so many other Greeks) for the patronage of a powerful Asiatic king.[19]

In Athens, though, his family's fortunes were more turbulent. In Miltiades' absence his estates at Laciadae had passed to his younger half-brother, Cimon I. Like Miltiades, Cimon was besotted with horses and chariot racing, but here similarities ended. Nicknamed 'the Simpleton' (in Greek, Coálemos), he failed to navigate the treacherous shoals of political life under Peisistratus. His position as effective head of the

Philaids brought danger, for the tyrant, nervous of being overthrown, was alive to any threat. Peisistratus had already exiled some Alcmaeonids, and perhaps around 540 he banished Cimon too—quite why, we do not know. Nor do we know where Cimon went. If he wished to preserve good relations with Peisistratus, it is unlikely that Miltiades was keen to house him. Wherever Cimon ended up, it was comfortable enough to accommodate his horses, drivers, grooms and chariot-technicians. For, in 532 he took his team to the Olympic Games, where in the heat of a fraught August morning he won the olive crown; and four years later he returned to win again with the same horses. But this time, the Simpleton showed cunning, not only dedicating his win to Peisistratus but naming the tyrant as the real victor. His blatant sycophancy paid off; Peisistratus was reconciled with his one-time enemy; and Cimon, his household and his champion mares returned to Attica. 'Me, I can think of nothing sweeter than my native land', Homer had once declared, and it was hard to find a Greek who disagreed—how sweet Laciadae now seemed to Cimon, how sweet its grass to his fine horses. Yet, four years later, they again went to Olympia and once more galloped home to victory. At three successive games now they had proved their mettle. It was a record only one man in the past had equalled and few could ever hope to beat. Cimon's name and Athens' fame would surely be immortal.[20]

By now a new spirit gripped the city. Thanks to some well-thought-through reforms, Peisistratus had turned Athens from a somewhat parochial backwater to a city fit for its age, refurbishing its fabric and bolstering its sense of community and identity. A fine new gatehouse now gave onto the Acropolis. An aqueduct fed public fountains in the once-parched Agora and so made water readily available to every citizen, not just to those with closely-guarded private wells. And freshly-minted silver coins, each proudly stamped with both Athena's bird, the owl, and the first letters of the city's name, 'ATHE', would soon proclaim to all the world a burgeoning economy. Athens' growing confidence was proclaimed in other ways, too. Already in 566 when the Philaid Hippocleides was Chief Archon (before Peisistratus had seized the reins of power), the Greater Panathenaea, a ten-day civic festival, had been inaugurated, a dazzling mélange of processions, ceremonies and sacrifice in honour of Athena, accompanied by athletic games open to competitors from across the entire Greek-speaking world intended to rival even the Olympics.

Now, ever keen to promote Attica's growing reputation, Peisistratus not only did everything within his power to enhance the festival still further, he proselytized, too, the blessings of the Mysteries, rites sacred to Demeter, Persephone and Dionysus, which promised a blissful afterlife to men and women, slave and free (as long as they spoke Greek) in ceremonies held at Eleusis some twelve miles west of Athens, where he enlarged the Initiation Hall and embellished the sanctuary. In Athens itself, Peisistratus instituted a festival of Dionysus, god of growth and transformation, with processions and competitive performances of a newly-established art form, tragic drama, where, wearing masks and sumptuous costumes, with stylized singing, speech and choreography, an actor and chorus staged freshly-written plays, with subject matter sometimes based on myth, sometimes reflecting real contemporary events.[21]

Whether enriching Athens or enticing visitors and pilgrims from abroad, Peisistratus was constantly aware, too, of the need to expand his international powerbase and foster overseas alliances. To help achieve his last successful bid for tyranny, in the mid-540s, he had drawn on a wide circle of foreign friends from Argos and Sparta in the Peloponnese to the island cities of Naxos and Euboean Eretria and the fertile mainland plains of Thessaly. But while such alliances were still important, key to maintaining Athens' prosperity while ensuring citizens could eat remained the sea lanes from the east, the most important of which was the Hellespont. For the time being, Lampsacus, which had so comprehensively resisted Miltiades' attack, remained unassailable, but just south of the western entrance to the channel, Sigeum was a different proposition. Ever since its foundation by colonists from Mytilene in nearby Lesbos, Athenians had viewed Sigeum as a potential prize. For a century they had fought to have it, jubilant when, following an inconclusive war in the late seventh century, international arbitration ruled in their favour, frustrated when the Mytileneans regained it some sixty years later. But Peisistratus was determined. A squadron of Athenian ships beached in the Troad; a troop of heavy-armoured infantry poured out; battle; bloodshed; and Sigeum was once more in Athens' hands; and to ensure the town remained in his possession, he sent his son, Hegesistratus, the product of his second marriage, to govern it. The name 'Sigeum' meant 'the Place of Silence', but this was a loud proclamation to the world of Peisistratus' expansionist ambitions. For ten years Greeks of the Heroic

Age had fought a stone's throw from Sigeum, at Troy, the town that then controlled the western access to the Hellespont; now, thanks not just to this victory but to Miltiades' continuing sway over the Chersonese, Athens was tightening her grip on the entire waterway.[22]

But Peisistratus could not live forever, and in 527, already in his seventies, he died. He was succeeded (as was the way with tyrants throughout Greece) by his eldest son, Hippias, a superstitious man now in his early forties, who had stood squarely at his father's side. Now he gladly shared the burdens and perks of power with his cultured brother Hipparchus, an enlightened sponsor of the Arts, who, when not erecting moralizing inscriptions throughout Attica, was cementing Athens' reputation as a cultural hub by commissioning an elegant (if outsize) Temple of Olympian Zeus on the banks of the River Ilissus and extending his patronage to groundbreaking poet-musicians of international repute: men such as Lasus of Hermione, who composed poems without employing the letter s; Simonides of Teos, renowned both for his choral compositions and verses sung to the lyre's accompaniment; and Anacreon of Ceos. So famous was Anacreon that, no sooner had his former patron, Polycrates of Samos, died, than Hipparchus sent a trireme to convey the poet to Athens, where his urbane, witty verses seemed to encapsulate the sophisticated hedonism of court life: 'Eros, the lust god, golden haired, throws his purple ball at me and calls me out to play with a girl in raggletaggle sandals. But she mocks me for my grey hair. And besides—being from Lesbos—she has eyes only for another girl.'[23]

But beneath the civilized veneer, bitter jealousies remained, perceived rivalries still bred suspicion, and the period of transition from Peisistratus to his sons seemed to some an ideal time to settle grievances. One night shortly after the old tyrant's death, as Cimon Coálemos was walking through the Agora's administrative quarter, he was set upon and killed. His murderers were never found.[24]

In Athens, Cimon's death thrust his son Miltiades IV (the Younger), now in his early thirties, centre stage, elevating him effectively to head of the family. Under normal circumstances his elder brother, Stesagoras, would have assumed the role, but he had already joined his uncle in the Chersonese, and there he elected to remain. Indeed, the messenger who brought him news of Cimon's death may well have furnished a description of his funeral as well. And what a funeral it was. Somehow the Philaids had circumvented long-standing legal prohibitions on flamboyant lamentation and performed a ceremony of Homeric grandeur. In the early hours before the dawn, from their mansion in Melite, a silent slow procession with Miltiades at its head wound its way beside the wagon on which the body of his father Cimon lay, now washed in oils and dressed in gorgeous robes, through dark streets to a burial plot on Coele Road outside the city boundaries. Drawing Cimon's hearse were his faithful mares, their manes and tails shorn close in ritual mourning, united with their master on his final journey. And there outside Melite Gate, in the guttering light of smoky torches under velvet night-time skies, intoning prayers and pouring the prescribed libations, and with Miltiades' speech praising their heroic ancestors still ringing in their ears, they laid Cimon Coálemos, three-time Olympic victor, in his tomb. Then they slaughtered the four horses, buried them across the road from their proud master, and piled high mounds above both graves. Later they set up bronze statues of the horses, a permanent memorial of Philaid fame.[25]

It was a blatantly elitist ceremony, an unashamedly patrician statement of dynastic power. But if the newly installed tyrant, Hippias, and his adjutant brother Hipparchus saw it as provocative, a threat to their own status, they prudently turned a blind eye. They needed to placate the mighty Philaids, especially as rumours were circulating of their own involvement in Cimon's assassination. So, both then and in the years that followed, they did everything they could to woo Miltiades IV and win his family's support in Athens and abroad. Accordingly, when Miltiades the Elder, tyrant of the Chersonese, died childless the next year, they accepted without demur that his seat should naturally pass to his nephew Stesagoras, the eldest son of Cimon Coálemos. Moreover, a year later they engineered or (at the very least) sanctioned, Miltiades IV's appointment as Chief Archon of Athens, the city's leading official (before Peisistratus' coup, the head of state), who oversaw both the probouleutic Council and the decision-making Assembly which agreed or rubber-stamped the Council's resolutions. And if that were not enough, Hippias arranged for Miltiades to marry the modest Archedice, his daughter. No tighter bond between two families could be imagined, no closer, more expedient embrace. So, when Archedice produced a son and heir, Metiochus, the grandson of both Cimon Coálemos and Hippias, all Athens saw him for what he was: the physical embodiment of a strong dynastic union.[26]

While the Philaids prospered at home, in the Chersonese, Stesagoras consolidated his position. After all, it was not he, but his uncle, whom the Delphic oracle had authorized to rule the Dolonci, and he needed to do all he could to stress his family ties. This he achieved in the best aristocratic tradition by establishing and presiding over annual rituals and sacrifices, athletic games and chariot races (the Thracians were themselves great horsemen, and chariot racing was in their blood), all held at the hero shrine he dedicated to his uncle, which honoured him as founder of the Chersonesian state. However, as he toured his new demesne and gazed across the churning waters of the Hellespont to clear-seen Lampsacus, Stesagoras knew that there was still unfinished business. As long as that city remained autonomous, the sea lanes were not safe. It was his duty to succeed where his uncle failed. But his cross-channel raids provoked counter-attacks, and the situation spiralled into full-blown conflict. In Cardia, Stesagoras called a council of war, encouraged when his advisors ushered in a Lampsacene, whom they assured him was a valuable deserter. But, as he approached the throne, the man drew a hand axe from his clothing, ran screaming at Stesagoras and crashed the blade into his skull.[27]

In Athens news of his death was met with grim anxiety. Despite the continued presence of many whose loyalty was steadfast, the leaderless Chersonese was in imminent danger. There was no time to lose. Stesagoras' successor must be dispatched at once, and there was one clear candidate: his younger brother, Miltiades IV. So, with the blessing of his brothers-in-law, and accompanied by wife and son and household slaves, Miltiades boarded one of Athens' precious triremes, new state-of-the-art warships that only ten years earlier had proved their mettle in the seas off the Nile Delta, and ordered his helmsman to make course for the Chersonese. The time had come for him to assume the role of tyrant.[28]

In Cardia the atmosphere was volatile. Clearly there were leading Thracians—men who connived or sympathized with Stesagoras' assassination—who could not be trusted. But if Stesagoras, an old hand in the Chersonese, had failed to protect himself against them, how could Miltiades, a newcomer? His first days were crucial, and his greatest asset was that few (if any) knew his character. So, immediately upon his arrival, he locked himself in the palace, saw no-one, and did nothing, which perplexed his Thracian subjects. What was he doing? Was he mourning his dead brother? As time passed and there was still no sign of their new ruler, the leading Dolonci agreed that etiquette dictated they should visit Miltiades in his grief and pay respects. However, once they were admitted to the royal audience chamber, instead of Miltiades, armed guards filed in and, before they could fully grasp what was happening, every man had been arrested. It was a spectacular show of power and intent, a daring coup relying on psychology, surprise and surgical violence, tactics that would stand Miltiades in good stead in the future. But he was not finished yet. Even as his hostages were led away, the palace doors swung open, and Miltiades made his first public appearance before his new subjects—and flanking him were 500 well-paid bodyguards. He had heard from his wife and father how Peisistratus had once used a private army to maintain control in Athens; and he had learned his lesson well. There would be no more trouble in the Chersonese.[29]

But Miltiades and his backers in Athens knew that force must be accompanied by diplomacy. The stability of the Chersonese relied not only on strong ties with neighbouring Thrace, but on resetting relations across the Hellespont with hostile Lampsacus, and experience suggested that a common solution might resolve both issues: marriage. In the context of the age, it was usual for high-born women to be used as pawns in the power game of politics, traded by male relatives, wedded or divorced when expedient as public proof of family or state alliances, hard evidence of private deals cemented to meet pragmatic needs. And pragmatism now dictated that Miltiades divorce Archedice. For both must be free to remarry.[30]

Months of diplomatic talks had revealed that the powerful Odrysian Thracian king Olorus, whose lands extended west along the North Aegean coast including the much-coveted gold mines of Pangaeum, was amenable to strengthening his ties with Athens, impressed by Miltiades' no-nonsense treatment of his subjects, and possessed of a daughter of marriageable age, princess Hegesipyle. Although in the long run their union would bring Miltiades great dividends (not least, lucrative gold-mining concessions), unlike in Athens, where the father of the bride gave a dowry to her husband on their wedding day, in Thrace the husband bought the bride for whatever sum her status might command. The price of a princess can only be imagined. Nor might a first-time bride be the pure unblemished virgin an Athenian would by rights expect. Whether justified or not, Greeks told with gusto how adolescent Thracian girls were given free rein to indulge their unbridled sexuality, which was why their husbands were subsequently obliged to keep a very watchful eye. But her breeding and connections, not her chastity, were important to Miltiades. Past indiscretions could be set aside. Far more indelible and (to a Greek) indecorous were Hegesipyle's tattoos on arms, legs, neck and torso, for the higher a Thracian's status the more tattoos they bore: bands of dots and chevrons; stylized rosettes; deer and other animals. And then there was the wedding feast. If Thracian royal banquets were unbridled bacchanals—where lavish gifts were given to the king, where tables groaned with platters heaped with meat, where drinking horns were passed from guest to guest and wine flowed in prodigious quantities, where acrobats somersaulted, clowns capered, musicians performed warlike tunes, where lewd jokes met loud laughter, where heads swam, speech blurred, eyes lost focus—Thracian royal wedding banquets took excess to almost unimaginable heights. Stout-heartedly, Miltiades met the challenge of Olorus' hospitality head-on, and back in Cardia, he and his princess produced first a son, named after his grandfather, Cimon, and then three daughters, whom they brought up half-Greek, half-Thracian, wholly royal.[31]

As for Archedice, Miltiades' former wife, securing an alliance was her role, too. While negotiations had been going on between Miltiades and Olorus, her father, Hippias, had been engaging in increasingly amicable discussions with Hippoclus, tyrant of Lampsacus. Hostilities suspended, a settlement was reached, and as evidence of the new rapprochement, at a ceremony attended by representatives of both families and dignitaries from both cities, Archedice was married to Hippoclus' son, Aeantides. In time they, too, produced an heir and, had circumstances remained stable, the potential for political and economic harmony offered by this nexus of domestic ties might well have been formidable (Archedice's father, Hippias, ruling Athens; her son Metiochus, growing up in Cardia with Miltiades, the son-in-law of King Olorus; her husband, Aeantides, lording it in Lampsacus). But circumstances were not stable, either internationally or domestically. Within a few years, hard-won security achieved by delicate negotiations would be swept away in chaos.[32]

On Aegean coasts and islands, change was in the air as political upheaval rocked city-states—and not least, Athens. On a fine summer morning, anticipation palpable, citizens were gathering for the parade that formed the spiritual heart of the Great Panathenaic Festival. Beginning outside Athens' north-west gates a long line of worshippers dressed in their best robes—men and women, citizens and foreign residents, with representatives of influential families at their head, led by Hippias, Hipparchus, and their households—would file through the streets from the cramped Cerameicus (the industrial heartland where potters' kilns and metalworkers' furnaces jostled side by side with cheap bordellos a stone's throw from the public cemetery). Across the Agora it made its way, winding up the steep road round the Acropolis, before it passed beneath the monumental gateway erected by Peisistratus and so onto the sacred rock itself. Here stood a forest of fine marble statues, Asiatic in their artistry (elegant girls with plaited hair and almond eyes, young men on horseback, sphinxes with folded wings, all with enigmatic smiles playing round their lips), and towering over them the new Temple of Athena Polias, its freshly-painted pedimental sculptures showing a battle between gods and anarchic giants, with Athena at their centre wielding her spear and shaking her snake-fringed breastplate, her aegis possessed of devastating powers. To the east of the temple stretched the altar where, on this special day, a hundred cattle would be slaughtered in pious offering. But this in itself was not the climax of the celebration. For within the temple stood a statue of the goddess carved from olive wood, so ancient that it was believed to have fallen from the sky, a gift from the gods to the Athenians, so numinous that it was thought to harbour magic to protect the city for as long as the city revered it. So, today, as they did each year on Athena's birthday, the Athenians would present the statue with a gift, a new robe woven by young girls hand-picked from noble families, its fabric worked with scenes from legend—the same scenes shown on the temple's pediment—the Battle of the Gods and Giants, the victory of order over chaos.[33]

Already Hippias, surrounded by his bodyguards, had arrived outside the city gate and was conversing with friends, relaxed, exchanging jokes, when a man came sprinting down the hard-earth road, breathless, distraught. His news was devastating. Out of nowhere, two thugs had attacked Hipparchus and knifed him to death. The younger assassin had been killed already, the older was still on the run. It might be part of a well-orchestrated plot. Not even Hippias was safe. But the tyrant kept his cool. Rather than race to his dead brother's side, he ordered every man to stack his shield and all his weapons (legitimately borne in the procession) and stand by for further instruction. As they did, his bodyguards watched on, noting carefully who openly was carrying traditional

The fifth-century-B.C. statues of Harmodius and Aristogeiton in Athens' Agora inspired paintings such as this from an Athenian red-figure vase (c. 400 B.C.).

long spears, and who bore clandestine knives and daggers. Then, with the weapons in, they rounded up the suspects. But it was only when the second assassin was discovered, arrested and interrogated under torture, that details of the plot emerged.[34]

Both from the relatively minor Gephyraei family (originally from Tanagra in Boeotia), the assassins, Harmodius and Aristogeiton, were lovers. But Hipparchus, too, was obsessed with the handsome young Harmodius. With a song by the court poet Anacreon perhaps looping in his brain—'Boy with a maiden's looks, I seek you out, but you've no eyes for me. You don't know you're a charioteer, and that you're holding in your hands the reins to my very soul'—he had been pestering Harmodius to transfer his affections to him. As an incentive for the boy to yield (and a promise of benefits to come), he arranged for Harmodius' sister to play the prestigious role of basket carrier in the Panathenaic Procession, which would enhance the kudos of the Gephyraei, and might even lead to her attracting a high-status husband. But by the time re-hearsals for the festival came round, Harmodius had so roundly rebuffed Hipparchus that, when the girl arrived, animated and excited, he coldly declared that there had clearly been some error, that she had never been invited, that a girl like her was not fit to take part in such an important festival. Now, incensed, Harmodius and his lover, together with a small band of trusted friends, conspired to kill not just Hipparchus, but his brother, Hippias, as well, and put an end to their regime. But when the day came, they panicked. Seeing a co-conspirator in close conversation with Hippias, they thought they had been unmasked, but rather than abandon their plan completely, they found Hipparchus near the Agora and vented their rage on him. It was a pivotal day in Athens' history. With elegant Hipparchus dead, Hippias was plagued by paranoia. At a stroke, his once relaxed administration, under which Athens had flour-ished as a beacon of the Arts, became a bleak totalitarian nightmare.[35]

With popular resentment growing, past allies distanced themselves from Hippias, while potential rivals fled the city—not least the Alcmae-onids. Once they had been ardent allies of Peisistratus. Indeed, for a brief spell their present family head, the charismatic Cleisthenes, had been the tyrant's brother-in-law, and he had subsequently served as Chief Archon in the first year of the brothers' regime (immediately before Mil-tiades IV). Now, though, they began busily to rewrite history, claiming that under Peisistratus the entire family, freedom lovers all, had de-camped with all their wealth from Athens to fight a rear-guard action in defence of liberty. It helped that they could boast a strong record of opposing tyranny. A century earlier, when a strutting young Olympic victor, Cylon, tried to seize the state, Megacles, then head of the Alc-maeonids, led a popular movement to oppose him. But, while he suc-cessfully ousted Cylon (who fled to safety), Megacles overplayed his hand. During negotiations with Cylon's followers he had sworn an oath to spare them if they surrendered peacefully. Instead he bound them in shackles, led them to the coast, and executed every one of them, an act of such sacrilege that even Cylon's enemies, not to mention any who still secretly sympathized with the would-be tyrant, considered Megacles to be be-yond the pale. And in the decades that followed rumours abounded that the Alcmaeonids were accursed, which was why it was now so important for Cleisthenes, in exile from Hippias' increasingly ruthless regime, to parade his piety.[36]

More than thirty years previously, Apollo's temple at Delphi had been destroyed by fire, prompting an appeal across the Mediterranean to help raise the vast sum needed to rebuild it. Now, thanks to his financial acumen and the promise of a substantial contribution, Cleisthenes succeeded in winning the contract to oversee the work and, when the extent of his largesse became apparent (instead of the agreed limestone, he paid to import expensive Parian marble for the facade), no-one at Delphi could resist him. Already, just a year after Hipparchus' murder, he and his fellow Alcmaeonids had fortified a hilltop north of Athens in an attempt to lead an insurrection against Hippias, but they were quickly beaten back. Now, though, with Delphi on his side, things seemed decidedly more rosy—not least because whenever Spartan delegates came to consult the oracle, the priestess prefaced each response by urging them to take the lead in liberating Athens.[37]

A first Spartan invasion—from the sea—was beaten back by Hippias and his crack cavalry, mercenaries from Thessaly, who thundered across the plain, scattering Spartan hoplites disembarking from their ships at Phalerum, and cutting down their general. But next year the Spartans returned in force, this time by land, their king, Cleomenes, at their head. Just inside Attica they routed the Thessalian cavalry, Hippias' mercenaries, who at once abandoned the tyrant and, leaving forty of their number dead, spurred their horses homewards. As for Hippias, he bundled his children out of Attica, barricaded himself inside the Acropolis and prepared for what he hoped would be a short and inconclusive siege. But the Spartans discovered his children, held them as hostages and gave him an ultimatum: leave within five days or they die. So, having dominated Athens for half a century, Peisistratus' family (the Peisistratids) slunk off to exile—to Sigeum, where Hippias' brother Hegesistratus ruled as tyrant across the Hellespont from the Thracian Chersonese.[38]

Even now Athens was not at rest. Yes, the tyrant had been ousted. But who would replace him? What kind of regime? It was Cleisthenes who proposed the answer. An astute political thinker, he had observed how fragile Hippias' grasp on power became once he lost popular support. So, partly to ensure his own position as the People's darling, and partly to diminish his rivals, as soon as it was safe for him to return home, Cleisthenes bruited his role in Athens' liberation while at the same time championing a proposal to commission from the leading sculptor, Antenor, life-sized bronze statues of Harmodius and Aristogeiton, now hailed for their murder of Hipparchus as liberating 'tyrannicides', to be set up in pride of place in the Agora (the only human beings as yet to be so honoured). And with his star blazing brightly in the stratosphere, Cleisthenes set about changing Athens' constitution.[39]

At the heart of his reforms was the concept of *isonomia,* parity (literally, strict mathematical equality) before the law, which (albeit to a relatively limited extent) granted each citizen, regardless of wealth or status, equal privileges and opportunities, introducing sortition—random appointment by lot, not preference—as the means of filling many public offices, removing the deliberative Council from the hands of the elite, increasing the frequency of meetings of the popular Assembly (now Athens' major decision-making body), and instituting drastic innovations that would change how every citizen viewed his relationship with his fellows. For as long as anyone could remember, factional strife had plagued Attica's stability, as residents of its disparate geographic areas and their aristocratic leaders sought to promote their interests at the expense of others—sailors and fishermen from the coast, farmers from the agricultural plain, and communities from beyond the scrubby Pentelic hills, not to mention the growing artisan and mercantile population within the city itself. Eighty years earlier, the great lawgiver Solon had tried to address these problems (as well as problems of class tensions) with reforms of his own, which equated opportunity with wealth rather than birth, but they were simply not sufficiently radical or wide-ranging to succeed in the longer run and they had since been overtaken by the Peisistratid tyranny. So Cleisthenes knew—and Athens accepted—that, if his new dispensation had any chance of lasting, extreme measures would be required.

Previously, Athenians had been divided into four tribes, based supposedly on blood relationship, each dominated by a handful of powerful families. Now Cleisthenes enlarged the number of these tribes to ten and redistributed citizens between them. Moreover, to help minimize regional and inter-family frictions, so characteristic of the past century, he stipulated that each tribe be formed of residents from at least three of the 139 or 140 *demes* (village units or urban districts), each from a different area of Attica: the coast, the city, and the agricultural inland. These *demes* and tribes would form the backbone of the new Athenian constitution. From now on, each would have its own local government and submit delegates to fill state offices, of which some, such as military command, were chosen by vote, and others—from Council membership to supervising markets to waste disposal—by lot. Furthermore, to ensure tribal loyalty, citizens would now compete by tribe for prizes in the games, sit by tribe in theatre audiences, and fight by tribe in Athens' battle line. To add gravitas to this new order, Cleisthenes sent a list of a hundred Attic heroes to the oracle at Delphi, requesting that Apollo himself choose ten, each of which would champion and give his name to one of the new tribes. Even if they themselves were now assigned to the Oeneid Tribe (named after an obscure son of Dionysus), when they heard that another had been named for Ajax, the Philaids must have felt a frisson of family pride.[40]

Despite Apollo's imprimatur, however, not everyone in Greece or Athens was convinced. Notwithstanding his being appointed Chief Archon, Cleisthenes' main rival, Isagoras, an old-school aristocrat, was particularly anxious. The tyranny of Hippias had been bad enough; the potential tyranny of the People—the lower classes—promised to be disastrous. So he, too, like Cleisthenes before him, appealed to Sparta, where he found sympathetic ears. With their own constitution anchored unshakeably in a centuries-old notion of strong government by a rich landowning elite, the Spartans were congenitally suspicious of anything that might place power in the hands of the peasant- or working classes. To them *isonomia* was anathema. So, for the second time in two years, King Cleomenes led his army into Attica. But before setting out, he sent a messenger to Athens: woe betide Cleisthenes or any of his cursed family if they were still there when he arrived. The Alcmaeonids beat a prudent exit. Within weeks they were joined in exile by members of 700 other leading families, denounced by Isagoras, Cleomenes' preening puppet, who, backed by Spartan spears and swords, began gloatingly to unpick all Cleisthenes' reforms.

But he had forgotten his mythology. Just as Pandora could not return the 'countless woes' that fluttered from her fateful amphora once she had lifted its lid, so Isagoras found himself powerless to resist the combined will of the Athenians. Like Cylon and his cohorts before him, Isagoras, Cleomenes, and their supporters were forced to retreat to the Acropolis. But even here they were not safe. The Acropolis was surrounded, and with food and water running dangerously low, Cleomenes and Isagoras bowed to the inevitable. They surrendered after just three days on condition that they be allowed to leave in safety. Their followers were less fortunate. In an orgy of recrimination they were rounded up and executed. The People had spoken; their will could not be crushed; *isonomia* was here to stay; and with his fellow exiles Cleisthenes, its architect, rode home in triumph.[41]

But still Athens' enemies were determined to crush her, and not least Sparta. Accustomed to being acknowledged as Greece's leading polis, her treatment at the hands of Athens' revolutionary—if not anarchic—populist regime rankled. Such treatment needed to be punished. So she dispatched secret envoys to Athens' near neighbours—Corinth, the wealthy trading centre to the west; Boeotia, the powerful state on Athens' northern border; and dynamic Chalcis, a city on Euboea, the long island nestling off the east coast of Attica. And at the time appointed, soldiers took their long spears from the wall hooks and hefted burnished shields, and armies poured from all sides into Attica, their intention to crush the power of Athens' upstart People and install Isagoras as tyrant.[42]

For the Athenians the stakes could not be higher. But they could not fight on every front at once. So, leaving their northern and eastern flanks dangerously exposed, they marched west to Eleusis, where the combined heavy infantry of Sparta and Corinth was drawn up in grim order, bronze helmets lowered, shields raised, spear-tips protruding, razor-sharp, like a hedge of deadly thorns. Now the Athenians, too, formed ranks. Now they, too, were ready, staring out across the narrow strip of no-man's-land, where in the briefest moment they would kill or be killed for the sake of their new constitution. And then, a miracle: an order barked, and relaxation rippling through Corinthian lines as their hoplites turned and simply walked away; and next the Spartan joint kings, Cleomenes and Demaratus, arguing, debating, quarrelling, until Demaratus issued the command to his detachment, and they, too, turned and left; soon only Cleomenes remained, Isagoras glaring at his side, his men uneasy at how readily their comrades had deserted them; and now they, too, were gone. Later, the Corinthians maintained that they had seen the error of their ways, that they could not condone imposing tyranny on Athens. Perhaps this really was the reason—and if (as often happened before battle) they simply got cold feet, they were unlikely to admit it.[43]

For now, though, all that mattered was that this enemy was gone. But there were still Boeotians to contend with, and the men of Chalcis. So the Athenians swung round and marched with haste back to their city, then on, across the saddle of Pentelicon, towards the swirling waters of Euripus that separate the mainland from Euboea, where the enemy was due to muster. They caught the Boeotians first, and with the fire of victory already in their bellies unleashed carnage, slaughtering any who resisted and rounding up the rest. And then they crossed to Chalcis and, on the same day before nightfall, crushed its army, too. Undoubtedly (each man of them believed) these triumphs were a sure sign of the power of their new constitution. Now they were fighting for themselves, not some resented overlord and, as hymns rang out on the Acropolis accompanying the dedication to Athena of a fine bronze chariot and horses in token of their victory, it must have seemed as if no hostile force on earth could possibly resist them.[44]

Yet still those hostile forces tried. Simmering with hatred, the Boeotians conspired with the islanders of Aegina, requesting that they loan to them the statues of Aeacus and his sons, with whose aid they were convinced they would beat Athens. They were wrong. Then they asked for military aid instead, and while the Athenians were occupied in fighting back Boeotia's troops, warships from Aegina slid into Athens' port at Phalerum, wrecking dockyards, torching houses, wreaking havoc in a string of nearby villages. The Spartans, too, were planning vengeance. With tempers still frayed following the stand down at Eleusis, they washed their hands of Isagoras, and instead invited Hippias as guest of honour to a council of their allies with a view to reinstating him in Athens. But, emboldened by the delegates from Corinth, who refused to get involved, the other representatives, too, vetoed the idea, and Hippias sailed back in dudgeon to Sigeum. Yet his trip to Sparta had stirred something in his loins. Why should he not return to rule in Athens? After all, his father, Peisistratus, had been expelled twice, and twice he had returned. If Sparta and the Greeks would not help him, there were others who would. Not least the newly-installed governor, who was even now transforming Croesus' erstwhile capital at Sardis into the regional administrative hub of a vast and fast-expanding empire.[45]

For in the past few decades not only Lydia but the broad expanse of lands that stretched far to the east and south and west—fertile plains and snow-capped mountains, home to nomadic farmers and proud residents of ancient cities, Babylon, Egyptian Thebes, Ecbatana and Sardis, even Greek settlements across the long Aegean coast—vast swathes had fallen to the seemingly unstoppable onrush of a dynamic new regime that in under fifty years had risen from obscure tribesmen to be rulers of the greatest empire that the world had ever seen: the Persians. Surely *they* could help Hippias regain his heritage. Surely they could bring him home again to Athens. It was not long before the ageing tyrant found his way to Sardis to try to work his magic on its Persian governor.[46]

But he was not alone in seeking Persian help. Perhaps led by their hero Cleisthenes, the Athenians, attacked from every side, sent a delegation of their own to Sardis. There in the hushed audience chamber they were ushered, bowing low as they had been instructed, into the presence of the satrap, the Great King's viceroy, enthroned in majesty, armed guards on either side, and incense heavy in the air. Their plea for aid was met with sympathy. Of course, the Persians would help. All that the Great King needed in exchange was a simple sign of goodwill, a gift of two jars, one filled with Attic earth, the other with Attic water. Delightedly the delegates agreed. The deal was done, and the alliance sealed. Security against their enemies was guaranteed. But when they got back home and explained the terms, they were met with ashen horror. For did they not know what it meant to offer earth and water to the Persians? Had they not learned that this was how conquered peoples pledged their loyalty to Persia's empire? Had they not realised that, by agreeing to this gift, they had surrendered newly-liberated Athens without a blow being struck, without an arrow fired, to a foreigner, a king, the most autocratic despot in the world? Did they not understand that—now no longer free—Athens had agreed to be a vassal state of Persia?[47]

2

WHEN THE PERSIANS CAME

Relaxing well-fed by the fire in winter, sipping
sweet wine on a soft couch, nibbling at nuts,
these are the sorts of questions you should ask:
'Friend, what's your name, and where do you come
    from? How old are you now—
and how old *were* you when the Persians came?'

Xenophanes, fr. 21

THE THRACIAN CHERSONESE, 505 B.C.

Miltiades knew all about the Persians. He had already served them well.
Indeed—like many others (like the Athenians, had they delivered on
their promises of giving earth and water)—he was by now a Persian
vassal, his loyalty pledged solemnly to the Persian Great King, his territory now part of the vast Persian Empire that had erupted as if from nowhere less than fifty years before, a fireball that had overwhelmed so
many hostile armies, engulfed so many ancient kingdoms and torn apart
so many adamantine certainties that its future seemed unstoppable.

The detonator was what should have been a minor war, a mission undertaken by the Median king Astyages, whose realm stretched from
Anatolia to Bactria and from the Caspian and Black seas south to the
Arabian and Persian gulfs. His campaign was against a rebel leader, his
own grandson, Cyrus, recently enthroned as King of Anshan in the
southern state of Pars, where his once nomadic people had migrated
centuries before. But Astyages' general, Harpagus, betrayed him, his
army defected to Cyrus, and after only a few years of fighting Cyrus, vic-

torious, entered Ecbatana, the ancient Median capital perched high on a plateau in the folds of the towering Zagros Mountains. As a contemporary chronicle records, 'he seized the palace and removed the gold and silver and the treasures of Astyages, and took them back to Anshan'. Yet instead of punishing Astyages, Cyrus, a brilliant strategist, showed clemency, cementing ties with his grandfather's regime through marriage and diplomacy, transferring the administration of the kingdom to his loyalists with almost seamless skill.[1]

However, Cyrus was not content with simply annexing Media. Just three years following his victory, he was embroiled in fighting his new western neighbour, a neighbour with which Miltiades and many Greeks had warm relations and close bonds: the kingdom of Lydia. Niggling cross-border aggravations escalated into full-scale war. According to the Greeks, Croesus (the Lydian potentate, whose wife was sister to the erstwhile Median king, Astyages), itching to crush the upstart Cyrus, sent to Delphi to ask what he should do. The oracle's reply emboldened him. 'Cross the River Halys' (the border between Lydia and Persia), it said, 'and you will destroy a mighty empire.' So Croesus crossed the lazy Halys' red waters, but battle ended in frustrating stalemate, and with winter nearing he withdrew to Sardis to await the new campaigning season, by which time he hoped to swell his army with committed allies.[2]

But Cyrus did not wait for spring. Through snow and rain he marched on Sardis where he ranged his forces on the plain. Outnumbering them two to one, Croesus was confident, but as his men poured through the gates and out into the fertile fields—Lydians and Phrygians, Egyptians, Babylonians, Greeks from Ionia and cities on the Hellespont, infantry and cavalry and shock-troops riding chariots—he found that he had underestimated Cyrus' brilliance. Unflinchingly the Persians awaited in a close-drawn square formation, reinforced by mobile towers whose tops were lined with archers, and as Croesus' extended battle line swung to attack the sides, Cyrus ordered his well-drilled regiments to peel off from the rear, encircling the Lydians in a devastating pincer movement as squalls of arrows rained down from the towers. At the same time, he unleashed his secret weapon: a battalion of cavalry mounted on snorting camels, whose sight and smell scared Lydia's horses. As panic flooded through his army, Croesus fled. For two weeks he cowered in his palace perched on the vertiginous clifftop until Persian scouts found a way up; and Croesus' rule was over. This time Cyrus was less merciful. Some claimed that the Lydian king lived out his life as an advisor to his Persian captor, but according to another chronicle Cyrus 'killed the king, seized his possessions, and installed a garrison of his own'. Whatever his fate, Greeks knew the real reason that Croesus was defeated. Thanks to his great confidence, he had misinterpreted the Delphic oracle. Yes, he had crossed the Halys and destroyed a mighty empire, but that mighty empire was his own.[3]

However, for Greeks their oracle's infallibility was little consolation for the stark new geopolitics: established only three or four years earlier in Ecbatana some fifteen hundred miles away, the Persian Empire now effectively controlled Greek poleis on the coasts of Asia Minor and the Hellespont. When news reached the Greek mainland, only the Spartans intervened: as befitted their accepted role as leader of the Greeks, they sent diplomats to Cyrus, now ensconced in Croesus' palace, warning that, if he harmed any of the Asiatic Greeks who had previously been treated well by Croesus' beneficent regime, they personally would punish him. Cyrus' response was telling: 'And just who are these Spartans?' Even when he found out, he was undisturbed, dismissing Greeks as shopkeepers, men who 'swear to anything and break their oaths at market', before issuing a chilling threat. 'If I have anything to do with it, soon such men will not be blabbing about troubles in Ionia. They'll be blabbing about troubles of their own.'[4]

Given such an attitude, it was perhaps not unexpected that, although once willing supporters of the urbane Croesus, many Ionian Greeks felt reluctant to bow before the altogether more combative Cyrus; so when Pactyes, a Lydian grandee charged with shipping captured gold and treasure east to Persia's heartlands, preferred to keep it for himself and rebel against his Persian overlords, he found in the Ionians willing, if short-sighted allies. For Cyrus did not take insurrection lightly. Within weeks his Persian army had poured back to Sardis, and Pactyes was on the run. Now it was the Greeks who harboured him who faced Persian ire, and while islanders of Chios bowed to the inevitable and prudently betrayed the Lydian, returning him in chains to Sardis, black smoke belched high into the pale blue air from cities that had shown more pluck—Priene nestling on Mount Mycale, above the wide Bay of Miletus; Magnesia on the banks of the Meander River—as peoples were enslaved, their buildings ransacked, their freedom ground into the red, crumbling earth.[5]

Even when his general fell ill and died soon after, Cyrus considered it so vital to subdue the Asiatic Greeks—punishment, he proclaimed, for not supporting his war with Croesus, but possibly because he simply distrusted them—that he appointed Harpagus, a Mede but his most trusted general, to spearhead the campaign. As siege works rose and cities fell, the Persian Great King tightened his iron grip on the entire coastline from Phoenicia north to Lycia—where citizens of Xanthus preferred suicide to capture—and from Caria north again to Greek Ionia. As Harpagus approached, cold existential terror spread. In Teos, birthplace of the poet Anacreon, they poured down to the rocky harbour, bundling possessions into boats, and sailed across the sea to make new homes in Thracian Abdera; the citizens of Phocaea fled as well, slipping away by night for a long voyage west that after many years would see them settle at Marseille, though some were so consumed by homesickness that they returned to find their idyll of a city overrun. Only rich Miletus, claimed as a colony by Athens, was permitted to maintain its independence in recognition (it was said) of good deeds once done to the Medes by its son, Thales, the great rational philosopher. In fact, the decision was strategic: Cyrus needed at least one Ionian city he could trust.[6]

For there were still more worlds to conquer. Inland to the south lay Babylon, whose resurgent empire had enjoyed a close accord with Lydia and Media, and whose lands stretched westwards to Phoenicia and the sea. A few years after ousting Croesus, Cyrus launched his new campaign. As frightened country dwellers poured into the city, statues of gods strapped next to household goods on backs of mules and oxen, Persian sappers diverted the River Tigris before, smashing through the great defensive wall linking that river to the Euphrates fifty miles from Babylon, Cyrus led his troops to a decisive victory. Resistance crumbled. Within days he was entering the ancient city with its wide boulevards, plush palaces and towering ziggurat, and another province had been added to the Persian Empire.[7]

Not even this slaked Cyrus' thirst for conquest and, with the three former great western Asiatic empires—Media, Lydia and Babylon—now under his command, he turned his gaze far east beyond the Caspian Sea, where across the River Araxes great plains 'stretching to infinity' were home to the nomadic Massagetae and their fearsome Queen Tomyris. But for Cyrus the ensuing battle ('the most bloody fought between two foreign armies') was his last. Now in his seventieth year, the thirtieth of his extraordinary reign, he fell in the confusion of fighting. His body was retrieved, encased in wax and carried back in reverence to Pasargadae, where near the sprawling palace he had constructed in his ancient homeland of Anshan, 'the universal king, the Great King, the mighty king, the king of Babylon, of Sumer and Akkad, the king of the four quarters of the world' was buried in a simple tomb.[8]

That his empire did not implode was evidence that Cyrus, the military genius, was an even more astute administrator. Unless provoked, he chose not just to spare defeated nations but to ensure they were well governed, often maintaining their familiar established constitutions. Indeed, from Babylon and Sardis to Ionia, once regime change was accepted, many new Persian subjects discovered that for the most part daily life was much the same. Ionians could still worship their ancestral gods; their rulers—Persian loyalists, yes, and answerable to Persian satraps, but still local Greeks—were no worse than they were before; and, even if they *were* compelled to pay taxes to the Great King, the benefits of Persian peace to trade and commerce were enormous. As the cynical poet-cum-philosopher Xenophanes observed: 'They learned useless luxury from Lydia and as long as they were free from hateful tyranny they swarmed the markets in their purple robes, at least a thousand at a time, preening, proud of long well-barbered tresses, drenched in the perfume of exotic oils.' So, while Cyrus' successor, his son Cambyses, increased Persian sway still further, annexing Lower Egypt before pushing west to Libya and south to the First Cataract, some Ionians were more than happy to embrace the new regime—not least Polycrates of Samos, who tore up a lucrative alliance with the pharaoh and furnished forty freshly-manufactured triremes for Cambyses' fleet.[9]

Yet at heart the empire was still not secure. When Cambyses turned back for home, he was assassinated. It was part of a much wider plot. In Media the Magi, a powerful religious caste, unhappy with constant warfare, had already staged a coup, installing Bardiya, Cambyses' brother, on the throne, and for seven months they flexed their muscles, courting the people, suspending military expeditions for three years and cancelling the taxes that would fund them. For Persia's nobility it was intolerable. As summer drew to an uneasy close, six high-level conspirators asked an ambitious, energetic officer, who, though only thirty years of age, had served both Cyrus and Cambyses, to join their cabal: Darius, whose ancestry was distantly enmeshed with that of the royal family. At

The Behistun Inscription from Western Iran shows captive rebels approaching Darius, who is trampling Bardiya's body while gazing at a winged figure representing Ahura Mazda.

once he turned plot into audacious action: thanks to their status, the conspirators were admitted without question to the palace, but a pettifogging eunuch refused them access to the king. Darius' response was unequivocal. He drew his sword and ran the eunuch through, and while his six companions despatched the eunuch's colleagues, he burst into the inner chamber. Moments later he emerged into the palace courtyard, brandishing Bardiya's severed head, inciting crowds of Persians to take vengeance on the Magi. For they, he said, had been behind a terrible conspiracy: they had installed a puppet king—not the royal heir, Bardiya (assassinated, he claimed, months before), but his doppelgänger (whose head he was now holding)—in an attempt to hijack Persia's destiny. The Magi were agents of the Evil One, the Lie. They must be rounded up and massacred. As for Darius, shortly to assume the throne himself, 'I prayed to Ahura Mazda, and Ahura Mazda gave me aid.'[10]

Since the story of the doppelgänger was almost certainly a fiction, Darius' appeal to Ahura Mazda was at best disingenuous, at worst downright blasphemous. For Ahura Mazda was the god of truth, the animating spirit behind the Persian project's great world vision. According to their prophet Zoroaster (perhaps Cyrus' contemporary), the universe was split into two warring factions: on one side was Ahura Mazda, the overarching force of truth and justice, embodied in the purity of fire;

on the other, the corrosive Angra Mainyu, lord of demons, who delights in the Great Falsehood, the Lie. With Persia's mission to promote the one and help destroy the other, the three pillars of a Persian's education (riding, archery and speaking truth) were designed precisely to support it. Even hunting and horticulture, precious pastimes of a Persian nobleman, were not aimed simply at pleasure. Wild, savage beasts were hosts of Angra Mainyu and so must be eradicated, the wildest and most savage in intricately choreographed ceremonies staged in theatrical royal hunting parks. Wild, untamed countryside must also be subdued, turned into fertile farmland or high-walled pleasure gardens (literally 'paradises', the Greek form of a Persian word), well-watered, geometric, beautifully manicured, with shrubs and trees imported from across the empire, microcosms of the ideal world of truth and harmony—and, while for now it might be politic (and relatively harmless) to let subject states keep worshipping their idols, sacred animals and anthropomorphic gods, there were other servants of the Lie who must be brought to heel: demons and men who swore one thing, then did another, who opposed the spreading of the Truth. Cyrus had not been joking when he condemned Greek shopkeepers for their duplicity.[11]

Darius' royal name, in Persian 'Dārayawuš', meant 'defender of the good', but his accession to the Persian throne did not result immediately in harmony. Instead, unstable now, the empire fractured as ambitious potentates and would-be princes whipped up rebellion from Babylon to Bactria. Yet Darius was nothing if not energetic. Coordinating the swiftest of responses, he galvanized lieutenants, dispatched trusted generals, and led a crack army of loyalists to a whirlwind of victories, crisscrossing his vast territories at lightning speed with devastating force. Within little over a year, insurgent territories had once more fallen under his command, and soon all Asia Minor (as well as Libya and much of Egypt) was either subject or allied to Darius. His efficiency was breathtaking. So was the ruthlessness with which he punished those responsible. In his own chronicle inscribed high on a rock face he recorded the fate of one insurgent: 'I sliced off his nose, his ears, his tongue. I blinded him. I kept him tied up at the gates and all could see him. Then at Ecbatana I impaled him on a stake. And within the army camp I flayed his close confederates.' Wherever a rebel leader was caught alive, the ritual was repeated with grim regularity.[12]

Ionian Greeks, too, were caught up in the revolt. Seizing his opportunity, their satrap, Oroetes, refused to help Darius in his hour of need, declared independence, invaded neighbouring Hellespontine Phrygia, slaughtered its governor and annexed the province. But still he wanted more. Glittering just offshore was the island of Samos, with its sumptuous Sanctuary of Hera, not to mention engineering marvels—an aqueduct hewn through the mountain, an enviable harbour bounded by a mighty mole—and Polycrates, its pro-Persian tyrant, was so unsuspecting. He accepted an invitation to Oroetes' court, where instead of a royal welcome he was nailed to a stake and left to die beneath the harsh sun and driving rain. Nonetheless, Oroetes' bodyguards stayed loyal—not to the jumped-up satrap but to the King of Kings and to the dream of empire. So when an envoy brought orders from Darius, they obeyed him to a man and killed Oroetes. With Lydia and Phrygia, Ionia was back in Persian hands. So now was Samos, and, shortly after, Chios, too. Inexorably, unerringly, the empire was spreading west. Well might Darius publicize his boasts: 'Ahura Mazda and such other gods as are came to my aid because I was not evil; I did not lie; I did not oppress; nor did my family. I walked the path of righteousness and justice.' Surely such a man might rule the world.[13]

For a while, however, thoughts of expansion must be set aside. Like Cyrus before him, Darius was indefatigable, as brilliant at ruling his existing lands as he was at adding more through war. Now he reorganized his empire, establishing clear chains of command, improving communications between outlying provinces and imperial palaces, creating dedicated royal roads, each with regularly spaced caravanserai where messengers could find fresh horses on which to gallop onwards with their news. He struck gold coins, too, 'darics', which bore his image in the guise of a crowned, running archer, and ordered censuses of all his provinces to calculate what tribute or taxation to exact. And while (like Cyrus) he generally let local populations lead their age-old lifestyles, in charge of each of his now twenty or more provinces he set his representatives on earth, his satraps. Their palaces were royal courts in miniature, their persons treated with almost divine respect, just less than that accorded the Great King himself, though none could make a major policy decision. Only Darius could do that. For he was Ahura Mazda's chosen one. And what he said was law.[14]

So, when Darius planned a new campaign, all had to spring to action. This was why, when he announced his wish to annex the Black Sea coastline and the steppe far to the north—and his intention that Ionian Greeks must play a major role—a frenzy of activity swept through his western cities. And not just them. Included in the muster was Miltiades IV, tyrant of the Thracian Chersonese. Quite how he came to join the expedition is unknown. So far (before 513) the Persians had made no military forays north of the Hellespont, but Miltiades had watched their steady progress, and had seen how resistance had been crushed and rebels punished, so perhaps, sensing how the winds were blowing, he cannily, astutely, offered to support Darius. Indeed, not to take part might diminish his political standing and personal kudos, since the expedition's roll call listed every proud Greek tyrant in the region. Tasked with organizing them was Histiaeus, tyrant of Miletus, a man of great energy and ambition, whose city held a privileged position in regard to Persia, whose glittering lieutenants numbered not only Hippoclus, tyrant of Lampsacus (father-in-law of Miltiades' ex-wife, Archedice), but the tyrants of Samos, Chios, Phocaea, Abydus on the Hellespont, Proconnesus and Cyzicus on the Propontis, and (further east) Byzantium, the gateway to their destination, the Black Sea.[15]

All were required to furnish ships and muster near the Black Sea's mouth upstream from Chalcedon, a city on the eastern shore of the Bosporus, until Darius and his land troops joined them. For, before the Great King and his army—said by some (improbably) to number 700,000 men—could pass from Asia to Europe, a bridge must be constructed across the turbulent dark waters. And to build it, the high command had chosen a Greek engineer, Mandrocles of Samos, the island that was a showcase for technological achievement. If the racing currents of the Bosporus were hazardous, the design he chose was tried and tested: a pontoon of ships, their bows upstream, hulls lashed together with strong ropes, across which a broad, high-sided wooden walkway was laid down. Darius was delighted. Fresh from a reconnaissance cruise along the northern Black Sea coast, he showered Mandrocles with gifts before calling a council of war.[16]

This was perhaps the first time that Miltiades had been admitted to the Great King's presence, and the experience was carefully stage-managed to inspire a sense of awe. Despite being a seasoned fighter, a hardened cavalry officer, an implacable commander capable of long forced marches to win merciless campaigns, Ahura Mazda's chosen one, Darius, embraced the theatricality of kingship. As he entered the room— on carpets, since his feet could never be allowed to touch bare earth—his generals and officers, his crowds of courtiers, interpreters and secretaries performed the ritual of *proskynesis*, all kneeling, bowing low until their foreheads touched the ground, kissing their right hands, extending right arms forwards to the king, a ritual of acknowledgement that showed their subjugation. Meanwhile, long robed, Darius, head encased in a gold crown, his hair and beard immaculately dressed in ringlets glistening with perfumed oil, watched on, enthroned, a lotus flower in one hand, a sceptre in the other, his soft shoes resting on a golden footstool, beneath a purple canopy embroidered with the wings that symbolized Ahura Mazda, while flanking him, spears raised, implacable, emotionless, tough officers of the Guard whom Greeks knew as the Immortals stood to attention. And then, the whispered sibilance of their interpreters rustling in his subjects' ears, the Great King spoke. But, although Darius may have asked to hear his generals' opinions, all understood that in the end there was only one opinion that mattered: the Great King's. To argue, let alone to contradict would not only challenge etiquette, it could be suicidal. Not that in this meeting there was much said that was controversial. The strategy was clear. While Darius and his troops proceeded overland, the Greeks must sail around the Black Sea coast until they reached the Danube, turn ships into another pontoon bridge and await the army's coming.[17]

Then, while Darius was escorted to a vantage point from which he might admire his Persians crossing to another continent—tens of thousands of foot soldiers from across the empire, cavalry, long, creaking baggage trains, including brightly painted carts and wagons laden with the rich necessities of Persian court life from jewellery and fine furniture to well-sealed jars of water drawn from the River Choaspes near Susa (for the Great King could drink no other)—the Greek fleet pushed out from the escarpments of the eastern Bosporus and tacked north, hugging the Black Sea's western seaboard. With lush green fertile plains, it was a coastline some of them knew well—especially Milesians, for in past centuries they had established colonies along these shores from Apollonia to Istria, and beyond the Danube's mouth on the peninsula that Greeks called Tauris, trading posts from which staples such as wheat were shipped back home, outposts where Greeks might meet and interact with

A Scythian archer wearing a highly patterned jacket and
trousers draws an arrow for his bow (Attic red-figure vase,
520–500 B.C.).

Thracians and Scythians, cities which now seemed likely to be subsumed
into the relentlessly expanding Persian Empire.[18]

Yet things did not go to plan. When he reached the Danube bridge,
Darius told the Greeks to stay and guard it—he would be back in sixty
days at most—so, as his multitude moved off to disappear across the far
horizon, Ionia's most powerful men (and many of its greatest egos) settled down to feast and drink together, triremes lashed between two riverbanks, at the bidding of the Persian Great King. But when the sixty
days were up, it was not Darius, who came riding to the riverbank. It was
the Scythians, whose lands he had invaded, whose opposition he had
been so confident of crushing.[19]

For many Ionians these Scythians (as Greeks called them) were almost
mythical. Nomads, who migrated with their herds across the grasslands

of the steppe, their families travelling in caravans of covered wagons, they were ferocious fighters, archers who fired deadly volleys from the backs of galloping ponies, who scalped and skinned defeated enemies, and at banquets drank from skulls of fallen adversaries. Reports of royal burials gave spice to their grim reputation: how the cortege was accompanied by self-mutilating mourners, cutting ears and lacerating arms, driving arrows through their own left hands; how at the royal cemetery they strangled concubines and cooks and chamberlains and other household staff, and slaughtered horses, and interred them in a high-heaped mound beside the king; how they returned exactly twelve months later to despatch a further fifty servants and a further fifty horses, before eviscerating them and stuffing them with straw and setting up these ghastly effigies to guard their fallen king and the treasures buried with him.[20]

While to Darius it made sound strategic sense to neutralize such fearsome neighbours—neighbours who had given the Medes much trouble in the past—no less a motive for his expedition was the lure of gold, which Scythians were famed for owning in abundance. Far to the north, they said, where thick clouds of feathers swirled like snow forever, griffins guarded hoards of Scythian gold, while in the tribal heartlands sentinels kept constant watch over mystic royal regalia said to have fallen from the skies, a sign of their gods' approval—a golden plough, a golden yoke, a golden cup, a golden battleaxe, objects of such transcendental awe that each year the king made sacrifices in their honour. Indeed, the quality of Scythian and Scytho-Greek metalwork was unparalleled: gold pectorals adorned with delicately incised trees and leaves; gold plaques showing fighting warriors, or panthers, griffins mauling fallen horses; and a massive cauldron displayed west of Tauris, its bronze bowl four inches thick, which held 5,000 gallons.[21]

But it was not of artistry that the Ionians first thought as they saw the horsemen bearing down on them, their ponies' hooves thudding like so many drumbeats on the summer earth, their padded felt coats billowing behind them, their leather trousers tucked into soft boots, their quivers full of arrows rattling on their backs. A hasty call to arms; buckling breastplates; snatching spears; racing into ranks as, helmets down, shields up, they braced for the attack. But none came. Instead, the Scythians drew rein and shouted their proposal. Darius and his men, they said, were beaten down, exhausted. As fast as they advanced, the Scythians withdrew, leading them frustrating miles across the plains, refusing to give battle, sending instead taunting messages, until even the Great King, ambitious as he was, admitted his campaign was futile. He had left behind the sick and wounded; he was marching to the bridge. But the Scythians had outflanked him to bring seductive military advice: 'Destroy the bridge and go. Now! Quickly! Thank the gods and Scythians for your freedom. We'll deal with your former master. We shall ensure he never marches against anyone again.'[22]

As the Scythians let their horses graze the long grass on the riverbank, the tyrants huddled in hasty council. According to Herodotus, Miltiades—whose Chersonese had not yet fallen to the Persians, and who (we might assume) was loath for it to do so—spoke passionately: they should take the Scythians' advice; they should destroy the bridge; they should liberate Ionia. But cooler heads prevailed. To a man the tyrants owed their seats to Darius. Without him citizens were certain to rebel, for democracy, they said, was in the air. Without the Persians, their days were numbered. Such arguments, however, are anachronistic: for one thing, at the time (three years before Hippias was expelled from Athens) there *were* no Greek democracies; the concept had yet to be invented. So if there was, indeed, a debate by the Danube, it did not involve democracy. Nor can Miltiades have counselled such betrayal. He must have known that the Ionians would never heed him: afraid of their own subjects the tyrants may have been, but they were still more frightened of Darius, especially since all remembered how he had treated the rebel grandee in Sardis.[23]

Yet, for the sake of appearances, to get them off their backs and guard against attack should things turn nasty, they pretended to accept the Scythians' advice. They made a show of starting to dismantle the broad walkways, removing those triremes closest to the shore but, when the Scythian horsemen, satisfied, wheeled round and galloped off in search of straggling invaders, the Greeks slowed to a stop. That night in their encampment on the river's western bank, they were awakened by an urgent call. Darius and his Persians were on the farther shore, alarmed to find a section of the bridge demolished. And the Scythians were on their tail. The missing triremes were manoeuvred into place; planks were thrown down, tired soldiers marshalled speedily across; and then, as soon as the last man was over, after many hours of anxious waiting, the walkway was pulled up, ropes were cut, sleek ships nosed downstream for the sea, and the retreat began.[24]

Not that Darius wished to let it seem like a retreat. He was still resolved to add new lands to his existing empire—European lands at that—and if the Scythians would not oblige, there were others who surely would. So, instead of retracing his steps across the Bosporus bridge, he struck out along the shores of the Propontis, and so came to the Chersonese, where in true Persian tradition Miltiades was forced to offer right royal entertainment, feeding and watering his army and their animals, hosting the Great King at sumptuous banquets. And when Darius did at last depart, sailing with the Ionian fleet across the Hellespont from Sestus before marching inland to Sardis, he left behind his general, Megabazus, along with 80,000 troops. If Miltiades had joined the Scythian campaign as a free agent, his status had been quietly reversed. Almost by accident, the Chersonese had passed incontrovertibly to Persian hands. Almost by default, homes and administrative buildings in Cardia and Pactye and Agora had been appropriated for the use of Persian functionaries and staff. Almost without knowing it, Miltiades had become a vassal of the Persian Great King. And not just Miltiades. After subduing such cities as were still resisting on the Propontis' northern shores, Megabazus turned west. To Thrace, the lands of Miltiades' father-in-law, King Olorus, where, if Olorus was unwilling, Miltiades, with first-hand experience of both Persian ruthlessness and Persian leniency, must have been quick to encourage his capitulation.[25]

Others, however, were less pliable. As Megabazus and his men tramped west, warlike tribesmen blocked his way. But the Persians circumvented them and fell on towns and villages, before (on Darius' express instructions) escorting captives back through the Chersonese to Asia and a life of exile far from their ancestral lands—though, thanks to their expertise and knowledge of the seams, the tribespeople who worked Pangaeum's gold mines were allowed to stay in place. Meanwhile, a Persian detachment entered Macedonia, where at the royal palace they demanded earth and water. The canny King Amyntas weighed his options and did not refuse. Indeed, he went further, sealing his alliance by marrying his daughter to the officer in charge. And if her brother, the lithe, swift-footed Alexander, disapproved, there was little he could do. Even as a young man he was as much a politician as his father, no matter what tales he spun later.[26]

With the northern Aegean coast now under Persian command, for Megabazus there remained one item of outstanding business. In recognition of his service on campaign, Darius had appointed Histiaeus (the former tyrant of Miletus) to rule new northern territories, specifically Myrcinus on a lake near the mouth of the River Strymon. It was a settlement alive with possibilities, close to silver mines and forests of tall pine trees, from whose wood warships might be built and long oars planed. But when he saw how Histiaeus lost no time in forming close alliances with local Greeks and Thracians, erecting sturdy walls around Myrcinus, blockading Thasos with its seams of gold, Megabazus was suspicious. It would not take much, he thought, for Myrcinus' wealth to go to Histiaeus' head, or—despite his loyalty on the Danube—for newly-subjugated Thracians to recognize in him a rebel leader. An urgent communiqué to the Great King, still holding court at Sardis, was followed by a royal dispatch delivered to Myrcinus: on second thought, Darius wrote, he valued Histiaeus so highly that, when he returned to Susa (as he shortly would) he would require his presence there as friend and counsellor. So, to Megabazus' undisguised delight, Histiaeus accompanied him east, and while Persia's new coastal commander was deftly quashing uprisings in Byzantium and Chalcedon, securing the Troad and capturing the Aegean islands of Lemnos and Imbros (enslaving those who showed resistance now or in the past), Thracians and Macedonians settled into new lives as beneficiaries of Persian Peace.[27]

As did Miltiades. But his position must have seemed progressively anomalous—sent to govern the Dolonci on behalf of Athens, he was now a vassal of the Persians, a tyrant, whose native city was rejecting tyranny—and while for a brief moment it appeared that Athens, too, would offer Persia earth and water, when those gifts were not forthcoming, Miltiades' connection with his homeland must have seemed so tenuous as to be almost non-existent. True, there were still those on the mainland who did not seem to mind that fellow Greeks had links to Persia. While no Asiatic Greeks appear on Olympic victors lists during this period, when Alexander, Prince of Macedon, another vassal of Darius, applied to compete in 504, insisting that, through descent from Heracles, he was of true-Greek, Argive blood, the authorities (albeit controversially) admitted him to the Games, and he celebrated equal first place in the footrace.[28]

Alexander was not alone in trying to make his mark on mainland Greece. From his capital at Susa, Darius was sending out his spies, and fast Phoenician ships were heading west to reconnoitre. Across well-travelled sea lanes past jagged, pale blue islands they reached Greece's eastern coast to cruise on leisurely, observers sitting beneath awnings dictating notes to secretaries, recording likely landing beaches, listing towns and settlements. And on they sailed, hugging the Peloponnese, around Cape Malea, to where long promontories stretched out into the sea like ribbons, and imposing mountains marched inland in broken columns, before swinging northwards to the mouth of the Corinthian Gulf, past Zacynthus and Cercyra (Corfu), and so on further west to scout the shores of Italy. With many Greek advisors—men such as Hippias, still yearning to return to Athens, and other exiles who had gravitated to his court—Darius knew how matters stood in Greece, a mishmash of rival, warring states, where enmities ran so deep that it would be unthinkable for most to form the loosest of alliances, and where even within cities factions were so violently opposed that it was likely there would be as many who supported Persia as opposed her. What the Great King had not counted on, however, was that these very factions would cause his great project to stall.[29]

The problem, when it came, was precipitated by Darius' appointee as tyrant of Miletus, Histiaeus' son-in-law, the slippery, sly, self-important Aristagoras. For some time, conquest of the Cyclades had been high on Persia's agenda, not only for its own sake but as the preliminary to a seaborne invasion of mainland Greece, and in 499 when democrats on wealthy Naxos (fired by the Athenians' example) rose against their rulers, who in turn fled to Miletus and their ally, Aristagoras, the moment seemed ripe for exploitation. For Aristagoras was more than just an ally. His relationship with members of the Naxian nobility was one technically known as *xenia,* a bond of loyalty and trust between specific leading individuals of two city-states, which obliged them to promote each other's interests in peacetime and do no harm to one another's property or person in war. More crucially, it could be called upon in circumstances such as those in which the Naxian aristocrats now found themselves when, their city taken over by a hostile force, they required assistance to restore the status quo.[30]

To the scheming Aristagoras it must have seemed a blessing from the gods, a chance not just to aid his *xenoi,* but to ingratiate himself still further with his Persian overlords. As he pointed out to Artaphernes, one of Darius' brothers, now satrap in Sardis, while Naxos was a fine prize in itself—the most prosperous of all Aegean islands, fertile, wealthy, slave-rich—it could also be strategically crucial. With Naxos captured, its dependencies—Paros, Andros and the Cyclades—would fall easily to Persia, after which it would be simplicity itself to take Euboea off the coast of Greece, and then cross to the mainland. Moreover, the Naxian exiles had even sworn to fund the campaign themselves. It all seemed predestined—and seductive. No wonder that Darius gave it his blessing. But even more important was the sheer scale of materiel and manpower that he then allotted the campaign: 200 triremes, a formidable land force, and to command them his own cousin, the experienced and battle-toughened Megabates. For this was to be no longer simply a bid to reinstate some exiled noblemen. It was to be the first act in the Persian annexation of all Greece.[31]

Even from the start there was friction. When he learned that it was Megabates and not he giving orders, the naive Aristagoras was peeved; when the Persian punished an Ionian commander for lax discipline, the stubborn Aristagoras countermanded him; and when at last they sailed for Naxos, their plans were so well known that they found the islanders prepared, shut in behind their walls with enough food to withstand a lengthy siege. Aristagoras was incensed. He had staked his reputation and sunk much of his own wealth into the venture and as months passed and the end of the safe sailing season (when they must lift the siege) came ever closer, as morale evaporated with their dwindling supplies, he petulantly accused Megabates of deliberately sabotaging the campaign out of personal animosity. So when, after four months, the disgruntled Persian troops shuffled back on board their ships, as triremes hoisted sails and Aristagoras returned home not just empty-handed but in considerable disgrace, he was convinced that his days as tyrant of Miletus were numbered and that Megabates, debriefing to Darius, would frame him as scapegoat.[32]

There was only one way Aristagoras could find to save his skin and let him keep his status, a devious way, a dangerous way: rebellion from Persia. At Miletus his close advisors backed his motion almost unanimously, and with no time to lose an agent was dispatched to Myous at the head of the great bay where the fleet, just now returned from Naxos, was drawn up on the shore. His mission was to lure the ships' commanders, Ionian tyrants to a man, back to Miletus. From there each was transported under close arrest to his home city accompanied by a messenger proclaiming that, inspired by the examples of heroic Naxos and Athens, Aristagoras was standing down as tyrant of his own free will, introducing a democratic constitution, championing his people's independence from the Persians, and inviting every citizen of every subject state to help throw off oppression's yoke. With his indefatigable leadership they would be free. It was such a heady rallying call, and it was so infectious that—across Ionia and the Aegean islands, through the Hellespont as far east as Byzantium and Chalcedon—all who heard it, the disaffected and the voiceless, the majority who for generations had been governed by a few rich families, and who yearned for the new dispensation, People Power, democracy, rose to arms and drove out their overlords. As rebellion spread, Aristagoras, self-appointed first among equals, took it upon himself to sail to Greece to stir up passions and secure support not just for the immediate revolt but for a campaign to the heart of Persia, for total war.[33]

His first audience was with the Spartans, de facto leaders of the mainland Greeks, who a generation or so back had sent a strongly-worded warning to the Great King Cyrus swearing to support their Asiatic cousins if he harmed them. Now, in a meeting with their interventionist King Cleomenes, Aristagoras explained that those Asiatic cousins needed Sparta's support more than ever; he described how easy it would be for Spartans, 'the deadliest fighting force in all the world', to defeat pigeon-hearted Persians, whose weapons were bows and short swords, whose armour was turbans and trousers; and with a final flourish he produced a map of Persia engraved on bronze, 'showing every sea and river', on which he pointed out the road the Spartan army might then take through countries rich in crops and cattle until it came to Susa and the Persian treasury, a just reward for victory. All this, he promised, could be Sparta's for the taking. But then he made a fatal error. When Cleomenes asked how long it took to march to Susa from the coast, Aristagoras (without thinking) told the truth: three months.[34]

Immediately, Cleomenes' demeanour changed. For the army to be so long absent from Sparta was simply unthinkable. Yes, they had once intervened on Samos in a bid to overthrow Polycrates, but even then a siege of forty days had been as much as they could stomach, and they left, their mission unaccomplished; yes, they had intervened in Athens in a bid to stifle her democracy; and yes, too, they were fighting constantly with neighbours such as Argos; but for the most part Sparta's army must stay close to home. Dangerously outnumbered by their native helot serfs, free Spartans lived in constant fear of an uprising, which was why they had committed to keep constant vigilance, maintain peak fitness, and ensure that their citizen-militia could rapidly respond to any sign of trouble. Aristagoras' proposals were unconscionable, his subsequent attempts at bribery were stonily rebuffed and he was instructed to leave Sparta before sunset.[35]

But the determined Aristagoras was undismayed. At Sparta's port of Gytheum he instructed his helmsman to turn his trireme's prow for Athens, and there on the warm slopes of Pnyx Hill (where—in a natural outdoor auditorium above the Agora in full view of the fragrant hills of Attica and the glittering Acropolis—the still newly-formed democracy held regular assemblies) he put his proposition to the People. Once more he began by belittling Persia's military competence ('they have no shields, no spears') and waxing lyrical on Persian wealth, but this time he took care to tailor his appeal to his specific audience. Drawing on Miletus' (mythical) status as an Athenian colony, he called upon them to defend their fellow countrymen in their struggle to throw off the yoke of tyranny and live as Athens lived—in democratic freedom. His audience—4,000 to 6,000 faces, eager, credulous, turned fervently towards him—was transfixed, as Aristagoras gave ever more extravagant assurances. 'He promised whatever came into his head', Herodotus would later sneer, before reflecting pithily that it was so much easier to persuade Athens' entire citizenry than one Spartan king. But persuade them Aristagoras did. After all, they were ebullient. Their democracy was under ten years old. Just seven years earlier they had driven off four armies in as many days. They were unstoppable. They certainly would step up to the plate.[36]

So, come spring, a small flotilla of Greek warships nosed out of harbour and sailed east towards the sunrise. Twenty were from Athens (most of the city's fleet), and five from Eretria, the only other ally Aristagoras could find, a town with grassy pastures and a sloping beach on Euboea's west coast, overlooking Attica across the straits: twenty-five triremes, a mere eighth of the size of Darius' fleet in his assault on Naxos; but many of his ships had been Ionian, and now they, too, were in rebel hands. So, when they reached Miletus with its three imposing harbours at the mouth of a vast bay, the sight of the Ionians, mobilized and mustered, fired the new arrivals' zeal still more. But they had little time to rest after the voyage or to enjoy the city's luxury. Almost immediately they were on their way, waved off by wily Aristagoras, who had chosen to remain behind the better to coordinate the great campaign. North to Ephesus the triremes sailed, and there, their numbers swollen further, hoplites disembarked, struck out upcountry, crossed the ridge of Mount Tmolus and, unopposed, reached their objective: Sardis.[37]

The satrap, Artaphernes, barricaded behind ramparts in the upper city with his bodyguards, mounted a grim defence, pouring deluges of arrows down on the attackers, but the relatively unprotected lower town—with narrow streets and workshops, huddled houses and the sacred precinct of the Goddess Cybele—offered easy pickings, not least the gold refineries on the banks of the River Pactolus. So, while some allied Greeks tried desperately to find a way to breach the citadel, others, drunk with lust for plunder, began ransacking homes and workshops. As they upended braziers and toppled lamps, one of the houses caught alight and, flames fanned by breezes from Mount Tmolus, an inferno quickly spread through thatched roofs and wooden walls to tear through jostling houses. Now it had leapt the River Pactolus, a ring of fire surrounding the broad central square, where screaming citizens were pouring from their homes, the only place that offered any hope of safety. Now, though, the Lydians of Sardis no longer cowered before the Greeks. Blazing with anger they turned to fight. With black smoke rolling through the burning streets and white-hot cinders falling from the skies, there was little that the Greeks could do except retreat, and as they fell back, choking, to the ridges of Tmolus, and looked down on the roiling city, they could see the firestorm ripping through the sanctuary of Cybele as the ancient temple crashed in ruins and its treasures sank beneath the glowing ash.[38]

They had no desire to stay a moment longer. The next day saw the allied Greeks, soot-blackened, trudging back towards the coast. But on the plain that curved down to the sea near Ephesus the Persians caught up with them—not just the troops from Sardis, but contingents from across all Lydia and Phrygia, who had arrived too late to save the city, but were bent on retribution. As well-trained Persian cavalry thundered down on them, and infantry—albeit with their short swords and their turbans and their trousers—marched still closer in what seemed like never-ending numbers, the Greeks knew they had little hope. Those fortunate and fast enough to make it to their ships cast off and sailed for safety. The Athenians did not hesitate. Like the Eretrians, they raced with all speed west for their homeland's welcome waters, where they washed their hands of the Ionian Revolt and blocked their ears to further pleas for help. It was a luxury no Asiatic Greek possessed. The die was cast, and in the knowledge that, should ambitions fail, reprisals would be merciless, all they could do was ratchet up hostilities, show unity and hold their nerve.[39]

Miltiades, too, was answering the call, expelling Persian bureaucrats, declaring independence in the Chersonese—but, while rebellion offered him a perfect pretext, his agenda was startlingly different from that of his Asiatic colleagues. Yes, his aim was to take back islands occupied by Persia, but not to liberate them. Instead, in a show of spectacular (and typically Greek) self-interest, he would use the growing crisis as an opportunity to bring them firmly under his own control. For centuries, animosity had simmered between Athens and the men of Lemnos, an island that for fifteen years had been a Persian subject. However, legends—and the Delphic oracle—suggested that its fate was to become Athenian. They told how Lemnian raiders once abducted Attic women but became so incensed at their resulting sons' domineering nature that they slaughtered every one of them and so incurred the anger of the gods. Crops failed; cattle died; the Lemnians sent delegates to Delphi to demand advice. 'Submit to whatever punishment the Athenians see fit', came the reply. But when they learned that the terms demanded they surrender the island, they replied that they would hand it over only when a ship could sail with a northerly wind from Attica to Lemnos in a single day, which all who heard it were convinced was both a nautical and geographical impossibility. They were wrong. With Persia's attentions focussed on Ionia, and the Ionian fleet occupied elsewhere, with the warm dry breath of the north-easterly meltemi billowing his sails, Miltiades' five triremes sped out from Attic territory on the south tip of the Chersonese and across the sea to the city of Hephaestia on Lemnos' north coast. Whether because the townsfolk were impressed by his audacity, or because they longed to shake off Persian rule, or realizing that Miltiades had met the terms of their response to the oracle's command, they willingly surrendered. The city of Myrina on the west coast with its azure bay and knobbly hills was less accommodating, yet even it could not withstand a siege, and soon Miltiades controlled all Lemnos before, fanned by the winds of victory, he returned to Imbros and took that island, too. Which was when he showed his diplomatic mettle: rather than claiming them as his own, Miltiades announced that both his newly-captured territories belonged to Athens. It was such a clever move. Just as his father, Cimon Coálemos, returned from exile by dedicating his second Olympic chariot victory to Peisistratus, so Miltiades had gone a long way to restoring his position in the hearts and minds of the Athenian People. Yes, he was still a tyrant, and yes, he had served the Persians, but his gift of the islands to Athens proved he was still a patriot.[40]

Sadly for them, the Ionians possessed neither Miltiades' luck nor his strategic nous. Despite putting up a spirited defence for almost four more years, and winning a momentous victory in Caria that saw the Persian offensive stall, their enemy was simply too powerful. Aristagoras, architect of the rebellion, bowed to the inevitable and fled to Myrcinus, the city on the Strymon, which Darius had once granted Histiaeus, before summoning him to Susa. Now, though, his suspicions soothed, the Great King sent Histiaeus back to Ionia in the belief that he could end the troubles. In Sardis Artaphernes was less gullible. When the Greek arrived at the regenerated city on the last leg of his journey to the coast, the satrap made it clear exactly whom he held responsible for the revolt: 'You made the shoe,' he snarled, 'that Aristagoras put on.' His were not the only doubts. Few in Ionia now trusted Histiaeus, but only the Lesbians harnessed his talents: giving him eight triremes, they sent him as far away as possible—to the Bosporus to intercept ships heading out from the Black Sea.[41]

So Histiaeus was absent in 494 when the rest of the Ionian fleet, 353 triremes, gathered at Ladé, the low, humped island at the entrance to Miletus Bay. News that the Persian army was converging on Miletus, the jewel in Ionia's crown, the city where the seeds of revolution had been sown, soon became reality. Within days the city was besieged, while offshore 600 Phoenician warships blockaded harbours and patrolled the seas. Soon little rowing boats were slipping over from the mainland with messages from deposed tyrants to their fellow citizens: disband and Persia will spare you; fight and she will show no mercy. No wonder then that, after a week's standoff, with stories of young men castrated and desperate girls dragged off to harems ringing ever louder in their ears, so many Greeks had little stomach for doing battle; that, as Phoenician warships closed in, most of the Samian triremes peeled off and turned for home; or that crews from Lesbos followed them, and most of the allied fleet. Only the Chians' hundred ships remained to face the enemy and fight; at last they, too, the few survivors, fled for safety, but when their oarsmen and marines, exhausted and dishevelled, came to Ephesus, they were mistaken for invaders and massacred. In Miletus, too, the streets soon ran with blood. In little time the Persians had broken through the walls, and their revenge was absolute. With chilling efficiency they cleared roadways and squares and smashed house doors, killing every man they found and rounding up the women before marching captives off to Susa, from where Darius dispatched them to the Persian Gulf to live new lives as exiles in the marshlands of the River Tigris. As for Miletus, it was sacked; Apollo's oracle and sanctuary at Didyma, connected to the city by a Sacred Way, was looted and then burned; and the country was resettled with loyal Persians. The first city of Ionia, the special one, the trusted one, had paid the price for infidelity and following the Lie.[42]

With Miletus fallen, the rebellion was over. Of course there were loose ends. But that autumn Histiaeus was captured and decapitated, and his head sent to Darius, who mourned the death of his old friend. And next spring the Phoenician fleet slipped moorings at Miletus and skimmed across the glassy sea to subjugate and punish first Chios, then Lesbos and then Tenedos. Along the east Aegean coasts and south shores of the Hellespont, round the Propontis and on each bank of the Bosporus, Greek cities burned; and next would come the Chersonese.

In his palace at Cardia, Miltiades already knew that it was just a matter of the shortest time before his kingdom, too, was overrun, and—if the Persians caught him and his family—they could not escape the punishment that had been meted out on other rebels. There was just one solution. They must return to Athens. So they packed what they could into their five triremes—bullion and treasure, family heirlooms that none could bear to lose—before, accompanied by essential staff, servants, slaves and bodyguards, they nervously embarked and, with the Chersonese's south coast falling to the Persians, and the Phoenician fleet already garrisoning Tenedos, they raced for Imbros, from where they might reach Lemnos, Scyros and Euboea, and then home. But only four of the five triremes reached Imbros. The ship captained by Metiochus, Miltiades' elder son, was captured by Phoenicians, though perhaps the young man let himself be taken. Perhaps he thought it for the best. He was, after all, the grandson of hated Hippias, the last tyrant of Athens. He could scarcely expect a hero's welcome. Better to join his grandfather as a Persian courtier than risk the People's retribution. Perhaps he had already received reassurances from Hippias that the Great King would treat him well. If so, he was not disappointed. In Persia Darius lavished gifts on him—a house with land, a Persian wife—and when Metiochus had children of his own he brought them up not as Athenians or Greeks or Thracians, but as good truth-telling Persians.[43]

But when Miltiades and his wife, the Princess Hegesipyle, together with his one remaining son, Cimon, and three young daughters, stepped ashore at Athens' ancient port of Phalerum and (followed by their Thracian retinue) travelled as a family for the first time on the road across the insect-ridden marshes south of Athens to their townhouse on Pnyx Hill and their ancestral holdings at Laciadae, they found the atmosphere subdued and ominous. A few months earlier the city's leading playwright, Phrynichus, had tried to stage a drama that explored the capture of Miletus by the Persians. The audience was scandalized. Amid tears and howls of indignation, the play was stopped, its author fined, and an edict passed forbidding any future staging, since 'it caused them to remember their own problems'. Not that they could forget.[44]

For in Persia Darius was remembering, too. When he heard of Athens' role in the destruction of the sanctuary at Sardis and the burning of the town, the avenging Archer King had fired an arrow high into the sky and prayed to Ahura Mazda that he might rain down punishment on the Athenians. And he commanded his chief chamberlain to repeat to him three times at dinner every day: 'Remember the Athenians'. It was not only their sacrilege, their desecration, their impiety that had earned his certain punishment. It was their perfidy as well. For had not these same Athenians promised to give earth and water to his satrap? Had they not sworn to join the Persian Empire? Had they not broken their word? Had they not lied? Were they not, in fact, servants of the Lie, devoted to the Evil One, to Angra Mainyu, the Lord of Demons? Must they not be destroyed? The cities of the liars of Ionia were ablaze already. With their punishment the rule of Persian Truth was being restored. Now, though, it must spread further. The fate that had befallen treacherous Miletus must fall on Athens, too.[45]

3

TRIALS OF STRENGTH

You revelled in good fortune once
when Fate brought that your way.
So now show courage in the face of trouble.

Theognis, 355–356

ATHENS, 493 B.C.

For seventeen-year-old Cimon, newly arrived in his ancestral homeland, Athens must have seemed bewildering and alienating. Her sheer
opulence was unlike anything he had been used to in the Thracian
Chersonese—not least the sparkling Acropolis, with its glittering
temples, clearly seen from Pnyx Hill, like the shining hub of the great
heaving city, itself alive with vendors' cries from market stalls, the creak
of wagons on the sea road, and the rhythmic clack of metalwork that
drifted with the smoke from furnaces and potters' kilns down in the
Cerameicus. Much must have struck Miltiades, too, as unfamiliar—from
the swagger of common citizens, now masters of their fate and answerable to no-one, to how, parading democratic sympathies, even the
wealthiest were dressing down (no more chic oriental robes for *them* or
gorgeous eastern fabrics), to the fervid atmosphere of the Assembly so
close to his town house—and much must have seemed downright ominous. At drinking parties, where songs once lauded ancient heroes, re-
petitive, politically-correct new verses now seemed inescapable:

> I'll carry my sword wreathed in myrtle
> like Harmodius and Aristogeiton,

when they slew the tyrant
and brought *isonomia* to Athens.

I'll carry my sword wreathed in myrtle
like Harmodius and Aristogeiton,
when at Athena's festival
they slew the tyrant, Hipparchus.

Your fame will live forever,
dearest Harmodius and Aristogeiton,
for you slew the tyrant
and brought *isonomia* to Athens.[1]

Had Miltiades given it much thought, he might have reflected on how these drinking songs traced the introduction of *isonomia* not to the wealthy Cleisthenes (whom they did not name) or to the overthrow of Hippias by the returning Alcmaeonids (helped by Sparta) but to the street killing of Hipparchus (whom they wrongly identified as 'the tyrant') by two otherwise anonymous men from a relatively humble family some twenty years before. They were, in other words, profoundly political, promulgating a distinctly democratic version of recent history that not only downplayed but airbrushed out the part played by the aristocratic elite (and Sparta). This was not to say that the elite had been removed from politics. On the contrary, they still held solid power bases within local communities; they could still command deep loyalties; and, as survivors of the reigns of Peisistratus and Hippias, they possessed sufficient nous and determination to adapt to the challenges of democracy. But having established this new, still fragile status quo, there were some among them who feared that the presence of a powerful interloper—the newly returned Miltiades, head of the forceful Philaids—might soon disturb it. So they scrambled to find a means to destroy him, and, while drinking songs' lyrics might not give them their due, their spirit gave them hope.

At parties celebrating his return, it cannot have escaped Miltiades that most of these new songs extolled the killing of a tyrant, a status he himself had held until a few weeks earlier. So, with old enemies ranged increasingly against him, when the summons came it cannot have been unexpected. He was to face trial on the charge of ruling as a tyrant in the Chersonese. If convicted, his punishment would be influenced by his accusers. The least he could expect was a heavy fine. More likely by far was exile, even death. As he left the family house on Pnyx Hill and walked the lanes to the courthouse, he knew that this one day—and Athenian trials did last no longer than a day—would determine not just his own fate but his family's. All that his son, Cimon, could do (too young to set foot in the Agora, let alone attend a trial) was stay at home and try to keep his mother and his sisters calm. Besides, if he attended, this son of a Thracian princess might be too strong a physical reminder of how alien, how foreign Miltiades had become; and it might tip the balance against him.[2]

Miltiades' trial, held open-air on the Areopagus, before a court of archons and ex-archons, the conservative elite of Athens, was a day of high drama. The arguments of the prosecution, who spoke first, must be imagined, but they were no doubt calibrated carefully to contrast the democratic credentials of those landed aristocrats who had played a leading role in the events of the past twenty years, risking lives and livelihoods on behalf of the People to withstand Hippias and his Spartan backers, with the privileged life led by Miltiades, Hippias' puppet, tyrant of the Thracian Chersonese. No doubt they included emotional appeals to Athens' new constitution, to the heroism of Harmodius and Aristogeiton, to how it would insult their memory if, having rid themselves of one tyrant, Athenians allowed another back onto their soil.

Miltiades' response, too, is unknown, but it was perhaps now that those tales of how he stood up to the Persians first fired the popular imagination: how he urged the Ionians to destroy the Danube bridge, how he captured islands from the Persians—Lemnos, Imbros—and made them instead Athenian; how, rather than be ruled by Persia, he had risked all to return to Athens and stand by his city in her hour of need. For he was sure to have reminded avid listeners that even now Phoenician warships were scouting the Greek coast. Even now, angered by Athens' role in the Ionian Revolt, and the burning of Cybele's temple, not to mention broken promises of gifts of earth and water, the Persian Great King was planning his revenge. Even now, Persia posed an existential threat. And the man to face it, the man who knew the workings of the Persian military mind at first hand from the Scythian campaign, the man who had already smashed the Persians in the north Aegean? That man was Miltiades. Athens needed him. Her People must acquit him. If not with these arguments, then with others very like them, Miltiades inspired his audience, and much to his enemies' chagrin that evening he walked free, acquitted and exonerated, no longer simply a fugitive, whom many Athenians had never seen (so long had he ruled the Chersonese), but a clearly charismatic orator, an inspirational, far-sighted leader, on whom they might rely in troubled days that surely lay ahead. His enemies' political manoeuvring had backfired. At the first opportunity the People elected him one of their ten generals, a position he would hold until he died.[3]

For his family the transition to Athenian life was not so seamless. At seventeen, the easy-going Cimon, already physically imposing, his handsome features framed by a fine mop of thick curls, was finding that his Thracian upbringing was setting him apart. No matter what his schooling in Cardia might have been, no matter what his character or how fine his singing voice, many contemporaries, loath to admit him into their charmed inner circle, did all they could to undermine him. Egged on by fathers who were piqued at how enthusiastically the People were rehabilitating Miltiades, the gilded youth of Athens brayed chauvinistically that Cimon was uncouth, poorly read, uneducated, lacking in eloquence and in the mercurial quick-wittedness innate in true Athenians. You could tell, they said, he was the grandson of Coálemus, a man who had been good for nothing except racing chariots, a man who lived up to his nickname, 'Simpleton'. And as for Cimon's character, his appetites for drink and girls were positively Thracian.[4]

Indeed, being half-Thracian posed problems. At a time when friendship bonds were forged and political alliances were tempered in the sweaty, testosterone-rank atmosphere of daily physical workouts, only true-blooded Athenians were permitted access to the elite gymnasia, one by the city's western wall near the sanctuary of Apollo Lyceius ('Wolfish Apollo'), the other by a dusty olive grove a mile north-east of Athens beside the shrine of the hero Academus. Boys of mixed parentage were segregated, forced to make do with the gymnasium at Cynosarges on the banks of the Ilissus next to a temple of the half-divine, half-mortal Heracles. Although to be barred from the Lyceum and Academy gymnasia must have rankled, it was not a total barrier to high society. Almost a generation earlier another young man of mixed parentage had circumvented strict convention by inviting true-born Athenians to train with him at Cynosarges, thanks to which the gymnasium achieved considerable cachet of its own. He was probably still training there when Cimon was a member. Bull-necked, self-confident, his hair cut short in the style of the working classes, he was immediately recognisable, a fervent patriot but in every other way Cimon's antithesis, the self-made son of a self-made father, well-read, a seasoned orator, hungry for power regardless of what rules he broke to win it, ready to lie and cheat if that was what it took. He was Themistocles, and at only thirty years of age he was already serving as Chief Archon.[5]

Themistocles was the archetypal man of the People. Since his teens, when Hippias was overthrown, his ambition was to make his mark in the Assembly. Not for him the study of poetry and music that formed the core of conventional Athenian education. Rather he honed forensic skills, haranguing friends with lengthy declamations, composing speeches as if for courts of law. Two stories circulated about these early years. One told how his teacher, seeing how driven the boy was, predicted he would make his mark on Athens—but for good or ill he could not say. In the other, Themistocles was walking by the seashore with his father, Neocles, when they saw the hulks of decommissioned warships left on the beach to rot. 'That', said Neocles, 'is how the People treat their leaders, too, when they no longer have a use for them.' The warning fell on deaf ears, and by early adulthood Themistocles was building a political powerbase among the poorer citizens, his popularity enhanced not just by his prodigious memory which meant he could recall the names of everyone he met, but by promising reforms more radical than any seen before and pledging that, in power, he would show favour to his friends. Whether pounding the baking Agora, glad-handing crowds that swarmed to the Assembly, or backslapping lounging customers in barbers' shops where men of every age met to joke and gossip and talk politics, he lost no opportunity to show his face and advance his manifesto. As befitted an arch-democrat, he even bought a house in the rough Cerameicus (Potters' Quarter), making it seem suddenly the only place to be by persuading a celebrity musician to rehearse there. As was the case with his gymnasium, chic visitors, who once avoided the district at all costs, now flocked to see him.[6]

Even given his determination and long years of campaigning, it must have come as a surprise—indeed, a shock to his patrician rivals—when, as soon as he turned thirty and became eligible, Themistocles was elected to the key office of Chief Archon, a powerful role that saw him preside over meetings of the People's Council and Assembly, and led automatically (once his year of office was over) to membership of the

Council of the Areopagus, the court that tried Miltiades, once the supreme legislature and still one of the most important administrative bodies in Athens. Now, it was not his personality but his policies that set Themistocles apart. For him equal opportunities were not enough. The entire focus of Athenian endeavour must be changed to give the growing population access to regular lucrative employment. And he fervently believed that in order to achieve this, the city must become a major naval power.[7]

For centuries Athenians, had traded with the Mediterranean and beyond from the little port of Phalerum, some five miles distant from their city's centre, but Themistocles' ambitions called for new facilities on a much grander scale. Perhaps inspired by the example of three-harboured Miletus, he chose for his new enterprise a hilly promontory nearby to the west, already home to the town of Piraeus, which was similarly endowed with three natural harbours. When equipped with wharves and warehouses, the westernmost and widest would suit commercial shipping, while the perfect horseshoe crescent bay at Zea would be home to the warfleet that Themistocles was determined would guarantee Athens' future greatness. For warships would be needed to ensure safe passage for merchantmen and especially the crucial grain ships (that, with Persia in control of many eastern entrepôts and trade routes, were now coming increasingly from Sicily and the Greek west). As each trireme required a crew of 170 oarsmen, not to mention helmsmen, boatswains and marines, even a warfleet of an extra hundred ships (if it could be funded) would give employment to nigh on 20,000 citizens. And since the sailing season was the six or so summer months, those crews would not be drawn from relatively wealthy landowners or peasant farmers but from the urban poor, Themistocles' constituents, which would enhance not just their living standards but Themistocles' political career.[8]

For aristocrats such as Miltiades and his rivals, the Alcmaeonids, this projected extension of the People's power had troubling long-term implications, but more immediately worrisome was news from across the sea that the Persians were once more mobilizing. With no firm intelligence about their goal, Athenians feared the worst. Surely the mission was to march on Athens and Eretria, cities that had aided the Ionian Revolt and torched Cybele's temple in Sardis. Surely this was the hammer blow that they had been expecting since Miletus fell, the beginning of the endgame which, if Persia won, would see not just slaughter and slavery, but Hippias, the Persian lackey, reinstated as 'tyrannos', or 'satrap'—his title would not matter; what mattered was the end of their democracy.

To lead the expedition, Darius chose the brilliant young Mardonius, son of one of the six co-conspirators who had helped him win the throne some thirty years before, his royal son-in-law, the recently appointed satrap of Lydia. Here Mardonius had shown considerable acumen in handling the crushed Ionians: while ensuring that, as newly reinstated members of the Persian family, the 'Yauna' ('Ionians', as Persians called all Greeks) once again paid tribute, he allowed many to adopt a democratic constitution so that in spirit if not fact they might believe that they enjoyed a similar autonomy to their mainland cousins. It was a canny move, the gift of a carrot following the wielding of a bloody stick, a tactic to secure his rear as he struck north across the Hellespont and west for Europe. For his first objective was to bring the north Aegean back into the Persian fold.[9]

With every merchant ship that docked at Phalerum, the news grew grimmer by the day: Persia's fleet had ferried a huge army into Europe; the Chersonese, all Thrace was back in Persian hands; Thasos, rich in gold, had fallen; and now Mardonius was in Macedonia, feasting at Aegae, 'City of Goats', in the palace of King Alexander, who had succeeded to the throne some six years earlier, as amenable as his father to Persian blandishments—or simply just pragmatic. It was as if Ionia's revolt had never happened. And all it had achieved was for Darius' determination to be stronger, for his grip on his Greek subjects to be tighter, for his will to punish Athens to be more entrenched. And now Mardonius was only weeks away in Macedonia, and tension in Athens was rising. But suddenly, the unexpected: as Mardonius pushed west into the rugged heartland, his encampment was overrun at night by mountain tribesmen. Mardonius himself was badly wounded and many of his men were killed, but still he stayed until he was victorious; then he returned to Aegae, where he sent an order to his fleet, which had been stationed at Acanthus just west of Chalcidice, to join him.[10]

As they put to sea and coasted down the easternmost of three extended promontories that form the long Chalcidice peninsula, the great bulk of Mount Athos rising, wooded and majestic to their starboard, crews and helmsmen felt the winds begin to rise. But there was nowhere to land; now they were rounding the cape, grey cliffs plunging to the sea, and rollers smashing, surf exploding, hard rain battering the hulls. Helpless, the helmsmen tried to seer a steady course, but it was useless. First one vessel foundered on the rocks, then more, until the sea was churning flotsam from 300 ships, and the drifting corpses of 20,000 men—or so reports would have it. Herodotus recorded what he heard: 'Some of the Persians were snatched by sea-monsters, which infest the waters around Athos, and devoured; others were dashed against rocks; others, who could not swim, were drowned; still others died of hypothermia.' Faced with such disaster, Mardonius was forced to change his plans. He returned to Asia and the ministrations of a good physician. It was not the last time Greece's seas and storm winds would prove staunch allies to her people.[11]

Yet Darius was undeterred. Ships and men could be replaced. What mattered was that Thrace and Macedonia had been reclaimed. And, if the seas round Athos proved treacherous, there were other ways (as Aristagoras once pointed out) to mainland Greece. So the next year he sent demands for fealty, which at Athens were accompanied by an ultimatum: surrender earth and water, as once promised, or face devastating military consequences. With the example of Miletus seared in the imagination, many were minded to comply: not least rich landowners, so comfortable with eastern lifestyles, for whom Persian patronage seemed so much more appealing than the spread of People Power, or (worse) the sharp edge of a Persian scimitar; not least, too, the family of Hippias, some of whom still lived in Athens (one, indeed, against all odds had recently been Chief Archon and many of them longed to see the tyrant reinstated). Others, though, were adamant. The demand must not be met. And their voices won the day. The Persians were rebuffed—and more. Tradition later told how the ambassadors were thrown into the dismal bowels of the 'barathrum', a deep pit where criminals were cast alive with no means of sustenance and no hope of escape. And the man who proposed this punishment? Miltiades. If true, the grisly episode suggests that, knowing how opinion in Athens was divided, he was determined to commit an outrage of such grave proportions that there could be no going back. Nor was he alone. Arriving in Sparta with similar demands, other Persians were said to have been thrown into a well. They had come for earth and water. They received their fill of one in Athens, while in Sparta they received the other.[12]

Yet Athens and Sparta were not Greece, and while they seemed united in their stance, many more cities were ready to capitulate. True to the maxim that an enemy's enemy is a friend, foes of the Athenians and Spartans, embittered by years of warfare and attrition, and hoping that regime change would enable them to settle ancient scores, were showing signs of, if not welcoming, at least tolerating Persia. Worryingly for Athens, they included neighbouring Boeotia to the north, parts of Euboea to the east, and Aegina, whose silhouette, a dancing dolphin, could be clearly seen from the Acropolis. When Darius' ambassadors landed at its quayside, they were met by a flock of fawning islanders, huddled round their spokesman Crius, a burly former wrestler whose name meant 'Ram', readily agreeing to the Persians' demands; and when they left, they took with them two well-plugged amphoras, one filled with the island's earth, the other with its water. The Spartan king, Cleomenes, was incandescent. For years his city had been recognized as the most powerful in all Greece, so for Aegina to make such a decision unilaterally without consulting him was unacceptable. So he boarded a warship and sailed full speed to Aegina. But Crius and his cronies were intransigent. Cleomenes, they said, was an Athenian lackey. He did not speak for Sparta, and they would take no orders from the likes of him.[13]

In truth the Spartans were divided, too. Unlike fellow Greeks in almost every way, theirs was an eccentric constitution, not least because at any time they had not one king but two. Each belonging to a powerful family (the Agiads, who claimed seniority, and Eurypontids), both traced descent from Heracles, and while in theory they were tempered by a board of five annually-elected ephors ('overseers'), with whom they exchanged monthly oaths to act within the law and uphold harmony, in fact it was not unknown for kings to use their power and majesty to thwart it. Such was the situation now. Since the debacle of their attack on Attica seventeen years earlier, when the Spartan joint king Demaratus and his Corinthian allies abandoned Cleomenes at Eleusis (prompting a Spartan law that thenceforth only one king must lead any one army on campaigns, while the other would normally stay at home), feelings between the two men had been running high. So, on his return to Sparta, Cleomenes accused Demaratus of undermining his mission to Aegina. Perhaps he was justified. Perhaps (like some Athenian aristocrats) Demaratus, whose place within the international elite had been cemented by his victory in the Olympic four-horse chariot race, did indeed feel less hostile towards Persia than many of his fellow citizens. At any rate, the atmosphere in Sparta was becoming more tense by the day, as Cleomenes did all he could to compromise his colleague.[14]

At last he found a way. There were still some old men, former ephors, who recalled how, when Demaratus' father, King Ariston, learned of his son's birth, he was observed counting on his fingers the months since his wedding and muttering, 'the boy cannot be mine'. Despite his queen's protestations, another member of the family, Leotychidas, backed up the claims. With Sparta in turmoil, a delegation went to Delphi to consult Apollo. The answer, delivered through his priestess, was unequivocal: Demaratus was not Ariston's son. He had no right to rule. So Demaratus was deposed, and Leotychidas raised to the throne. At last, too late, the truth came out. Cleomenes had bribed the Delphic priestess and one of the officials. Both were immediately dismissed. The Spartan kings, however, kept their thrones, and Leotychidas accompanied Cleomenes to Aegina, where, presenting a united front, the two men ordered the islanders to surrender Crius and nine others, whom they shipped as hostages to Athens, a sign of their goodwill.[15]

While Aegina's readiness to side with Persia was troubling, more threatening for Sparta was the position taken by her near neighbour, Argos. For centuries, as both proud cities vied to lead the Peloponnese, border raids had escalated into wars. Just three years earlier, inspired by an oracle declaring that he was destined to take Argos, Cleomenes had launched an invasion of his own. Landing on the beach at Sepeia near Tiryns (from where Heracles, his ancestor, had once set out to perform his labours), he found the Argive army. For days neither side was willing to attack. Instead, breakfast over, they drew up into desultory lines to wait until the trumpet sounded lunch, when they would fall out, enjoy a leisurely, untroubled meal, take up position once more in the afternoon and break again for dinner. But when he realised that the Argives were simply mirroring the Spartans, following the patterns of their trumpet calls, Cleomenes found a means to break the deadlock. He passed the order through his ranks that, while they should appear to stand down at lunchtime, they should wait until the enemy was eating and attack. Caught unawares, the Argives turned and ran. Those who were not hacked down took refuge in a grove, where they found themselves surrounded by the Spartans.[16]

Once more there was a stalemate, until some Argive prisoners agreed to tell Cleomenes the names of friends now snared inside the wood.

Armed with a list, the Spartan herald called to them one by one. Their relatives, he said, had ransomed them, and they were free to go. One at a time each man emerged and was escorted off by Spartan guards, but when a suspicious Argive climbed a tree to find out what was happening, he shouted to his credulous companions that, instead of being sent back to Argos, the fifty who had left had all been slaughtered. Trapped and terrified, no-one moved. But then smoke began to billow and flames crackled through dry brushwood, and there was no escape. Cleomenes had ordered his helot serfs to set fire to the grove. Surrounded by a wall of Spartan shields, to a man 6,000 Argives burned alive. The flower of Argos, an entire generation, had been wiped out.

But Cleomenes failed to follow up his victory. Told by a shocked prisoner that the grove was sacred to the hero, Argos, he despaired: surely this was what the oracle had meant; this was the Argos he was fated to capture; and if he tried to take the city, he would fail. His mood was not improved when he tried to sacrifice at Hera's sanctuary a few miles inland from the site of his atrocity. That the priest refused him entrance was of little matter—priests were human and could easily be dragged away by Spartan soldiers—but when a flame shot from the breast of Hera's statue, Cleomenes knew that it was time to leave. Back in Sparta, he was put on trial. Fortunately for him, the Spartans were exceptionally superstitious, and the authorities accepted his interpretation of the statue omen (that the gods had intervened) as sufficient reason for his failing to take Argos. Less tolerable was that now, already three years later, Argos—the second greatest city in the Peloponnese—was refusing to stand firm beside them against Persia. Not that Argos yet possessed a major army. To fill the places of their slaughtered citizens until their sons were old enough they had been forced to empower slaves and serfs and elevate them to positions of authority. No wonder that, faced with such humiliation, still reeling from Cleomenes' brutality (it was a war crime to kill men in the protection of a sanctuary), they had no stomach for assisting Sparta.

In the early summer, the word came that all Greece had been expecting: intelligence from spies and traders of a Persian army mustering on Cilicia's Aleian plain and a fresh fleet at the coast to meet them; two crack commanders—Artaphernes, a brother of the Great King; Datis, a top Median admiral—promoted to replace Mardonius, still convalescing from his injuries; Hippias, an old man now but still ambitious, buoyed by his readings of the omens, preparing to embark with them, already certain he would realize his dream of once more ruling Athens. As weeks passed, more reports came, bulletins that pounded into Athens, thick as hail: the army, 25,000 strong, complete with cavalry and horses, had boarded special transport ships; and now the fleet, 400 merchantmen, 200 triremes, had sailed north to Ionia from where, against all expectations—for surely they would take a northern arc up past the Hellespont and Thrace and down the eastern coast of mainland Greece—they suddenly swung west from Samos and set course for Naxos.[17]

Not only was Naxos wealthy, the island bore testimony, too, to an Athenian's treachery. As all Greeks knew, it was here that the legendary King Theseus discarded Ariadne, despite her helping him to slay the Minotaur. But of far greater significance to Persians, it was Naxos' resistance nine years earlier that had inspired the Yauna to revolt. Now, in revenge for that fiasco, Naxos must be not just conquered but mercilessly punished. As watchmen saw the Persian sails, dark, looming rectangles against the morning sea, the islanders abandoned homes and farmsteads, fishing nets spread out on harbour walls, workshops, and looms, and ran, small children clutched in tight embrace, towards the hills. Already the first Persians were landing; already the old, frail and slow were overtaken, some to be butchered, others led away to slavery; and as, lungs bursting, pulses pounding, those who did escape up stony sheep tracks turned to look down to their city, they saw Persian soldiers ransacking their homes and sanctuaries, efficiently removing strongboxes and statues, rounding up flocks and cattle, slaughtering them for the feast that followed. At last, at dawn, with most ships ready to depart, and pitch-soaked firebrands in their hands, detachments fanned through lanes and alleyways, torching workshops, homes and temples, and flames began to ripple, and smoke began to rise, and an acrid pall began to drift across the sea. For the Persians this was a perfect purging: as the sun's fire rose into the sky and Ahura Mazda blazed in majesty, on earth fire cleansed the rebel city; order was restored; the purifying process had begun.[18]

From smouldering Naxos it was only a short way to Delos, the most holy island in the Cyclades, where once Apollo had been born and now, around a sacred lake beneath the low Mount Cynthus, a lavish sanctuary was glittering in the baking sun, its temples rich with offerings, their dazzling forecourts forested with statues. Its population feared the worst. They put to sea and scrabbled to the safety of the hills on nearby Tenos to watch Persia's fleet sail unopposed to Delos. But it did not land there. Instead, it anchored just across the narrow strait at Rhenea, from where, dressed in their finest robes, with Persian guards weighed down by heavy boxes, an exclusive group of men was ferried to the island. At its head were Datis and Artaphernes, but beside them as an honoured guest was Hippias.[19]

A generation earlier, Peisistratus, his father, alert to Delos' significance, presided over rituals to purify the island, the spiritual heart of the Ionian Greeks, who shared ethnicity with Athens, and began a splendid colonnaded temple to Apollo. Now, onto the altar opposite its open doors, beside a towering statue of the archer god, Datis ordered that the contents of the crates be emptied and then burned: 300 talents of pure frankincense, whose sweet smoke, so unlike the bitter cloud that had engulfed unyielding Naxos, rose high into the sky to hang, a haze of piety, a mark of Persian respect to the Greek sun god, the equivalent of their Ahura Mazda. Darius showed specific reverence to Apollo. He had already shown his disapproval of the satrap of Ionia for taxing 'Apollo's sacred gardeners', requiring them to 'work unconsecrated land', but now his favour to the god could be combined with honouring his trusted servant, Hippias, a mark of goodwill to the man who would soon be ruling Athens, once that city had been shown the error of her ways. As the Persian fleet cast off on their short voyage north, an earthquake rumbled through the island. For superstitious Hippias, remembering how Apollo had vowed to 'cause Delos to shudder as it never shuddered in the past', it seemed the best of omens: the gods had accepted Persia's offering of incense; they would shake Greece to its roots.[20]

With Boeotia hostile to the north and Aegina keen to see them worsted to the south, the noose was tightening round Athens. Soon news came that the Persians, the safety of their rear ensured by hostages from ports passed on their way, had landed on Euboea at Carystus, just forty miles from Athens. At first its people would not bow to the invaders. Unlike the Naxians and Delians, they barricaded themselves bravely behind city walls and hunkered down for a long siege. But when they saw their crops destroyed and livestock butchered, they lost heart and came to terms. For Datis it was a sweet victory, and since Carystus was not implicated in the Ionians' revolt from Persia, he could be lenient, for he had achieved his purpose: he now possessed a crucial base from which to attack each of the two hateful cities that had helped the rebels when they set fire to Sardis: from Carystus he could pivot either north towards Eretria or west to Athens. Wishing rightly to consolidate Euboea, he chose to pivot north.[21]

Not that his intentions were immediately clear. As Persia's fleet sailed up the Euripus channel it might equally be making for the eastern coast of Attica, but, until they landed, there was little that Miltiades or any of his fellow generals could do. To try to second-guess the Persians could prove disastrous. Deploy on the east coast, and the enemy could sail around Cape Sunium and slip into Phalerum or Piraeus before the army could be back to face them. Better—if more nerve wracking—to play a waiting game. Better to stay on guard, coiled, ready to respond to whatever Datis and his Persians might throw at them. Indeed, there were already 4,000 Athenians on hand, poised to aid Eretria, men who had colonized Chalcis' fertile fields after that city's crushing in the heady early days of democracy. But as they talked tactics with their allies, these settlers became increasingly concerned. It was not at all apparent that Eretrians were speaking with one voice: while one faction stood prepared to fight, the other (more pragmatic or more cowardly) was arguing for taking to the mountains, for doing as the Delians had done, for running, for surviving. There were even rumoured to be others ready, if the price were right, to betray their city to the enemy. At last one of their spokesmen gave his sensible if fatalistic advice: the situation was so volatile, the response of the Eretrians so unpredictable, that the Athenians would be best advised to leave the city to its fate. No point in sacrificing their much-needed men for an uncertain cause.[22]

As the Athenians crossed over to the mainland, Persia's fleet hove into view. Within a short while, transport ships were beached, ramps set in place, and horses led ashore to be saddled, mounted, galloped across the hard wet sand to loosen muscles following the long sea voyage. Then infantry, too, disembarked, men in their thousands from across the Persian Empire, as well as Greeks—Ionians, Aeolians—some press-ganged into serving the Great King, others obeying willingly. Within Eretria a vote was carried to remain and face a siege, so for six days they patrolled the parapets, pelting the attacking Persians with javelins, firing fusillades of arrows from the city walls until the sun sank red across the water and the blue hills of Attica beyond, and fighting finished for the night. But on the seventh day they were betrayed. The city gates were opened, and the Persians poured in. And now again they did their systematic work of rounding up survivors, corralling them, transporting them across the sea to Persia to work as slaves for foreign masters, of looting treasures from sanctuaries, and, when they were completely bare, of burning every temple to the ground. Eretria had had the gall to join a lawless expedition aimed at undermining the Great King, and now the Great King's vengeance was complete: Eretria was no more.[23]

Yet there remained one city on which Persian revenge had still to fall. Across the straits lay Attica and the enticing silhouette of Mount Pentelicon, and beyond that clear horizon Athens, surely, like Eretria, low-hanging, luscious fruit, ripe for the plucking. As Herodotus succinctly wrote: 'Having taken Eretria in hand, and rested a few days, they sailed to Attica, exalting in their victory, and confident that they would do to the Athenians as they had done to the Eretrians.' As the first Persian ships left Euboea to start their voyage south, watchmen on the Attic hills would have been excused for thinking that their route would take them all the way to Sunium then west towards Piraeus or Phalerum, where troops would disembark, fight their way up to Athens and besiege the city. Instead, after just a few miles, the ships changed course. And as they did, their goal became clear. They were heading for the same flatlands and sandy beaches of eastern Attica where the Peisistratids once owned estates; where Peisistratus himself once landed with a foreign army—hoplites from Naxos, Thebes and Argos, cavalry from Thessaly—before smashing the Athenian opposition and establishing himself for the third and final time as tyrant; where Hippias hoped that history would repeat itself. They were heading for the plain of Marathon. Soon they were setting up their bivouacs, as once more Persian cavalry galloped their manoeuvres on the hard sand south of the sheltered waters where, protected by a headland, their ships were dragged onto the beach.[24]

For months Miltiades and his nine elected colleagues, generals on the board of Athens' democratic high command, had been planning for this moment. But still they were unprepared. Attempts to rally an alliance had proved singularly futile. Only the little polis of Plataea on the southern border of Boeotia, an Athenian ally for almost thirty years, had responded to their call, agreeing to send a thousand hoplites to join Athens' army of 10,000. From Sparta, so far, nothing except fine assurances. Yes, they would come to Athens' aid, but only when the time was right: they had considerations of their own to think of. Soon, though, it might be too late.[25]

So in a final bid to prod their ally into action the generals dispatched a messenger, Pheidippides, a long-distance runner who would pound the dusty earth along the coast of the Saronic Gulf, across the Isthmus of Corinth, on into the Argolid and through the mountain passes of Arcadia, down into Laconia and the bridge across the reedy River Eurotas before, in Sparta at the Spartan Council, he would make a last appeal to Sparta's kings and ephors. By the time he got there forty-eight hours after setting off, it might all be over. By the time the Spartans came to help, Athens might not exist. But it was worth the risk. It was worth any risk at all.[26]

Meanwhile, outnumbered more than two to one, and with the fate not only of Miletus but Eretria and Naxos at the forefront of their minds, Athens' hoplites made prayer and sacrifice. Their desperation was apparent in their bargaining with gods, not least their vow to Artemis, Apollo's sister: if she helped the city win, they would sacrifice a goat for every Persian killed. And then, hymns sung, libations poured, beasts slaughtered and their bones and fat burned on the altar of Athena Polias high on the warm Acropolis, the army trudged across the hills to Marathon.[27]

Not trained to march in step, it was a ragtag band made up of poets and businessmen and farmers, anyone and everyone who could afford a suit of armour—a bronze helmet, five pounds in weight, complete with nose- and cheek guards that enclosed the skull; a bronze breastplate, thirty to forty pounds in weight, tied at the sides with leather straps; a skirt of leather thongs that hung from waist to knee above the tunic; bronze greaves bent tight round calves and shins; a round shield, three feet in diameter, weighing sixteen pounds, its wooden core faced with a sheet of bronze on which were painted personal devices (gorgon's heads; birds; animals); an eight-foot ash or cornel spear, tipped with a razor-sharp iron spearhead, an iron spike at its butt; and a short iron sword with a two-foot blade, sheathed in a leather baldric. Most if not all brought a batman, a slave responsible for carrying and maintaining equipment, helping strap on armour, pitching tents, cooking meals. Undoubtedly there was a host of light-armed troops as well, men whose finances did not stretch to armour, but who were good with slings and bows, all keen to do their bit for Attica. Then there were priests and animal handlers, a vital part of any expedition, since before each battle sacrifices needed to be made and portents read—if omens were unfavourable, there would be no fighting; there were aulós players, too, and trumpeters; and there were the ten generals elected, one from each tribe, and with them the War Archon (a political, non-military official, assigned to his office by lot). This year the post had fallen to Callimachus, whose name at least was providential. It meant 'Good Fighting'. But more experienced and of far greater authority were his generals, of whom one was recognized as being supreme: Miltiades, the Persian expert, who knew Persian tactics at first hand. And with him perhaps (since as many warriors of fighting age as possible were mobilized) marched Cimon, now almost twenty years of age, on his first campaign, the most vital that Athenians had ever undertaken.[28]

From the saddle between wooded Parnes and Pentelicon, the Athenians and Plataeans dropped down to dunes south-west of Marathon, to take up their position on land sacred to the hero, Heracles. Like Callimachus' name it was propitious, for legend told how Heracles once stole from Crete a powerful bull, which rose dripping from the sea, Poseidon's gift to Crete's King Minos, intended by the god to be a sacrificial offering. But Minos was so enamoured of the beast that he spared it. Too late he realized his error. Mating with the queen, the bull had sired the Minotaur before escaping to rampage throughout the Cretan countryside. So, when Heracles offered to remove it to Greece as one of his twelve Labours, the king agreed. In Greece, too, the bull wreaked destruction until, at Marathon, Theseus captured it, dragged it to Athens and sacrificed it on the altar of Athena before, a pious Athenian, he sailed to Crete and slew the Minotaur, defying all odds to triumph over a foreign king. Looking out across the plain teeming with so many thousand Persians, many a Greek hoplite must have prayed that such an outcome would be theirs.[29]

So the waiting game began. Neither side had reason to attack immediately. For Datis and Artaphernes, the longer the delay the more chance that the Greeks would lose their nerve, especially if Persian cavalry kept riding close to fire off arrows and trade insults. Meanwhile, opinion among Athens' generals was split between those ready to risk all in battle and others who advised surrender. Even when Miltiades delivered an impassioned speech to the war council, it took Callimachus' casting vote to ensure that they would stay and fight. The Athenians were far from being united. Not only that: the Persians knew well, and Hippias knew better, that in Athens—even among those who currently professed hostility—there were not a few who, when the time was right, would readily switch sides; there were, indeed, some in the city primed to open Athens' gates, as the traitors at Eretria had opened theirs, if the Persians arrived victorious. Even among those willing to defend their city and their constitution, many—perhaps most—held little hope for victory. The Persians' reputation, the ease with which they had overrun Eretria and Naxos and countless other poleis, not to mention Egypt, Lydia and Media, meant that the chance of an Athenian victory was slim. Not only did the Persians outnumber the Greek army at least two to one, their terrifying cavalry would hamper any Greek advance, punching holes into their battle line, exploiting weaknesses, turning defeat into a massacre.[30]

A well-timed message from Datis divided the Athenians still further. Displaying his knowledge of Athens' mythological history (gleaned no doubt from Hippias), the Great King's general reminded them that Theseus' father, King Aegeus, had sired a son called Medus by the sorceress Medea, who went on to found the kingdom of the Medes. As a result, he said, he would show clemency to his Greek cousins. If the Athenians surrendered, he would forgive their crimes at Sardis; but if they fought, they must endure their fate. Again, Miltiades stood firm. Citing the same myth, he bade the messenger return to Datis with the reply that, since Medus, an Athenian, had once been king of Media, it was more appropriate that Datis should surrender, for no Mede had ruled Athens.[31]

Only Miltiades had experience of Persia defeated: in Scythia he had witnessed at first hand Darius' desperate dash across the Danube bridge; in the Chersonese he had expelled Persian officials; on Lemnos and Imbros he had trounced Persian garrisons. He knew that they were not invincible. But still, logistics were against him and his fellow generals. Quite simply, in terms of numbers and resources they were outclassed. As they awoke each morning and watched the Persians, so confident, so self-assured, and just a mile away, all they could do was wait and hope— hope for a miracle, and wait for the arrival of the Spartans. Even when Pheidippides returned alone—breathless and blistered and so dazed from his long run that he spoke convincingly of having met the god, Pan, in the mountains of Arcadia, and made a solemn vow that for all future time Athenians would honour him—they still did not lose trust in the

Spartans, despite being told that they were celebrating their Carneia Festival in honour of Apollo, which meant that they could not embark on war until the night of the full moon: it would be ten days before they could set out for Marathon. In truth, the Spartans were reluctant to venture far from home. Even so depopulated after Sepeia, Argos remained a danger; and Sparta's helot serfs were always threatening rebellion; besides, the polis had not properly recovered from the crisis of Demaratus' deposition and Cleomenes' continuing attempts to bolster his own power. But the Athenian and Plataean hoplites needed that mirage, that fantasy of seeing the Spartans in their red cloaks marching down the hills to join them, and as the days wore on and the moon grew fatter every night-time, they clung still tighter to their hopes.[32]

Then suddenly one morning everything changed. Waking to the blinding August sun breasting the pale mountains of Euboea, across the plain they saw a scene of tightly disciplined activity: soldiers striking tents and heading for the sea, others packing their equipment into boxes as transport ships manoeuvred to the shore and horses were led patiently up ramps into their stall-lined holds. Far from giving battle here at Marathon, the Persians were set on sailing round to Athens, where they would find their quislings ready to receive them, the city unprotected. Horror rippling through the ranks, all eyes turned towards Miltiades. Since each of the ten generals—rivals such as the radical Themistocles and Aristides, a highly-principled conservative—held equal powers, they rotated the supreme command each day. Already, when their turn came, several had willingly allowed Miltiades to take the role, but by pure chance this was his allotted day, and with no time to lose he rose to the occasion. In fact, unwittingly the Persians had done him a great service. By embarking their horses early, they had deprived themselves of cavalry, which could have wreaked such havoc. Moreover, the infantry seemed unprepared for battle. There could be no better time to fight. In the Chersonese, when he first assumed the role of tyrant, the combination of surprise and surgical violence had led to victory; here, too, at Marathon such tactics might just work again.[33]

So, sacrifices made and omens read, as hoplites hurriedly strapped on their armour, Miltiades passed on his orders and nodded to the trumpeter to sound the signal. Then, with a mile between them and the Persians, the Greeks began their grim advance. To try to cover the whole plain, their line was desperately extended: on the right wing, in the place of honour, strode Callimachus; on the left the thousand Plataeans; and in the centre, where the ranks were thinnest, was Miltiades. By now the enemy had seen them, and, with still more than fifteen minutes before the sides would clash, they were readying themselves to meet them. Already, Persian archers were stringing bows and, as the Greeks came into range, deluges of arrows rained down from the sky. It was now that Miltiades' tactics came into play. Abandoning the usual close ranks of an advancing phalanx, he gave the order: 'Run!' And, shields held high against the hail of missiles, spears poised to thrust and stab, the Greeks crashed forward in a wave of bronze, each man cocooned within his helmet, his hearing muffled, vision tunnelled by his cheek guards and his narrow eye-slits, shield pummelled now by sword blades, and so buoyed by adrenaline he neither knew nor cared whether the blood that splashed hot on his face and arms was another's or his own. Each man's focus was now centred on his personal experience.

One, Epizelus, later said he saw a towering figure, heavy-armoured, with a bristling beard bear down on him, but just at the last moment the enemy's sword swerved, and the Athenian was spared. But in his terror he was struck profoundly blind. Another fought beside his faithful hunting dog. Another, Callias, hereditary Torchbearer at the Eleusinian Mysteries, plunged into battle in his priestly robes, his long hair tied back in a ribbon. Still others swore they saw the apparition of King Theseus in hoplite armour harrying the Persians; others saw Heracles, and others still Athena; and there were even those who seemed to see a local peasant, dressed in rags and slashing at the Persians with his plough, but when they sought him afterwards, he was nowhere to be found—only from Apollo's oracle did they subsequently learn he was a local deity, Echetlus, and they must worship him.[34]

Now the two Athenian wings had overrun their counterparts, but instead of offering pursuit, they wheeled back in, as ordered, to attack the enemy centre, where crack battalions of Persians and Sacae (grim Scythians from far beyond the Caspian Sea) were forcing the Athenians' thin lines to give ground towards the hills. And now another god appeared to lend his aid: Pan, whom the Greeks believed sowed his eponymous panic. Sensing themselves inside an ever tightening trap, the Persians felt the tide of battle turn. Hemmed in on every side, their one thought was of survival, but as they tried to fight their way back to the ships, many were forced into marshes at the northern edges of the plain. More were cut down in the bloody surf. And still the Greeks surged on. Wading deep into the sea, they tried to board the Persian ships. One, a young man, Cynegeirus, grabbed a stern, ready to leap up, but an axe blow lopped his hand off at the wrist, and he fell to bleed his life out in the churning waves. But with seven ships already taken by the Greeks, and the remaining Persian fleet now out to sea, and with those of the enemy who were still flailing in the marshes being systematically despatched, Miltiades gave the order to stop fighting.[35]

For Athens remained in mortal danger. With a fair wind the first Persian ships could be at Phalerum within ten hours of sailing. If they found the city unprotected, the victory at Marathon would be in vain. For the Athenians to march the twenty-five or so miles overland would take perhaps eight hours, so even if they set off now they might still be too late. But it was crucial that they try. With no time to lose, Miltiades assembled his euphoric men. Assigning the trusted Aristides and his tribe to guard the plain from looters and complete the slaughter of the enemy trapped and wounded, he set off with the rest of his Plataeans and Athenians on their forced march back across the baking hills, loud with the thrum of insects, on their last-gasp mission to save Athens. When they reached the banks of the Ilissus, where they meant to set up camp at Cynosarges, they learned to their relief that, while Persian ships were anchoring off Phalerum, so far there had been no attempt to land. But, given the long beaches and the flat expanses south of Athens, so suited for their cavalry—and given, too, that some claimed to have seen signals flashed from treacherous collaborators in the city (surely the accursed Alcmaeonids)—it seemed just a matter of time before another battle must be joined. So, for desperate hours, perhaps throughout the humid night beneath the now full August moon, exhausted soldiers kept their watch, until they saw the ships put out to sea and hoist their sails and steer for Sunium—not to make landfall elsewhere in Attica (as many must have feared) but to keep on east until they came to Asia. Against all hope the Persians were gone.[36]

Too late the Spartan reinforcements came—2,000 hoplites, who whether through design or accident, arrived only once the threat was over, the day after the battle—and with them the Athenians returned to Marathon. As they surveyed the battlefield, the sheer scale of the victory sank in: around 6,400 Persian dead consigned to hastily-dug pits for the loss of precisely 192 Athenians and an unnumbered handful of

Miltiades may have worn this Corinthian-style helmet at Marathon. Discovered at Olympia, its inscription reads, 'Miltiades dedicated to Zeus'.

Plataeans. It had indeed been a massacre. But of Persians, not Greeks. At Marathon itself, the victors made solemn sacrifice before burying their dead beneath two grave mounds, one for each city, Plataea's ten feet tall, that of Athens (the so-called Soros) four times higher, adorned with ten marble slabs, one for each tribe, which memorialized the names of the fallen. In time another slab would be erected, the epitaph it bore commemorating Athens' victory, one city saving all of Greece:

> At Marathon Athenians fought in the first ranks for Greece,
> and scattered the power of gold-garnished Persians.

Where the enemy had turned in flight they set up, too, a trophy, a column, carved from marble from Pentelicon, while elsewhere on the battlefield they would raise another monument, this time in honour of a single man, Miltiades, whose bravery and prowess the hoplites honoured beyond all others', to whom above all they assigned their victory and salvation.[37]

As for Miltiades, he knew whom he must thank. While in a cave on the Acropolis' north-west slope the People consecrated a new sanctuary to Pan, the god of wild things, who had sown such terror into Persian breasts, he raised a statue to the god at Marathon itself, at the very place where thanks to his intervention the battle pivoted:

> Miltiades set up this statue to me, Pan, the goat-hooved Arcadian,
> who fought against the Persians and stood as Athens' ally.

He made a dedication at Olympia as well, at the Panhellenic sanctuary of Zeus, deep in the Peloponnese: the helmet he had worn at Marathon, his name incised on its left cheek guard. But when he suggested to the Athenian Assembly that he be honoured with an olive crown like a triumphant athlete, his rivals intervened. This was a step too far. One of his adversaries was the hulking Sophanes, a leading citizen from the Attic *deme* of Decelea, whose kudos rose immeasurably when he killed Aegina's general in single combat in that island's ongoing war with Athens. Standing tall amid his fellow citizens, he bellowed that only when Miltiades had won a victory against the Persians single-handedly should he be singled out for such an honour. The citizens were delighted. No matter if they owed their victory to one man's tactics, it was the People as a body who had won it (though the hoplite class would never truly share their glory with the non-combatant poor). If anyone was owed the People's recognition it was their representative, the War Archon Callimachus, who, in his official role, had vowed to set up a thank offering to Athena in event of victory, and sacrificed his life for Athens on the battlefield. Erecting an Ionic column topped by a fifteen-foot-tall winged Victory adorned with metal fittings to stand proud on the Acropolis, the People fulfilled his vow and on their own behalf remembered him:

> Callimachus of Aphidnae dedicated me to Athena,
> who mediates with the immortal gods of Mount Olympus,
> Callimachus, Athenians' War Archon, who fought
> at Marathon for all the Greeks:
> this monument is given by the sons of Athens.

As for their vow to sacrifice to Artemis a goat for every Persian killed, so many enemy were slain that they were forced to fulfil it in instalments: the goddess must accept 500 goats a year.[38]

But it was at Delphi, one of the greatest Panhellenic sanctuaries, that Athens proclaimed victory most loudly. Delphi, so Greeks believed, lay at the centre of the earth, where aeons earlier, flying from the two facing limits of the world, two eagles met, the place marked by an egg-shaped stone (dropped from the skies by Zeus) that landed close to where Apollo's temple later stood. This was the *omphalos*, the navel of the world, just yards from which Athenians now celebrated victory at Marathon and

An inscription on the platform of the Treasury of the Athenians at Delphi
proclaims: 'The men of Athens [dedicate this] to Apollo, the first fruits
from the Persians at the Battle of Marathon'.

staked their claim to Delphic glory by constructing an exquisite treasury,
in form a miniature temple, constructed out of Attic marble freighted all
the way from Mount Pentelicon, to stand a stone's throw from the Temple
of Apollo completed just a generation earlier by Athenian Alcmaeonids.

The metopes of the new Treasury proclaimed the glory of Athenians'
ancestral hero, Theseus, whose exploits for the first time ever in a sculp-
tural grouping were boldly linked with those of Heracles. For now like
those heroes, both of whom their hoplites had seen fighting on their
side at Marathon, Athenians could boast of ridding their land of a savage,
brutish enemy and ensuring that their civilized Greek democratic values
prevailed; and to emphasise their message further they not only hung
captured Persian shields beneath the Temple of Apollo's metopes, they
carved an inscription on the platform upon which their proud new Treasury now stood: 'The men of Athens [dedicate this] to Apollo, the first-
fruits from the Persians at the Battle of Marathon'. Positioned beside the
omphalos at the top of a steep rise that dominated the approach to Apollo's shining temple beneath which it stood, the glittering Treasury,

crammed full of precious artefacts from already ancient marble statues
to gold and jewellery captured from the Persians, broadcast Athens'
growing confidence: the city that almost single-handedly had faced off
the Persians and won, the city whose freedom had been underpinned
not only by her men but by her heroes, the city whose democratic values
were a beacon to all humanity was claiming what it felt to be its rightful
place at the very heart of Greece and of the world.[39]

By any standards, the victory at Marathon, so unexpected and against
such odds, was monumental, and many Athenians were content to bask in
their own glory. After such a thorough trouncing, Persia must have surely
learned its lesson. The threat was over. The Great King would never dare
to try again. Others had other reasons to preserve the status quo—men
who still harboured a nostalgia for the days before democracy and yearned
for a time when they might dawn again. No matter that old Hippias had
not survived the journey back to Asia. The gods had ceased to favour him
when he was driven out of Athens. It was not fated that he should return.
Indeed, a joke soon went the rounds that, on the eve of his arrival with the
Persians in Attica, Hippias had dreamt that he was sleeping with his
mother, which he interpreted as foretelling his restoration to the throne;
but as soon as he landed, he sneezed so violently that he dislodged a tooth;
searching in vain to find it in the sand, he realised his error: 'This land
does not belong to us, and we shall never manage to subdue it. My tooth
possesses the only portion that is mine.' It was a harmless enough anecdote, but it trivialized a real and present danger not just from Hippias'
sympathizers still in Athens (who only recently were said to have flashed
signals to the enemy) but from Persia, whose wrath remained unslaked,
whose power was undiminished, whose resources seemed almost infinite.
Among those who did recognize this grim reality was Miltiades.[40]

Elected general again the next year, the one-time foreign tyrant wooed
his democratic fellow citizens. Their prowess at Marathon was awe-
inspiring, yes—but now was no time to sit on their collective laurels.
Rather, with victory behind them, they must embark on an exciting expedition. Its goal for now must be kept secret: it would not do for the
enemy to be prepared. But, if the People put their trust in him and followed where he led, he could assure them that not only would the fight
be easy but it would bring enormous profit to the city. The People needed
no persuading. A forest of hands, and they assigned Miltiades no fewer
than 70 triremes, most of Athens' fleet, which meant a force of almost

14,000 men; and when the spring brought tranquil seas, they swarmed to Phalerum and cast off on their new adventure. But when, a few months later, the ships sailed back again, it was immediately apparent that the campaign had been a failure. Not only were the troops dejected, Miltiades himself was carried from his flagship on a stretcher, his knee smashed and his leg already gangrenous. It was the moment that his enemies had been waiting for, and without delay Xanthippus, an ambitious, strutting young patrician, his cachet recently enhanced by a well-judged marriage to a proud Alcmaeonid heiress, filed charges with the magistrates: Miltiades had deceived the People; if found guilty, he must be executed. So for the second time in four years a procession filed from the house on Pnyx Hill across the valley to the Areopagus: family and friends, well-wishers and supporters, and carried in their midst Miltiades himself, weak, wounded, feverish.[41]

The prosecution case was simple. Miltiades had promised not just victory but cash. He had failed to deliver either. In fact, he had cost Athens' coffers dearly, since it was the state, not he, who paid the wages for the many thousands who had been involved. Besides, by refusing to reveal his goal in advance, Miltiades had acted overbearingly, high-handedly, undemocratically—in short, like the tyrant he had really always been. So, forget his part in victory over Persia: this new debacle was proof positive of what patriotic Alcmaeonids (keen to counter rumours of shield-flashing after Marathon) had known for years. The city had successfully got rid of Hippias. Now it must rid itself of Miltiades as well. The fleet had sailed to Paros. Why? Allegedly because the island had collaborated with the Persians and sent a ship and hoplites to fight the Greeks at Marathon. But that was only an excuse. In fact, Miltiades nursed a vendetta of his own against a Parian leader, who had insulted him before a Persian grandee. And what did Miltiades achieve on Paros? Nothing! He had demanded 100 talents not to blockade the island, but the money never materialized, the blockade failed. Perhaps he had been bribed by the Great King? And then there was his sacrilege. (How the 'accursed' Alcmaeonids must have relished such a charge.) For was Miltiades not lured by a priestess to the sanctuary of Demeter, the Earth Goddess, with assurances that only if he went there would he take the city? And when he found the gate locked, had he not climbed over the sanctuary wall? And once on sacred soil, seized by terror, had he not panicked, fled; had he not tried to jump the wall, but fallen, torn his knee and leg? Was this not why he was now lying on his stretcher, because of his impiety, because Demeter, the Earth Goddess, had herself punished him?[42]

Miltiades was too ill to speak. Instead, frail and delirious, he lay on a couch as his cousin, Teisagoras, mounted his defence. Even had he been privy to Miltiades' grand strategy (perhaps he meant to subdue other collaborating islands, too; perhaps he saw Paros merely as a stepping-stone on a much longer voyage east to plunder Asia), the campaign had ended so disastrously that to dwell on it would hardly help his argument. Instead, he reminded the court of Miltiades' record: how he had captured Lemnos and Imbros and brought the islands under Athens' rule; how he had led them just the year before to victory at Marathon; how this very day they owed Miltiades their freedom and their lives.[43]

Xanthippus was a coruscating orator; Teisagoras was not; Miltiades was found guilty as charged. But despite the prosecution's passionate demands, the Council of the Areopagus would not condemn their general to death. Instead they imposed a massive fine: 50 talents, half the sum Miltiades had asked of Paros, perhaps the total bill for the failed expedition. Until it was paid in full, the fast-failing Miltiades must be confined in one of the cramped, dank cells of the state prison. But even as Cimon was racing home to open strongboxes and calculate what assets he might sell to meet the fine, he must have known that there was little hope his father would recover. The only remedy was amputation, and Miltiades was much too weak.[44]

So just a few days later, with a tragic sense of the inevitable, Cimon and his mother and his sisters and his wider family and friends, crowded inside the stuffy, stinking cell to watch Miltiades, hero of Marathon, his mind gone and his body drenched in sweat, take his last laboured breath. As they gathered round the corpse, some must have recalled the maxim, 'consider no man's life to have been happy until you see how he has died'. An archon at an early age, the husband to the daughters of a tyrant and a king, a ruler in his own right and a brilliant general, Miltiades had died disgraced and plunged in debt. And now it was left to his son and heir to pay it off. Even as he closed his father's eyes, and blanched to see the women tear their hair and scratch their cheeks, and hear them raise their ritual wails of lamentation, Cimon, recently turned twenty-one but with experience beyond his years, knew that for good or ill he had come into his inheritance.

II

ATHENA'S BRIDLE

4

BETWEEN TWO WARS

I wish the aulós would forget its warlike purpose
and be dedicated only to carousal
and the tussling of young men,
tipsy, brawling at their lovers' doors.

Pratinas, fr. 3

ATHENS, 489 B.C.

Miltiades' death, so sudden and in such circumstances, turned Cimon's world on its head. Just four years earlier, his status had been that of the younger son without reason to expect to step so soon into his father's shoes. Now, with his elder brother living the louche life of an expatriate in Persian lands, he found himself not only catapulted unexpectedly into the heart of Athenian political life, but at the same time mired in crippling debt and scandal. It was precisely what Xanthippus had intended, for, as champion of the rival Alcmaeonids (the family not just reputed to be cursed but—worse—since Marathon accused of being pro-Persian), it was in Xanthippus' interests to deflect the People's outrage. And, while he could easily have demanded Miltiades' execution, it was so much more expedient (since it was clear that the convicted general was dying anyway) to demand the imposition of a fine in the sure knowledge that, passed on to the next generation, it would humiliate both father and son (the one condemned to return to his cramped prison cell, where he soon died; the other compelled to take his place in Athens' jail as surety while Miltiades' corpse was released for burial, and he amassed sufficient money to pay off the fine). At least in the short term the sentence would seriously inconvenience Cimon at a time when he would otherwise be focussing exclusively on taking on his role as leader of the Philaids.[1]

For even in democratic Athens, the city of supposed equals, money talked. Despite recent constitutional changes, there had been no attempt to redistribute wealth and there was no direct personal taxation. The gulf between rich and poor remained as great as it had ever been, and the lifestyle of the super-rich was unimaginable to the average citizen. Nonetheless, these plutocrats were still expected to contribute to the common good—through *leitourgia* (liturgy), a mechanism by which wealthy individuals bore the cost of certain public services from their own pockets. Ranging from funding choruses in festivals of Dionysus to paying for public meals for fellow demesmen at other such religious festivals to sponsoring official delegations to the Games, not to mention equipping and maintaining triremes, while many of these liturgies involved considerable expenditure, they provided the elite with much-coveted opportunities not just to demonstrate their bounty to the People (and thereby win political support or ward off enmity) but to flaunt their wealth and vie for kudos. Of course they could—and did—still flaunt their wealth and vie for kudos in the Panhellenic Games, where to win a horse- or a chariot race remained every ambitious aristocrat's dream; but to excel in the performance of a liturgy enabled them not just to shine but to appear as pious democrats before the People, to advertise their personal investment in the common weal. So by imposing such a heavy fine on Cimon, Xanthippus and his coterie were cleverly constricting him, impeding his path to public life, frustrating his ambitions to play a part in city politics.[2]

If he had powerful enemies, however, Cimon had powerful friends and allies, too. With his swashbuckling determination, dynamic leadership and forceful magnetism, not to mention his victory at Marathon, Miltiades had attracted some of the most influential men of Athens to his circle, and now that his death had left a vacuum, they were determined to do all they could to help his son and heir. Perhaps most influential of them all was Aristides, one of the generals at Marathon and now in 489 elected Chief Archon. Still only thirty, Aristides had a reputation for outstanding moral probity that would earn him the nickname, 'the Just'. Politically incorruptible and fiercely independent, as a boy he

had been close to the reformer, Cleisthenes, but, while he embraced democracy, he was suspicious of new firebrand populists such as Themistocles, and determined that traditional values not be discarded simply
because they might be thought aristocratic. Athens' moral bellwether,
he was a cool-headed general, whose objective, unequivocal support for
Miltiades in fraught war councils before Marathon helped stiffen wa-
vering resolve, and when Miltiades ordered him and his tribe not to
march back to Athens with him potentially to face the Persians, but to
stay on the battlefield to guard the booty, far from being a slight on his
military expertise, it was evidence that there was no-one he could trust
more not to pilfer. How fortuitous for Cimon, then, adrift in a strange,
hostile, cut-throat city, his assets weakened and his rivals circling like
hungry dogs, that he should find in Aristides, its chief magistrate, a
friend and mentor.[3]

Equally fortuitous was the friendship of Aristides' cousin, the wealthy,
exuberant, yet politically astute Callias, who, hitching up his priestly vestments, had also fought with such panache at Marathon. Perhaps ten
years Cimon's senior, Callias like him was from an old flamboyant family.
Seventy-five years earlier, his grandfather had carried off the olive crown
at the Olympic horse race (while his four-horse chariot took second
place), in celebration of which he named his first (and only) son Hipponicus (Horse Victory). But there was more to Callias the Elder than
his love of horses. He possessed a shrewd financial mind. When Peisistratus was first expelled from Athens and compelled to liquidate his
assets in a hurry, Callias the Elder bought them up, adding new properties to his already burgeoning portfolio—he owned estates around the
family home at Alopece, a desirable, upmarket village north of Athens;
and it was he perhaps who made another shrewd investment, buying the
right to hire out slaves to work some of the state-owned silver mines at
Laurium just up the coast from Sunium.[4]

In other ways, too, Callias the Elder's roots ran deep within the bedrock of Athenian society. As a leading member of the ancient Ceryces
('Heralds'), one of two Athenian families who oversaw the general administration and annual performance of the Eleusinian Mysteries, he
held the prestigious inherited post of Torchbearer, in which role he revealed the sacred light of truth. This gave him great prestige, while fees
from initiates further swelled his fortune. Which was not to say that Callias the Elder was not a pious man; he may even have extended his own

quest for mystic truth by sailing south to Egypt for the long hot trek across the desert to the oasis oracle of Zeus Ammon at Siwah, the first Athenian to do so. In his private life, too, Callias the Elder was a pioneer. In an age when fathers chose their sons-in-law with careful diligence, he let each of his three daughters choose her husband, a move that was perhaps at least in part a public declaration that he had no need to use them to cement political or social alliances. One chose their neighbour, Lysimachus, and with him had a son: Aristides.[5]

On Callias the Elder's death, Hipponicus inherited not just his wealth, estates and business interests, but his religious office, too. He guarded them all jealously, and passed them at his own death to his eldest (and perhaps only) son, named from his grandfather, Callias. It was not all that the young man inherited: his views on marriage, too, were unconventional. Perhaps at the house on Pnyx Hill or at the lush Laciadae estate or in the jostle of a state procession or at an otherwise unremarkable religious ritual, he saw and fell in love with Cimon's sister, Elpinice, and asked for her hand in marriage. It was a daring thing to do: the wedding of an eligible bachelor, one of the richest men in Athens, would under any circumstances be subject to intensive scrutiny and gossip; so, to choose as bride the daughter of the disgraced Miltiades, the sister of the outsider, Cimon, still struggling to integrate into Athenian society, and to ally himself so blatantly with the Philaids, whom others had worked so hard to neutralize, was to take a controversial stance politically and socially, challenging Xanthippus and his allies, while rehabilitating Cimon and his family. No wonder Cimon readily agreed. Just as importantly for Callias, so did Elpinice.[6]

Forced by convention to lead lives of domestic drudgery, condemned by a lack of education to harbour few ambitions other than to become perfect wives and mothers, most contemporary Athenian citizen-class women existed in the shadow of their menfolk. Not Elpinice. Possessed of a keen mind, she held strong opinions and was not afraid to express them. In addition, unshackled by the etiquette of strict Athenian society, and now in her mid-teens, this daughter of a Thracian princess was beautiful, bewitching and exotic. Indeed, both clever and alluring, she embodied everything that petty-minded men found threatening and troubling in a woman, and she became an easy butt of slanders. No sooner was Miltiades dead and buried than Cimon's enemies oozed nasty rumours: the siblings lived as man and wife, slept in the same bed, indulged in incest. That it was untrue was irrelevant. It made for such salacious fantasies and conjured up such titillating images of Thracian depravity.[7]

Such slanders did not worry Callias. He knew the lengths to which malicious enemies and idle tongues would go. Already there were those who muttered that his wealth was due to underhand insider trading (his ancestor, they said, had learned that Solon meant to cancel all debts on a given date, hurriedly exchanged on all the land he could with promises of later payment and, when Solon's legislation was enacted, sat back to enjoy his ill-gotten fortune). Rumours circulated, too, about Callias himself, not least his conduct after Marathon, when, a member of Aristides' tribe, he was left to guard the battlefield. As he strode along the beach (his enemies maintained), his beard flowing, priestly vestments billowing, a Persian survivor mistook him for a king, prostrated himself trembling before him and took him to a shallow trench where vast quantities of gold were buried—at which Callias stole the treasure for himself and slaughtered his informant on the spot. (In fact, his nickname, 'Trench-Rich', was a reference to his mining interests at Laurium.)[8]

So Callias knew all about 'alternative facts'. He shrugged off rumours of Elpinice's immorality, and the wedding went ahead in style. Perhaps the most dazzlingly expensive of its day, the marriage marked more than just the union of two people; it marked an alliance between two of Athens' wealthiest, most influential families, the Philaids and Ceryces, and with crowds of onlookers milling around Cimon's door to catch a glimpse as bride and groom set off for Callias' rich town house no expense was spared. The sight that greeted them at dusk was worth the wait, as Elpinice, her head and face wreathed in a shimmering red starry veil, her dress bejewelled, her body hung with gold, was lifted up onto the wagon (hung lavishly with flowers and garlands), and Callias in costly robes climbed up beside her, and in the flickering torchlight the procession—family and friends, in all their finery, and excited crowds of running children—wound its way through echoing night-time streets.[9]

Pressed up against the still-warm walls, onlookers exchanged confusing tittle-tattle. Given how lavish the ceremony was, and the enormous fine that Cimon had to pay, was it not possible—was it not true—that, instead of Cimon giving Callias a dowry for Elpinice as was Athenian custom, Callias had paid off the fine and bought his bride from Cimon? Was there any basis for this outré allegation? In Thrace husbands did pay a marriage settlement, so perhaps to honour the traditions of

Elpinice's maternal ancestors Callias in Athens did the same. More likely, though, the story was a calculated slur designed either to discredit Callias by suggesting that he was 'going Thracian', or to debase Cimon by insinuating that poverty was forcing him to prostitute his sister. No such slanders attached themselves to the subsequent marriages of his two younger—and apparently more reticent—sisters, both (probably) to members of the family of Melesias, a wealthy Olympic wrestler, athlete and trainer from Alopece. By then Cimon's position in society was so established that his wealth was not an issue. Yet, how poor *was* he after paying his father's fine? For most Athenians a fine of 50 talents (a quarter of even Callias' wealth) was almost unimaginable, and few who saw or heard of the procession could probably believe that Cimon's wealth remained so large that he could possibly have funded it or given a dowry to match. But Miltiades had ruled the Chersonese, where he amassed great riches, most of which he brought to Athens when he fled. If few fellow citizens could guess what he was worth, it is impossible for us to know today. Rumours of Cimon's poverty were based on likelihood, not knowledge. There certainly is no suggestion that he led an impoverished lifestyle.[10]

Quite the opposite. For Cimon moved in exalted circles. In his favour was his passion for horses and horse riding—inherited from both his grandfathers and shared by the elite of every culture of his age—while membership of Athens' small, exclusive cavalry force inevitably built bonds of comradeship. Meanwhile, his easy grace and humour, relaxed charisma and unforced affability not only charmed his fellow men but earned him a reputation—again, perhaps, founded upon little more than jealous gossip—for seducing women, too. Always, though (his rivals would insinuate), there was more than a whiff of the foreigner about him. Caricaturing him as a cavalier patrician playboy, a rakish ladies' man, a roué with a Thracian appetite for alcohol, ill-educated, unrefined, and unaccomplished in the liberal Arts, by temperament and nature more Spartan than Athenian, his detractors sought to drive a wedge between him and the common citizen, whose support Cimon would need if he were ever to succeed in the Assembly.[11]

But Cimon was not alone in finding himself undermined. In the decade after Marathon, the propertied elite in general were subject to increasingly virulent attacks from populist opponents and, fearing for the future, many brokered unexpected alliances. Old families must stick to-

A bridegroom takes his veiled bride by the wrist as he
leads her from her house to his (Attic red-figure pyxis,
470–460 B.C.).

gether; few were older than the Philaids; and, if Cimon was rough
around the edges, he was still charismatic, having so clearly inherited
his father's nose for politics and his aura of authority. Moreover, although
relatively young, he was of marriageable age, and marriage had for centuries shored up the establishment. So it was hardly unexpected when
the announcement came that Cimon was himself engaged to a patrician
heiress. Far less predictable was her identity: she was an Alcmaeonid,
related, albeit by marriage, to Miltiades' nemesis, Xanthippus. But sometimes such inconveniences must be overlooked. Descended from the
venerable Megacles I and his son Alcmaeon (who had once stuffed his
clothing with Croesus' gold dust) her pedigree was impeccable. Even
her name shone with significance: 'Isodice' meant much the same as
isonomia, 'equal justice for all', the policy of her great-uncle, Cleisthenes.

What no-one could ever have foreseen was that she would be the love of Cimon's life.[12]

Perhaps brokered by Cleisthenes' old friend Aristides, the marriage was inspired, for it placed Cimon at the centre of a nexus of important ties, binding together Athens' three most powerful families—the Philaids, the Alcmaeonids and, through Elpinice, the Ceryces—at a time when radicals such as Themistocles were shaking up the very fabric of the city. For the political landscape was changing at a quite unprecedented rate. Four years after Marathon, riding the wave of People power, Themistocles pushed through revisions to the constitution. Already he (or his confederates) had stripped the landed families of their hold over the archonship, opening the office up to anyone from the top two property bands—be he experienced or inept, intelligent or naive— selected through the usual means of lottery. Even religious festivals were democratized, with the Great Dionysia recast in a populist mould.

Since its introduction under Peisistratus, this celebration of drama, dance and music had been built around performances of choral hymns (or dithyrambs), tragedies and satyr plays (parodic dramas that inverted ideas from mythology). Now, as a sign of how much the old world was fragmenting, another far more controversial genre was introduced into the festival: comedy. Hard-hitting political satire, often set in a madcap world of make-believe, but always rooted firmly in the real (if heightened) mores of contemporary society, Athenian comedy included frequent jeering mockery of prominent men seated in the audience and derision of their policies and records, sometimes portraying them as characters on stage in excoriating, cruel impersonations that with well-turned phrases could ridicule a decent, upright citizen and shred his hard-won reputation. Now suddenly the establishment elite, with no right of redress whatsoever, found themselves the butt of taunting ridicule as audiences, thousands strong, hooted and squawked and crowed with laughter, jabbing fingers, laughing till their sides were sore and tears ran down their bearded cheeks, in a vicious, yet state-sponsored jamboree protected by *parrhesia*, free speech, one of the cornerstones of the Cleisthenic dispensation.[13]

In other ways, too, new laws were being used to undermine the aristocracy. One clause had been carefully included to ensure that no one individual could gain such dominance that he tried to seize the reins of government and install himself as tyrant. The mechanism was simple.

Each year a motion was put forward to determine if there was anyone the People wanted to remove from Attica. If there was a majority in favour of the proposition, a second vote was held sixty days later. This time it was a secret ballot, for this time it was personal: this time each citizen had to write or scratch his chosen victim's name on a piece of broken pottery and place it in an urn. If a minimum of 6,000 votes were cast, the vote was declared valid. The urns were emptied, the ballots counted, the results read out. Whoever topped the poll and so 'won' this reverse election was given just ten days to put his affairs in order and leave Athens for ten years—albeit in the knowledge that his property would be preserved intact, he could engage in business from abroad, and after the ten years were up he could return with no stigma attached. Named from the potsherds used for voting (*ostraka* in Greek), the mechanism was called ostracism.[14]

For the first twenty years of Athens' democratic dispensation it lay dormant. Now, though, Themistocles and his populist supporters, realizing its potential as a means of picking off their enemies, appropriated ostracism for their own political ends. They took aim first on the remnants of Peisistratus' family, one of whom bore the hated name, Hipparchus. Thick-skinned and steadfast, in the wake of Hippias' exile he had somehow clung on in Athens, turning a deaf ear to songs praising the so-called tyrannicides, who knifed his namesake, and a blind eye to their heroic statues. He had even held the office of Chief Archon. Since Marathon, however, everything had changed. After all, brave citizens had sacrificed their lives to stop the Persians from returning Hippias, their puppet, to rule Athens. Why should they still allow his relatives to live the good life, hold office, pass resolutions in the Council of the Areopagus, tell them what to do? For populists seeking to experiment, to see whether they could harness ostracism as a weapon, Hipparchus made an easy target. For tyranny was in his blood, and tyranny must be expunged. So they set to work preparing fertile ground, sowing rumours, stoking scandals, husbanding their cause, until the day came in late January for the annual vote: to hold or not to hold an ostracism. When the citizens on Pnyx Hill raised their hands, their verdict was clear. Athens' first recorded ostracism was underway.[15]

At sunrise two months later, approaches to the Agora were already thronged with people, as officials supervised the final preparations. Much of the area had been roped off, a vast enclosure fed by ten funnelling entranceways, one for each tribe, each with huge voting urns already set in place, observers hovering, keen-eyed to ensure fair play. But others, too, were scouring the gathering crowds, or standing domineeringly beside the gates, agents and supporters of rival politicians and their factions, musclemen exhorting voters not to ostracize their candidate but to condemn another man instead, touts armed with big bags bulging with pre-written potsherds, to be pressed into the hands of the illiterate, along with weaselly assurances that they really did bear the name the voter asked for. And then the trumpet call, the herald's proclamation, and the poll was open: men jostling and shoving through roped-off corridors, jokes, curses, hollow clacks as the first sherds were cast, replaced by a more muffled pattering as they rained inexorably down and urns became more full. It need not have taken long before the streets were empty and the Agora a throng of people—city dwellers, country folk, men up from Phalerum or Sunium or Marathon, all there to play their part in this curious new practice, all keen to find out whether the result had gone their way. Another trumpet call; the chatter fading into silence; then the herald read out the results; and, as Themistocles had planned, the name that topped the poll: Hipparchus. Within ten days he was gone. Most of his family went with him, for all could read the signs. They were not welcome in new, modern Athens and, despite the clause that said he could come back once his ten years were over, Hipparchus never returned. The Peisistratids had been eradicated. The experiment had worked. Democracy had won the day.

The populists were cock-a-hoop. They had set a precedent. With the mass of Athens' populace behind them, they could use ostracism to rid themselves of hateful grandees, one a year, not only weakening the aristocracy, but strengthening their own hand, wresting ever greater power for themselves. With the Peisistratids removed, they turned their sights on the Alcmaeonids, for were not they, too, tainted? First by the curse; and then again by rumours crystallizing into strong beliefs of their collusion with the Persians and Hippias, flashing signals as the enemy sailed round from Marathon. That an Alcmaeonid, Cleisthenes, had written the new democratic constitution seemed irrelevant, especially if he was really implicated in the treacherous agreement two decades earlier to offer earth and water to the Persians. So for the next three years the pattern was repeated: the decision every January to hold an ostracism; the vote in March; the expulsion of an Alcmaeonid or an Alcmaeonid associate.

The first to feel the People's disapproval was Cimon's father-in-law, Megacles, the nephew of Cleisthenes himself. Comments scratched on *ostraka* revealed what motivated voters: some sneered at his wealth, his greed, his racing stables; others cited the curse. Next was a man recorded in the annals simply as the 'Medizer' or 'Persian Sympathizer'; and finally another Alcmaeonid, Xanthippus, Mitiades' prosecutor.[16] Seeing his bête noire bundled out of Attica, Cimon cannot but have felt some satisfaction. Seeing his own name scratched on *ostraka* may have pleased him, too, for this showed that he was making his mark felt in public, whether, like Xanthippus, cutting his teeth as a prosecutor, or speaking in Assembly debates to support his friend and mentor, Aristides. But his satisfaction was short-lived.[17]

Just two years later, it was Aristides' turn to feel the People's wrath. Even now, his character shone through. As he mingled with the crowds outside the cordons, it was later said he was approached by an illiterate peasant from far out of town, a man who never came to the Assembly and did not know its politicians. The stranger approached Aristides and, clutching his blank piece of pottery, asked him to write a name. Whose? 'Aristides.' Why? 'Because I'm sick and tired of hearing everybody calling him "the Just"'. True to his nature, Aristides took the sherd, wrote his own name, and gave it to the peasant to add to the growing pile of votes that would condemn him. Entertaining though the story is, it was not for his integrity that Aristides was ostracized. Rather it was because, just months before, he had short-sightedly opposed Themistocles' most pressing policy and tried to block a measure that in a few short years would save not only Athens but all Greece from Persian subjugation.[18]

For almost three millennia, men had been mining (intermittently) the hills of south-eastern Attica round Laurium, where veins of silver snaked through the dark rock, but it was Hippias who first exploited the resource politically, and struck official, high-grade silver coinage—one side stamped with an image of Athena, the other with her bird, the owl— that quickly spun throughout the Greek world and beyond, a mark of Athens' growing prosperity. State-owned, the mines were leased to wealthy moguls such as Callias, whose teams of slaves worked in nightmarish conditions, squeezing through networks of grim, claustrophobic tunnels, airless, sweltering, lit only by the flickering of oil lamps, while on the surface rocks were ground and washed, and industrial refineries glowed in the heat of furnaces as silver was extracted by cupellation from the enveloping lead. Wretched and ragged, the best these slaves could hope for was a quick and early death to bring release from such back-breaking toil: sent shackled into narrow shafts for ten-hour shifts day in night out, mouths parched, lungs filled with fine limestone dust, few miners survived long. But their masters and the democrats of Athens cared little for their suffering: such slaves were easily replaceable; what mattered was the silver; what mattered was the profit; what mattered was their growing wealth. Then, seven years after Marathon, one of the teams of miners emerged into the sunlight with tantalizing news. They had discovered a new vein of silver unlike any seen before, a seam with the potential to make Athens rich beyond her wildest dreams.[19]

The news set the city reeling: here was yet another sign of how the gods loved Athens. First the political miracle: democracy; then the military miracle: defeating first aggressive Greeks and then the might of Persia; and now the economic miracle: the very land of Attica bestowing such largesse on its people that overnight they had become potentially the richest men in Greece. Even before the implications could sink in, the Council summoned the Assembly to debate how best to use the revenue—two and a half tons, 100 talents of pure silver for the first year alone. As they climbed onto Pnyx Hill and watched the sun edge golden over Mount Hymettus, silhouetting the Acropolis where, beside the Temple of Athene Polias, within its skeleton of scaffolding a new temple was rising, a thank offering for victory at Marathon, citizens were fantasizing how this windfall from the gods would change their lives. For in a democracy, where every individual was a stakeholder, each man must naturally receive an equal dividend. Which was what Aristides, flaunting his sense of justice and his commitment to the principles of *isonomia,* duly stood up and proposed to rapturous applause not only from his natural support base, the landowning patricians, but from the artisans, the peasant farmers, the great body of the struggling poor, who stood to gain proportionately so much more, 10 drachmas each, more than a good month's wages—and, what was more, they stood to gain it every year.[20]

The vote was simply a formality, but before it could be held there was still one man who wished to speak—the People's champion, Themistocles. Surely he would throw his weight behind the general consensus and endorse enriching his supporters. It was the only democratic thing to do. But as his arguments unfolded, logical, far-reaching, and expressed

Carved around 410 B.C., the so-called Lenormant Relief from the
Athenian Acropolis shows part of a trireme, its crew straining at
the oars.

with such unerring clarity that to refute them was impossible, the men
of Athens found themselves first questioning then reconsidering their
original stance. For, instead of pandering to popularity, Themistocles
challenged the Assembly to defer immediate gratification and think to
the longer term, to use the money in a way that would not just bolster
national security and standing but increase future trade and lead to
greater personal prosperity—to build a fleet, 200 new triremes, with
which they could defeat their island neighbour, Aegina, secure trade
routes and bring employment to more than 34,000 mariners and countless shipbuilders. For years, Themistocles had been reiterating his conviction that Athens' future greatness lay at sea. Already in Phalerum's
dockyards and warehouses and Piraeus' newly-rising wharves his vision
was beginning to bear fruit. But Athens had never possessed the means
fully to turn that vision into reality—until now.

And with the deadly fleet of hostile Aegina lording it in the Saronic
Gulf, now was the time to do it. Just a few years earlier, had not Aegina's
ships attacked and captured the Athenian state trireme as it sailed,

garlanded and gilded for a religious festival, along the Attic coast to Sunium? And then, to take reprisals, had not Athenians been forced to hire—to hire!—from Corinth a fleet of twenty warships? And did they not arrive a day too late; had not Aegina learned their plans; had not Athens' democratic allies on the island been compelled to flee; was not the whole thing a disaster? And more. Had not the enemy swooped down on Athens' ships and captured four with all their crews? And now as a result of her controlling shipping lanes was not Aegina taking vital trade from the Athenians? And there was nothing anyone could do. But build one hundred new triremes, and the fleet would increase threefold; Aegina would be easy prey; Athens' honour and the honour of her gods would be restored; trade would flow unimpeded into Piraeus' new, fast-growing port facilities; and the Athenian People would prosper.[21]

It was a passionate, persuasive speech, and the Assembly erupted in approval, with no longer any thought for private gain. But some were still unhappy (among them perhaps Cimon), aristocrats who saw the implications of Themistocles' suggestion, how it could undermine their long-held standing as protectors of the state. Until then it had always been the rich elite, men who could afford their panoplies of armour, who had chiefly borne the brunt of war and fought to save their city. Every victory, not least the recent victory at Marathon, had been won by landed hoplites, and there were some who thought that—just as (in Homeric Hector's words) 'war is man's business', not a woman's—war was the business of aristocrats, not commoners. To place Athens' security in the hands of indigent oarsmen was to take *isonomia* to new and dangerous extremes, to overturn the status quo, to tear apart the very fabric of society—as Themistocles knew well. Besides, think of the training it would take for crews to become competent, let alone battle ready. What would happen to their businesses or smallholdings during their enforced absence? Even (more importantly for the elite) if, in the future, the fleet put to sea in those months from mid-March to September when the sea was calm, months when seeds were sown and harvests taken in, what impact might that have on Attica's farmlands and landowners' estates? Was Themistocles' proposal actually a ruse to redistribute wealth, designed specifically to undermine the wealthy? Especially as it had been, and still was, the rich who must fund not just the warfleet's upkeep but its oarsmen's wages. Was this, in fact, not simply a means to salve Themistocles' own ego, which had taken such a bruising after Marathon? All knew he was consumed by jealousy when Miltiades was vaunted as the People's hero; all knew he could not sleep, but stayed away from every victory celebration; all knew that he had vowed revenge. Was that, then, what this was all about: Themistocles' revenge against his dead rival, Miltiades, and Aristides, whom he hated even more—Aristides whose proposal would enrich each citizen?[22]

Yet their patrician voices went unheard, drowned out by the great roar of the majority, silenced by the multitude of hands raised in confident enthusiasm as the vote was taken and the decision made, a decision that all knew would change the course of Athens' history, though few if any knew by how much—and by the time of the next year's ostracism Themistocles had heaped such scorn on his defeated enemies that some of his followers were even parroting his claims that his opponents tried to block his bill because (like the reviled Peisistratids and cursed Alcmaeonids) they were so vigorously anti-democratic as to be pro-Persian. At least one voter in the ostracism scratched on his potsherd, 'Aristides— brother of Datis' (Persia's commander at Marathon).[23]

By then a frenzy of construction was engulfing Athens, Phalerum, and ever-growing Piraeus, for, if to build one trireme was a complex operation, to build two hundred meant minutely detailed planning, meticulous management and the training and employment of diverse teams of specialists. First introduced by the Phoenician navy and adopted by Corinthians, the trireme was a triumph of technology, a state-of-the-art weapon that in the right hands and right conditions could inflict crippling damage on any warship of traditional design. Sleek, slim and deadly, with a draft of just three feet, each measured 120 feet from prow to stern and 20 feet in width. But what made it unique were the three banks of oars from which it took its name (*trieres* in Greek), three tiers of rowing benches, the uppermost installed in an outrigger projecting from the hull. While it hoisted sails for long sea voyages, for speed (especially in battle) it was powered by the muscles of 170 well-drilled oarsmen, blades rising, falling, slicing the water with such precision that it seemed the ship was one single organism, a winged sea monster, its stern curving like a feathered tail, its prow inlaid with staring painted marble eyes above a lethal bronze-sheathed beak. Three-pronged, like Poseidon's trident, and jutting just below the waterline, when, at a maximum velocity of ten knots, it smashed with murderous momentum into a hostile ship, this beak would punch a hole into its hull, swamping it with water, immobilizing it immediately. This was a crucial moment for the trireme's crew. Delay too long, and they would be entangled with the wallowing enemy, unable to withdraw. So, no sooner had the strike been made than the order came to back off, to reverse at speed, to pull away from the stricken ship as quickly as they could, while the helmsman locked onto his next target. Only he and the marines on deck could tell where their course was taking them. Facing the stern, the oarsmen could see little—those on the sunless lower benches least of all—and all must place blind trust in orders barely heard above the din of battle and the creak of timber and the pounding of their own blood in their ears, relying for their lives on their commander's competence and the condition of their ship.[24]

Which was why it was so crucial to ensure that each of the new triremes was constructed to the highest standard. The decision made and plans drawn up, procurement officers began negotiating contracts in Attica and friendly states across the Aegean and beyond. Most urgently required was timber—oak for the keel and curving stern- and stem posts, green pinewood planed and bent to shape before being tied and pegged around the skeleton that curved from both sides of the keel. Then, with the shell complete, stout linen cords were threaded through the planks to form a sturdy network that would reinforce the hull and help protect it from the slap and batter of the sea. So would the ribs, which now were lowered and secured, and the thick cables that were stretched from stern to prow beneath the rowing frame, kept ever taut to stop the hull from warping and preserve its structural integrity. Then, with the frame complete, the outriggers were fixed in place, each with stretched linen canvases protecting crews from missiles and the baking sun.

As rows of ships took shape on wooden stocks down by the seashore—six to eight triremes every month, each given a fine female name to suit its personality—elsewhere other teams of carpenters were cutting, shaping, planing 40,000 lengths of fir: oars to propel the triremes. It seemed as if all Athens was engaged in this one enterprise. Nearby bronze-workers were mixing tons of tin and copper, melting down old useless artefacts—misshapen bowls, bent swords and broken statues—pouring red-hot metal into individual clay moulds, each formed from wax to the exact shape of one specific wooden beak projecting from one prow, onto which the dedicated bronze sheath would be slid, secured with long bronze nails, the trireme's trident, its one reason to exist. Iron smelters, too, were stoking furnaces to fashion pairs of anchors that would stabilize the trireme's prow when it was dragged stern-first onto the beach, and grappling hooks for use in battle or when captured ships were tugged back to the shore. And then there were the goldsmiths, called to gild two hundred figureheads, each a statue of Athena, the fleet's protecting goddess, her shield and helmet flashing in the sun, the snake-fringed *aegis* draped across her chest resplendent with the severed Gorgon's head, grim, grinning.[25]

At looms in private houses, too, women were weaving for the fleet rectangles of pale linen cloth that would be sewn together for the sails, while from hemp, papyrus or esparto grass, others plaited rope—some to bind these sails to slender yardarms, others for rigging and mooring lines. And from denuded hillsides wagons packed with jars of resin from burned pine trees lurched through city streets, and on down the white road across the marshland to Phalerum, where the black pitch would be smeared on dried-out hulls, protection against a mollusc, the teredo or 'shipworm' that infested the warm seas, the most deadly threat of all, whose larvae could bore deep into untreated wooden planks to lodge there as the creature grew until it reached a foot in length, by which time a trireme was so riddled that it might suddenly and simply disintegrate.

Yet, while precautions could be taken to ensure that ships were not consumed from within by a hidden enemy, it was harder to safeguard a city. Harder still to safeguard Greece. As skirmishes between Athens and Aegina proclaimed, despite the threat from Persia, Greek poleis were no nearer than before to shelving petty differences, let alone to entering negotiations that might result in a united front, as egos, singular and collective, dominated foreign and domestic policies.

In Sparta the crisis that had seen King Demaratus deposed had worsened in the aftermath of Marathon. The first sign of trouble came at the Gymnopaediae, a festival for Apollo held in the summer heat in Sparta's central agora, when martial arts were set aside in favour of ball games and choral dancing, a ten-day celebration at which the great and good from all Greece were made welcome, fêted and shown Spartan hospitality, perhaps the city's most important politico-religious gathering. Although no longer king, Demaratus had accepted his demotion to a lesser office, in which role he had just sat down to watch the festival unfold, when a Spartan swaggered up to him, a lackey of his replacement, Leotychidas, on whose behalf he asked loudly: 'How does it feel to be a humble civil servant after ruling as a king?' Heard by foreigners and Spartans alike, it was an insult and a challenge designed to humiliate and provoke. But, if Leotychidas hoped to goad his rival into an unseemly act of violence, he was disappointed. Nonetheless his jibe sank home. 'Only I have filled both offices; Leotychidas has not,' muttered Demaratus lamely, before standing and addressing the spectators: 'This question heralds either countless pains or countless benefits for Sparta.' With which gnomic utterance, he covered his head with his cloak, stalked out of the theatre, sacrificed an ox to Zeus, bade farewell to his still-lovely mother and, pretending to be going to Delphi to consult the oracle, went into exile—to Persia, where, like Hippias before him, he vowed loyalty to the Great King, accepted gifts of lands and cities and (equally importantly) respect, and swore to help bring Sparta under Persian control.[26]

Leotychidas was not the only Spartan to put ego before diplomacy. His fellow king, Cleomenes, did, too, and to a quite spectacular degree. When it was revealed that he had bribed Apollo's oracle to help oust Demaratus, god-fearing Spartans were appalled. But before they could try him, Cleomenes escaped first to the court of the Aleuadae of Larissa, the dominant pro-Persian ruling family of Thessaly, then to the jagged mountains of Arcadia that bordered Spartan territory. There he stirred dreams of conquest. This was the Arcadians' best chance, he argued, to defeat their irksome neighbours. Secure Cleomenes on Sparta's throne, and the Spartan threat would be no more; march beside him, and he would reward them handsomely. Then at a solemn ceremony he led their generals in swearing oaths on the icy River Styx, the river of the dead whose waters oozed to drip down from a chill rock face. His plan to attack Sparta had been sealed.[27]

But before he could launch his invasion, a messenger slipped through mountain passes and into Cleomenes' quarters: the Spartans had forgiven him. 'Come home, and rule again as king.' It was undoubtedly a ruse, but Cleomenes, convinced of his own greatness and his indispensability, agreed. Forgetting thoughts of conquest, he abandoned the Arcadians and rode back to the Eurotas valley. But the Spartans were watching, weighing his behaviour, and when they saw him jabbing with his stick at everyone he met, they knew it was a sure and certain sign of madness. Only one treatment was possible: place him in the stocks until his sanity returned. But even in jail he was despotic, demanding to be brought a knife. They found him later, dead. They said that he had cut himself methodically, slicing his flesh into strips, working upwards from his ankles to his thighs, slashing his hips, carving his belly until, from loss of blood, he died. They claimed that it was suicide. More likely it was a grotesque execution, whose method was designed to fit his crime: he had intended to turn countless blades and spear-points against Sparta; instead, in his madness, so the story went, he had turned a Spartan blade—his own blade—countless times upon himself.[28]

To many Spartans, and certainly Cleomenes' successor, his half-brother, Leonidas, that two kings—one plotting in Arcadia, the other working for the Great King in luxurious self-banishment in Persia—were prepared to place personal ambition over country was unthinkably un-Spartan. Immediately from birth, every experience a Spartan underwent, every lesson that he learned was designed to ensure he would protect the state. For, unlike other poleis, Sparta feared attack not only from abroad but even more from inside her own borders—from her serfs, the servile underclass of helots—a fear so omnipresent that they even built a sanctuary to Phobus, god of fear. Whereas in other states most slaves were foreigners won in war or bought in markets, helots were Greeks, the native population of Laconia and Messenia, the two fertile lands controlled by Sparta on either side of Taygetus, the mountain spine that tumbles from Arcadia south down to the sea. Conquered centuries before by Spartans, the helots were allowed to live in their old homes, to farm their former lands, to marry and have families, but now they must pay heavy taxes to their overlords and perform countless other services, from routine agricultural production to (on occasion) even fighting for Sparta in battle. Yet, as Greeks, they yearned for their birthright of freedom, and several times they had rebelled en masse. Back in the seventh century, abetted by Argos, Messenian helots poured through Taygetus' passes down into Laconia, but despite defeating Sparta's army, they were forced back to their fastness on Mount Eira, and a ten-year siege. At last the Spartans offered terms: some helots, women and children, were allowed safe passage to Italy and exile; the rest were forced back to their fields; the revolt was over, but its shockwaves would shape Sparta for centuries.[29]

Outnumbered by helots, yet determined to ensure their own security, the Spartans abandoned former political and social arrangements. From now on theirs would be a purely military state, in constant conflict with its helot population against whom it declared war at the start of every year. Whereas previously they enjoyed a buoyant, open society, now they could have no time for anything but their security. Not that this was easy to maintain. Living not in one central conurbation but in five scattered villages, one of which, Amyclae, some four miles from their low acropolis, was the centre of a major annual religious festival (the Hyacinthia), it was impractical to think of building walls as other cities did—especially since their potentially most dangerous enemy lived within their boundaries. Instead, they would rely on their communal strength, shared shields and spears, to protect their families from their serfs, while securing their borders against external threats. From now on Sparta's overriding purpose must be to train fighting men, a dedicated citizen army. Even keeping the economy afloat was not allowed to be a major preoccupation: while the Spartans did exercise some direct control over their helot farmers, as well as possessing hunting grounds and other amenities within helot territory, they passed on responsibility for manufacturing and commerce to Perioikoi ('those who live all around'), a relatively free, if still tightly controlled, subordinate population who—apart from the constraints of existing within the borders of the Spartan state—lived far more like ordinary Greeks elsewhere than the Spartans did themselves. It was a startling response, a bewilderingly counter-intuitive solution: instead of promoting the domesticity that they were striving to protect, they renounced the pleasures of family life, surrendered private purpose to the public good and embarked on constant training.[30]

The community now regulated everything. While in poleis such as Athens fathers or heads of families might (for reasons of economics, health or gender) choose whether newborns lived or died, in Sparta a grimly independent board of inspectors assessed babies for physical defects, condemning weaklings to be exposed to die in a ravine that tunnelled into Mount Taygetus. While children fit enough to live were then kept at home to be suckled, weaned and given basic training, at the age of seven every Spartan boy (except each royal heir to the joint throne) joined what became known as the *agogē* ('upbringing'), an obsessive residential education system that, while it included literacy, poetry and music, taught only songs and verses that instilled tough, patriotic fervour, with dancing lessons to promote not just agility but strength and spatial awareness, essential virtues in the battle line. The system's one aim was to toughen young men physically and mentally, to train them to withstand pain and hardship, how to forage, how to steal, above all how to kill. It was a system aimed at stripping them of all emotion even if it meant removing their humanity, that turned them into cold-hearted machines, that brutalized them and transformed them into sociopaths. As they passed through each phase of their training, wearing the same tunic in the bitter snows of winter or the scorching summer heat, they were kept on the most meagre rations, sleeping by night in dormitories on tough reeds they had pulled with their own bleeding hands from the banks of the chill-flowing Eurotas (no knives permitted for this exercise), by day enduring endless gruelling drills in tight-knit groups, whose very name, *agelai* or *bouai* ('herds' or 'packs'), proclaimed the will to make them 'animal in nature'. As boys matured and turned eighteen, when in extremis they might serve alongside adults in the army, some elite few were enrolled in the *Crypteia*, the 'Secret Service Corps', tasked with spying on helots and killing any they suspected of showing signs of independence, such as being in the wrong place at the wrong time.[31]

Two years later (unless blackballed, and denied a place within society), at twenty they were admitted into messes, *sussitia*, or *suskania* ('common tents'), contributing provisions from their own estates, eating their notorious black broth (a mélange of vinegar, boiled blood and salted pork, appreciated, it was said, only by those who bathed in the Eurotas). Now, too, they became fully-fledged *homoioi*, Identicals or Peers, honed units, ready to stand in Sparta's shield wall, hair long, faces bearded with only the upper lip shaved smooth, wearing the feared red cloaks and tunics that would not reveal their own spilt blood, part of the 'scarlet and bronze' battle line that terrified their enemies, a lucky few enrolled in the royal bodyguard, 300 strong, the iciest, most merciless of all. Now they could marry, usually in their late twenties, wedding girls who (uniquely in the Greek world) had also undergone a rigorous public education, trained in calisthenics and gymnastics, their bodies toughened to produce strong children, their wits whetted so that they could hold their own in Sparta's notoriously laconic conversations. Now a Spartan could have sons who would repeat the cycle, Identicals who would replace their father when his strength failed. Now, too, he could sit in the assembly, held on the seventh of each month, Apollo's day, listening to gruff speeches (for too much eloquence of any kind was suspect), demonstrating his approval not with a show of hands but by shouting (the same method used to elect their top officials).[32]

Introduced in the seventh century, but supposed to have been rooted in laws laid down by the semi-mythical Lycurgus, Sparta's constitution was partly democratic, in that it ensured an equal 'vote' in the assembly to each member of its citizenry, and formally granted to all an equal citizenship (dependent on election as an Identical to a common mess). In fact, however, most power lay in three higher tiers of government, but even now its balance was changing. At the apex of the constitution were two joint kings of supposedly divine descent, each wielding equal power, each trained not just in skills necessary for an effective general (his most important role) and a successful ruler, but in arcane religious knowledge required for one destined to be a conduit between pious Spartans and their gods.[33]

It was to let them pursue such specialized education that each king's eldest son was excused membership of the *agogē*, but following Cleomenes' attempted power grabs neither his successor, Leonidas, nor Leotychidas, who replaced disgraced Demaratus, had received the requisite royal training—which was why the next two tiers of government were now more crucial than before. Most influential was the ephorate, consisting of five 'ephors' (overseers) elected annually for one year only. Sitting as judges, guiding policy and inspecting and controlling almost every aspect of daily life, the ephors' power trumped even that of the combined joint kings. Finally there was the Gerousia ('senate'), the upper house, elected by public acclamation, its membership formed of twenty-eight Identicals aged over sixty, who, sitting with the kings, debated motions to be ratified by the Assembly, and, sitting with the ephors, acted as a supreme court to try errant kings.

Notwithstanding their compulsive introspection and chronic obsession with homeland security, Sparta was the most important polis in all Greece. Throughout the seventh and sixth centuries B.C. rulers of most other states had shared many Spartan values, not least the central concepts of obedience to the law, respect for an established order and a high regard for bravery and courage, virtues that were the bedrock of the 'kalokagathoi', the 'beautiful and good', as the Athenian elite of 'Eupatrids' ('descendants of good fathers') were wont to call themselves. Even with the introduction of democracy, old-school Athenian aristocrats (men of Cimon's circle) admired Sparta's constitutional stability founded (they might argue) on restricting citizenship to the elite and establishing a hierarchy in which everyone knew their place. While sophisticated Athenians might lament Spartans' lack of culture, unlike in Athens, where comic writers caused their audiences to mock the aristocracy, Spartans found humour in getting helots drunk and laughing at their inebriated antics. However, other leading Greeks who might encounter them knew that rumours of uncouth naivety were exaggerated: he might not say much, but with one brief cutting sentence a Spartan could invariably be relied upon to expose shortcomings in the most carefully constructed argument. They knew, too, that much of what foreigners believed about Sparta was, in part, a carefully curated myth, painstakingly designed to add to the mystique—or the mirage—of this most eccentric city-state. And many wished that their own polis still shared Spartan values.[34]

It was not surprising, then, that with their reputation for integrity allied to military might Spartans were recognized as arbitrators in international disputes and leaders of a league of mainly Peloponnesian poleis (with the notable and deliberate exclusion of Argos) or, despite their absence from Marathon, as the natural coordinator of any Greek response to further threats from Persia. So, when reports began to trickle west across the sea from Sardis, delegates from anxious mainland cities made their troubled journey south across the mountain folds to the Eurotas. For the news was chilling. The Great King was again assembling an army; its size was unimaginable; its objective was the overthrow of Greece.[35]

The Persians had been drawing up plans for years. Despite his setback at Marathon, Darius' determination had not wavered. Still every day and every night his servant's breath against his ear reminded him: 'Remember the Athenians'. So, almost as soon as Datis, his defeated general, limped home with his unwelcome news, Darius began preparing for another expedition, whose size would equal or surpass the army he had mustered to attack the Scythians, a force that must be unstoppable, whose victory must be inevitable. For riding at the head of this new holy war against oath-breaking, temple-burning Greeks would be not some functionary, some unenlightened general, but Ahura Mazda's representative on earth, the Great King, the King of Kings, the tough, experienced commander-in-chief: the battle-scarred Darius himself. For three years envoys had criss-crossed the empire, riding long roads and trackless grasslands to enlist divisions and platoons from every subjugated nation, while logistics officers reconnoitred routes by which the army and its baggage trains would pass, liaising with local functionaries, arranging food dumps, finding the best locations for encampments. And then, a sure sign that the campaign was imminent, throughout the empire he increased taxation specifically to fund the war effort.[36]

But at a stroke the Great King's plans were overturned. A rebellion against the hike in taxes rocked Egypt, one of Persia's richest provinces, whose grain supply was vital both to the empire and to the expedition. Then, as plans were being drawn up to quash it, in the hushed palace at Persepolis, Darius fell seriously ill. For thirty days his family fretted by his bedside while knots of courtiers whispered in cool corridors and prized Greek doctors did all they could to treat him, but as winter closed over the royal residence the Great King breathed his last. With lavish grief and loud lamentation his body was smeared with wax and borne in ritual procession to his rock-cut tomb a few miles north, where inscriptions proclaimed the piety and character of 'a good horseman . . . a good archer . . . a good spearman':

> My one wish is for the good. I am no friend to any man who loves the Lie. I am not quick-tempered. When I am moved to anger, I keep myself in check through my strong will. I control my impulses at all times . . . Ahura Mazda bestowed my expertise upon me . . . Human, learn well what kind of man I am, the nature of my expertise, how I excel. Trust all that you have heard, and hear all that you are told. Human, do not be led to disbelieve my deeds . . . Obey the laws; may all men learn how to obey.[37]

Like everything within the well-run empire, the succession had been planned meticulously, so, heads shaved, and with Ahura Mazda's sacred fires extinguished on their altars, after the proper period of mourning, perhaps at the spring equinox, the Persian New Year, a glittering procession set off from Persepolis on the short journey north to Pasargadae, the empire's spiritual heart—courtiers and eunuchs, wives and princes, generals and the royal bodyguard, the 10,000 'Immortals' with their belted robes and carefully coiffed beards, and at its hub the golden chariot and its so-precious passenger, the tall, imperious, dark-eyed crown prince, now thirty-two years old, Darius' favourite (though not eldest) son, the 'greatest, second only to his father', through his mother, Queen Atossa, the grandson of great Cyrus himself.[38]

Held in the sanctuary of the goddess Anahita in Cyrus' dazzling palace in lush, well-irrigated parkland, the ceremony saw the young prince with his priests and chosen dignitaries climb the impressive staircase to the inner sanctum, where, hidden from public view but in the presence of the goddess, he ate a ritual meal—pistachios, figs—and drank a draught of yoghurt before, dressed in splendid robes once worn by Cyrus, he reappeared to greet the waiting throng: their new Great King, Khshāyarsha, whose name meant 'Ruler of the Heroes', whom Greeks called Xerxes, who proclaimed himself in an inscription on the stairs to his great audience hall at Persepolis 'one king over many kings, one general over many generals', and who, in an inscription in his queen's apartments there, declared his seamless succession in the formula that is by now familiar: 'When Darius, my father, died, I assumed the throne through the will of Ahura Mazda'.[39]

Yet even as Ahura Mazda's altar fires were being relit across the empire, and platters laden high with gourmet delicacies circulated at his lavish coronation banquet, Xerxes was weighing the realities of kingship and the pressures that were pressing heavy on his shoulders—not just the uprising in Egypt or the revolt that had erupted opportunistically in Babylon, both of which he must attend to urgently, but the expectation that, like Darius and Cyrus before him, he would increase Persia's territories, and the specific obligation, too, to finish work his father had begun, to carry the torch west, to annex Greece. Egypt was easy, Babylon less so, and it was not until stability was sufficiently restored that the new king could revisit old ambitions. Much planning had been done already by Darius, but still troops needed to be levied, supplies secured, and strategy discussed with generals. Yet, as summer gave way to autumn, and dark rainclouds massed over the mountains, Xerxes migrated with top-ranking officers and advisors such as Demaratus, together with many of his key court personnel, to Sardis and the palace that had once belonged to Croesus, where the plain between Mount Tmolus and Lake Gyges with its rash of grave mounds by its reedy shores was already being inexorably colonized by vast tented encampments, as men from every corner of the empire, responding to the call-up, congregated for the new campaign: Persians with fish-scale armour, wicker shields and bows; turbaned Cissians; Assyrians with studded wooden clubs; feared Sacae with tall pointed caps and battleaxes; Indians and Bactrians; archers from Arabia and Ethiopia, shoulders draped with lion- and leopard skins, bodies smeared half white, half red, their spear-tips deadly shards of sharpened antelope horn; Asiatic Ethiopians with crane-skin shields, their strange headdresses formed from horses' scalps, the ears erect, the mane swept up to form tall rigid crests; leather-clad Libyans; Thracians with fox-skin hats; Pisidians with bronze-horned helmets; Lygians and Cappadocians; men from plains and mountains, from the Mediterranean's shores east into the heart of Asia; 170,000 infantry; 8,000 cavalry; 2,000 camels and chariots. In time these would be augmented as the expedition passed through or near their territories by 30,000 Thracians and Greeks.[40]

And scouting the sprawling tented city, ears bewildered by the multitude of languages, nostrils twitching as smoke from campfires mingled with exotic spices, brains bewildered as they computed the sheer numbers that they saw—numbers for which they had no words in their own language—three Greek spies sent out from Sparta and the recently formed Allied League prowled the plain, their apprehension growing with the knowledge that few back home would trust the truth of their reports: they would accuse them of exaggerating, embellishing, perhaps of never really going to Sardis in the first place, of not accomplishing their mission, of making it all up. But their activities aroused suspicion. A tap on the shoulder, and they were frogmarched to headquarters, beaten, tortured and condemned to death—once the order had been given royal approval. But Xerxes did not approve. He was already planning how best to sow fear in the hearts of mainland Greeks. He knew the benefits of terror. So he ordered his entourage to give the spies a tour of the encampment, show them everything there was to see, furnish them with comprehensive details of his fleet (1,207 triremes, not to mention countless transport ships) and send them back to Sparta to report. Which was how, first shivering beneath the snow-veiled peaks of Mount Taygetus in the Gerousia, then at a hastily convened assembly of ashen delegates from allied mainland states (including, perhaps, Callias, one of Sparta's *proxenoi* in Athens, and Cimon, whose sympathy for Sparta and expertise in Spartan matters may already have been recognized), the three men came to tell their story.[41]

And so the news reached Athens. As they huddled on Pnyx Hill beneath grey winter skies, straining to hear words snatched away by gusting winds, few of the hoplite veterans of Marathon or oarsmen, newly-trained, hands hard and calloused from long hours of practice at the rowing benches, can have doubted what the coming year would bring: invasion; war; destruction; maybe death; perhaps the end of Athens and her proud democracy. And as they gazed across to the Acropolis they must have wondered with a bleak sense of foreboding whether in just twelve months' time its graceful Temple of Athena Polias or the elegantly-rising pillars of the goddess' new shrine, its bronze chariots and its marble statues of sophisticated, smiling youths and girls would still exist or whether—like Miletus, Naxos and Eretria—it would all be torched, consumed in Persian fire.

5

DEDICATION

Nemesis, winged goddess, blue-eyed unbalancer
of life, you, child of Justice—
you rein in the empty whinnying of men
with your adamantine bridle . . .

Mesomedes, *Hymn to Nemesis*, 1–4

ATHENS, SPRING 480 B.C.

In meeting after meeting of the popular Assembly, as new reports came through, the sheer scale of the danger facing Athens grew ever more apparent. It was not just the enormous Persian army mustering at Sardis that was worrying, or the formidable Phoenician fleet—augmented now with ships from Egypt, Cyprus, Caria and Lycia, Cilicia, Pamphylia and Greek Ionia; it was not even the massive food dumps stockpiled at intervals along the newly laid-down road through Thrace to Macedonia, or bridges built to span the River Strymon, or even engineering works across the isthmus at Mount Athos. What was most worrying of all was their domestic disarray and the disunity of Greece. What was most devastating was their lack of preparation.[1]

While the Persians had utilized the previous ten years to plan their campaign, court potential allies and orchestrate logistics, Greeks had frittered away the decade squabbling. Not least Athenians (for all that they might like to see themselves as wise, far-sighted democrats). Whether bickering with nearby Aegina or quarrelling among themselves to see which of their best politicians they could ostracize, ostrich-like, even the posturing Themistocles had largely ignored the growing threat from Persia—despite what he might later claim. Now, though, all must change. With Thrace and Macedonia already Persian subjects, it was vital that not just mainland Greece but as many colonies as possible should unite in the kind of military alliance that, while familiar from epic tales of Troy, had never yet been fashioned in reality. If such a coalition could be formed it might just be able to withstand attack. But *could* it be formed? Already many poleis were actively considering a Persian alliance as a means of subjugating hated neighbours. To change their minds, to fight as members of a Greek confederacy would need tortuous negotiation and painstaking diplomacy. It would also require time. And time was running out.

The first steps were taken at a meeting held at Isthmia near Corinth, where, in an unprecedented show of solidarity, old enemies such as Athens, Aegina and Megara swore to suspend hostilities and unite in common cause, a promise repeated by not just Sparta and her foe, Tegea, but twenty or so other poleis ranging in size and influence from resplendent Corinth and resurgent Naxos to tiny habitations such as Epidaurus and Hermione on the north-east shores of the Peloponnese, and Mycenae, the once-glittering capital of Homer's Agamemnon, now little more than a rural backwater. Then, confident that they could at least trust one another, they dispatched high-profile delegations, one west to Sicily and the court of Gelon, the powerful Syracusan tyrannos, another south to Crete and a third to Argos. All returned disappointed.[2]

The Argives were always going to be difficult. Implacably opposed to Sparta, they still seethed at the memory of Sepeia and the massacre of their 6,000 men, a war crime for which no reparation had been offered. Yet now the Spartan butchers were expecting their cooperation. How times had changed. Nor was it just Spartans who were behaving arrogantly. Where had the other poleis been when Argos needed *them?* Nonetheless the Argive councillors proclaimed their willingness to join the coalition—on two conditions: Sparta must agree to a thirty-year truce with Argos, and Argos must share joint command with Sparta. They had good reasons for these stipulations: with so many Argives dead at Sepeia, if more fell fighting Persians, Argos would be vulnerable to Sparta for a generation; moreover, accepting Spartan leadership would mean publicly conceding supremacy; and finally, there was no guarantee that the Spartans would not abuse their command, perhaps even placing Argive troops deliberately in harm's way as a means of further decimating their manpower. For the Spartans, however, such terms were unacceptable. Incensed, they snarled that, while Argos had just one king, they had two who would ensure that he was constantly outvoted. It was a foolish, petty squabble, for, although she was still seriously depleted, to include Argos within the fold would have added significantly to Greece's overall security, while to keep her outside nursing thoughts of vengeance was to leave strategic territories dangerously exposed and risk the Persians making landfall unopposed in the Peloponnese. Which was undoubtedly why, when challenged, the envoys made such wild excuses: the Delphic oracle, they said, had warned Argos against joining the alliance; the Great King, they maintained, had used mythology (as Datis tried to do at Marathon) to persuade the Argives that, through their local hero, Perseus, they and the Persians were cousins; the Argives (they insisted, when all other pretexts failed) had themselves persuaded Xerxes to invade Greece simply to help crush Sparta in revenge for Sepeia. Spiteful and unedifying as these claims were, they did little to enhance morale.[3]

The other delegates' reports were equally disheartening. In Crete, where Sparta normally enjoyed close ties, a coalition of cities had refused to give their answer before first consulting Delphi. The oracle's reply had been disquieting: the ghost of Crete's (mythological) King Minos would turn on them its anger if they helped the Greeks, just as it plagued them in times past, when (despite his aiding them at Troy) Greek allies had neglected to avenge his death in Sicily.[4]

Meanwhile in Sicily, Gelon, the tough tyrannnos of Syracuse, was proving equally intransigent. Now in his eleventh year of rule, Gelon had clawed his way to power through ruthlessness and guile. A decorated general from Gela (on Sicily's south coast), he seized power in the chaos of a democratic uprising, before riding to the rescue of Syracuse's landed families, when the urban poor and slaves rebelled against them. At the sight of his approaching army they surrendered but, rather than restore the power of the elite, Gelon made himself tyrannos, placed his brother on Gela's throne and imposed his brutal will on eastern Sicily. Determined to make Syracuse a major economic powerhouse, in the same year that Athenians were celebrating Laurium's new silver seam, he emptied local cities of entire populations and sold their poor as slaves. Yet, strong though Gelon was, a still stronger force was threatening: with a foothold in the north-west, it was Carthage's ambition to control all Sicily. The previous year, the tyrannos of Himera, deposed, had fled to Carthage, where (like Hippias in Persia) he requested military aid to reinstate him. For Carthaginians, who still enjoyed close ties with their ancestral homeland of Phoenicia, the timing could not have been better: with Xerxes poised to invade Greece, their two campaigns could be coordinated to devastating effect. Once news came that the Persians were nearing Attica, Carthage would launch an offensive on Sicily: 200 warships, 3,000 transport vessels, 300,000 men. If both operations succeeded, by the year's end not just mainland Greece but Sicily would be in Persian or Phoenician hands. True, a few Greek outposts would survive in southern Italy or isolated on the coasts of France, Spain and North Africa, but in time they too would fall. And Asiatic power would spread to the Atlantic.[5]

Not that Gelon wanted to admit that he was worried. Neither Greece's delegates nor his domestic audience must sense his apprehension. Instead he gave a shrewd reply. Mirroring the Cretans (albeit unconsciously), he recalled with sadness the signal failure of Greece (by which he meant specifically Sparta) to help him thirty years before when, although threatened by the Carthaginians, he sought vengeance for the death of Sparta's prince Dorieus at the hands of Gela's neighbours, the Egestans. It was a calculated insult aimed deliberately to offend, for Dorieus was King Leonidas' brother, and Leonidas' failure to avenge him could be interpreted as evidence of negligence—or cowardice. But Gelon would forget the past; he would be generous; he would supply 200 ships and 20,000 hoplites, 2,000 heavy cavalry, 2,000 light horsemen, 2,000 archers and 2,000 slingers, and what was more he would provide all food and pay for the entire Greek army for as long as the war should last. There was just one condition: he, Gelon, must assume supreme command of the whole army. The Spartan delegates erupted in fury. 'Agamemnon' (legendary leader of the Greeks at Troy) 'would spin in his grave to hear that Spartans were commanded by mere Syracusans!' If Gelon was unwilling to take second place, he need not help at all.[6]

But still Gelon was not finished. Feigning sincerity, he made a second offer: despite his contribution being much larger than the mainland Greeks', he would be content simply to command on land while Sparta led at sea, or, if the Greeks preferred, vice versa. This time it was the Athenian ambassador who lost his temper—democratic Athens had not built her fleet to take orders from a tyrant. As he ranted apoplectically about how Homer praised Athenians for being the best at marshalling their men at Troy, men born from the very soil of Attica, men who, alone of Greeks, had never left their homeland, the meeting broke up in acrimony. 'It seems', said Gelon with wry insight, 'that you have many who would lead, but none who would be led. You want everything your way and you refuse to compromise. Best, then, go home without delay, and tell the Greeks that they have lost the springtime of their year.' It was the outcome that he had been engineering all along. Confronted by the Carthaginian threat, Gelon never meant to send his troops to Greece, but this way he retained his kudos, while exposing the weakness of the Greek position.

Although, returning, they did manage to salvage something of their pride by extracting promises of help from Corcyra, when they reported to the League, like their colleagues rebuffed by Argos, they resorted to excuses. Discovering that Gelon (anticipating war with Carthage) had shipped valuables to Delphi for security, they confidently claimed that his intention was, if Xerxes won in Greece, to give them all to him along with earth and water, but, if he failed, to bring them home again. Once more a potential ally (who had admittedly behaved high-handedly) was slandered for withholding his support, when in the circumstances it would have been impossible to offer it. Perhaps it did the allies good to let off steam, but the stark truth was that all three missions had been failures. There were no more allies now than there had been before.[7]

Indeed, there were potentially far fewer. From Sardis, Xerxes had already sent detailed inventories of his invasion force accompanied by requests for earth and water to every polis on the Greek mainland and islands—apart from two: Athens and Sparta. Given their treatment of previous envoys, they deserved no second chance. From many others, though, the fateful pairs of amphorae were carried east, gifts of men who knew their history, how Persia enslaved those who resisted but treated those who yielded with respect, allowing them (in name at least) to keep their constitutions, property and lands intact in return for paying their taxes. Now that they had learned the sheer scale of the Great King's army and the number of his ships, now they had weighed the odds, even many who had previously in patriotic speeches vowed to die before relinquishing their freedom realized that it was futile to resist, preferring not simply an easy life but life itself. In Herodotus' pithy words, 'most had no belly for the fight and so instead enthusiastically threw in their lot with Persia'.[8]

With Greek support haemorrhaging almost by the day, Xerxes' mastery of earth and water became even more apparent. For three years from Elaeus, 'Town of Olives', on the south tip of the Chersonese, a settlement once governed by Miltiades, gangs of labourers had been shipped west in shifts to the low scrubland that linked Mount Athos to the Thracian mainland, their mission: to carve through the isthmus a canal, one and a half miles long, 100 feet in width, through which two triremes might row side by side. It was not the first canal the Persians had built. In Egypt, Darius had set engineers to work on a canal east from the Delta to the Great Bitter Lake and thence south to the Red Sea, some 60 miles long, 150 feet wide and deep enough to take the draught of heavy merchant ships. His motives then were purely economic; Xerxes' were more complex. Yes, Persia's fleet had been destroyed by storm winds as it tried to round Mount Athos thirteen years before, and perhaps he was unwilling to repeat the risk. But if that were his only reason he could have hauled his ships across the isthmus. Instead, he wished to prove a point and make a strong, persuasive statement: let any polis that refused him earth and water know that Xerxes was so powerful that his ships could sail through land as if upon the waters of the sea, just as his troops could march across the water. As a later Greek would comment, 'he wanted to unleash shock and awe.'[9]

While Persian officers were proudly touring the canal, admiring its gently sloping sides, appreciating how long breakwaters that stretched into the sea would stop its mouths from silting, at the Hellespont another engineering feat was underway. Thirty-five years earlier Darius bridged the Bosporus and Danube to campaign in Scythia. Now Xerxes was constructing two bridges of his own across the Hellespont. Each had its own function: one, almost two and a half miles in length, and sited where the channel narrows between Abydus on the Asiatic shores and a rocky headland just south-west of Sestus on the European Chersonese, was specifically for military use; the other, two miles long, downstream, was for the baggage train. Ingeniously constructed so that sections could be temporarily swung out of place whenever convoys needed to pass through from the Black Sea, both were pontoons: 674 ships in total (360 for the military bridge, 314 for the other), triremes and smaller warships lashed together, bows facing the swift current, each moored by anchors fore and aft. Once all were in position and secure, thick, heavy cables (six for each bridge: four woven from papyrus, two from flax that weighed a hundredweight a yard) were heaved across from one shore to another, then stretched taut with massive windlasses. Next wooden walkways were laid down, their surfaces strewn with brushwood before being packed with hard-tamped earth, their sides fenced with tall parapets for safety and to ensure the animals—horses and camels, oxen and donkeys—did not panic at the sight of rushing water. Panic, after all, was what the Greeks were meant to feel, not the invading Persians.[10]

Yet instead of giving way to fear, many Greeks were trying to convince themselves that, by attempting to bend nature to his will, Xerxes was not just showing his megalomania but proving himself guilty of hubris, of transgressing the limits of human endeavour, of risking the gods' anger and the punishment of Nemesis, goddess of revenge. For all Greeks knew the gods' views on canals. When citizens of Cnidus tried to save their promontory from Persian attack by cutting a channel through its narrow neck, Apollo, lord of Delphi, intervened, injuring workmen and issuing an oracle: 'Stop digging! Zeus would have made an island here, if that was what he wanted.' Nor was this the only sign of Xerxes' madness. When a squall destroyed the still-unfinished bridges, ripping ships from mooring, Greeks delighted in imagining the Great King's tantrums, how he had the engineers decapitated, how he ordered that the Hellespont be branded like a slave with hot irons, that chains be thrown into its waters, that it receive 300 lashes as he shouted to the winds: 'Foul water! This is your master's justice for treating him unjustly, who never was unjust to you. King Xerxes *will* cross you, whether you wish it or not.'[11]

There had been further evidence of the Great King's insanity. Marching to Sardis, Xerxes became so besotted with a plane tree that he draped it with jewels and positioned one of his own bodyguard to watch over it forever. For Persians liked plane trees—so much that, when a Lydian grandee, Pythias, the richest man in Asia, second only to the Great King, wished to delight Darius, he gave him a golden model of a plane tree. Wishing subsequently to delight Xerxes, too, he offered to finance the entire expedition. But this did not save his family. The offer was rebuffed, and when Pythias asked that his eldest son be excused from serving on campaign, Xerxes exploded in rage, had the young man sliced in half, and placed the two parts of his split cadaver on either side of the road from Sardis, a putrefying, fly-blown warning, evidence (if evidence were needed) of his unyielding power. Yet, despite it all, the gods still ruled supreme. At the start of his campaign at the spring equinox, as Xerxes' army, setting off, struck out to snake between the rotting remnants of Pythias' son's corpse (or so the Greeks maintained), the sky darkened, day turned into night—a solar eclipse that Magi struggled to interpret as predicting the eclipse of Greece, but Greeks knew was the anger of the gods against the vaunting Persian king. It was not the only portent. As Xerxes neared the Hellespont (advised by his Greek retinue) he made a symbolic detour—to Troy, where, as Magi poured libations to its fallen heroes, he sacrificed 1,000 oxen, vowing to avenge the Greek sack of the city. 'But that night terror fell on all his camp', and in the morning the Scamander river, famous in Homeric epic, failed to provide sufficient water for the Persian army.[12]

Such portents (true or manufactured) may have breathed a ghost of hope into Greek hearts, yet there were other concrete reasons why Greek naval strategists might feel—albeit marginally—less pessimistic. For in building his two bridges, Xerxes had taken more than half his warships out of action. Though the odds were still stacked dangerously against them, the Greeks, albeit with fewer than 400 triremes (and a further 60 promised from Corcyra) now faced a fleet of not 1,207 ships as they once feared, but 533. Even so, it was cold comfort: each report and rumour that spiralled up the hard-packed road across the marshland from the quays of Phalerum and Piraeus, made the sheer size and spectacle of Xerxes' army on the march more terrifying. Eyewitnesses described how behind the creaking baggage train—pack animals and wagons, some transporting concubines and eunuchs, others female cooks—men marched from every nation in the Persian Empire, a deluge of foreign tribesmen torn from far-off villages, who poured across the plains and flooded through quiet country lanes and orchards heavy in full blossom. At last, as the polyglot procession's final units passed from sight, and all that remained was silence and birdsong, dumbstruck onlookers— peasants working nearby fields, shepherds on far-off hillsides—tried to take in the sheer enormity of what they had just seen. But then new sounds—the tramp of marching feet, the clop of hooves, the jangling of bridles—and 1,000 horsemen, Persia's elite cavalry, rode into view. Behind them: 1,000 infantry, their hair well-coifed, their beards well-curled, each wearing long robes falling to their ankles, each carrying his spear reversed so that, instead of its sharp point, its butt, a golden pomegranate, glinted in the sun. And then, despite the sheer mass of humanity that they had seen file by, the most arresting sight of all: ten sacred horses born and bred on the Nisaean Plain, all beautifully caparisoned, each led by its own groom; a golden chariot, sacred to Ahura Mazda, in which no mortal man might ride, drawn by eight horses of the purest white, their charioteer walking by their side; a second chariot no less ornate, drawn by Nisaean horses, in which rode two men: the charioteer, son of one of Darius' six co-assassins; and, resplendent in majesty, the Great King himself, Xerxes, embodiment of empire. A small convoy of covered carriages, and then a further 1,000 infantry, a further 1,000 horsemen, and the road was quiet once more. But even now it was not over: a brief respite, and a second sea of troops broke into view, as many as had gone before, their numbers unimaginable.[13]

It took them seven days and seven nights continuously to cross the Hellespont and march across the Chersonese to the broad plain at Doriscus, where they encamped and regrouped, where ships were hauled ashore to let hulls dry before they were recaulked. Then, men rested and repairs complete, Xerxes reviewed his fleet and army. As he rode his chariot past ranks of well-armed soldiers, his secretaries taking constant notes beside him, or sailed in a Phoenician trireme to inspect the fleet, he had every reason to be satisfied. He had completed the first phase of his invasion. He had reached Europe without incident. With Ahura Mazda's goodwill, with much of mainland Greece already on his side, and with leading Greeks in even hostile cities ready to trade patriotic sentiment for Persian gold, it should not take long before he added the entire Greek mainland to his empire.[14]

Yet, with nothing left to lose, Athens, Sparta and the rest of the Greek League held firm, trying desperately to look for ways to stop the Persians sweeping unopposed into their heartlands. One problem was Thessaly, whose broad plains stretched south from the snow-capped peaks of Ossa and Olympus to the Gulf of Pagasae, its southern tip just seven miles across the water from Euboea. Thessaly's ruling family, the Aleuadae, had already pledged support to Xerxes. Like every other state in Greece, however, Thessaly was riven by rivalry, and to many the Aleuadae were anathema. To them the situation, dangerous as it was, seemed to offer opportunities so, even before Xerxes crossed the Hellespont, they sailed south to a meeting of the League, where they urged the allied Greeks to send an army to the Vale of Tempe, where the River Peneus pours white and cold through mountain gorges, a narrow pass that would, they argued, be the perfect place to make a stand against the Persians—and if at the same time they effected a regime change (which they must do to protect their rear) they would enjoy all Thessaly's support. For League members, eager to clutch even the most flimsy straw, it made for an appealing plan. With Tempe more than 250 miles away, where better to halt Xerxes?[15]

Without hesitating or considering logistics, they embarked 10,000 hoplites onto troop ships, sailed round to Halos on the Gulf of Pagasae (avoiding open waters and Phoenician triremes—a sure sign of their nervousness) and marched overland through Thessaly to Tempe. In overall command was a Spartan, but leading the Athenian contingent was their darling of the hour, the general-cum-politician who wielded more power in the city than any other man, the radical populist, whose heart was wedded to the sea but who now led battalions of wealthy old-school hoplites: Themistocles. For the Thessalian dissidents, landowning horsemen trotting gleefully beside them, it was a pleasing show of strength but, when they reached the River Peneus and started to consider their position, the Greeks became less sanguine by the hour. For one thing, having failed to neutralize the Aleuadae, they risked being attacked from their rear—especially since Persia's navy could offload troops on unprotected beaches to the south; for another, they had misjudged their timing. With Xerxes only just now crossing into Europe, it could be weeks or months before he reached the pass, and for the Greeks to stay that long was probably unfeasible, not least because it would require reliable supply lines. Still more concerning was a message sent from Alexander, king of neighbouring Macedonia, who, while assuring the Greek generals of his respect and friendship (and his deep regret that he himself could not join with them to resist the Persians; his hands were tied), outlined again (in case they had forgotten) the size of Xerxes' army and the number of his ships, and at last got to the point: there was at least one other well-known mountain pass that led from Macedonia to Thessaly; Xerxes had no need to fight; he would simply make a detour.[16]

With ill grace the Greeks struck camp and stomped back to their ships, as angry with themselves for failing to complete even the most limited reconnaissance or consider the most basic logistics as they were with the Thessalians for misleading them. As for the Thessalians, abandoned, they bowed to the inevitable and reconciled themselves with the Aleuadae.

At a stroke the entire Greek eastern mainland as far south as the Gulf of Malia and the Oetaean Mountains, which marched in tumbling ridges to cascade into the sea at the steaming, sulphurous rock pools of Thermopylae, had pledged support for Persia. The net was drawing in, the options lessening. With every day that passed it seemed increasingly inevitable that, barring a miracle, in just a few months Attica would be ground under Xerxes' slippered heel.

The atmosphere in Athens was febrile. If human information gathering and human aid proved unreliable, they must enlist divine help and intelligence. At no time was Apollo's oracle more needed. So, now that Delphi's sanctuary (which stayed steadfastly shut over winter) was once more welcoming petitioners—though only on one day a month, the seventh day, the date that marked Apollo's birth, his sacred number—a delegation wound its way across the mountains, its donkeys heavy-laden with rich gifts for the god and his officiating priests. They knew that at a previous consultation Apollo had advised Argives and Cretans not to ally themselves with the Greek League. They may even have suspected that Apollo, or at the very least his priests, were in the pay of Persia. But for Athens to have any hope of survival, for Athenian morale not to crumble, they could not afford to go back home without a favourable response, no matter how ambiguous.[17]

First came the preliminary meeting with the priests, the gifts and the assessment of their worth, the confirmation that the question warranted consideration, the publication of the consultation timetable. Placed early in the list, the anxious delegates were still obliged to wait for arcane rites to be performed before their question could be put: for the priestess, Aristonice, to purify herself at dawn in the Castalian Spring; for her to wind her way surrounded by her retinue of priests back up the Sacred Road past treasuries and sanctuaries, through the great doors into the temple, where in echoing half-light she burned barley meal and bay leaves, an offering to Apollo; and for the priests outside to sacrifice a trembling goat on the great altar, the first of many animals that would be killed that day. Then, these preliminaries accomplished, at the temple's inner hearth the first petitioners made sacrifice, before proceeding deeper into the dark building where, concealed behind a curtain, the priestess, crouching in her cauldron atop a sacred tripod, suspended between earth and heaven, had already entered her prophetic trance.[18]

The Delphic priestess sits in her cauldron atop a tripod, clutching a bowl and sprig of bay, as a petitioner approaches to question her (Attic red-figure kylix, c. 430 B.C.).

Even before Athens' delegates had settled on the wooden benches, Aristonice began to moan her angry divination as the priests interpreted:

> Time-wasters! Why sit here? Flee to the furthest corners of the earth!
> Leave your homes and the Acropolis that your city circles like a wheel!
> The head will not remain in place, no, nor the body,
> neither feet nor hands nor torso.
> All is ruined. Fire and Ares, rushing god of war,
> who bears down on you in his Syrian chariot, will lay you low.
> He will shatter many other high-towered citadels—not yours alone—
> and consign many sanctuaries of deathless gods to all-consuming fire.
> Gods stand sweating, trembling in fear as over rooftops
> black blood surges: they know that suffering is inescapable.
> So leave my sanctuary, and veil your heads as you prepare to suffer.[19]

Choked with such images of death, the delegates blundered out into the sunlight. Surely they should return immediately to Athens to report Apollo's words. But the prophecy, the future was so bleak. As they wandered, dazed, across the broad piazza, one of Delphi's great and good approached them with advice: forget convention that the oracle could not be challenged; carry sacred olive branches back inside the temple; approach Apollo in the guise of suppliants; demand a better prophecy. It was a daring proposition, but they embraced it with enthusiasm. With or without the priests' permission, they forced their way into the inner sanctum and crashed onto the benches, a new determination in their hearts, a new fire in their bellies. 'Give us a better answer,' they demanded, before issuing a warning: 'If you do not, we'll never leave your temple—no, we'll stay until we die.' At which, miraculously, the priestess moaned once more, and muttered in her otherworldly tongue:

> Athena cannot completely win over the heart of Olympian Zeus
> though she begs him incessantly with many prayers and all her guile.
> Yet I shall give you this second response, adamantine and
>   unchangeable:
> although the rest of Attica and all the
> sacred gullies of Cithaeron shall be overrun,
> wide-seeing Zeus shall give Athena one inviolable stronghold,
> for you and for your children: the wooden wall.
> So, do not wait for the great hordes of cavalry and infantry from Asia.
> Do not stay still. Turn. Withdraw.
> The day will come when you will face him.
> God-like Salamis, you will bring death to women's sons
> when grain is scattered or the harvest gathered in.[20]

Inspired by their obdurate unwillingness to countenance defeat, or by their sheer audacity, or by their threat to desecrate his temple with their deaths, in the dark of their despair the sun god Apollo (or his priests) had offered the Athenians a glancing glint of hope. Despite all odds, despite the seeming certainty that Athens would be taken and all Attica would fall, Athena had not abandoned them. As the memorial on the Acropolis to Callimachus, war leader at Marathon, had promised, she had mediated 'with the immortal gods of Mount Olympus'. But what did the details mean? What of the reference to Salamis? To which women's sons—Persians or Greeks—would Salamis bring death? And what was the wooden wall that 'wide-seeing Zeus' (in Greek 'euruopa Zeus', a play on 'European', a hint that he was on their side?) had granted the Athenians as their stronghold? When the delegates returned to Pnyx Hill and read out the oracle's response, transcribed with care at Delphi, these questions were immediately seized upon for passionate debate.

But, while arguments became increasingly arcane, and professional interpreters were summoned to give expert judgement on the implication of such adjectives as 'god-like', for pious, if hard-headed, strategists there was just one question of importance: what did Apollo mean by the wooden wall? With the confident authority of time-serving specialists who do not expect their viewpoints to be challenged, the oracle-interpreters pronounced that, since their Acropolis had once been surrounded by a brushwood fence, the god was clearly urging the Athenians to take refuge on the rock that since time immemorial had been their citadel. Pillars of the community, their exposition met with some approval, especially from those whose policy had never really been to fight. But then Themistocles stood up. Fresh from the debacle in the Vale of Tempe, reluctant to risk defending a divided city or let himself be willingly besieged, and fired by the realization that the god of prophecy was endorsing his own cherished policy, he explained with cool poise and complete assurance that the wooden wall was not some ancient palisade that nobody had heard of, but the hull of every new ship in the navy, for Apollo plainly meant them to leave Athens, evacuate all Attica and fight their way to victory at sea.[21]

Supporting Themistocles was his natural constituency, the city's poor, men who had little to lose in the event of an evacuation, patriots for whom the ideal of Athens lay not in physical possessions but in camaraderie established on rowing benches, in freedom from tyranny, in the hard-won equality of democracy. For them their leader's policy was inspired. Others, though, had so much more invested in the fabric of the city and her farmlands: landowners, whose families for centuries had cultivated fields and olive groves; smallholders, who had raised children clearing stones or terracing warm hillsides; priests and priestesses and devout worshippers, who knew how much the gods and heroes loved the land and landscape of Attica, who had spent their lifetimes tending local shrines, who could not bear to see them falling to the Persians. And then there was the ideological divide between old-school hoplites, men who had marched so recently through Thessaly, proud that they would fight for Greece in a traditional pitched battle, and new radicals placing so much faith in an untried navy, ships that had never once been launched in anger. Faced with such polarizing interpretations of 'the wooden wall' and the need to make a choice on which the future of the city and her people would depend, the Assembly adjourned without a vote. It was time to go home and reflect. The danger was paralysis, that, in the face of fear, they could not agree on a policy. As they trudged back to their houses or stood in small knots by street corners, many must have hoped the gods might send a sign that would unite them.

Then at sunrise in the Cerameicus by the Sacred Gate, where state processions congregated before setting out, a group of young men gathered, each dressed in gleaming robes, hair glistening with oil, skin golden, muscles toned from hours spent at gymnasia, each man the scion of an elite Athenian family. And at their centre: Cimon. It was he who had sent word to meet him here, who had assembled this exclusive company of fellow aristocrats and brother cavalrymen. Here, too, was Callias, here young Alcmaeonids, linked to Cimon not just by marriage but by ideology, here representatives of every leading dynasty in Attica, men who had drunk and played together, raced chariots and ridden horses on the beach, watched plays by Phrynichus and sung the lyrics of Anacreon, men who owed everything to Athens' past and longed to shape her future. When they were all assembled, Cimon, reverently carrying his horse's bridle as if it were some holy offering, gave the word and led them, focussed and impassive, in through the Sacred Gate along the well-worn road until they reached the Agora.[22]

Already they had attracted followers, and soon a growing crowd was filing up the slope behind them, past the Areopagus and so on up the ramp that led to the Acropolis. As they emerged onto the rock, they saw slightly to their right the scaffolding around the half-built temple, started just a few years earlier, a thank offering to Athena for her help at Marathon. And there in front of them: the Temple of Athena Polias, the most sacred building in all Attica, adorned with sculptures showing the victory of Greece's gods in battle, and housing Athens' greatest treasure, the statue of the goddess hewn from olive wood, the icon given by the gods that centuries before had fallen from the skies. With great solemnity, the men processed on to the temple doors, beside which the old priestess sat drowsing in the morning sun. A whispered conversation, and—permission granted—Cimon with his closest comrades entered the hushed sanctum. Then, as crowds watched mesmerised beside the marble threshold, he gently laid the bridle down before the ancient statue. A moment's pause, a moment's contemplation before Cimon lifted from a wall hook a shield dedicated from a bygone victory (perhaps from Marathon) and, sliding his left arm into its strap and folding his fingers round its handle, stepped back outside and silently acknowledged the onlookers. Then he turned and walked away. But not towards the Agora. Instead he kept on striding down the slope towards the gate that led out to the road across the marshland to the sea. Wordless, his gesture was profoundly eloquent, its impact as significant in its own way as that of Athens' envoys who dared to stand up to Apollo, or of Cleisthenes who for his city's good renounced ancestral rights in the interests of the People. For, as spokesman for the gilded youth of Attica, Cimon had symbolically resigned his role as cavalryman to proclaim, instead, his will to fight at sea, a shield-bearing marine on the deck of one of Athens' triremes. And more: he and his aristocratic partners had staged a powerful demonstration of their backing for their rival in domestic politics, the scourge of the elite, but nonetheless the strategist who offered Attica her greatest hope—perhaps her only hope—if not of victory then of survival. By giving kudos to Themistocles, Cimon, the semi-Thracian incomer, had shown his powers to unite, to lead, and put an end to the political paralysis.[23]

At the next Assembly, Themistocles, inspired by Cimon's altruism, made a concession of his own, proposing the recall from exile of the four men he had ostracized (though since only two returned—Xanthippus and Aristides—his gesture vividly exposed the fault lines fissuring the city). Then, with class harmony as close as it would ever be, the vote was taken, the decision made: given the sheer size of Xerxes' army, and with little hope of saving Attica and Athens from invasion, the countryside and city must be abandoned, its inhabitants—perhaps 100,000 women, children, men over the fighting age of fifty-five, citizens and foreign residents and slaves—evacuated to three destinations: 'godlike' Salamis, Troezen across the Saronic Gulf on the Peloponnesian coast (where Athens' hero Theseus had spent his early years) and Aegina, once, pro-Persian, Athens' bitter enemy, now a declared ally. The logistics required painstaking planning. Every seaworthy vessel—from recently-built triremes, many still sweet with the scent of fresh-cut wood and newly-applied pitch, to patched-up fishing boats rowed round from Marathon and Attica's east coast—was pressed into service as long columns of frightened refugees poured down to Athens and Piraeus from outlying towns and villages with orders to report by tribe or *deme* to designated officers at booths and stalls strung out along the seafront. Cimon and Elpinice, the one abandoning beloved farmlands at Laciadae, the other quitting Callias' sumptuous Acharnian estates, must have experienced a sense of déjà vu: it was just thirteen years since Persian ships had forced them to evacuate the Chersonese, thirteen years since they had seen their elder brother, who perhaps was even now advising the Great King, thirteen years in which their father had been glorified and vilified, in which they had adapted stubbornly to Athens' ways, in which they had made Attica their home. Now, with all Athens clamouring and surging round them, desperate, disorientated—mothers searching panic-stricken for straying children, parents hugging sons they knew might die, peasants passionately trying to persuade unyielding bureaucrats to let them take their crates of chickens or their goats or sheep— they cannot have been alone in wondering if they would ever see Athens again. Some, trusting the professionals' interpretation of 'the wooden wall', refused to leave, preferring to barricade themselves with priests and priestesses and similarly stubborn dyed-in-the-wool conservatives inside the Acropolis, but they were comparatively few in number, and as they watched the convoys ply their way across the waters back and forth for seemingly unending days, around them city streets grew quieter, just stray dogs left behind now and the chattering of birds.[24]

Meanwhile at Isthmia plans were taking shape to buy the allies time. Xerxes had scheduled his campaign well, for this was an Olympic year, when not just athletes and trainers but the great and good of every Greek-speaking polis from the Black Sea's coast to Sicily would congregate at the sanctuary of Zeus Olympius for five days straddling the full moon, this year on the nineteenth of August. Monarchs, tyrants, democrats and their supporters, they came not just for the athletic and equestrian contests (though they were the most prestigious in their world) but to honour Zeus with rituals and sacrifices, feasting and processions. They came, too, to meet with each other and exchange ideas, to discuss great matters of political significance, to listen to philosophers and poets. And they came because the rhythm of the four-year cycle kept strong the heartbeat of Hellenism, the pulse that gave the Greek diaspora identity, community and continuity, a cultural and ethnic unity. And at no time in the Olympic festival's three-centuries-old history had it ever been more crucial to keep that unity alive, or to ensure their compact with their gods. So now, despite (indeed, because of) the existential threat now looming on their borders, instead of strapping on their armour as summer heat became more searing by the day Greek men of fighting age from every polis great and small, from mainland cities and from islands, set out on their long journeys to Olympia, while many others stayed at home to celebrate more local festivals.[25]

It was what Xerxes had been counting on. Like his Greek specialist—like Demaratus—he remembered how, because of a religious festival, the Spartans had missed Marathon: now, thanks to the Olympics, many other Greeks might fail to march at all. Which was why he had been so conspicuously frittering his time in Thrace and Macedonia. Which was why, too, as the August moon began to wax, he gave the order to advance. Alarming for allied Greeks, unwelcome to those generals still at the Isthmus of Corinth, the news was far from unexpected. But already they had formed their strategy, and days before had acted on it. With so much of the mainland north of the isthmus either declared for Persia or (in the case of Attica) evacuated, it was their intention to concentrate on defending the Peloponnese. At less than four miles wide the isthmus linking the two land masses seemed the obvious place to do so. However, with no real efforts made to fortify this narrow strip of land, and so many richer Greeks (the cavalry and hoplite class) engaged in crucial rituals, their plan was to play for time, to bar, or at the very least impede, the Persians by blocking the main route south, where it narrowed at Thermopylae, and cutting off the sea lanes round Euboea. It was a strategy that played to their strengths: to hold Thermopylae for any length of time would require between 5,000 and 7,000 hoplites, and, while the fleet would need just short of 50,000 oarsmen, most of these, coming from poorer classes, remained at hand, while the roughly 4,000 marines (men such as Cimon) and generals such as Themistocles had willingly foregone the lure of the Olympic olive crown to compete in a far greater struggle, whose prize (as they already realised) was the preservation of their freedom and identity.

Despite Athens' contribution of more ships than any other state, protocol demanded that a Spartan be appointed to command them. Thus, although Themistocles had charge of the Athenian contingent, Eurybiades was appointed Admiral of the Fleet, while Leonidas (one of Sparta's two kings) led the land forces—Spartans and Corinthians, Mantineans and Tegeans, villagers from Mycenae, fighters from Thespiae and Phocis, even 400 Theban patriots opposed to their pro-Persian government. Ten years previously, detained by the Carneia Festival, Spartans arrived late at Marathon, for them a source of shame, for Athens a great propaganda coup. Now, with the Carneia fast approaching, yet determined to take centre stage, the Spartans weighed politics and piety and, loath to deprive Apollo of all worshippers, opted for a compromise: accompanying Leonidas would be 300 stony-eyed Identicals, a royal bodyguard, to form the backbone of the allied force. Each knew that none was likely to return—not least Leonidas himself, at sixty now a hardened veteran of innumerable campaigns, a man of dark, sardonic humour who, willingly accepting leadership, believed a recent oracle predicted both his death and Sparta's consequent salvation. Now, hefting his shield, and telling his wife, Gorgo, daughter of the long-disgraced Cleomenes, to 'marry a good man and bear good children', Leonidas and his handpicked regiment (all fathers of at least one son to carry on his bloodline) struck out north-east until they reached a causeway running over noisome marshland (man-made to make much of the one-hundred-yard-wide strip of land impassable) with, to their left, steep bramble-covered slopes and, to their right, the sea. It was near here (legend told) that Heracles, Leonidas' ancestor, died, wracked in agony, because he wrapped himself unwittingly in an acid-impregnated robe; the steaming sulphurous pools pockmarking this unearthly landscape were said to have been formed from his still-suppurating wounds. It was these pools that gave the place its name, 'Hot Gates', 'Thermopylae', and in the long days of bored tension as they waited for the Persians, the stench of sulphur was to permeate Greeks' tents and hair and clothing.[26]

Meanwhile, the fleet sailed through the straits to Artemisium, a cape on Euboea's northern coast: 271 ships in varying condition, many of their crews quite inexperienced, all that could be spared to face Xerxes' 533 vessels while Attica's evacuation remained incomplete, though in time perhaps a further 200 triremes would be available to reinforce them or patrol the coast. But no sooner had they reached the narrow beach at Artemisium, with the mountains of Magnesia pale blue across the strait, than early in the morning an Athenian patrol ship came tacking in from the north-west. Together with two other triremes, it had been off the eastern coast of Scopelus when unexpectedly ten black Phoenician warships appeared out of the morning mists. As its crew turned to flee, building a speedy rhythm with their oars, marines on deck looked back to see first one and then the other allied vessel rammed and captured, before—if they really could believe their eyes—the bravest man from the first ship was dragged on board an enemy trireme, bundled kicking to the prow and sacrificed to some outlandish god, throat cut, blood belching black into the sea. It was a sobering experience. No longer a vague, abstract threat, the Persians' knife-blades had become reality. With Greek blood spilt and Greek ships captured, the invasion proper had begun; and on low hills behind the beach, lookouts kept constant watch, believing that at any moment the Persian fleet would round the distant headland and pour into the azure channel.[27]

For days the waiting seemed to stretch to breaking point, the everyday normality of sourcing food and water interspersed with rowing drills, the dull fear of death at sea never far from each man's mind. At last, word from the watchers. But not of Persians. The weather had been still and humid, baking hot, but now the air was drier, visibility much sharper; now they could see little clouds begin to form high over the far mountains. For local sailors it could only mean one thing: the Meltemi were on their way, Etesian winds that tear from Thrace for up to six days reaching speeds of sixty miles an hour and clashing with already deadly currents as they funnel through the straits, stirring the sea into a lethal maelstrom that seethes 'like a boiling cauldron'. Even for ships drawn up on shore at exposed beaches such as Artemisium these gales could spell disaster. Despite the Persian threat, the fleet had just one option: to make prayers and offerings to Boreas, god of the north wind, before withdrawing with all speed south to Chalcis to ride out the storm.[28]

For three days they fretted as grey breakers lashed the coast and hot winds howled, but on the fourth, as quickly as it had begun, the storm abated and, assured by local boatmen, they returned to Artemisium, where within hours scouting vessels brought news of the Great King's navy. Most of Persia's fleet had been lying at anchor off the eastern coast in neat lines eight ships deep when the Meltemi struck. While some captains managed to control their ships, bucking, rolling in the swell, steering them to shore and dragging them high up the beaches, many could not, and soon much of the Magnesian coastline from rocks known as the 'Ovens' broiling beneath the huge bulk of Mount Pelion to beaches stretching north to Casthanea were strewn with wrecks and wreckage, their crews attacked by local villagers, their treasure chests and gold and silver goblets dragged out of the surf and ransacked. Not even urgent prayers from Xerxes' Magi to the local sea nymph, Thetis, mother of Troy's bitter enemy, Achilles, could help control the storm and, when at last the gales died down and surviving ships were mustered, the Persians discovered the grim truth: they had lost almost a third of their warfleet, perhaps 150 ships. Their numerical advantage had been smashed on Greece's shoals and beaches. Boreas, the Greek wind god, had done his work. Yet even as the Greeks were sailing back to Artemisium, the Persian fleet regrouped and made its way around the cape; and now it was facing them across the strait, strung out in coves and harbours at Aphetae, baying for revenge. But still some ships were straggling, and when one disorientated squadron mistook the Greeks for Persians, it made easy prey. Its captains, captured, were interrogated and shipped off to the Isthmus, the fruits of an albeit easy victory, while at Artemisium Greek priests and generals made prayers and votive offerings to Poseidon, sea god and Saviour.[29]

But they were not yet home and dry. Far from it. Almost immediately, a tiny fishing boat came labouring across the channel; at its oars a professional diver, the bombastic Scyllias, who had spent the past days looting Persian wrecks. Now he brought valuable intelligence to Eurybiades and the Greek fleet. The Persians had sent a squadron of 200 ships to loop south down Euboea's eastern coast, its mission: to swoop round the island's southern tip, then hairpin north again, through the Euripus straits past Chalcis, before emerging west of Artemisium, where in a pincer movement coordinated closely with the remainder of the fleet at Aphetae it would crush the Greeks so mercilessly that 'not even a fire-signaller was left alive'. The news left many on the Greek side stunned and terrified. They hastily convened a war council, but their arguments have been distorted in the telling. Later it was said that there was talk of getting out as quickly as they could, of sailing to the Isthmus, escaping to the hills, forgetting hopes of victory at sea. It was said that Eurybiades was keen to sail immediately, despite Euboean pleas not to abandon them before they moved their families to safety, while the Corinthian commander, Adeimantus, was ready unilaterally to flee for home. There were even rumours, repeated so frequently and with such confidence that they took on a patina of truth, that islanders had bribed Themistocles, the one commander arguing to stay. He used the money (so they said) to bribe first Eurybiades then Adeimantus, hoarding the remainder (they maintained) in secret for himself. (Even in times of heroic struggle Greeks assigned the basest motives to their leaders.) Yet there were strong strategic arguments for staying: abandoning Artemisium would not just gift Euboea to the enemy, but let the Persians (already massing in the plain north of Thermopylae) land unopposed south of the pass and attack Leonidas and his troops from the rear, wasting their lives and squandering the vital days that they were buying for fellow, festival-going Greeks. So, if there were internal tensions (as almost certainly there were), the Greek commanders (bribed or not) were sufficiently mature to shelve their differences and stay. It was a brave decision for men who had no way of knowing how their crews—untried, untested—would perform in battle. For months they had drilled hard and often, but now the time had come to put their training to the test. Now it was time to face the enemy.[30]

That night by the light of the almost full moon, Greek ships slid out across the ghostly sea south towards Chalcis to lurk in wait for the Persian detachment that even now was wheeling round the island. Meanwhile another trireme raced at top speed for Cape Sunium to contact the rest of the Athenian fleet lying off the coast of Attica with a request to come in haste to Artemisium. Then, these preliminaries in place, the Greeks at Artemisium sat back and waited while the sun rose white and shadows shortened and cicadas screamed ever louder on the hillsides. By late afternoon, with still no news from Chalcis, their generals gave the order to embark and put to sea in tight formation, shooting out from Artemisium across the channel to the mainland coast, where the Persians were anchored, strung out along the shoreline not expecting an attack. Still reeling from the storm, with many ships still damaged, the Persians scrambled to respond, and soon they too were in the straits, their two wings fanning out and curving round to smash into the Greek fleet from the rear. It was exactly what the Greeks had been expecting. A trumpet call, an order passed, and in a well-rehearsed manoeuvre triremes peeled off from either wing, swung round, backed oars, until in a tight circle each ram-tipped prow was bristling outwards, each eye on each side of each bow unblinking, a strong wall so impenetrable that all the Persians could do was stand off, vigilant, while here and there a Greek ship darted out, conducted a surgical strike and rapidly returned to the formation. It was a battle of attrition and in the end, just as the Greeks had calculated joining battle so late in the afternoon, the sun began to set and it was over. Or so the Persians thought. But as they wheeled towards the shore, Greek triremes overtook a Persian squadron, thirty ships from Salamis in Cyprus, surrounded them and cut them off, and forced them back to Artemisium. The first clash at sea was over and, while neither side had scored a major victory, neither had been defeated, which for the Greeks was a considerable boost to their morale.

Then as the sun set low across the entrance to the Gulf of Pagasae the winds got up again, this time from the south-east, a sirocco, screaming, bringing lashing rain as thunder shook Magnesia and crashed in deafening explosions above the cloud-thick peaks of Pelion. Drawn up on the beach at Artemisium, the Greek fleet was relatively unaffected but the storm winds caught the Persians at anchor in steep, rocky coves, or riding in the open sea, swamping vessels, driving them ashore, churning the seething waves with flotsam and the bodies of the dead, as all the while the crack and boom of thunder rolled and lightning bursts revealed the night-time horrors, and sailors who had ridden out the storm just days before were seized once more with panic. And then, as quickly as it came, the storm died down; dawn came; the sea gave up its dead. Neither fleet sailed out that morning, their generals assessing what might be learned from their encounter on the previous afternoon, their carpenters repairing damages to hulls or oars, their crews regaining their composure. But by mid-afternoon the Greek fleet received reinforcements—fifty-three triremes reassigned from their evacuation duties. Moreover, two swift boats sped in to Artemisium with welcome news. One came from the mainland: with his army backing up along the coastline of the Malian Gulf and supplies beginning to run out, Xerxes had ordered an attack across the causeway at Thermopylae. To no avail. Protected by a stone wall, equipped with better armour and with the treacherous terrain as ally, the Greeks had experienced little difficulty in beating them off and, while they suffered casualties, these were nothing in comparison to Persia's dead. The strategy was working. There was no reason to suppose they could not hold the pass indefinitely. The news the second boat's crew brought was even more appreciated. The previous night's storm had caught the Persian ships sent round Euboea. Tacking by moonlight round the southern coast, steering by stars, they lost their bearings beneath massing clouds, and, in unknown waters, were swept helplessly against the island's rocky shore, hulls breached and timbers smashed. Once more the weather had put paid to Persian strategy. To celebrate, the Greek fleet put to sea once more and swept through the straits unopposed, their only prey a stray Cilician squadron, which they rammed with glee before returning back to base to celebrate their victory in the glow of the full moon and give thanks for 'the god's intervention calculated to ensure that Persia's fleet was rendered equal to the Greeks' and was no longer so superior'.[31]

But next morning—waters calm and little breeze—the Persian ships put out to sea, a hollow crescent seeking their Greek prey. At Artemisium the Greeks were waiting on board quietly, patiently, and now their captains gave the order to advance, their long oars feathering the swell, each crew aware that this time nightfall would bring no early end to fighting, and that the hours ahead were crucial to their country's fate. As distances between them shortened, oarsmen picked up speed and helmsmen set their course, while on narrow decks marines—men such as Cimon—braced themselves for impact. And then it came: the thump as ram smashed into hull, the crack of wood, the snap of oars, the cries of sailors, as a stricken trireme, water gushing cold through splintered timbers, wallowed helplessly and showers of javelins rained down. Strung out along the straits ships were colliding, as others wove their intricate manoeuvres, trying to dodge attack or wheeling for the best position that would let them build momentum as they powered in for the kill, always seeking to avoid a chance glance, always aware that if they overshot they risked slicing off their oars against the enemy ship's stern and ending up a sitting target. For long hours, with the baking sun reflected in the mirror of the sea, those on deck watched Persian triremes closing on their ships, sometimes so close they fouled each others' oars, while below them in the heat of bending bodies trapped in hollow hulls, men sleek with sweat strained at the rowlocks. All most could see were their companions' gleaming backs; all most could hear were orders passed along the line from increasingly parched throats; but all feared the same thing: the sudden ingress of a three-pronged snout, the rush of water, and the helplessness, a choking drowning far from shore, no burial, just drifting in the current till the waters cast the corpse ashore and seabirds feasted.

Then unexpectedly the Persian trumpet sounded the retreat and it was over. Scouring the sea for corpses or survivors, the Greeks limped back to Artemisium unconquered. Their losses had been high, but the Persians' were higher, and even with half of their surviving vessels damaged, the Greeks could still claim victory. But any pleasure was short-lived. Another message from the mainland, and the mood turned black. At Thermopylae the Persians had found a path across the mountains. The night before, Xerxes' Immortals, 10,000 well-trained men, had marched beneath the full moon through rugged gullies and thick forests of dark oak up onto the high plateau, where they surprised the sleeping Phocians whom Leonidas had sent to guard the place, and who now simply ran away. By morning they had reached the road behind the Greek position, though too late to catch them all: when a runner brought news of their approach, many allies, rather than face certain death, had packed their bags in haste and slipped into the night. Only the Spartans stayed, and with them Thespians and Thebans, whose lands lay north of the Isthmus, who knew that they were all that stood between their families and death, though they knew they could not stand for long. No-one could tell quite what had happened—there were so few survivors; although it had been fierce, it had been swift, a massacre, a wipeout, a sacrifice of blood made on not just the last day of the great Spartan Carneia, but the central day of the Olympics, when far to the south Greeks sacrificed one hundred oxen to their great god, Zeus, and one athlete powered to victory in two footraces (as in time he would celebrate a third). Yet, although the victor's name—Astylus—entered history, in his defeat, the Spartan king, Leonidas, eclipsed him. He had done his duty. He had bought time.[32]

This was why the Persian fleet had put an early end to their sea battle. When they heard of Xerxes' victory it was possible that many Greeks would simply surrender. Even if they did not, there was nothing for them now at Artemisium. Their future lay at the Isthmus. They would not stay. The Greeks knew it, too, and setting campfires burning in the night to fool the enemy, they manned their broken warships and pushed out down Euripus' strait, where Euboea's brooding hills stood silent, silhouetted to their larboard, before gliding past the plain of Marathon, already haunted with so many memories. And so, as the rising sun threw into sharp relief the distant mountains of the Peloponnese, they rounded Sunium and, hugging southern Attica, looked inland to the still-gleaming Acropolis, before, past Phalerum and past Piraeus, abandoned and deserted now, they nosed into the channel to their new, if temporary, berth. And so they came to god-like Salamis.[33]

6

##

FIRESTORM

Let us go to Salamis to fight for the beguiling isle
and free ourselves from grim dishonour.

Solon, fr. 3

SALAMIS, LATE AUGUST 480 B.C.

Salamis was crowded. In past weeks refugees from Athens had already
swollen its island population, and now the Greek fleet—around 75,000
oarsmen and marines—was inflating it still further. Food and water were
in short supply, and, as the waiting game dragged on and August's heat
showed no signs of abating, nerves stretched to breaking point. News
from the mainland did not help. From Thermopylae, where Leonidas'
fly-blown head was rotting on a stake, Xerxes had swung south to
Phocis, a territory that, in part through hatred for its pro-Persian neighbour, Thessaly, refused demands for earth and water. Now, to gratify
Thessalian allies, the Persians unleashed slaughter, working their way
systematically through the Cephisus valley, looting towns and villages,
torching temples, massacring such men who through age, infirmity or
misplaced trust in their own fighting powers had not fled to the hills,
gang-raping girls to death. Then, with Phocis burning, the Great King's
troops poured into the broad flatlands of Boeotia, receiving fawning welcome from the great and good of Thebes, gleeful at the thought that
Attica, their ancient enemy, deserted now—still, silent, eerie—would
soon be torched and roiling.[1]

Meanwhile, the Persian fleet, complacent now the allies had departed, crossed to Euboea and unchecked, ransacked not just the hill town, Histiaea, but lovely coastal villages, before cruising leisurely down the gulf, through the Euripus channel and on for Sunium. As they nosed in search of water into lapping coves and sandy inlets, where sluggish streams debouched into the sea, ships' captains were surprised to see slogans painted in tall letters on the rocks, a message from Themistocles to the Ionians that—though it smacked of desperation—was cleverly designed to sow doubt into every reader's heart:

> It's wrong for you to fight against your fatherland and enslave Greece! Better to fight *with* us. If that's impossible, don't fight at all—and ask the Carians to do the same. If both these courses are impossible, and you're so constricted that you cannot disengage, remember our close blood ties; remember that our hatred of the Persians stems from helping *you;* and don't fight well!

How bravely, the Phoenician captains wondered, *would* Ionians and Carians join battle when the moment came?[2]

How bravely, for that matter, would the allies fight? In war council meetings held on Salamis, rifts between champions of two mutually conflicting strategies became increasingly more dangerous as many Peloponnesians—especially the anxious Adeimantus, Corinth's general—argued for moving the fleet westwards to the Isthmus, where the army was assembled in force. Rightly nervous of being blockaded in the straits of Salamis, as old-school strategists they were convinced that for the war to be well won its decisive battle should be fought on land: only a hoplite victory would force a Persian retreat. Already key parts of the road from Attica had been destroyed or blocked to hinder Xerxes from deploying at speed, while stretches of the Isthmus' almost four-mile width were being walled off to funnel any Persian attack and minimize the allies' numerical disadvantage. While their army was engaging the Great King on land (Adeimantus and his friends maintained), the fleet would guard the coastline and prevent the enemy from launching an amphibious assault on the north-east Peloponnese, from where they could attack the Isthmus from the rear.[3]

For Themistocles and the Athenians this made no sense at all. With Argos at best neutral and at worst distinctly hostile, there was no certainty that—even if they *could* prevent a Persian landing—Sparta's ancient enemy would not march north and catch the allies in a well-coordinated pincer movement. Meanwhile, by the time the Persians reached the Isthmus more cities would have fallen: not only Megara, but Salamis itself, where Athenian civilians were taking refuge. Were they to sacrifice them meekly to the enemy? Why stake all on a hoplite battle at the Isthmus, when it made so much greater sense to face the Persians at sea, especially since the Great King's fleet was so depleted and the allies had already proved their skill to face and beat it? Besides, experience at Artemisium had shown that Greeks fought best not on the open sea but in more confined waterways—such as the straits of Salamis. And while the Argives might throw in their lot with Persia, Ionians and Carians in Xerxes' fleet might well switch sides when they saw the allies winning. Moreover, the impact of an allied victory at sea would be enormous, for, while so far the Great King's timings had proved uncannily astute—his march south coinciding with religious festivals when Greeks were loath to commit armies fully to the field—now, by September, time was running out. Neither conquered Attica nor ravaged Phocis could feed the Persian army, nor could the rich wheat fields of friendly Thessaly and Boeotia, and with seas soon too rough for sailing, provisions could not be shipped to Greece. Xerxes' strategy required a swift conclusion, smashing the allied army, breaking through the Isthmus, occupying first Corinth and then Sparta. Which he might do. But if—again that 'if'—the allies faced down his fleet, it might just give him pause; it might stall his momentum; it might buy time and let them fight another day, for each day they survived would bring autumn closer and with it the imperative for Xerxes to withdraw his hungry army north to eke out his depleted food dumps—or maybe even home to Asia.[4]

For days there was inertia in the allied camp. With Attica abandoned and Persia's fleet already occupying Athens' harbours, there was only one course of action that the allies could agree on. Under cover of night, a fast ship shot from Salamis for nearby Aegina. On board was Aristides, recently recalled from exile; with him his trusted friend and ally, Cimon, for their mission was to bring back Cimon's ancestors, Peleus and Telamon, the sons of Aeacus, embodied in their talismanic icons. As they hurried through the city's muffled streets, the moon already waxing once again, both men must have recalled the force these relics from another age possessed, relics whose power warring cities had already tried to harness in the past, and that, allied now, they prayed would save them in their trials to come—as they prayed that the sacred statue of Athena Polias, so carefully, so piously and so reluctantly removed from the Athenian Acropolis, would help to save them, too.[5]

But, far from the Acropolis, the statue could not save its temple. The Persians flooded into Attica, burned villages and homesteads, streamed unchecked through city gates and swirled around the rock, looking for a way to scale it. Surely those Athenians who still remained, their trust anchored in the brushwood wall, had no hope of survival. But still they refused to surrender. As the Great King established his command post on the Areopagus, where in legend Amazons, raiders like Xerxes from the east, encamped when they came seeking vengeance of their own, the stalwarts did all they could to resist, extinguishing the blazing pitch-soaked arrows thumping down into their barricades, rolling rocks onto attackers' heads and spurning offers of safe passage made by men they once knew well—Peisistratids who now did Persia's bidding, among them perhaps Hipparchus, ostracized with scarce a thought just seven years before. But not even the Acropolis was impregnable to Persian mountaineers. They scaled its almost sheer face on the eastern side, where no-one thought a route was possible and, once up, pounded, bellowing their terrifying war cries, towards the hapless Greeks. Many ran into the Temple of Athena Polias for sanctuary; others chose to leap from the cliff edge to certain death; but, as attackers threw open the great gates to the Acropolis, their waiting comrades surged onto the rock. No-one was spared, neither men nor women, old nor young: despite the temple's sanctuary they were slaughtered, every one. Then gold and silver offerings were stripped from shrines, and statues wrenched from pedestals, and all was carried down into the Agora to be catalogued and crated up for shipping. And then the fires were lit.[6]

Allied troops on Salamis, and refugees who packed the beaches of the northern Peloponnese or lined the shores of Aegina—all could see the thick pall belching high in the September air and drifting, listless, on the breeze, while far off, in blazing heat, marble cracked and rafters fell and terracotta roof tiles crashed down on charred, faceless corpses, and a city's history and hopes collapsed in ashes. No-one who watched, ululating through their tears, or stunned and silent, disbelieving, could have any doubt of its significance. It was the end of an old order. And, unless they stood firm, unless they stood united, unless they managed somehow to defeat the seemingly invincible invaders, it was a fate that before many months were out would befall each citizen and city in the Greek resistance. But next afternoon a rumour circulated. Where it came from no-one knew. Perhaps a boat had sailed to Salamis from Athens. Not that it mattered. What mattered was the news itself. For that morning (so they said) the Great King had commanded his Peisistratid lackeys to climb onto the still-smoking Acropolis (in his view cleansed now of the demons of the Lie) to sacrifice to Athena, and while they were there they witnessed a miracle. From the blackened stump of the gnarled olive tree that grew out of the rock, where legend claimed Athena had herself planted it, a new green shoot, some eighteen inches long, had sprouted in the night. For the Athenians on Salamis it was a sign: their city might be burned, but its vitality remained. Like the olive tree it could regenerate. The goddess had vouchsafed a portent, and, taken with Apollo's prophecy, the promise of success at god-like Salamis, it gave them heart.[7]

But still the allied Greeks were far from being united. When, a few days after torching Athens, Xerxes turned his focus towards Salamis, tensions were palpable—especially when Persian engineers assembled on the farther shore and began methodically to build a causeway out towards a nearby islet, while elsewhere merchant ships swung out into the channel before being anchored and then lashed together in clear preparation to create a pontoon bridge. All knew the Persians' capabilities, how they had spanned the Hellespont and dug a channel through Mount Athos. Surely it would not be long before the army was marching onto Salamis. While Athenian aristocrats as disparate as Aristides, Xanthippus and the young Cimon kept counsel, the Spartan, Eurybiadas, commander-in-chief of allied naval forces, so lost his temper with Themistocles for speaking out of turn, ignoring protocol, that he had to be restrained from striking him with his staff, while the high-born Corinthian Adeimantus, who loathed the populist Athenian, exasperated at his refusal to abandon Salamis, exploded in fury. He would not, he said, take orders from a man without a city. It was perhaps the turning point of the debate. Just as ten years earlier Phrynichus' *Capture of Miletus* reminded Athens of her troubles, so now a careless jibe gave the assembled generals pause. As did Themistocles' reply. Stones and bricks did not matter to Athenians, he said, and they would not permit themselves to be enslaved for the sake of lifeless things. 'But still we have the greatest city in all Greece—200 triremes that even now stand ready to help save you, if you would be saved. But if you leave us exposed again, Greece will discover that Athenians have got themselves a city that is free and a land that's better than the one they left behind.' Like the Phocaeans and the townspeople of Teos in Ionia, who had fled the Persians before them, they would simply sail west; they would found a second Athens, while, deprived of more than half their fleet, the Spartans and Corinthians, alone no match for Xerxes, would be defeated. As Themistocles stopped speaking, tremors shook the island and the straits began to boil—a sign to every ally that Poseidon, god of earthquakes and the sea, had given his approval. The generals had been outmanoeuvred. Thanks to an accident of nature, Themistocles had won the day.[8]

Yet how long would consensus hold? It was vital to fight soon. But it was not going to be easy. Why should the enemy engage the allied fleet? At a meeting of his high command, one of Xerxes' admirals, an indefatigable Greek, Queen Artemisia of Caria, made a strong case to play a waiting game: in only a short time, she promised, the factious Greek alliance would be sure to fracture as, desperate to save their skins, city after city sued for terms. It was such sound advice, and it betrayed a keen understanding of Greek character. Yet time was not on Xerxes' side. Like Themistocles, he was eager for a swift conclusion, especially since news was reaching him of troubles elsewhere in his empire, which required his presence there. So, when he learned that a sympathetic agent, a Persian prisoner of war who had been captured by the Greeks, had slipped unseen across the straits with a message of goodwill from Themistocles, the Great King was delighted. Especially as his words chimed so precisely with Artemisia's predictions: the allies, at each others' throats, were preparing to sail away that night; as for Themistocles, he wished to aid the Persians, switch sides and fight for Xerxes. It was, of course, a ruse. The agent was Themistocles' loyal slave, who, once his fictitious news had been conveyed, raced back to Salamis. But the stratagem had worked. The trap was sprung. The Persians swarmed into action.[9]

In stealth that night beneath the full moon's glare, a merciless unit of well-armed infantry was disembarked onto the rocky islet of Psyttaleia at the eastern entrance to the Straits of Salamis, where Persia's fleet lay anchored, while a squadron swung round the island to blockade the channel to the west. And so they waited, alert for any movement in the bay, in constant readiness for battle should the allies cut and run. All night they waited in the straits, captains careful to ensure their ships stayed static in the snaking currents, oarsmen feathering the waves, lookouts straining through the darkness for allied triremes on the move. When daybreak came they were still waiting. And when, at sunrise, surrounded by secretaries, Xerxes settled on his ornate throne beneath a golden canopy on the steep hillside overlooking Salamis (its gentle hills, alive with doves, already golden in the growing light), the great bay still lay calm and empty. The allies had stayed where they were. But surely not for long. On land long files of Persian infantry and horsemen were winding down the coast road west towards the Isthmus—their orders: to create as much commotion as they could, to scuff up clouds of dust to advertise their passage; their purpose: to terrify the Spartans and Corinthians watching from the beach at Salamis, to make them think the Isthmus was under threat, to trick them into leaving, lure them out to sea, to draw them, unsuspecting, into the ambush that awaited them around the hidden capes.[10]

But Themistocles turned even this to his advantage. Since his slave returned the night before, he had been working feverishly to share his plans with colleagues and ensure that they endorsed them. Aided by Aristides, Cimon and their entourage, he visited the generals, convincing them that now events were underway they must bow to the inevitable, accept that battle must be joined and embrace Themistocles' plans. By daybreak it was time to tell the men. At a general assembly Themistocles rose to speak. It was a barnstorming performance, full of fine sentiment, putting fire in his audiences' bellies: 'Forward, Greeks! Set free your fatherland! Set free your wives and children. Set free your fathers' gods, and spirits of your ancestors. The contest is at hand and all is to be won!' As for the sight and sound of Persians marching on the distant shore—by design or accident, the day Themistocles had chosen to give battle coincided with the date on which in peacetime worshippers would file along the Sacred Way from Athens to Eleusis singing sacred hymns before they underwent initiation in the Mysteries, whose promises of rebirth after death were closely linked to cycles of the agricultural year. The tramping men, he claimed (and how the oarsmen wanted to believe him), were not enemy but ghostly celebrants; their marching songs were songs of praise to Dionysus, god of metamorphosis, god of regeneration; it was a sign the gods were on the allies' side; they should recall Apollo's prophecy—victory at god-like Salamis, 'when grain was scattered or the harvest gathered in'—and Athena's olive tree destroyed by fire but sprouting once again.[11]

As sacrifices were performed and trumpets blared, oarsmen and helmsmen, hoplites and archers, roused to a fervour of patriotic zeal, and chanting Themistocles' stirring refrain, 'Forward, Greeks! Set free your fatherland!', swarmed onto their triremes, and put to sea—first the Corinthians, speeding west to intercept the Persian squadron that had sailed round Salamis and stop it entering the bay. To Xerxes watching from Mount Aegaleus, however, this sudden flurry of activity meant something else entirely: this was the moment he was waiting for—the Greeks were trying to flee. At once he passed the order to his men to row in haste into the bay to follow them. It was precisely what Themistocles had counted on. As the leading Persian vessels poured through the narrows, just 800 yards in width, the uncompleted pontoon making it still narrower, the allied fleet arced out to meet them, Themistocles and his Athenians on the left wing, the Spartan Eurybiadas on the right. Almost at once, amid the chanting and the trumpet calls, the thud of oars, the creak of timber, and the slapping of the sea, came the rasping crunch of bronze beak tearing through a wooden hull, so unmistakable, as an Athenian, Ameinias, rammed a Phoenician ship at speed, sweet vengeance for his brother Cynegeirus' death at Marathon, where in the surf he bled his life away, his hand sliced off by a Persian axe. Then moments later, down the line, an Aeginetan ship—the same ship that had fetched the relics of Aeacus' family—found its target. The battle had begun. The Persians—the Great King himself—had been outfoxed. But while Xerxes, with his panoramic view, could watch each sinuous manoeuvre as ships shoved and rammed and circled in the crowded bay below, on board all that the helmsmen and marines could see was whatever was immediately around them. Below deck, oarsmen could see nothing but each other. No wonder, then, that none could tell precisely what was happening—only a few snatched images: Ameinias at his trireme's bow, spear slick with blood from having skewered the Persian admiral; a delicately-carved Phoenician sternpost smashed; a Persian vessel captured and towed off, its crew dead in the water; and ghostly apparitions, too: a spectral woman coming to the allies' aid; Peleus and Telemon, Aeacus' warrior sons, wraithlike above the shores of Salamis, stretching arms in exhortation—and then the breeze began to blow, as it blew every day, around nine in the morning, and a heavy swell began to roll in from the sea, as Themistocles knew it would.[12]

For the Persians it spelled disaster. Exposed to the full force of rising waves, their ships, top-heavy, wallowed uncontrollably, slewing round in an entanglement of oars, hulls undefended from Greek rams, manoeuvres impeded by their own merchant ships lashed ready for the pontoon bridge across the straits. Once more the Greek wind gods had intervened—and Pan, the god of panic. Aware of their predicament, their inability to fight in such conditions against nimble Greeks, all that the Persians could think of was escape. It did not matter how. Seeing a stricken vessel in her path, the Carian queen, Artemisia, rammed it aside, despite its being one of her own fleet. Her callousness worked doubly in her favour. In desperate pursuit, Ameinias believed she had switched sides, broke off his chase and let her sail to safety, while he returned to the grim business of the bay, where waters were befouled with Persian wreckage and the corpses of their dead, while from decks of allied triremes marines skewered survivors, 'jabbing them with broken oars or bits of broken wood as if they were a shoal of tuna fish, as screams and shrieking spread across the sea, until black night descended and hid it all from view'. On the islet of Psyttaleia, too, where Persians had landed in the night, the fighting was intense. Here, Aristides and his hoplites (among them, Cimon, whose ardent bravery was long remembered) leapt onto the rocky shore and, brandishing their spears, pushed back the enemy, shoving, slicing, stabbing, slaughtering them to a man, before scouring the blood-streaked shoreline for shipwrecked Persians trying to crawl to land and despatching them as well. The battle had turned into a rout; shores and reefs were rank with corpses; and as surviving Persian vessels wallowed eastwards to the shelter of Piraeus, and Xerxes, incandescent, rained down punishment on his defeated generals, triumphant Greeks, elated by unexpected victory, tugged captured triremes back to Salamis.[13]

But they could not relax. By sunrise Persia's vanguard could be near the Isthmus, where fighting might erupt at any moment. But while Peloponnesians were keen to set off west to help their countrymen, Themistocles refused to sail from Salamis. The refugees still needed his protection; Xerxes' fleet still posed a threat; and work to bridge the narrows was continuing. It was vital that the allies should stay put and hold their nerve. Yet, as his sailors whiled the day away, scouring the coast for Persian corpses, wading out into the surf to strip gold bracelets from cold arms, rings from stiffened fingers, torques from marbling necks,

Themistocles was weighing another, even greater danger that not one
of his colleagues seemed aware of: in the Hellespont Xerxes had effectively a fresh fleet: the 674 ships used to construct his two pontoons. If
just one bridge were dismantled and the warships recommissioned,
the allies would face not only overwhelming odds on land but fresh dangers at sea. Which was why, next day, he was particularly anxious when
a boat came scudding in with news: the Persian fleet was gone. But where?
According to intelligence: Ionia, then north towards the Hellespont. At
once the allies, too, embarked—for Salamis was safe now; Persia's operation at the Isthmus had been aborted; and work on the pontoon had
stopped—their triremes set off in pursuit, and by nightfall they had
reached pro-Persian Andros.[14]

But there they stalled. The Persians had eluded them, and, while Themistocles was for pressing on to the Hellespont, his allies overruled
him. Xerxes would not dismantle his vital bridges, they argued, since it
was across them that, now defeated, he would march out of Greece.
Better to preserve them. Better, if they could, to construct more. Faced
with their unwillingness to sail further, there was nothing that Themistocles could do. Frustrated, he turned his anger on the islanders of Andros, declaring that, as Greeks, they must contribute to the welfare of
all Greece. They must contribute to the allies' war chests. The Andrians
refused: they had no money. As they told Themistocles, when he warned
darkly of two Athenian gods, Persuasion and Compulsion, who would
enforce his claims, their own gods, Poverty and Powerlessness, meant
they simply had no funds to give him. The Athenian arch-democrat was
furious. Such cheek demanded a response, so just days after he had led
the allied fleet to battle in the name of Greece's freedom, allied troops
laid siege to the Greek town of Andros, sending messengers to other
towns and islands (including Paros and Carystus, collaborators both),
demanding cash with threats that, if they failed to pay, they would be
starved into submission. The threats worked; and as Themistocles' own
private coffers filled with cash from grateful exiles, too, news came that
the allies had been praying for: Xerxes and his Persians had left Attica;
they were marching north; soon they would reach Thessaly, soon Macedonia and Thrace; soon they would be back in Asia Minor. The victory
at Salamis had done its work. For now at least the threat was over.[15]

Jubilant, the allies lifted their siege of Andros and scudded back across
the roughening waters to the mainland. For Athenians docking at Pi-

raeus and filing up the road between the marshes the silhouette of the Acropolis, shorn now of all its buildings, made for a sombre sight, but it was only when they climbed onto the rock itself, disturbing acrid clouds of ash, and picked through charred and twisted corpses lying amidst the rubble—ruined temples, shattered sculptures, blackened pottery, with here and there a statue group that somehow had escaped the looting still incongruously intact—that the sheer scale of the devastation hit them. Of Peisistratus' great entrance portal, of the temple started with such optimism after Marathon, of the Temple of Athena Polias, before whose ancient statue Cimon laid his bridle only months before, all that survived were toppled columns and charred walls—the only sign of life: the green shoots sprouting from the charred stump of the sacred olive tree. Throughout Attica more sanctuaries lay ruined, stripped of their valuables, vandalized, pillaged, raped of sanctity, while in the Agora, where public buildings, symbols of democracy, had been despoiled, there sat an empty plinth, a sight as overwhelming as any plundered temple. For here had stood the statues of Harmodius and Aristogeiton, the tyrant-slayers, who had heralded democracy, now carted as trophies back to Susa and the heart of Persia's empire.[16]

Not everything was lost, however. With the help of Greece's gods and heroes, victory had been won—and not just on the mainland. In Sicily on the very day when Salamis was fought (or so romantic calculations would suggest) Gelon, tyrannus of Syracuse, had crushed the Carthaginian invaders at Himera, killing their general, massacring men, enslaving many thousand prisoners. The Persian-Punic axis had been shattered, and in the west (for now) the threat was lifted. Meanwhile in Athens and the surrounding countryside most homes, though damaged and defaced, seemed sufficiently sound structurally for families to return—and so the process of repopulating Attica began: triremes and transport ships criss-crossing the Saronic Gulf, women and children tentatively picking through desecrated homesteads, farmers yoking ploughs and turning the neglected soil, sowing seeds for next year's harvest; and when all were home the sailors hauled their ships on shore to dry, and shipwrights made repairs.[17]

For high-ranking officers, however, such as Themistocles and Aristides there was urgent business to be done. With the other allied generals they must meet at the Isthmus to choose whom to honour with the prize for bravery at Salamis. On Poseidon's great altar each placed two *ostraca*, each containing two names ranked in order, one of a city, the other of the individual each deemed to have done most to ensure victory. The results were fascinating. Despite providing over half the fleet, despite the willing sacrifices of her people, despite the energy and insight of her generals, Athens won no prize. Instead the city prize went to Aegina, which a decade earlier had willingly submitted to the Persians. Meanwhile in the individual category, most generals inscribed their own names first, with the result that there emerged no outright winner. So by default the prize went to the runner-up: Themistocles, whom everyone had placed a grudging second.[18]

If they felt snubbed (and they had every right to), the Athenians still pluckily joined in the celebrations, donating lavishly to funds for offerings to the protecting gods of Greece—a bronze Zeus at Olympia; at Delphi a gold-and-silver statue of a youth, eighteen feet high, a trireme's figurehead gripped tightly in his outstretched hand, a dedication to Apollo—all paid for from the spoils of war (and, when Apollo's priests rebuked the men of Aegina because they thought their city's gift too mean, many Athenians must have experienced a sense of schadenfreude). Athenians were present, too, to see a Persian warship dragged ashore to be displayed in triumph at Poseidon's sanctuary at the Isthmus, where with sacrifices, hymns and clouds of incense it was consecrated as an offering of thanks. Two other captured triremes were similarly dedicated—one at Poseidon's ruined temple on Cape Sunium, the other on Salamis itself, a tribute to the hero, Ajax, grandson of Aeacus, who had played his role in Greece's victory, the potent ancestor of Cimon and the Philaids.[19]

As celebrations unfolded, news came of how their gods continued to support the allied Greeks. Throughout his retreat (as gleefully exaggerated bulletins maintained) Xerxes had encountered ever greater hardships: without sufficient food, his army—forced to eat whatever vegetation they could find, stripping trees of leaves and bark, grubbing up weeds and grasses—fell victim to disease and dysentery; in northern Macedonia, where he had left Ahura Mazda's golden chariot and its team of sacred horses for safekeeping, he found they had been stolen by marauding Thracians; as his army crossed the frozen River Strymon, the ice gave way beneath so many marching feet, and men and horses drowned in its chill waters; and at the Hellespont (for the allies the sweetest news of all) he found his pontoon bridges had been swept away

by gales, their cables snapped, their walkways splintered, their ships torn
from their moorings and swept along the raging channel to be dashed
in pieces on the rocks, forcing his army to be ferried across to Asia by
sea. The fresh ships that Themistocles had feared were wrecked. For now,
at least, the Persian fleet was finished. Until new triremes could be built
there would be no seaborne invasions.[20]

At a stroke the military dynamic had been altered. Any remaining
threat now lay on land—but there still was a major threat. For Xerxes
had not evacuated all his troops from Greece. While he hastened homewards (to reassure the empire of his safety and deal with insurrections
in his provinces), he left up to 100,000 men in Macedonia with his
trusted general, Mardonius (whose ships storm winds had smashed to
pieces off Mount Athos ten years earlier). Before departing, the Great
King made it clear that his intention to take Greece remained steadfast.
When leaders of a Spartan embassy demanded satisfaction for the killing
of Leonidas, slain at Thermopylae 'fighting in defence of Greece', Xerxes,
lolling on his golden throne, stretched out his arm, pointed at his general and drawled, 'Mardonius will make sure the Spartans get the satisfaction they deserve.' His words needed no deciphering. Nor did it take
a strategist to realize that, in the absence of Persia's fleet, the remainder
of the war would be fought out on land by hoplites and cavalry, the
wealthy and well-off—in Athens, men whose loyalties lay not with Themistocles but with old-school aristocrats, men such as Xanthippus,
Aristides and Cimon, men joined by nexuses of friendships, marriage
and the shared interests of class.[21]

For now, though, Themistocles seemed curiously unperturbed by
shifts in the balance of domestic power, preoccupied as he was with his
new-found love of all things Spartan. In what was perhaps a calculated
move orchestrated with like-minded Athenians and designed deliberately to inflate his already sizeable ego, the Spartans hosted Themistocles on a state visit, awarded him an olive crown in recognition of his
strategic acumen and, when he left, gave him their most streamlined
racing chariot and a bodyguard of 300 young Identicals to escort him
to their border as if he were a king. Back in Athens' Assembly, self-worth
ballooning by the day, Themistocles took to slapping down all opposition, sneering at whoever tried to contradict him—'Without Themistocles at Salamis, where would you be now?'—concocting tales of how he
had precipitated Xerxes' swift retreat (thanks to the gullible Great King

believing yet another of his wily messages) and, despite the virtual destruction of the Persian fleet, insisting that the next year's fighting would
be mostly done at sea, a mantra that chimed with that of his new Spartan
friends, who, still loath to commit troops beyond the Isthmus, seemed
happy to leave Attica exposed and vulnerable to enemy attack.[22]

But Athenians were not content with such a strategy, as the shrewd
Mardonius knew well. An experienced tactician, he far preferred to win
wars without fighting and now, with the allies once more divided, he saw
an opportunity to sow further discord. He dispatched the oleaginous,
protean Alexander, King of Macedon, to Athens with a suspiciously mag-
nanimous offer. The Great King, he announced, was ready to let bygones be bygones, to forget Persia's injuries at Athens' hands. He was
willing to grant the Athenians not just their own land but the territories of any other mainland poleis they might wish for. *And* they could
keep their democratic constitution. *And*—what was more—he would
personally fund the rebuilding of any temples he had burned. If Athens
came to terms, and 'without deception or deceit' became his ally, her
people could preserve their freedom. In other words, no earth, no water
and no vassal status; rather a relationship of equals—as long as, come
spring, Athenians agreed to fight alongside Persia against Sparta and
such Greeks as might resist. For many in the Assembly, not least farmers
who had just sown crops or tradesmen repairing looted city shops and
offices or pious citizens who gazed towards the blackened, scorched
Acropolis, it was a tantalizing proposition, especially since Sparta (whose
envoys the Athenians had purposefully invited to the meeting) was
making it so clear that she had no intention whatsoever of defending
them. No wonder that, no sooner had the Macedonian stopped speaking,
his vision of feuding armies fighting for a wasteland Attica chilling his
audience's blood, his peroration ringing in their ears—'it is no small
thing to be the only Greeks to whom the Great King offers friendship,
whose offences he is ready to forgive'—than the Spartans argued passionately (if briefly) that, despite war being of Athens' making, it now
involved them all; freedom-loving Athenians must not enslave fellow
Greeks; in sympathy for Attica's plight, Sparta and her allies would support all Attica's non-combatants throughout the war's duration.[23]

In fact, they need not have feared. To his fellow citizens' approval,
Athens' spokesman gave his reply: yes, they loved freedom, and yes, the
Persians outnumbered them, but 'for as long as the sun keeps its course

in the sky' they would never surrender: rather, 'we shall fight him without ceasing, trusting in our allies, in our gods and heroes, whom he scorned, when he burned their statues and their temples.' It was every Athenian's duty to avenge this desecration. It was his duty, too, to fight for fellow-Greeks, with whom they were united by 'one blood, one language, our shared sanctuaries, our sacrifices, our shared way of life'. Moreover, it was Sparta's duty in the coming year not merely to house refugees from fire-scorched Attica, but to prevent Persians reaching Attica at all—to march with the Athenians and all her allies to Boeotia and face Mardonius in one last battle.[24]

Passionate certainly, perhaps idealistic, the speech enthused the men of Athens, and while the Spartans trekked back to their icy mountains and the still chill Eurotas valley, they set about appointing their new generals. While they probably included the still-vaunting Themistocles, he was joined as colleagues by two men whom he had previously undermined, whose ostracism he had engineered a few years earlier: Xanthippus and Aristides, patricians both, and both well-versed in hoplite fighting. Both, too, were keenly conscious of the need for wooing Sparta, even when, come spring, as they had feared, with Peloponnesians still refusing to march beyond the Isthmus, sad flotillas of merchantmen and triremes and small fishing boats were forced to ply their way across the gulf once more weighed down by listless refugees. Squatting on Salamis, whiling their days away in crowded, cramped conditions, increasingly frightened, frustratingly impotent, apparently abandoned by their allies, some Athenians began to question the wisdom of their policy. So when a second envoy from Mardonius addressed them, offering the same generous terms as previously, it was not unsurprising that Lycidas, a local man, proposed that they accept them. For those more resolute, his words were not only abhorrent but positively blasphemous and, with Persia's envoy looking on, they picked up rocks, surrounded Lycidas and stoned him to death. When word spread, irate women marched to Lycidas' house, set it on fire and killed his wife and children as they tried to flee. There was no more talk of surrender.[25]

Yet equally, without their allies, it remained impossible to resist. So, in late June the Persian army came once more and ravaged Attica, while west across the Isthmus, Athens' allies (although not the Spartans, who remained at home) skulked sullen, brooding, bored, behind their trusted wall. But while they cowered and kicked their heels, their fleet did not remain at Salamis. They had devised a new, bold strategy: to take the war to Persia; to sail east to Samos, where the Great King's fleet had over-wintered; and (with the gods' help) to deal the enemy a blow of such great magnitude that they would never threaten mainland Greece again. So, crews eager for a chance to end the work begun at Salamis, winds warm in their sails, the triremes scudded out of port and turned their bronze snouts east towards the shores of Asia, while on Salamis Aristides pondered the old and seemingly insoluble problem: how to meet and beat the Persians in mainland Greece.[26]

Without the allies there was little hope of victory, and defensive Sparta had already signalled her reluctance to leave the safety of the Isthmus. However, there was a glimmer of hope. As he knew from private meetings, despite there being no alteration in official policy, Spartan attitudes were shifting—not least since no-one knew for how much longer Athens' populace could resist a growing temptation simply to admit defeat, throw in their lot with Persia and return to their now-battered but much-yearned-for homesteads. Equally, however, with the return of Aristides and Xanthippus, Athens no longer posed quite such an ideological threat to Sparta as she had before the war—despite his success at Salamis, Themistocles' authority was being tempered, while his state visit to Sparta showed that he was readily susceptible to blandishments (and even, perhaps, bribery). Besides, was it viable for Sparta to let all Greece beyond the Isthmus fall to Persia? How long before the Persians breached the wall and crossed into the Peloponnese? How long before they marched into Laconia? How long before Sparta's helots, realizing that their time had come, were wreaking revenge for centuries of oppression? Surely it was better to resolve the crisis swiftly and as far from home as possible. But even reaching the Isthmus might pose problems, since whichever road they took meant crossing lands patrolled on one side by Achaeans and by Argives on the other, Greeks, whom Mardonius was rumoured to have tasked with intercepting any Spartan marching north. If, then, the Spartans were to join the allies and face down the Persians without being first embroiled in fighting, Greek-on-Greek, they must hone a clever strategy. And to do that they must involve the incorrupt-ible Aristides.[27]

In receipt of top-secret messages assuring him that Sparta would indeed give battle, Aristides despatched a high-powered mission to Laconia. Leading it were three patricians, men whom Aristides trusted and whom (crucially) the Spartans held in high regard: an archon, a general—and (in his first recorded public post) his own loyal friend, Cimon. Discretion was vital. With the situation on a knife-edge and the enemy alert for any shift in strategy, no word of Sparta's volte-face must leak out. It must still seem to all the world that she remained intransigent. The mission had been timed with care. As they disembarked at Gytheum, Cimon and his colleagues found themselves surrounded by throngs of other foreigners from countless other cities, all setting out along the twenty-three-mile track inland to Amyclae, one of the most sacred sites in all Laconia, where at Apollo's sanctuary Spartans would celebrate the Hyacinthia. For legend told how, at Amyclae, when Apollo accidentally killed his mortal lover, Hyacinthus, his discus blown off course by the jealous West Wind, he released his friend from death and bore him, immortal, up to Mount Olympus, a handsome adult, though he died a boy. In time the two became imagined as one god, Apollo-Hyacinthus, to honour whom the Spartans built a towering throne, whose base housed both an altar and (behind bronze doors) a chamber, Hyacinthus' tomb, its sides adorned with brightly painted sculptures, above which rose a statue of Apollo with a spear and bow, some forty-five feet tall, encased in bronze. This was the focus of the three-day festival that started with mass mourning for the stricken hero, before giving way to singing contests, horse races and banquets, where wives and daughters dressed in party finery drove to Amyclae in gaily bedecked carriages to join their men in celebration of the risen Hyacinthus with his promise of rebirth and everlasting life. Like Athens' Eleusinian Mysteries, the Hyacinthia attracted visitors from the entire Greek-speaking world. Under normal circumstances it was a time when Spartan minds were 'full of festival and nothing else'. But these were not normal circumstances. This year, as well as honouring the god, the celebrations were a smokescreen for a risky subterfuge.[28]

The ephors let it be known that Cimon and his colleagues were complaining that, while Athenians had done their bit, refusing tempting offers from the Great King, they had received nothing from the Spartans in return. The time had come for Sparta to act, for the allies to face Mardonius on the Eleusinian plain. They let it be known, too, that they, the ephors, were prevaricating, always claiming they would come to a decision the next day, but even after nearly fifteen days there was no progress. So as festival-goers drifted back to Gytheum, few were surprised to learn that Athens' mission had been unsuccessful. Yet, as they rounded Malea and sped back north for Salamis, Cimon and his colleagues were more confident than they had been for months. Neither Persians nor Argives nor Achaeans nor any other hostile state had found out their intentions. But there were further moves to play. In a war council at Salamis, Aristides made a show of venting his frustration. His envoys, he complained, had bungled their instructions. He himself must travel down to Sparta. Which, with all eyes watching him, he did, while the Spartan army—5,000 Identicals and seven times as many helots, commanded by Pausanias (regent for Leonidas' underage son, Pleistarchus)— crept into the night and in a forced march hurried north. Even at Sparta, Aristides kept up the subterfuge. When he was told their army had departed, he professed not to believe it. In truth, he was simply going through the motions. Within hours he, too, was heading north at the head of 5,000 Perioikoi. The Spartans were stepping out to battle. The stalemate was over. And it was too late for either Argives or Achaeans to do anything about it.[29]

The news electrified Greeks and Persians alike. Both knew the endgame was afoot. But while Athens' generals were planning for a battle near Eleusis on the broad Thriasian Plain, Mardonius thought differently. For one thing, cavalry were central to his tactics and the terrain was not conducive to the kind of action that he had in mind. For another, with the allied fleet controlling the seas, he might find himself outflanked if the allies landed troops elsewhere in Attica. Far better, he calculated, to decamp to Boeotia, where, inland with friendly Thebes ready and willing to serve as a safe base, he could use the terrain to his best advantage and perhaps ensnare the allies with a flanking movement of his own. So, while his cavalry galloped out to Megara, ravaging the countryside and pinning down the allies, Mardonius retreated through the eastern hills of Attica on the old trade road across Mount Parnes and the wooded pass at Decelea, and thence into Boeotia, before striking west along the course of the Asopus, where the river leached through the parched plain past Plataea, the town whose hoplites had provided Athens with her only help at Marathon. But before leaving Attica, Mardonius exacted his revenge. After the Persians' first occupation, they had left much intact, intending to occupy the land themselves. Now, though, they destroyed whatever they could find—houses, any temples they had not already torched, even walls that marked field boundaries. When the orgy of spoliation was complete and the last Persian troops tramped out of Attica, all that remained of once-proud Athens were blackened ruins and the stumps of buildings smouldering in the summer sun.[30]

But at the Isthmus other troops were on the move. Out through the narrow gates in their defensive wall, on round the ruined coast road between towering cliffs and sea, the men of Sicyon and Corinth, Hermione, Tegea, Phlius, Epidaurus, Tiryns and Mycenae marched beside Spartan hoplites. Among the ashes of Eleusis they were joined by the Athenians, as well as islanders from Euboea—from Eretria and Chalcis—and from far-off Cephalonia. But while more than twenty poleis sent their men, the largest Greek force yet assembled, many more did not, preferring to play a waiting game, to discover who the victor was before offering support. Even among the allies few fully trusted one another to remain firm in the face of Persian attack. So at Eleusis, that place of awesome sanctity, the armies of each city offered sacrifice and swore a solemn oath of loyalty before, with trumpets blaring, they called down dire curses on the heads of any who would break it. Then, bellies full from feasting on the sacrificial beasts, and assembled in battalions according to their cities, the allied army, more than 100,000 strong, marched north towards Eleutherae and the folds of Mount Cithaeron, from where, breasting the last ridge at Erythrae, they looked down on the dusty plain. But it was not the little township of Plataea or the hamlets or the villages that seized the allies' focus, or the distant silhouettes of Mount Parnassus and Mount Helicon, blue in the summer haze; it was what lay across the listless river, a sight to give them pause, a square stockade, each wall a mile in length, the Persian headquarters, and the plain itself alive with men.[31]

But how to face them? Outnumbered by Persian infantry and no match for their cavalry, to give battle on the plain would be suicidal. Better to stay in the foothills of Cithaeron; better to guard the mountain passes to their rear; better to try to lure the Persians to fight where nature favoured Greeks, as they had fought at Salamis, or catch them unawares, as they had caught them and defeated them at Marathon; better to play the longer game; better to watch and wait—and win. As each contingent marched down the dust-dry road, their commander-in-chief, Pausanias, gave the word to veer off laterally across the rise and take up their positions, a wall of shimmering bronze shields and glinting helmets topped with horsehair crests, all facing down the slope. From across the riverbed

Mardonius saw them, and he did not hesitate. Even as the allies were falling into line, he passed orders to Masistius, his cavalry commander—tall, handsome, dashing, a true Persian nobleman, proud of his golden armour and his white Nisaean horse—to unleash carnage, and at once 5,000 horsemen were thundering across the baking plain, and on towards the allied line, loosing off clouds of arrows as they came, before they wheeled, regrouped and surged back on again. They targeted the men of Megara especially, pummelling them with missiles until they could endure no longer. Then at the last moment 300 crack Athenians accompanied by archers ran to their aid. Now arrows whistled back towards the Persians, and when one embedded itself in Masistius' horse's flank, the animal reared up and threw its rider. At once the allies surged to surround the fallen Persian, hacking, trying to kill him. But his golden armour kept him safe. At last a thrust down through his unprotected eye despatched him. As the cavalry withdrew, loath to launch any more attacks without receiving orders, the vaunting allies arranged Masistius' body on a wagon and paraded it before their battle lines, while across the trickling Asopus men shaved their heads in mourning and cut short their horses' manes and tails, and raised their wails of ritual lament for their lost and much-loved leader.[32]

It was a welcome boost to allied morale. Soon men were weaving epic tales of a Homeric struggle for Masistius' corpse to match the struggle at Thermopylae over the dead Leonidas or the fighting for Patroclus' remains at Troy. Yet, despite this early triumph, their situation remained dire, not least because here on the rise there was no access to fresh water. The position was untenable; they must move. So, ever vigilant, the allies marched west over rough ground before descending to form a three-mile front that stretched from the Spartan right wing (at Gargaphia Spring) to the Athenians on a low hill close to the Asopus. For eleven days they waited in the blinding August heat, encased in armour, in sweat-sodden tunics—days of boredom shot with spikes of fear whenever with remorseless regularity the ground pulsed to the dull beat of the hooves of Theban cavalry as they appeared from nowhere, deluging Athenian shields with storm bursts of slingshot and arrows, while to the east their Persian colleagues harried Spartans or strafed allied lines with missiles. If for the allies this was stalemate, for Mardonius the long wait represented strategy; with Greek attention focussed on resisting cavalry attacks, he sent riders round their flank and up into the passes of

Cithaeron, to intercept a baggage train—500 mules and drivers bringing food through to the allies. In an orgy of violence they slaughtered animals and men, save for a few whom they brought, bloodied, back to show the allies that the end was nigh. And three nights later through the darkness a horseman rode up close to the Athenian encampment and asked to speak with Aristides and his inner circle. It was the Macedonian king, Alexander, claiming once more to wish the allies well. Mardonius, he said, intended to attack next morning: while the omens for the Persians were unfavourable, they, too, were running out of food. If the allies remained where they were, all would be well. Dawn would bring victory.[33]

At once Aristides (believing Alexander) hurried to Pausanias, and with their chiefs of staff the two held hasty counsel. Their plans are lost in the confusion of history. Even veterans questioned by Herodotus, images of that next morning seared into their memories, were unclear what the tactics actually were. They recalled incessant troop manoeuvres, as Spartans marched to occupy the left wing, Athenians (the only Greeks to have defeated Persians in battle) to occupy the right where they would face Mardonius, before positions were switched once more when Mardonius, too, swapped wings. They remembered how next morning the Persian cavalry attacked; how they kept on attacking wave on wave throughout the long hot summer's day; how the Persians captured the Gargaphia Spring and fouled its waters; and how only as the sun set low beyond Mount Helicon did the attacks abate. Yet even darkness brought no rest. For now they were moving again: Spartans back towards high ground at Hysiae; Athenians marching through the early hours to join them; while the remainder of the allies fell back to a patch of ground protected on two sides by riverbeds, though in the darkness they became confused and ended up instead beside Plataea's walls. But most of all they recollected how at dawn the allies seemed so unprepared, so muddled and chaotic, so vulnerable, and so exposed—so, when the hoof beats came, an echo, a crescendo on the hardened earth, and phalanxes of cavalry exploded through the slanting light, they had no way of even knowing where their fellow allies were, no chance of forming a coherent battle line, no time to think at all. And then time ceased to matter.[34]

For, across the Asopus, sensing the allies' disarray, Mardonius gave the signal to advance. As they saw the Persians powering forward, the Thebans, too, took up their warcry and, shields raised, splashed on across

A Greek hoplite, his shield
bearing an image of the
winged horse Pegasus, slashes
with his sword at a fallen Persian
(Attic red-figure kylix, c. 480 B.C.).

the shallow river, intent on glutting centuries of hatred on the vulnerable Athenians. Now the rest of Mardonius' men were on the move—Sacae and Medians, Indians and Bactrians, Egyptians, Ethiopians, Phrygians and Thracians, as well as Macedonians and Greeks from Thessaly and Locris, Malis and Phocis—pouring in their myriads across the dusty plain. Separated by some miles, their lines of vision blocked by hills, the three allied armies—Spartans in the foothills to the east, Athenians trying manfully to reach them from the west, Corinthians and others near Plataea's walls—had no means of communicating, no way of gauging what was happening except in the narrow here and now, the rapidly contracting time and space before the enemy was on them and the brutal business of the war god Ares started.[35]

Already Mardonius' Persians had halted within firing range of Sparta's scarlet line, his infantrymen forming a tall screen of wicker shields while archers shot off deadly volleys to thrum and thump and clatter into the Spartan shield wall. But while helot ancillaries responded, sending hails of missiles of their own, and hoplites itched for combat, Pausanias refused to give the order to engage. A pious Spartan, he knew that it was suicidal to do battle until the gods sent favourable signs communicated through the entrails of sacrificial animals—and so far not one of the creatures that he slaughtered and whose viscera his priests examined gave the portents he desired. With increasing desperation more beasts were brought, more throats were slit, more bellies were sliced open, but still the gods held back. And still the swarms of arrows whistled through the August sky. Until at last, his hands and arms already glutinous with blood, one priest pronounced his satisfaction that the gods were on their side, and the Spartans heard the word they had been waiting for. As one they lowered their long spears, and with locked shields advanced. To a man they had been drilled for just this moment, hardened in the snows of Mount Taygetus, brought up to sing the battle songs of their national poet, Tyrtaeus:

> Each man must stand his ground with both feet
> rooted firmly to the earth, biting his lip firmly—
> thighs, shins, chest and shoulders
> covered by the bulging belly of his shield.
> In his right hand he must wield his deadly spear,
> while on his head his helmet crest—a thing of terror—bristles.
> He must be skilled in battle, in the savage arts of war,
> not trying to dodge the missiles—what is his shield for?—
> but getting close in, lunging with his spear
> or sword, cutting down the enemy.
> Set *your* foot against *his* foot; press shield on shield,
> helmet on helmet, crest on crest,
> and chest on chest; and bring the battle to the enemy,
> gripping your sword's hilt or long stabbing spear.[36]

So it was now at Plataea. As well-drilled Spartan men of bronze slammed into them, spears tearing easily through wicker shields and slicing flimsy armoured vests, the Persians fought gallantly, but they stood little chance. Out-trained and out-equipped they threw themselves against the Spartan line to be skewered on razor-sharp spear-points, to fall clutching their erupting guts, to be trampled as the Spartan line advanced. And then Mardonius himself, astride his white Nisaean warhorse, surrounded by his thousand bravest fighters, fell, and when they saw that he was gone, the heart went out of all his men. The Persians turned and fled. And the Spartans, remembering the Great King's smug prediction that Mardonius would give them satisfaction for the killing of Leonidas, poured after them.[37]

Meanwhile, among Athens' ranks good discipline prevailed. Somehow, despite being caught still mid-deployment, Aristides had managed to rally his men, passing orders down to each of the ten tribal commanders, ensuring they were ready when the waves of Theban hoplites smashed against them. And in the bloody scrimmage the Athenians, too, locked shields and shoved and jabbed and sliced; and in close combat they, too, face to snarling face and hand to blood-soaked hand, strained every sinew of their aching beings to press the Thebans back, to punch a hole through their tight phalanx and turn their enemy to flight; and in the end they, too, succeeded. Now the allies were racing in pursuit—Spartans; Athenians; those who had sheltered near the town itself and so avoided battle, since the Persian commander there had held back, watching to see what happened before, realising that the game was up, falling back swiftly to begin a forced march north to safety, abandoning his colleagues to the mercy of the allied Greeks. But the danger had not passed. As Thebans ran back to their city and the rest of the invaders dashed for the safety of their tall stockade, Theban cavalry were launching an effective rearguard action, galloping across Plataea's plain, cutting a swathe through the Greek allies, forcing many to retreat and scatter in the foothills of Cithaeron. But not Athenians or Spartans. Together they stormed the wooden palisade, forcing their way inside, unleashing such an orgy of unfettered butchery that by the time they had glutted their bloodlust, fewer than 3,000 of the enemy were left alive.[38]

And then the looting—helots (to whom the business was allotted) wading through the blood-swamped camp across the darkening plain, prising bracelets, chains, gold-hilted scimitars from bodies of the dead and dying, cutting rings from still-warm fingers, stripping tunics sewn with rich embroidery from staring corpses, scouring tents for gold and silver furniture, gold cups and goblets, golden bowls, and dragging off the wagons laden down with booty seized from Athens, rounding up the women who, willingly or not, had been sharing Persian beds. In time all would be allocated: a tithe awarded to Apollo at his sanctuary at Delphi, a tithe for Olympian Zeus, a tithe for Isthmian Poseidon, a further tithe for the commander-in-chief Pausanias, with the remainder divided between the rest. But among the spoils one relic caught the eye of every Greek: the vast tent that had served as Persia's command headquarters, that had housed Mardonius, so lavish and luxurious that few believed that it had not belonged to the Great King himself, left for his general when he fled to Asia. Hung with the choicest fabrics, strewn with soft carpets, and equipped with the most exquisite furniture, with glittering plates and jewel-encrusted drinking vessels, it represented the epitome of Persian luxury, a wealth of which most Greeks could only dream, and which as a result they condemned as barbarous, corrupt, effeminate.[39]

For ten days they stayed there, identifying and gathering the corpses of their dead, laying them out reverently on pyres, one for each city (though for the Spartans there were three: one for priests; another for Identicals; a third for the anonymous host of helots), heaping grave mounds high above each pile of ash, sacrificing to their gods, and celebrating victory—a double victory, since news soon came that on Ionia's west coast beneath towering Mount Mycale, commanded by Sparta's King Leotychidas and the Athenian Xanthippus, the allies had defeated Persia's army and torched the Persian fleet. The threat had been annihilated, but there was work still to be done. Not least at nearby Thebes, whose treachery (or the treachery of its pro-Persian faction) was inexcusable and which now must suffer the consequences. No matter that it was Greek or that mere months before Athenians had waxed so eloquently about how they could never betray fellow Greeks, united as they were by blood and language, gods and custom. No. Then they were trying to make the Spartans toe the line and march north of the Isthmus. Now that they had succeeded, now the Persian threat was gone, there was no more need for such romantic nonsense. Now Thebes was at their mercy, they could revert to their old polis politics, the status quo of Greek morality: to help friends and harm enemies, no matter their ethnicity. And so they made their ultimatum: surrender the pro-Persian faction or face siege, starvation, death. For three weeks Thebes held out as fellow Greeks roamed through Boeotia, raiding towns and villages and farmsteads from the mountains to the sea and to the shores of Lake Copais that rippled in the warm September breeze. At last the city could resist no longer; its people staged a coup; and, although many of its pro-Persian leaders somehow disappeared, sufficient others were surrendered to let the siege be lifted.[40]

So the allies dispersed—Spartans and Peloponnesians back beyond the Isthmus (where they executed Theban prisoners), Athenians to Attica. But not back home. They had no homes to go to. As they trudged through the soot-blackened countryside, past the debris of Eleusis, on up the Sacred Road across the shoulder of Aegaleus to where they could

look down across scorched fields to the Acropolis, its plateau empty now
of any shrines; as they came nearer still and passed the wreckage of once-
proud estates, scorched stumps of fruit trees at Laciadae, the country
house, from whose porch Miltiades the Elder hailed the Thracian envoys as they made their way from Delphi, now nothing but a pile of
rubble; as they picked their way through broken headstones in the
Cerameicus Cemetery and clambered over the detritus of the gates and
on into what once was their city, the true scale of devastation overwhelmed them. Where Athens had stood proud, nothing remained but
emptiness and otherworldly silence.

Yet, as Themistocles had pointed out the year before, Athens was not
simply a place; it was its people, for its people were its heart, its soul. And
while the fleet under Xanthippus was overwintering on the Hellespont,
besieging Persia's garrison at Sestus, the rest of Athens' population was
returning: the army, fresh from victory; the women and the children and
the elders, safe across the sea from Salamis. All were ready to rebuild,
to shape a new beginning, to create a new identity. It was, they knew,
their pluck, their energy, their democratic constitution that had made
them great before. Now it could make them great again. The past eighteen months had proved there was no force on earth that they could not
withstand. They had seen off the greatest empire the world had ever
known. What could they not do now? The city might be lying in ruins,
but Athens would live once more. Like the mythical bird, the phoenix,
that died in flames and rose again, fresh, energetic, young, Athens would
rise again, inspired by a new breed of leaders, their courage forged in
hellfires at Plataea and Mycale, Salamis and Artemisium; and at the forefront of them all would be the still-young man who had inspired his
people to make the hard decisions that would win the war, who consecrated his warhorse's bridle to Athena, who urged his fellow citizens to
fight at sea, the young man who in just a year, appointed general, would
spearhead Athens' new renaissance: Cimon.[41]

III

STRENGTHS OF MEN

7

HEGEMON

It is no small thing to call Athenians
experts in deploying the arts of war and strengths
of men.

Inscription on an Athenian herm

BYZANTIUM, 478 B.C.

The delegation that arrived at Cimon's office was not unexpected. Ever since the fleet sailed into harbour at Byzantium feelings had been running high. Quite simply the alliance was fracturing. At issue was the conduct of its commander-in-chief, Pausanias, the self-proclaimed hero of Plataea who, freed from the constraints of life in Sparta, his private wealth inflated from the tithe awarded to him from the spoils of battle, his sense of self-importance magnified by his unprecedented power, was lording it over fellow generals and soldiery alike in a quite insufferable manner. It might be acceptable in Laconia to punish soldiers by flogging them or forcing them to stand all day in the merciless sun with a heavy stone anchor on their shoulders, but it was not how to treat free Greeks. Nor could the allies tolerate being made to wait in line while Spartans helped themselves to rations—fodder for horses and pack animals; straw for their own bedding; even water—and woe betide any who tried to push in front: the only time this happened, the culprits found themselves on the receiving end of a cruel whipping, a punishment normally reserved for slaves. With colleagues, too, Pausanias' behaviour was increasingly high-handed, as he professed himself too busy to make time for meetings and flew into a rage with anyone who dared to disagree with him.[1]

If this were not bad enough, it was rumoured that Pausanias was collaborating with Xerxes. Even at Plataea the Spartan had been unashamedly obsessed with Persian luxury. Here, along with his headquarters tent, the allies had captured Mardonius' kitchen staff, whom they made prepare the kind of banquet favoured by the Persian general. For Pausanias the sight of gold and silver couches strewn with costly fabrics and tables groaning with what appeared to him impossibly exotic delicacies was a revelation. To conceal his wonder he made his helots cook a vat of Spartan gruel, and invited fellow generals to compare the meals, evidence (he declared) of Persian lunacy: 'They enjoy such a rich lifestyle, yet they came to rob us of our rags.' Now in the fleshpots of Byzantium, with sumptuous Persia tantalizingly nearby and the opportunity to swap black broth for Persian haute cuisine forever, Pausanias did not just turn gourmand, dress ostentatiously in Persian clothing or ride to hunt surrounded by an entourage of Persian and Egyptian bodyguards: he was rumoured to be corresponding secretly with Xerxes, offering to bring not only Sparta but all Greece under Persian control in exchange for marrying the Great King's daughter.[2]

The contrast between the authoritarian yet increasingly louche Spartan and the two affable yet highly disciplined Athenian generals could not have been more stark. Commanding thirty triremes, Athens' contribution to the allied fleet in the north-east Aegean and Propontis, these men were well aware of the importance of diplomacy and courtesy. That the experienced, trustworthy Aristides possessed both traits in abundance was well known; that his colleague, Cimon, still only in his early thirties, was not just ambitious but congenial, good-natured and approachable was becoming more apparent by the day. This may have been his first command, but he had learned from his father and his friends, many of them experienced generals; and, as head of the Philaids for the past ten years, he was already steeped in the arts of leadership. Now with Aristides at his side to offer friendly and invaluable advice he was dazzling Athenians and allies alike with his warm personality and charisma. So, as Pausanias' behaviour became ever more erratic and high-handed, Cimon and Aristides found themselves increasingly approached by representatives of newly liberated allied states complaining that they had simply replaced one tyrant with another. Surely something must be done; Pausanias must be dismissed; they must no longer have a Spartan general.[3]

These were only the most recent in a painful litany of grievances that had been building over the past year. In the immediate aftermath of Plataea rifts almost led to violence when both Sparta and Athens claimed the prize for valour and the right to erect the trophy, a captured suit of Persian armour displayed where the enemy first turned and fled. Their dispute was understandable. Thanks partly to Pausanias' chaotic tactics, the first stage of the battle had consisted of two separate encounters—one between Spartans and Persians, the other between Athenians and Thebans—while the Spartans could not subsequently have breached Mardonius' stockade without Athenian help. With neither prepared to concede the honour to the other, and Athens' generals protesting (perhaps rightly) that poor Spartan leadership had almost cost their lives, the atmosphere became so heated that many feared the two cities would come to blows on the very plain where they had just defeated Persia. Only Aristides' intervention calmed nerves sufficiently for a compromise to be proposed: the prize should go instead to the town outside whose walls victory had been won, Plataea, while Sparta and Athens should each erect trophies of their own.[4]

But even this did not end controversy. As after Salamis, offerings were consecrated at Olympia (a bronze statue of Zeus, fifteen feet tall) and Isthmia (a bronze Poseidon, nine and a half feet tall), but at Delphi—where, near their treasury beneath the Temple of Apollo, Athenians built a Stoa to house 'ropes' (perhaps the cables from Xerxes' Hellespontine bridges liberated by Xanthippus at Cardia) 'and figureheads of ships seized from the enemy'—the allies erected an ornate bronze column cast in the form of three snakes intertwining, seventeen and a half feet tall, whose jutting necks supported a gold cauldron. Sited near the Apollo's altar, the stone base of the column bore an inscription, its wording chosen by Pausanias himself: 'After defeating the Persians, the Greek commander-in-chief, Pausanias, dedicated this memorial to Apollo.' Even the Spartans were outraged. They hastily erased the lettering, and diplomatically incised the names of each of the cities that had fought as allies in the war, along with a couplet by Simonides: 'Greece's liberators dedicated this when they freed their cities from grim slavery.'[5]

It was not Simonides' only commission. Now an old man, Hippias' court poet found himself again in great demand. As battlefields became memorialized and state histories took shape, his verses were performed by choruses at festivals of thanksgiving and engraved on monuments throughout Greece. Like the Delphic serpent monument's revised inscription, many (epitaphs at Athenian and Spartan grave mounds at Plataea; the Corinthian mass grave on Salamis; a stele at Thermopylae) professed Greek unity:

> If the greatest part of bravery is to die a splendid death,
>> Fortune allotted this to us above all other men.
> For we strained every sinew to ensure that Greece was free
>> and now we lie here, vouched safe of a good name that will grow
>> not old.[6]

> These men adorned their fatherland with a glory that can never be
>> extinguished
>> before enveloping themselves in the blue-black cloud of death.
> Though they have died, they are not dead: their bravery brings them
>> glory
>> and leads them back to earth from Hades.[7]

> We are lying here, since we gave our lives to save all Greece
>> when she stood balanced on the razor's edge.[8]
> Here—against three million—
>> four thousand Peloponnesians once fought.[9]

Others such as the laconic epitaph to Sparta's dead at Thermopylae, were unashamedly partisan:

> Stranger, report this to the Spartans:
>> we're lying here following orders.[10]

That so many disparate Greek states had shelved their differences and served under one leader for one common cause had been a great accomplishment, but old rivalries remained, and in the honing of a narrative each polis did all it could to use its war record for self-promotion. In Athens, the handsome Sophocles, an accomplished wrestler and aspiring poet, at eighteen years old poised on the cusp of adulthood, 'naked, oiled, and accompanying himself on the lyre' was picked to lead the choral singing of an ode to exalt his city's role at Salamis, where Athens was now casting herself in the starring role, spotlighting the part played by Themistocles, sidelining Sparta's Eurybiades. The propaganda war had begun.[11]

In other ways, too, friction between the two states was growing. As soon as they came home—once funeral games had been performed to honour their war dead—Athenians began to rebuild city walls destroyed during the Persian occupation. But almost at once envoys from Sparta urged them to stop. Their arguments were at best disingenuous, at worst downright disquieting. There was no need, they said, for city walls at Athens or any other mainland city north of the Isthmus. Better to dismantle them, since, if Xerxes attacked again and captured them, he could use them for his own protection as he once did at Thebes. Besides, if the Persians did return, Sparta and her Peloponnesian allies would offer sanctuary to Athens' refugees, while the wall across the Isthmus would protect them. The Athenians politely agreed to discuss the Spartan proposition, but with the envoys barred from Pnyx Hill, Themistocles gave vent to incredulity. Although still relishing his flattering reception by the Spartans, he was not blind to their intent: they were not only putting Athens on notice that, in the event of further invasions, they and the Peloponnesians, reverting to their default strategy, would refuse to march north of the Isthmus, they were reminding the world that Sparta was Greece's hegemon, able to tell Athens what to do, keen to keep her rival weak, yet anxious lest Athenians' ambition (fuelled by their role in recent victories and buttressed by their navy) should upset the status quo. The situation required careful handling, but with the support of Aristides and his powerbase the guileful Themistocles knew what to do.[12]

The envoys were sent home with reassurances that Athens would consider their proposals and send a delegation of their own to Sparta to discuss the finer details. But no sooner were they out of sight than work began again, and efforts were redoubled. Racing against time, the entire population—men, women, children, foreigners and slaves—set to work collecting rubble, uprooting gravestones and transporting statues to the city boundaries, materials with which to build the walls. As the lower courses rose, Themistocles himself set off across the mountains to Laconia, fearful that if Sparta heard what the Athenians were doing, she would attack them. On his arrival, and still flattered by his hosts, he postponed official meetings, claiming that he was obliged to wait for colleagues, who were detained by urgent business but would join him shortly. But as days passed and no-one came, and as reports reached them that Athens' walls were rising, the Spartans, suspicious, sent representatives to find out what was happening. When they did not return, suspicions grew. Time dragged on until, at last, the rest of Athens' delegates arrived, among them Aristides, the man famed for his honesty. The walls, he said, were built; the Spartan representatives were being detained as hostages; and they would be released only when he and his fellow Athenians returned home safely. Not only had Athens defied Sparta, and publicly embarrassed her to boot, she had illegally detained Spartan citizens. But in the delicate days of post-war diplomacy, when preserving the alliance was paramount, there was little that the Spartans could do but claim the whole thing was a terrible misunderstanding: they had never intended to dictate terms to their Athenian friends, but simply to offer congenial advice. And if Athens disagreed, what of it? No need for any fuss. So the delegates went home, the hostages were released, and the Assembly approved Themistocles' proposals to build sturdy walls around Piraeus, too, the hub of the new navy, the basis of what they meant to be their future power.[13]

It was not just with Athenians that Spartan proposals went down badly. Following their victory at Mount Mycale, as Ionian cities made sacrifice in celebration of their new-won liberation, and Persians and Persian sympathizers fled into the night, Xanthippus, Leotychidas and their colleagues met on Samos to discuss Ionia's future. True to form, loath to countenance any long-term military commitment far from home, and perhaps seeing a way to stifle Athenian recovery and growth based on trans-Aegean trade, Leotychidas made a startling proposal: Ionians' security, he said, could not be guaranteed, since Xerxes would clearly try to punish them for revolting; so their lands would be potentially a flashpoint for renewed war with Persia; better to reduce the threat through a population exchange—removing all Greeks from Ionia and repatriating them in mainland Greek territories occupied by Persians or Persian collaborators, who would themselves be forcibly returned to Asia. The Peloponnesian generals voiced their approval. Xanthippus most vehemently did not: Dorian Spartans had no right to interfere with Ionians, many of whom were Athenian settlers. Besides, he might have added (though, to preserve a veneer of cordiality, he probably did not), it made no sense to gift Xerxes the coast of Asia Minor with its military harbours and rich commercial centres, since this would not only endanger nearby islands but cede control of the entire eastern Aegean. It would be strategically and economically disastrous, providing Persia with a springboard from which to launch renewed attacks on mainland Greece, potentially crippling maritime trade and threatening the free passage of wheat and other foodstuffs crucial to Athenian interests from the Black Sea. Besides, since Athens possessed a strong fleet (for the moment, stronger than the Persians') and a string of victories to its name, this was no time for passivity. Rather they must seize the moment, finish what they had begun, liberate Greek cities, cleanse Greece of Persian settlers, and wrest control of vital lands and waterways from Persia. Backed by the islanders, Xanthippus stood his ground, and, with the Peloponnesians, unwilling to prolong the argument, professing to have no real opinions either way, Leotychidas shelved his proposal. But it was not forgotten. Realizing how close they had come to being betrayed, the Ionians along with other islanders who had resisted the Great King, insisted that they be formally admitted to the Greek alliance, and (while Leotychidas, the Spartans and the Peloponnesians sailed home to overwinter) Xanthippus headed north for Sestus on the Hellespontine shores of the Thracian Chersonese, to besiege the Persian governor, the grasping Artaÿctes.[14]

This, then, was the background to Athenian elections the next spring, which saw Cimon for the first time appointed general. Despite his relative absence from the previous decade's records, he had clearly made his mark. As head of the Philaids, Miltiades' son (though not, of course, his only son—Cimon must never have forgotten the existence of his 'Persian' brother) enjoyed a potent birthright, while politicians such as Aristides were influential friends; but this was not enough for fellow tribesmen to elect him general. Instead, he must have spent his twenties in the public eye, arguing in lawcourts or on Pnyx Hill, his warm charisma winning popular support, his generosity attracting backers, catching the public eye through energy and vision. No matter that he had rough edges, that there was something of the Thracian about him. Nor did his purported heavy drinking or addictive womanizing (supposedly pursued despite his genuine devotion to Isodice) suggest he was unsuited to hold high command or office. There must have been strong evidence that private excess was eclipsed by sober aptitude for public service, a subtle acumen for delicate diplomacy and a stellar magnetism that inspired men to follow him wherever he might lead. All of these were qualities that Athens, locked for the foreseeable future into war with Persia, pledging to support Ionia, but undermined by her apparent ally, Sparta, so desperately needed. His role in the negotiations that saw Spartans march out to Plataea unmolested by the Argives or Achaeans was evidence enough that Cimon enjoyed Sparta's trust. Nor was he personally tarnished by the deceit surrounding the rebuilding of the city walls.[15]

Indeed, around this time he made a public show of his commitment both to championing Ionia and maintaining (or, more realistically, establishing) a balance of power between Athens and Sparta, while preserving good relations: when Isodice bore twin sons, Cimon shunned custom. Instead of naming them for recent ancestors, he called one Lacedaemonius ('Spartan') and the other Oulius ('Baleful'), an Ionian cult title of Apollo and possibly the name, too, of a mythical Athenian who had helped to colonize Ionia. A study in sensitive statecraft, the move cannot have gone unnoticed, further evidence of how innately qualified he was to hold high office. When, the year after Plataea, his fellow tribesmen elected Cimon general, he was only just over thirty.[16]

To have him serve as Aristides' colleague was an inspired decision. The two had worked well in the past, enjoying a warm relationship; now with the elder statesman's ongoing guidance Cimon could shine in his own right, while benefitting from wise counsel underpinned by strong moral principles. For, unlike the parvenu Themistocles, Aristides understood the need for ethical command. In the Assembly, Themistocles, resurgent now that he had both tricked the Spartans and won agreement to construct at least twenty new triremes each year, announced that he had formed a plan to make Athens supremely powerful—but it was so top secret that he could not voice it in public. Intrigued, the People told him to share his thoughts with Aristides: they would accept his judgement. The two men huddled in close conclave, then Aristides took the speaker's platform. The proposal he announced would indeed bring Athens huge benefits—but huge humiliation, too. So the motion was rejected, and for now Aristides told only his close confidants what Themistocles had recommended: to set fire to the other allies' ships, so that Athens' fleet could dominate not only Persia but the rest of Greece. In time, in a bid to undermine Themistocles, the details were allowed to leak. For now, though, even to suggest such treachery would prove incendiary: it was crucial to keep the allies loyal.[17]

So Aristides advised Cimon to treat them with respect and deference. Not that Cimon needed such advice. He was innately courteous and understood the value of friendship. Leaving Athens at midsummer, when their new appointments came into effect, the two generals sailed with thirty triremes (the remainder of the fleet having overwintered at Sestus) first to still-occupied Cyprus, where they lent support to cities trying to shake off Persia's yoke, then north to the Hellespont. By now Sestus was liberated: after a lengthy siege the starving Persians, including governors and garrisons of other local towns who gathered there for safety, escaped into the night—but not to freedom. One, who had governed Cardia, Cimon's childhood home, fled to the lands of Thracian Apsinthians, who captured him and sacrificed him to a local god. His was an easy death compared to that of Artaÿctes, Sestus' governor, caught with his family and bodyguard near Aegospotami. At the promontory close to Sestus near the European head of one of Xerxes' bridges, Xanthippus had him crucified, forcing the dying Persian to watch as citizens of nearby Elaeus stoned his son to death in punishment (they said) for Artaÿctes' desecration of the tomb of Protesilaus, the first Greek killed in the legendary Trojan War. At Cardia itself, Xanthippus found the cables from the Persian bridges, loaded them aboard his triremes and, now that his generalship was over, shipped them home with him to dedicate in thanks for victory.[18]

Although reprisals such as Artaÿctes' crucifixion may be commonplace in war, to some including Cimon it seemed a short-sighted approach. Rounding up Persian survivors, he and the allies took them to Byzantium which they captured after another siege and established as the base from which to conduct operations in the Propontis and the western Black Sea. Then they set about dividing the spoils, a process requiring tact and fairness. Responsibility for captives fell to Cimon. Herded, cowed, into the city's agora, they stood, still dressed in Persian finery, bracelets of precious metals encircling arms and ankles, costly necklaces draped round necks, long purple robes shot through with gold and silver thread hanging low in shimmering folds. Normally each prisoner—man, woman, child—would be allotted to a victor as his slave, but instead Cimon commanded them to strip off clothes and jewellery and leave them on one side of the square while they stood on the other. Then he invited the allies to decide whether they preferred to take the treasure or the people. Eyes feasting on the glittering mounds of costly artefacts, the allies chose the treasure, incredulous that young Cimon had so mismanaged such a simple exercise that he let them take the prize and left himself with almost nothing. But in the next weeks bands of travellers began to reach Byzantium, men from the south, from Phrygia and Lydia, relatives and friends of the prisoners of war and, admitted into Cimon's office, they negotiated hefty ransoms. By the time the last captive was liberated the canny Cimon had gathered sufficient money to fund Athens' fleet for four months, not to mention further strongboxes of gold that he sent home to swell the city's coffers; and, even after each man had received his share of booty, the portion left for Cimon himself as general increased his wealth considerably. A scheme worthy of Themistocles, it was a settlement of which he was inordinately proud, a tale on which he would dine out for many years to come.[19]

But while Cimon was conducting himself equitably (no-one *forced* the allies to make their unwise choice), his commander-in-chief, Pausanias, seemed uninterested in maintaining even a show of fairness or decency. As Spartan Identicals, following his swaggering example, wallowed in Byzantium's fleshpots, abusing residents and allies with disdain, a growing number of disgruntled Ionians filed complaints with Cimon and asked what might be done. In meeting after meeting, Cimon and Aristides considered evidence of Pausanias' outrageous punishments or allegations of collaboration with the enemy, but it was his treatment of a local girl that forced them to take action. Behaving like an overweening pasha, the Spartan was commanding any local girl who caught his fancy to be brought to him by night. One was Cleonice, the bashful daughter of Coronides, a Byzantine grandee and, when Pausanias' guard came to convey her to his general, she and her father were too frightened to refuse. Once at the door, shy, inexperienced and terrified, she asked the sentries to respect her modesty and remove the lamps before she crept inside. But the darkness was intense and, blundering blindly forwards, Cleonice knocked over a lamp-stand. Pausanias immediately awoke, instincts alert, his training kicking in, and fearing enemy attack, he snatched the dagger from beneath his pillow, found the intruder and stabbed her to death. For the allies it was the final straw. Within days two generals, one from Samos, the other a Chiote, deliberately rammed Pausanias' flagship as it was approaching port. The Spartan was livid. Such insubordination, such outright hostility demanded serious punishment—not just for the men responsible but for their cities. The generals were unrepentant. Standing proud, they answered their commander to his face that he should thank good fortune for his victory at Plataea (won by luck not skill), since it was respect for this alone that held Greeks back from bringing him to justice. When they then stalked off to Aristides' tent, many suspected that he backed their protest. In fact, he had no need to—he appreciated how morale was plummeting and he knew the need for urgent action. So he and Cimon penned a message to the ephors back in Sparta. Pausanias was bringing Sparta into disrepute; behaving like a tyrant, he was undermining the alliance; he must be recalled. The ephors sent a trireme to convey him home.[20]

By now many allies had endured as much of Spartan rule as they could stomach, and in Pausanias' absence the Ionians approached Athens' generals, asking them to take command. It was not a decision they could make lightly. Thanks to shared history and ethnicity, Ionians and Athenians were natural allies, but for decades Peloponnesians had been part of Sparta's league and they were unwilling to switch allegiances. Moreover, under normal circumstances such a move would be interpreted in Sparta as threatening her self-esteem, and so could lead to war. But these were not normal circumstances. The Spartans and other Peloponnesians had already made it clear the year before on Samos that they lacked enthusiasm for campaigning far away from home, that they would happily relinquish all responsibility for the Ionians, that now the Persians had been driven out of mainland Greece, all they wanted was to stay at home, relying for protection on the Isthmian wall. Cimon and Aristides must have corresponded with the ephors. They must have received assurances, for the ephors, horrified to see how just a few short months away from home could undermine even their regent's character, concerned lest others be corrupted, too, and ever mindful of the helot threat, must have considered the campaign to be more trouble than it was worth. So, when Pausanias' replacement reached Byzantium (accompanied by the minimum of staff) it was simply to sanction the inevitable, to pass on to Athens' generals the Spartans' blessing, and to sail away. It was a smooth, untrumpeted transition, a discreet changing of the guard. And while Pausanias did return to Byzantium, acquitted at home on all but the most minor charges, disciplined, yet far from chastened, it was as a private citizen, a louche expatriate, a fugitive without official papers who had managed to slip unseen from Sparta, drawn like an addict to the scene of his debaucheries, where, increasingly outlandish and eccentric, he was said to be still plotting with the Persians, until at last, placed under house arrest, the victor of Plataea was persuaded to depart to exile in the Troad.[21]

Meanwhile the Athenians, conscious of the sudden, unexpected power shift were mindful of the need to formalize arrangements with their allies. It was a golden moment, a game-changing opportunity, and it must be seized. Yet, since its consequences might be so far-reaching, how it was handled now was crucial. Months earlier, Sparta had been lording it as leader of the Greek mainland and eastern colonies, not just trying to stop Athens from rebuilding her city walls and seriously proposing removing the Ionians from much-loved homes in thriving trading ports, but treating her free allies with contempt like helot serfs. Now—unwilling or unable to bear the weight of her responsibilities, and perhaps blinded by this same contempt—she had not only ceded leadership to Athens but immeasurably boosted the Athenians' prestige, effectively recognizing them as the Spartans' equals, while with bewildering short-sightedness gifting them the opportunity to create an international power base. Yet, for any future league to be effective, its foundations needed to be strong and stable, built on trust and fairness, an alliance of equal partners—even if it was clear right from the start that as its chosen leader Athens would be more equal than the others. Leadership, equity and tact: these were the qualities most needed now. And the men who possessed them all in great abundance were the generals already in Byzantium, Cimon and Aristides, whose openness and generosity had moved the allies to transfer their allegiance to Athens in the first place.

With so much to do, it made sense for the two colleagues to apportion their newly-increased obligations, Cimon leading military operations and consolidating control of the crucial Bosporus and Hellespont, the fifty-three-year-old Aristides assuming responsibility for organizing the alliance. It was to be both defensive (to liberate those Asiatic Greek cities still subject to Persia and keep them free, by preventing another mainland invasion) and offensive (to exact revenge and extract compensation by plundering lands belonging to or sympathetic to the Great King, and so making good the huge financial losses of the recent War), objectives that would entail combined land and sea operations for years to come—for as long as Persia's empire should exist or constitute a threat to Greek freedom. Of course, a fleet and army, not to mention the administrative costs of running an alliance, needed to be paid for. So, Aristides began examining each member state's resources to assess its contribution to the common enterprise, and whether payment would be best met in the form of ships or money. Since Ionians

His head garlanded with bay leaves, Apollo strums his lyre as he
pours a libation (Attic white-ground kylix, c. 460 B.C.).

and many islanders were accustomed to paying tax to Persia, for which
purpose their wealth and assets had already been assessed just fifteen
years before, it seemed simplest for the most part for them to remit
the same amount in cash or kind to the new Greek alliance, which—
adding contributions from Athens and other poleis that had escaped
being annexed by the Persian Empire—resulted in a healthy annual
budget, estimated or targeted to be (in round figures) 460 talents. To
administer it, Athenians as League leaders would elect ten commis-
sioners each year, Hellenotamiae ('Greek Treasurers'), one from each
tribe, responsible to Athens' Council and Assembly for collecting the
cash contributions and depositing them securely in the alliance's central bank—the strong room of the Temple of Apollo on Delos.[22]

For Delos would represent the League's nerve centre and, although
for now funds would be stored and meetings held in or near the temple

built two generations earlier by Athens' tyrannus Peisistratus, one of the League's first decisions was to build a grand new temple worthy of the 'League of Athens and her Allies'. The choice of Delos was as inspired as it was obvious, a natural choice for a sea-based league. Easily protected by whoever ruled the waves, the island had been revered for centuries as the sacred heart of the Ionian Greeks, whose cities sent state-funded representatives in gaily-adorned ships to splendid festivals, 'Ionians in long flowing robes with their children and modest wives, remembering you [Apollo] in their boxing and their dancing and their song, delighting you in contests. To see Ionians thronged there, you would think them ageless and immortal, gazing on their beauty, delighting in the men and deep-bosomed women, in their sleek ships and their treasures.' For generations, mainlanders and islanders had vied to set up costly offerings, not least the Naxians who dedicated a colossal statue of Apollo and twelve proud marble lionesses crouching on a terrace overlooking a round shallow lake that danced with myriad mosquitoes, and a sacred palm tree beside which (it was said) the god himself had been born. Some generations later, Peisistratus had purified Delos, exhuming skeletal remains from near the lake before reburying them on the far side of the island, erecting both his temple and another towering statue of the god, carved from wood but faced in gold, just over twenty-six feet high, while Polycrates, the tyrannus of Samos, consecrated the nearby islet of Rhenea by linking it to Delos with a chain along which sacred energy could flow. When the Persians came, in deference to Apollo (or to Hippias) they had left everything untouched, so now—in contrast to smoke-blackened Athens—Delos remained glittering, intact, a place built on tradition, but redolent of self-belief and ripe to take its rightful place at the hub of the new ambitious League.[23]

So it was to Delos that delegates from all the allied cities came to mark a solemn ceremony, part religious ritual, part settlement of a political and military deal. Amid blood sacrifice and offerings burned on the altar (on which thirteen years before the Persians and Hippias consigned to flames 300 talents of sweet-scented frankincense, trusting this would bend Apollo's will to theirs, before their expectations turned to ash at Marathon) and with hymns ringing in their ears, the delegates filed down the short road to the Sacred Harbour for the swearing of oaths. Their precise wording has not survived, but their intent was clear: to bind the allies close to one another in their joint commitment to harm

Persia, and formalize the compact by which they placed themselves under the leadership of Athens. But perhaps still more significant than their wording was the symbolic act accompanying the vows. To underscore their permanence, as he repeated the formulaic words, each delegate followed Aristides, Athens' representative, and dropped a heavy lump of red-hot iron into the sea, declaring (as the waters hissed around it) that, until the metal rose and floated on the waves, in other words forever, his promise would remain unbroken. The ceremony must have lasted many hours as representatives of city after city stepped forward to recite the sacred formula, but, when all was over and the sun set low behind the lake, and delegates sat down to feast on sacrificial meat, the significance of that day's achievements must have been clear to everyone. They had created the most extensive military union the Greeks had ever known, as momentous as the mythological alliance before the Trojan War, a coalition with extraordinary potential; and too late the Spartans realized what they had done.[24]

When news from Delos reached the Eurotas valley, Sparta's proud warriors were furious. The ephors and old men of the Gerousia had betrayed them. They had once been lauded as the leaders of all Greece, but now they had allowed themselves to be outplayed, eclipsed, humiliated by the upstart democrats of Athens; they had meekly recognized the new League as commanders of the sea; they had ceded not just Byzantium and the Bosporus but Sestus and the Hellespont to the Athenians; they had seriously undermined their own prestige and jeopardized their country's safety. Alive to the growing dissent the Gerousia discussed the feasibility of war with Athens; and at the next Ecclesia the motion was debated with enthusiasm. While the newest generation of Spartan fighting men sat, sullen, simmering with rage, their fury matched by that of veterans of Plataea, Sepeia and countless other campaigns, waged to ensure their city's kudos and supremacy, the arguments were laid before them: politically, militarily and economically, what they had done made no sense at all. Years before, Apollo's oracle had warned against such folly, advising them to beware their leadership becoming 'lame'—surely the god had foreseen the current situation: for after Plataea, Sparta had commanded both the Peloponnesian League and the Ionians alike, the two legs of Greece; now they ruled only the Peloponnesians. This was not what Leonidas had died for, or his colleagues at Thermopylae, or those others, dead, in other battles against Persia or

Argos or other rogue Greek city-states; this was not why they had intervened in Athens thirty years before in their attempt to stifle Cleisthenes and his dreams of democracy.[25]

With the Ecclesia supporting action, the Gerousia convened once more, ready to pass a motion that would see Sparta and her still-loyal allies marching out to war. But at the last moment one of their number, Hetoemaridas, an aristocrat who traced his ancestry to Heracles, stood up to speak. Calmly he reminded fellow councillors of why they had withdrawn from leadership of the campaigning far off in the east: the helot situation meant they needed to stay close to home; and what would Sparta do with all the booty if they did resume command and capture Persian cities? They need only remember Pausanias to see how wealth corrupted. A war now would be fought against not only Athens but the entire Ionian League, while to control the sea would need a fleet at least as large as that of Athens—could they not imagine the social upheavals this would entail? Look at Athens, where, required to man ships, poor and sometimes landless citizens (a class absent from Sparta) had become a powerful political force. It was not in Sparta's interests to try to rule the waves. Better to let Athens bear the brunt of keeping the seas free from Persians and protecting Greece's shores. Let Athens bear the costs; let Athens take the risks; it was no threat to Sparta. Hearing Hetoemaridas' arguments laid out so calmly and concisely, his colleagues could do nothing but agree; and at the next Ecclesia (trained from birth to respect their elders, and accepting the wisdom of their arguments) the Identicals bowed to the Gerousia's decision. War with Athens and her League had been averted.[26]

If he needed further arguments to calm the Spartans' nerves, Hetoemaridas might have reminded them that in the League's commanders they had powerful friends. For, while the working class of Athens did indeed hold sway, the League was the creation of those two patricians, Aristides and Cimon, both of whom had shown goodwill to Sparta in the past. Indeed, Cimon found much in Sparta to admire, and often cited their example in debate, slapping down opponents with the frustrated exclamation, 'No! Spartans would *never* do anything like that!' For him, the ideal would have been for his beloved Sparta to exist in harmony with newly powerful Athens, just as the two cities' human incarnations, the twins Oulius and Lacedaemonius, lived together in his repaired mansion at Laciadae. Indeed, for Cimon, the oracle used by

Spartan hotheads to incite war with Athens could equally apply to the relationship between his own city and Sparta: in time he would describe them as the legs of Greece, or as two horses pulling the same chariot, who by working together could win victory, as he urged fellow citizens not to weaken Sparta and so 'let Greece go lame, or see Athens robbed of her yoke-mate'. Such sentiments delighted the Spartans, who helped bolster Cimon in these vital days, while his assurance that the League was meant purely to fight Persians, not threaten sympathetic Greeks, did much to allay Spartan fears. But on both sides some still entertained suspicions, not least Athenians who questioned whether Pausanias really had gone spectacularly native, and really was living in the Troad as a private citizen, or was in fact an agent on a secret mission to win Persian support for Sparta for a war against the League, and gold with which to fund it—if successful he would be hailed in Sparta as a hero; if not, he could be easily disowned. But on the whole, it made no sense for Athenians and Spartans to be at each other's throats, especially as there were still so many clear and present external threats, and, while twelve months or more were wasted planning for a war that did not come, by spring of the third year since Plataea, the League was ready for campaigning.[27]

By now, back in Persepolis where he was trying to forget the carnage of Salamis and his retreat from Attica by focussing on overseeing the building of a fine new palace, and despite his rumoured correspondence with Pausanias, the Great King had grown tired of his irritating western neighbours. But while Xerxes (for now) could turn his back on Greece, Greeks could not ignore the Persians. Persian outposts were still dotted across north Aegean coasts and, with worries of a war with Sparta shelved, stability and peace of mind dictated that all trace of them must be eradicated. It was time for Cimon to lead the new League (whose Ionians were keen to expunge memories of their collaboration with the Great King at Artemisium and Salamis) on their first major campaign. Like most of Cimon's operations, alluded to by ancient sources yet not elaborated, many details remain sketchy. As the League fleet swept north, it may have made strategic sense for him to swoop on Lemnos (as Miltiades, his father, did two decades earlier), driving out its Persian soldiery and bureaucrats, sending collaborators scampering for safety and reclaiming what had once been an Athenian possession. But his main goal was Eion, the fortress that Darius' general, Megabazus, had established on the site of a Greek settlement at the River Strymon's mouth to control the fertile Thracian plains and the nearby gold mines of Pangaeum. For Eion was not just a stronghold with a useful naval base but a thriving trading post, where produce from far northern hinterlands could find its way to the Aegean and beyond. And being close to the kingdom of his grandfather, Olorus, it lay in lands that Cimon knew well.[28]

Sited on a low hill on the river's eastern bank, well-walled and seemingly impregnable, Eion and its garrison had been entrusted to the capable command of Boges, one of Xerxes' most valued lieutenants, on whom the Great King constantly heaped praise, and whose eldest sons (now back in Persia) he treated with the utmost courtesy. As a result, the governor could now not countenance abandoning his post; so, as Cimon neared the shallow mouth of the green river with its mudflats and gently sloping beaches and—far off—the pale blue hills of Thrace, he found Boges and his small, brave band of Persians drawn up behind their wall of wicker shields, the summer sunlight jouncing on their spear tips and their golden jewellery. But the Greeks saw nothing to intimidate them. They had faced far greater numbers in more dangerous conditions. Bringing their ships to shore, they splashed onto the beach and up towards the enemy. And so it all began: the roar of Apollo's hymn, the paean war song, muffled in the close confines of their bronze helmets; the tunnel vision through the narrow sweat-soaked sockets; the slap of bronze greaves on knees and leather straps on thighs; the weight of shields; the heft of spears; the racing heartbeat; grim satisfaction as a blade tore home and the spume of blood that drenched their sword arms was another's, not their own. Pushed back, the Persians gave way, ran up the sandy road and fled inside their fortress, barred gates and raced onto the ramparts. But Cimon held back from an assault. Instead, he beached his triremes, bivouacked his men and made it clear that he was ready to conduct a lengthy siege. Then he sent a messenger to Boges: surrender, and the Greeks would grant him, his family and his men safe passage back to Persia. The reply was unequivocal: Xerxes had entrusted Eion to Boges; in Eion Boges would remain. There was only one way forward: siege.[29]

But while the Persians were pinned down, the allies need not be. Leaving troops to man the barricades, which would prevent all egress and protect the ships, Cimon, his ranks and coffers swollen thanks to the help of a far-sighted, generous Thessalian aristocrat, Menon of Phar-salus, led raids inland—up the broad Strymon valley, through narrow defiles, far into the foothills of the towering Thracian mountains—his target: the Edoni, tribesmen who, when Megabazus sent the native popu-lation into exile, had settled in abandoned villages and farmsteads, grateful for the opportunities the Persians provided them, ready to supply their benefactors with whatever produce they might need. Now it was their turn to be driven out. As they saw Cimon and his men ap-proaching, most simply melted back into the hillsides to begin their long trek back to their ancestral homes.[30]

There was no hurry to complete these operations. Each day that passed was one more day for Eion's food supplies to dwindle, as Boges weighed the consequences of starvation or surrender, while from allied camp-fires scents of cooking, tantalizing, drifted in the summer air. Cut off, surrounded, nowhere could hold out forever. Yet for those besieged there still remained another option. As weeks became months, and days began to shorten, black smoke belched behind the fortress walls. On Cimon's order the Ionians strapped on their armour, dashed up the hill and clambered unopposed onto the ramparts. Few would forget the sight that met them as they gazed down into Eion: a tall pyre built from bits of furniture, anything the Persians could find; atop it piles of treasure, gold and silver plate and jewellery; and Boges' household—his wife and their young children, his concubines and slaves—throats slit, eyes staring, thrown onto the blazing pyre, before Boges in one last heroic act of proud defiance climbed into the flames, to die, self-immolated, in Ahura Mazda's cleansing fire. As they picked their way through Eion's ashes, the allies found little left of value, only the emaciated remnants of its garrison, wide-eyed and terrified, many needing to be helped down to the sea, all needing to be fed and fattened before they could be sold as slaves.[31]

If the hoplites were disappointed by the absence of booty, for Cimon and Athens, Eion's liberation was a major coup. Although there were still Persians in Thrace—including parts of Cimon's native Chersonese—in this one campaign the League had not just robbed Xerxes of his reve-nues from Pangaeum's gold mines, funnelling them instead to Delos, they had extended their control over the north Aegean coast and re-established their regional presence, enabling themselves once more to reap the economic benefits of trade with Thrace. And while the need to rebuild Attica meant it was still too soon to send Athenian settlers to occupy an outpost by the Strymon, Cimon, half-Thracian, still had useful contacts in the region, who might repopulate evacuated villages and farm the land. In addition, seeing the way the wind was blowing, the islanders of Thasos had joined the League; with Paros, from where Thasos had been settled, they had once ruled Eion, and now they were well placed to keep an eye on it.[32]

No wonder, then, that Cimon and his men were greeted by enthusiastic crowds on their return to Athens. Their success confirmed what many in the city now believed: that the gods were on their side; that victory was their due; that their commitment to democracy had set them on the path to glory as the rightful leaders of the free Greek world. Signs of this confidence were seen throughout the city. Although (thanks to their decision not to rebuild temples burned by Xerxes until the threat of his return had been removed once and for all) on the Acropolis and elsewhere, only temporary wooden structures housed revered cult objects, the sanctuaries themselves had been cleaned up, with broken statues and smashed orientalising sculptures (out of fashion now that the Persian East was an anathema) buried in deep pits; and as within the newly-towering city walls householders supervised the reconstruction of domestic homes, public buildings were already springing up around the Agora, not least on its west side where the Council had its offices close to a new stoa. Here two bronze statues had been recently unveiled, which embodied Athens' swelling optimism. While previously statues of the human body had seemed static and demure, these were infused with life, each appearing to advance with daggers brandished in their upraised hands. Heroically nude (though one had a short cloak draped over his left arm), they seemed more gods than men, yet none doubted their identity. For they were set up where two other statues had once stood, statues that now stood in Susa, removed as trophies by the Great King—the statues of the two tyrannicides, Harmodius and Aristogeiton, honorary forefathers of Athenian democracy. In the wake of the Wars, their valour in cutting down Hipparchus, brother of that hated Persian-collaborator, Hippias, had assumed even greater significance, while their statues' theft showed how seriously even Athens' enemies regarded them. So now the stolen statues were replaced with fresh ones, modern substitutes that would herald a new age. And, if their style was bold and new, like newborn Athens they proclaimed a continuity—one

A group of three triumphant herms, each bearing
the head of Hermes and an exuberantly erect phallus,
is commemorated on this fragment of Attic red-figure
pottery.

of their two creators, Critius, had studied at the feet of Antenor, who
thirty years before had made the now-looted originals, while the other's
name, Nesiotes, 'The Islandman', propitious for a new sea-based League,
proclaimed a glorious future.[33]

They were not the only sculptures to adorn the transformed Agora.
Soon they were joined by three large triumphant herms, square pillars,
each topped with the bearded head of the god Hermes and adorned
with an exuberantly erect phallus, totemic talismans designed to ward
off evil. Other herms stood guard in front of private homes and public
buildings, together creating a magic web, an all-embracing amulet

protecting the whole city, but what made these three exceptional was that they were commissioned by popular vote as proud memorials of Cimon's victory at Eion, though (it being the fashion to attribute such successes to the People as a whole) Cimon's name was nowhere to be seen. Inscribed verses glorified Athens' triumph. One read:

> Those men were courageous, too, who fought at Eion
>> against Persians beside the Strymon's swirling waters.
> They first brought with them parching famine and chill Ares, god of war,
>> and discovered for their enemies death-dealing despair.

Another declared:

> The Athenians dedicated this in tribute to their generals,
>> for benefits bestowed and their great bravery.
> Whoever looks on this in future will be filled with greater courage
>> to fight with greater resolution for the common good.

The third proclaimed:

> Once from this city with the sons of Atreus
>> Menestheus led Athenians to the sacred plain of Troy.
> Homer records how—of all Greeks in their close-fitting armour—
>> he was the best at stationing his men for battle.
> So it is no small thing to call Athenians
>> experts in deploying both the arts of war and strengths of men.[34]

Linking Eion with that most glorious of Greek campaigns, the mythological Trojan War, this last inscription encapsulated how Greeks, particularly Athenians, were coming to view their struggle with the Persians. Like the legendary campaign, their war, too, from Marathon to Plataea and Mycale had lasted for approximately ten years. And while others were involved, it was Athenians who won the day at Marathon; it was Athenians who played a crucial part in every later battle (except, of course, Thermopylae, the one defeat—and that was chiefly down to Sparta); it was Athenians who now were spearheading the campaign to drive Persians from lands claimed by the Greeks and eradicate the threat of Persian invasion. So, it was right and proper to proclaim their role in art and sculpture—in Athens and abroad. The new statues of the tyrant-slayers and the nearby herms were just a start. Resurgent Athens must proclaim her new identity and hone the story of her destiny—to present herself as age-old, venerable, rooted in tradition, championed by heroes, loved by gods, while at the same time rightful leader of the Allied League, modern and radical, democratic, brave, ambitious to shape Greece's future. Since the days of Peisistratus they had known the value of propaganda. Now, though, they would be even more creative and, as they looked for ways to mark the new age and consolidate their standing at the head of an expanding coalition, they would find no-one more creative than Cimon.

8

SECURING ATHENS

Blessings be upon you, Theseus, for your nobility of
   spirit
and for treating us with care and justice.

Sophocles, *Oedipus at Colonus*, 1042–1043

ATHENS, 475 B.C.

The inspiration came from Delphi and Apollo, an oracle commanding
the Athenians to seek out and repatriate the bones of Theseus, their legendary king. Believed to have reigned many generations in the past,
before the Trojan War when men and monsters shared the earth, Theseus had for centuries been held in high esteem in Athens and beyond.
Poets sang of his exploits, artists painted them on vases, while Peisistratus
and Cleisthenes used Theseus to add legitimacy to their political ambitions, the one to strengthen links with Delos, the other to support re-
structuring the constitution, both moulding him into a civic hero, the
embodiment of all their Athens stood for. So his grip on the imagination grew, until now in the city there were men who swore that they had
seen him fighting by their side at Marathon, arrayed in shining armour,
steering Athens to a victory on which she might build in the future, just
as he delivered her from bondage in the past. For his was a stirring story,
a heady mix of swashbuckling adventure and hard politics, and his values
seemed tailor-made for this new age.[1]

Like Athenians, Theseus owed his existence to the sea—in his case
literally: his father was Poseidon or (in other versions of the legend)

Aegeus, Athens' king, who gave his name to the Aegean. Born in Troezen (the north-east Peloponnesian polis that had welcomed refugees from Athens from Persian-threatened Attica), when he came of age he walked to Athens, ridding the countryside of thugs and bandits, and ensuring safe passage for all. Once there, he tamed the fearsome Bull of Marathon (in recognition of which feat a statue of the creature stood now on the Athenian Acropolis) before, surviving her attempts to kill him, he drove out the foreign sorceress Medea (ancestress of Medes and Persians). This was not his only triumph over peoples whom Athenians were fast defining as the Other, 'barbarians', a term that once meant simply speakers of other languages who sounded to Greeks like bleating sheep, but that was now acquiring hostile connotations, as Persian temple-burning enemies became derided for being not just uncivilized and brutal but (in a bizarre twist of logic) effeminate and craven.[2]

For Theseus not only saved Athens from invading Amazons (those eastern female warriors who, though terrifying, like Persians, wore the ultimate in effete clothing, trousers), he crushed the Centaurs (hybrid horse-men) and took the fight to foreign lands, sailing to Delos (where he established sacred rites), before proving his patrimony to the Cretans (by retrieving a ring from the ocean's depths), slaying the Minotaur, the half-man, half-bull aberration that feasted upon Athens' youths and maidens, and overthrowing King Minos and his empire, the world's first thalassocracy. Moreover, it was Theseus who took possession of Eleusis and unified the scattered settlements of Attica under Athens' central control, an arrangement that he marked by founding the Panathenaic Festival. But all did not end well for Theseus. Recklessly he provoked the Spartans, stealing their princess, Helen (whose beauty later sparked the Trojan War), though she was just a child. Shortly afterwards, while trying to help a friend abduct Persephone, he was imprisoned in the Underworld for four long years, during which a rival usurped Athens' throne. Freed at last, now wounded, elderly and weakened, he fled to the island of Scyros with its crumpled hills and valleys, whose king feigned friendship before pushing him from a high cliff and hiding his body in a shallow grave. So it was on Scyros that Athenians must look to find his bones.[3]

Athens was not the first city that Apollo had advised to repatriate a legendary hero. Thanks to him, the Spartans had already brought home not just one but two. Seventy-five years earlier, intent on enslaving neighbouring Tegea, their confident Identical ancestors had been defeated, shackled and forced to till enemy fields. Campaigns to liberate them failed until the Delphic oracle in typically enigmatic language told them to find a location in Tegea where two winds were crushed by overwhelming force, and blow met blow, a place of toil and hardship; for there lay the body of Orestes, son of Agamemnon, Greece's general at Troy, and nephew of the Spartan Helen. The hero's presence was protecting Tegea, but transfer his remains to Sparta and he would switch allegiance. No-one knew the meaning of Apollo's words, but during a lull in fighting Lichas, a prominent Identical, pretending to have been forced to flee from Sparta, visited Tegea, where, in a blacksmith's forge, his host described how, as he dug a well, he found a coffin ten feet long containing a skeleton of remarkable proportions. Suddenly (bellows, hammer, anvil, toil) the oracle made sense: Orestes lay beneath the smithy! So the ambassador rented the forge, dug up the bones and brought them back to Sparta, where in a new shrine Orestes was worshipped as a hero—and within no time at all Tegea was defeated. Encouraged by Apollo the Spartans then repatriated the remains of Orestes' son, Tisamenus, this time from Helice on the Corinthian Gulf; and so her power increased. Indeed, across Greece, skeletons of varying size and authenticity were not infrequently dug up and either reverently returned to grateful cities (if they were deemed benevolent) or cast out beyond their borders (if they were not). And did not the relics of Cimon's ancestors, the Aeacidae, bring victory to the Athenians at Salamis? Apollo's bidding to bring Theseus back home was nothing new.[4]

But it did chime with political expediency. For Scyros was a bandit island, the haunt of ruthless pirates, cousins of tough mountain men from badlands in Dolopia, brigands who had embraced the Persian cause as a means of settling old scores and doing some killing. Now that the wars were over, they still lurked in dark shadows behind rocky headlands to shoot out from hidden coves and swoop on heavy-laden merchantmen—and woe betide the crews whose boats they captured. Less than twenty-five miles east of Euboea, Scyros commanded one of the main sea routes, so this was not a situation to be tolerated. To neutralize the threat of piracy and enforce law and order, it was crucial that Scyros be brought under control; and now, thanks to the oracle, Athenians had unimpeachable authority to do so. Indeed, Apollo seemed to be doing all he could to help them. A short while earlier, not content with raiding the high seas, the pirates had refined their freebooting techniques, impounding vessels that put in to their harbours, and appropriating anything they fancied. Among their victims was a Thessalian ship that docked at Ctesium, a port nestling beneath a rocky crag on Scyros' eastern shores. Somehow the crew escaped and brought their case before an international court at Delphi, which ruled that Scyros should pay compensation. The islanders refused: it was the Dolopian incomers who had actually boarded the ship, so it was they and not the native Scyrotes who should pay. As feuding families eyed each other with increasing hatred, one of them had what he thought was a brilliant idea: he would enlist the help of Athens; he would write to her League's leader; he would invite Cimon to sail to Scyros with his fleet and take possession of the island.[5]

The letter was a godsend. Not only did it legitimize an Athenian conquest of Scyros but, in punishing the pirates for attacking a Thessalian ship, it gave Athens a means of re-establishing relations with Thessaly that had soured during the Persian Wars—for, decades before the troubles, ties had been strong. Thessalian cavalrymen helped install Peisistratus as tyrannus; others served under Hippias; and if the Aleuadae family had capitulated easily and early to Xerxes, it was only because they calculated (rightly) that doing so would protect their lands from the kind of devastation he unleashed on Attica. After Plataea, however, the Aleuadae were suddenly exposed as pro-Persian collaborators who must bear the full force of the victors' righteous wrath, and Thessaly's broad fertile plains braced themselves for attack. Sure enough, it came— from Sparta, far from happy at how meekly she had ceded maritime control to Athens' Allied League, and yearning for a military victory to restore her wounded kudos. So, led by King Leotychidas (Xanthippus' colleague at the Battle of Mycale), they clasped their scarlet war cloaks round their necks and marched out north. But when weeks later they returned they were even more frustrated than before. They had been ready to give battle, but before a spear was thrown in anger, Leotychidas, like his predecessor Demaratus at Eleusis, issued orders to stand down. The Spartan authorities claimed he had been bribed; they claimed they had discovered a rich hoard of silver in his tent, a gift from the Aleuadae; they found him guilty and they exiled him, demolishing his house and eradicating every physical trace of him. So within three years of his triumphant victory over Persia, Leotychidas, humbled, was hounded out of Sparta, and in neighbouring Tegea, as close to home as he could be, the victor of Mycale grew old and died.[6]

For Athens, Sparta's military failure offered rich diplomatic opportunities, for, if Thessaly could not be won in battle, it could at least be wooed. By championing the Aleuadae, by righting an acknowledged wrong, by enforcing the decision of the international tribunal, Athens would win powerful friends and, if she did not punish them for siding with the enemy, it was because the new world order demanded a pragmatic form of politics. Sparta's botched attack had alienated the Aleuadae, but if, by aiding them, Athenians could regain grateful allies, then so be it. The invitation to the League to sail to Scyros was a perfect opportunity. With the Assembly's approval Cimon acted swiftly. The fleet was scrambled and, before the Dolopians could rally, Athenian triremes were anchored in their azure waters, allied hoplites surging through streets, arresting everyone they met, kicking in doors and windows, dragging startled householders into the flooding daylight where they let the native islanders go free but shackled the Dolopians and led them off to holding pens from where they could be shipped to slavery, their empty homes soon to be occupied by Athenian settlers.[7]

A triumphant message home proclaimed mission accomplished, another victory for the League, and not just over Scyros. As the Assembly considered the logistics of how best to colonize the island, the grateful Aleuadae, diplomatic ties renewed, were fêting Cimon, building a close friendship that he would shortly broadcast to the world when, on the birth of his third son, he named the baby Thettalus—the Thessalian—a name as redolent of his political world view as those of his two elder sons, Lacedaemonius and Oulius. For, while determined to increase Athens' power, the shrewd Cimon was constantly aware of the need for foreign ties and international cooperation. Just as the three boys would grow strong under their father's watchful eye on his Laciadae estate, so all Greece would prosper from his leadership.[8]

But this was for the future; on Scyros Cimon had unfinished business. He had yet to find the bones of Theseus. And the suspicious islanders refused to tell him where they were. Moreover, supposing (rightly) it was all a pretext to extend Athenian control across the island, they refused to allow Scyros to be searched. They had totally misjudged the situation. Athens was already in control, determined military units fanning out across the island, criss-crossing fertile valleys to the north, climbing rocky slopes, picking their way by sandy beaches lapped by rippling waves, the sun hot on their backs, the rasping of cicadas in their ears. But each day they came back empty-handed. It seemed a hopeless task. How could they find a pile of bones on an island eighty-one square miles in area and, even if they did, how could they know that they belonged to Theseus? It was now, plunged in despair, that (according to official accounts) the gods once more intervened. They sent Cimon a sign. Gazing out towards the Temple of Apollo on a hill near Ctesium, he saw an eagle perched on a low mound. As it pecked the ground, scraping the earth with its talons, gradually the truth began to dawn—the bird of Zeus was showing him where to dig. A bustle of activity; pickaxes; shovels; an ever-rising spoil heap; an ever-deeper hole; and then the sound of iron on hollow wood; the digging now more careful; a bronze sword and an ancient spear passed to the watchers; and a casket hauled out of the soil; the coffin crow-barred open to reveal its treasure: the skeleton of a towering man, taller by far than any of the current generation, clearly a hero from a bygone age. Cimon had found the bones of Theseus. And now he would escort them home, and with them not just bring new hope to his war-weary city but consolidate his own role as its leader.[9]

But first to choreograph the hero's homecoming. As messengers sped south to Athens to pass on the joyful news, Cimon caused his trireme to be cleansed and ritually purified, adorned with garlands, before the coffin was embarked. Then, with a following wind, sails bellying, ropes slapping in the warm salt breeze, and white foam hissing back in ripples from the bronze beak gleaming in the early autumn sun beneath the ship's two staring marble eyes, the helmsman steered his course: first south across the broad expanse of sea towards the southern mountains of Euboea, golden in the morning light; then round the promontory, west through the broad channel between Andros and Euboea and, keeping Ceos on the port bow, on towards the land mass, the hills of Attica so clearly seen now; past Sunium to starboard with its ruined temple on the headland, and as hills gave way to broad, flat, olive-studded plains that stretched down, silver, to the sea, Athens herself came into view, with her new walls and the age-old slopes of the Acropolis and Lycabettus Hill, and then ahead the low rise of Piraeus with its three enticing harbours. Their destination was perhaps Phalerum, from whose ancient port Theseus himself sailed on his quest to slay the Minotaur, a fitting site for this, his last homecoming. And what a homecoming it was. As little rowing boats came out to meet them, those on the trireme's deck could see the waterfront was packed with people, many wearing their best robes and dresses, their well-oiled hair secured in place by gold clips moulded like cicadas, their gaze fixed on the narrow hull and on the tall man with his mop of curls standing at its prow. For here was an excuse to celebrate, to preen, to put the horrors and the deprivations of the recent past behind them, to forget how, terrified and trembling, they had packed this very quay just five years earlier as they waited for the boats to ferry them across the gulf before the Persians came. And now their fortunes were reversed; now they were awaiting a returning hero.[10]

The procession to the city was part celebration, part state funeral. Laid on a bier strewn with flowers, a wagon drawn by well-groomed horses, and accompanied by an honour guard, the coffin, conveyed along the hard-tamped road across the marshes, was followed by a column of well-wishers—citizens and foreign residents, all with their wives and families. Once inside Athens it was taken to a temporary resting place (perhaps on the now-desolate Acropolis), where, with hymns and prayers, incense and sacrifice, priests received their lost king home. And while the elite might naturally embrace the honours paid to one so clearly of their class, remarkably arch-democrats could find it in their hearts to welcome him with genuine joy, too. While they still loathed monarchy of any sort—the autocracy of tyrants such as Hippias or the sovereignty of Persia's Great King—they managed to persuade themselves that Theseus had ruled as monarch in name only: yes, he had occupied the throne, but he governed by popular consent; he was benign, compassionate, approachable and just, first citizen perhaps, but first among equals. It was in no way inconsistent, then, to honour King Theseus while glorifying Harmodius and Aristogeiton, the tyrannicides, or to reverence his physical remains—especially since, having fought beside them with such single-mindedness at Marathon, his spirit would protect his people against threats to come.[11]

These ceremonies, however, marked just the start of Cimon's plans for Theseus. The conqueror of Scyros proposed to the Assembly the dedication of a sanctuary, a hero shrine to house the great man's physical remains. His suggestion was approved—as he no doubt anticipated. For thanks to the decision not (for the moment) to restore the sanctuaries

An Athenian kylix (drinking cup) of c. 440–430 B.C. celebrates the
deeds of Theseus, including (*centre*) his slaying of the Minotaur.
His pose top left is deliberately reminiscent of that of Aristogeiton
(see page 32).

sacked by Xerxes, unlike Sparta or Argos or Corinth, Athens possessed
no impressive temples. There may well have been temporary structures,
but in an age when colonnaded temples were a sign of status, such shacks
were poor reflections of the city's new-found power and prestige. Yet,
while they had undertaken not to rebuild ruined structures, nothing
prevented them from building new ones, and the construction of a
shrine to Theseus located not on the Acropolis but in the heart of the
lower city would do much to beautify the district, enhance Athens' cachet and fire patriotic zeal, especially since the subject matter of its associated artworks would proclaim not just Theseus' heroic deeds but the
valiant achievements of his descendants, the contemporary Athenians.
When they were finished and with sombre ceremonial the ancient bones
at last were laid to rest within the gleaming mausoleum, no-one could
have doubted their relevance. Two paintings depicted battles in which
Theseus had shown great gallantry. In one he was fighting the Amazons,

in the other, battle swirling around him, he was locked in conflict with the Centaurs, overcoming barbarism, championing order, ensuring the triumph of Greek civilization, just as a few years earlier (or so their co-alescing view of history would claim) Athenians overcame the savage bestiality of Persia. The third wall showed another scene from Theseus' hagiography, the episode in Crete when he dived into the sea to retrieve Minos' ring: the artist, Micon, showed the moment that he broke the water's surface, the ring held in his upraised hand, a gold crown on his head, the gift of Amphitrite, wife of the sea-god Poseidon, thanks to whom Athens ruled the waves. It was an episode that Bacchylides (nephew and heir of the acclaimed Simonides) wove into one of his exquisite songs of celebration—perhaps recalling Micon's painting or inspiring it—describing how, as the Athenian prince, his hair as curly as Cimon's, dived overboard:

> dolphins of the salt sea swiftly bore great Theseus
> down to the dwelling of his father—Poseidon, lord of horses—
> until he reached the great hall of the gods.
> He trembled then to see rich Nereus' shining daughters,
> light radiating from their gorgeous limbs like fire
> as ribbons shot with gold thread flew out from their hair,
> as they delighted in their dance with splashing feet.
> And in that splendid house he saw his father's much-loved wife,
> the venerable Amphitrite with her limpid eyes.
> She draped a purple cloak around him and set upon his curly hair
> the flawless garland, dark with roses,
> that cunning Aphrodite gave her on her wedding day
> (right-thinking mortals must believe whatever gods desire).
> Then Theseus emerged once more beside the white-prowed ship.[12]

The building of a hero shrine was in itself significant, but Cimon now went further, embedding reverence to Theseus deep in the rituals of an-nual festival. For generations in the autumn month of Pyanepsion (straddling our October and November), behind two boys on the cusp of manhood, each dressed in women's clothes and carrying vine branches, men had processed from Dionysus' temple in Athens to the Sanctuary of Athena Sciras in Phalerum, where long into the night they feasted before parading back next morning uttering alternate cries of joy and sorrow. Followed as it was by other ceremonies which saw young men enrolled as citizens, the ritual may originally have marked transi-

tion into adulthood, but for Cimon it had other connotations: the procession to Phalerum commemorated Theseus' journey to the sea before
he sailed to Crete with some of his accomplices disguised as girls to fool
the Cretans, while the procession back to Athens mirrored Theseus' return, his joy at freeing his city from her tribute to King Minos tinged
with sorrow at the news of his human father's suicide. (Wrongly believing
that Theseus was dead, Aegeus threw himself from either the Acropolis
or Cape Sunium.) Now, with Theseus-fever gripping Athens, Cimon
easily persuaded fellow citizens of the festival's 'true' meaning and that
changes should be introduced to make its links with Theseus more clear,
transforming a ceremony marking a specific rite of passage into a celebration not just of a civic hero but of victory over barbarism and the defeat of foreign powers, dominion over the sea (thanks to Theseus' relationship with Poseidon) and by extension the establishment of Athenian
hegemony.[13]

For equally important were Theseus' close links with the island at the
heart of Athens' new League, Delos. Among dances performed there at
Apollo's festival was one, the crane dance, said to have been choreographed by Theseus himself, its steps (mirroring the intricacies of
Crete's labyrinth) danced not just by Athenians but by 'Ionians in long-
flowing robes'. How well the crane dance suited current politics: where
Theseus of Athens led, Ionians quite literally must follow. Indeed, Bacchylides proclaimed this very message when he sang of the hero's voyage
south to Crete accompanied by not just Athenians but Ionians:

> The ship with its dark prow, unshakeable
> in the cacophony of battle, brought Theseus and two sets
> of seven glorious Ionian youths as it sliced the Cretan sea;
> and north winds filled the glistening sail,
> thanks to Athena's will,
> the glorious goddess of the warlike aegis.[14]

Nor was 'the ship with its dark prow' a mere poetic construct. Down
at Piraeus Athenians could view the very vessel in which Theseus had
sailed to Crete, now lovingly restored and launched each spring to ferry
official delegates to Apollo's annual festival on Delos. Small, thirty-oared,
its design belonged to the Iron Age (later than the legendary Theseus),
but to Athenians uninterested in clear chronologies of distant historical
events all that mattered was that it was ancient, and being ancient and

preserved it must have belonged to Theseus. So what had once been simply an ordinary warship assumed an aura of sanctity. Repaired, re-fitted every year, new timbers were inserted in the place of old until in time it became the subject of philosophical debate: with not one orig-inal timber still remaining could it really be considered to be Theseus' original ship? But for most Athenians such hair-splitting was irrelevant. What mattered was that it connected them to their heroic past. What mattered was that, in taking their ambassadors to Delos, it once more proclaimed Athens' pride of place, this time at the head of a new, bur-geoning League. But if, with his bones' repatriation, Theseus' star and that of Athens blazed again in the ascendant, the star of the great pag-eant's mastermind—Cimon—was blazing brightly, too. 'More than any other,' Plutarch was to write, 'this single achievement won him the People's love.'[15]

Cimon was not the only politician using public service to enhance pri-vate reputation or help encourage policies reflecting his world view. Since Plataea and Mycale, Themistocles had been pursuing his own dream of radical democracy, enhancing the People's power and status through constructing more triremes (employing shipwrights and more oarsmen) and developing Piraeus, whose improving port facilities re-flected and encouraged the growth of Athens' merchant navy, which—now that her warships were patrolling the waves—could ply the sea lanes with increasing confidence, exporting prized goods such as olive oil and pottery, while bringing back a growing variety of produce to the booming Agora, and boosting the Athenian economy. And if poets such as Bacchylides (as comfortable composing praise songs for Sicilian tyrannoi, victorious in Panhellenic Games, as for Ionian choirs at Delos) were pleased to channel Cimon's political outlook, others shared The-mistocles' perspective.

Among them was Phrynichus, whose *Capture of Miletus*, written in the aftermath of the Ionian Revolt, had so outraged Athenians that they fined him for reminding them of their own troubles. Which made his *Phoenician Women*, staged roughly when Cimon was taking Eion and sub-duing Scyros, all the more daring. Although its plot revolved round Greece's victory at Salamis, its setting (like that of his earlier tragedy) was a city reeling from the impact of military disaster—this time, Phoe-nician Sidon, home to the bulk of Xerxes' fleet. It opened with a eunuch carefully arranging chairs in Sidon's council chamber. Perhaps he is removing them now that the meeting has adjourned, for it quickly becomes clear that he has heard momentous news: the Phoenician fleet has been destroyed at Salamis; its crewmen are no more. As horror spreads throughout the city, widows and mothers of dead Phoenician sailors pour onto the stage to sing ritual laments. Only tantalizing fragments of the play survive: the eunuch's proclamation that 'all these are Persian possessions, but the Persians themselves have long ago departed'; a description of the battle, how 'men were slaughtered until evening fell'; bereft women 'singing threnodies accompanied by plucking harps'. As in the *Capture of Miletus,* here in *Phoenician Women* the audience is invited to share the grief of the disconsolate, to mourn a generation's loss, but now instead of Greeks, those grieving are the enemy. For if the plays' scenarios are similar, the situations motivating them were polar opposites—which was precisely Phrynichus' intent in writing his *Phoenician Women* and what made the play so powerful: seen together, the *Capture of Miletus* and *Phoenician Women* are a tragedy of retribution in two acts, of Persian hubris quashed by Greek bravery and pluck (and where the failure of the first play is forgotten in the triumph of the second). Moreover, considered as a pair, they proclaim a concept central to Greek thought, the concept of balance, where fully to appreciate a situation we must explore its opposite, as Homer did when he described city-sacking Odysseus responding to a song about his exploits in the Trojan War by weeping like a widow who has seen her husband killed and is herself about to be led off to slavery. More than even that, however, viewed simply in isolation, *Phoenician Women,* pivoting on its account of Salamis, underscored the mastery of Athens' seafaring class, the city poor, the People who had manned the rowing benches and achieved their famous victory. In highlighting their triumph rather than that of hoplites at Plataea, Phrynichus was both gratifying (most of) his viewers and proclaiming himself to be (like them) a true progressive democrat, all of which delighted the play's sponsor—Themistocles himself.[16]

The success of *Phoenician Women* inspired at least one other tragedy, *Persians,* presented four years later, exploring similar material from a similar perspective. Its author, Aeschylus, a veteran of the Persian Wars, had fought at Marathon (where his brother Cynegeirus died bleeding in the surf) and probably, too, at Salamis (where another brother, Ameinias, the trireme captain, covered himself in glory). It was to Salamis again that Aeschylus, now in his early fifties, turned to gratify the audience of Athens. Modelling his scenario on that of Phrynichus, he set his play in Susa, where Persian elders, gathered near Darius' tomb, fear for the safety of their men who set out months before with Xerxes, 'whose eyes flash with the clouded glare of a marauding dragon'. Now hearts fill with foreboding as at home 'in marriage beds wives weep with longing for their husbands, every Persian wife who watched her husband seize his spear and rush to war lamenting for him in her grief and longing, abandoned like a horse that's lost its yoke-mate'. The arrival of Atossa, the Queen Mother, Cyrus' daughter, and her description of an ominous dream increase their anxiety, but nothing can prepare them for news brought by a reluctant messenger or his description of the slaughter at Salamis and Xerxes' subsequent retreat. But Aeschylus, the master of dramatic tension, does not leave it there. In a spellbinding scene of necromancy, the Persian elders and Atossa call up Darius' ghost, which, proclaiming that his son's defeat was 'payment for his hubris and impiety' both in 'smashing wooden statues of the gods and setting fire to temples' and (curiously in view of Darius' own bridging of the Bosporus) 'binding the current of the Hellespont, a sacred stream', warns Persians 'never to march against Greek land again, even if your numbers are superior'. Salamis will not end Persian suffering, the ghost predicts: the 'oozing mess of blood spilled at Plataea' will serve as a reminder that 'mortals must not think too big'. As they watched Xerxes himself, robes torn in shame, weeping in antiphonal lament with his dispirited advisors, the Athenian audience could recall words spoken earlier in the play—how 'the very land is on the side of Greece'; how 'the gods protect the city of Athena'; how 'as long as she has men, the walls of Athens will be safe'; and how, questioning the messenger about Athens, Atossa learned not only of the city's 'flowing stream of silver, a treasury beneath the earth', or of its men, who 'stand tall, fighting with their shields and spears', but of its constitution. Demanding, 'Who herds them in place; who wields his will over their army?', she was informed: 'No man calls Athenians his slaves or vassals.'[17]

It was all such stirring stuff, made more remarkable because, while Persian names, real and fictitious, appeared aplenty scattered through the script—proud generals or slaughtered company commanders— Aeschylus singled out by name not one Athenian. Yes, he described Themistocles' ruse on the eve of battle, when he misled the Great King into thinking that the allies were ready to escape, but here even Themistocles was simply 'a Greek man from the Athenian army'. For Athens' victory was nothing if not democratic, won by all her sons, and no one individual must take the credit—though one up-and-coming politician could permit himself some personal satisfaction: thanks to his name being chosen by lot, the staging, lavish in its high production values, with ornate costumes and ghostly apparition, was paid for from the purse of one of Themistocles' most ardent acolytes, a radical young aristocrat, an Alcmaeonid with progressive democratic views, who (like some Aeschylean hero) was carrying ancestral grievances over into his own generation, looking for a way to bring down Cimon, as Xanthippus, his father, once led the prosecution to bring down Miltiades, a serious intellectual with a dangerous potential to stir up the rabble, a cocktail of contradictions: Pericles.[18]

Greek drama was competitive. At every festival three new tetralogies (three tragedies and a light-hearted 'satyr' play), each staged by specially selected playwrights, were judged by a ten-man citizen jury. Costumes, staging, music, choreography, as well as the performances of actors, singers, instrumentalists and dancers all influenced its verdict, but a major consideration must have been how much the script appealed to Athens' audience, of which the jury (randomly selected by lot from each of the ten tribes) was—at least in theory—representative. This was why jingoistic dramas such as *Persians* and *Phoenician Women*, their subject matter tailored to appeal to patriotic audiences, were so successful. It was arguably, too, why dramatists chose to focus on Salamis (a sea battle in which the great bulk of spectators—and therefore potential jury members—had personally fought as oarsmen) rather than the more exclusive hoplite victory at Plataea. So it was inevitable that, just as on Pnyx Hill ambitious politicians honed their arguments with care to bring the People's vote behind them, so in the theatre playwrights took great care to humour, if not flatter, audiences and subscribe to public sentiment to win first prize. Which may explain a curious disconnect—because, while theatregoers were enjoying Aeschylus' description of their own exploits at Salamis, their opinion of the 'Greek man from the Athenian army', the father of their fleet, the architect of victory, was undergoing a sea change. No longer viewed as Athens' shining hope, Themistocles was losing popularity. And as his star waned, Cimon's grew ever brighter.

In part it was because Themistocles had quite simply been left behind. While Cimon supported him and his policy of evacuating Athens in the face of existential threat, he did so because it made strategic sense, not because he held Themistocles, the man, in any great respect. Similarly, Cimon's mentor, Aristides, had placed national security before personal antipathy in the fraught days before Salamis, but in its aftermath he had repeatedly distanced himself from what he thought to be Themistocles' lack of ethics. Not that this stopped Themistocles from strutting on the international Greek stage, not least at the first post-war Olympic Games held four years after Salamis. Whereas the previous Olympics had been held beneath the looming shadow of invasion, with Leonidas already marching at the head of his doomed army to Thermopylae, the allied fleet assembling at Artemisium, and Sicily preparing for a Carthaginian attack, this festival of 476 B.C. was an exuberant display of triumph. Yet, as Scamandrius of Mytilene sprinted to victory in the footrace, and as Theagenes of Thasos emerged bloody but unbeaten from the pancration, a vicious combat sport, as Euthymus, the hulking Locrian, felled his opponent in the boxing ring for the second Games in succession, the one name on all lips remained that of Themistocles.

In a bid to build on his already sizeable prestige, the great populist, champion of Athens' poor, swaggered in style to Olympia, to take residence in a lavish pavilion, far grander and more ostentatious than Cimon's modest tent, before doing all he could to put his rival in the shade, hosting lavish dinners, and insisting that his guests admire his costly furniture and hangings, behaving like some vulgar parvenu, as he trumpeted his role not just as Greece's saviour but as the enemy of despotism everywhere—including at Olympia itself. For this year the new tyrannus of Syracuse had set up his own tent, as breathtaking in its splendour as Themistocles'. The brother of Gelon (who had died peacefully in bed just two years earlier), Hieron was using his wealth to bolster his prestige and establish himself as a key player on the Panhellenic stage. His presence (and his tent) provoked Themistocles to anger and, basking in acclaim, his ears still ringing from the rhapsodic ovation with which assembled Greeks had greeted his studied entrance into the packed stadium, the Athenian delivered an impassioned speech to any who would listen: a despot such as Hieron must not be welcomed at Olympia; his racing teams must be debarred; free Greeks must rally to the democratic cause, tear down the tyrant's tent and drive him from their festival. But few did listen. Guarded by thuggish bodyguards, the Syracusan's tent remained intact. Days later Hieron celebrated victory in the horse race and congratulated his friend and fellow tyrannos, Theron of Acragas, for his chariot team's triumph.[19]

Themistocles had miscalculated. He had forgotten that the Games transcended politics, that what made them special was their celebration of pure Hellenism, those ties of language, blood and custom that Athenians had vaunted three years earlier, and he himself had put such stress on since. For, while Sparta was intent on punishing Persian collaborators on the mainland, and the League of Athens and Ionia cleansed the Aegean of pro-Persian sympathizers, Themistocles had been arguing successfully that citizens of Argos, Thebes and Thessaly be readmitted to the Panhellenic Council despite some having remained neutral in the recent wars and others fighting stalwartly for Xerxes against the allied Greeks. Should any question his proposals he could, of course, stress that Ionians had served in Xerxes' fleet at Artemisium and Salamis, but now, exonerated, they were benefitting from the new world order. Not that he made too much of this argument in Athens. Instead he pointed out that of the thirty-one or so Greek poleis who had resisted Persia, most were Peloponnesians, members of a league controlled by Sparta; if the majority of northern mainland states were barred from joining the Panhellenic Council, Sparta would still dominate the rest; and with experience showing how readily the Peloponnesians abandoned Attica during the recent war (reluctant at all times to march beyond the Isthmus) for her security it was vital that Athens woo as many northern states as possible. Of course, this was not how he put it to the Peloponnesians. To them, instead of singling out the Spartans, he voiced his fear that the three most powerful cities in the anti-Persian alliance, Athens, Sparta and Corinth would dominate small states and try to carve up the Greek world for themselves.[20]

Not that Themistocles always followed his own strategy. When the Ionians invited Aristides and Cimon to lead them, neither felt any inclination to involve Themistocles, but this did not halt his ambitions. Around the time that Cimon was laying siege to Eion or repatriating the lost bones of Theseus, Themistocles himself may have campaigned against Carystus in south-east Euboea. The city had declared for Xerxes, and, although after Salamis it gave in to Themistocles' demands for money and subsequently dedicated a bronze bull at Delphi to celebrate Greek victory, its loyalty was questionable—which for Athenians was unacceptable since (like Scyros) its location held great strategic value, controlling shipping lanes from Ionia, the Hellespont and Thrace. It was crucial that these be secured. The operation involved only Athens— perhaps the League's fleet was elsewhere or Athens did not want League members fighting on Euboea. The sources are too scanty to tell. They speak only of a battle fought, a prominent Athenian cut down, his body buried where he fell—even how the campaign ended is unknown but, if Themistocles indeed was general, his absence from the record is significant.[21]

For Themistocles, the threat posed by Persia palled beside the dangers that he saw (despite her blandishments) in anti-democratic Sparta, and his lack of real enthusiasm for pursuing the Persian campaigns may have led him to be sidelined. Besides, the People were already tiring of his boasting how it was his stratagems alone that won the war, and many longed to see his downfall—not least Cimon. Politically and ethically his polar opposite, Cimon did all he could to undermine the radical Themistocles, joining fellow aristocrats such as Alcmaeon, family head of the Alcmaeonids, to attack him in the courts and the Assembly. Meanwhile, accusing Cimon of being a Spartan lackey, successful only thanks to Spartan backing, Themistocles reminded his power base, the city poor, that Cimon was a member of the social elite. Did the elite not favour oligarchic government like Sparta's? Was Cimon's wish for equal partnership between Athenians and Spartans not proof that he supported Sparta at least as much as Athens? Was this not actually why Sparta acquiesced so readily to Cimon's taking over the command of the alliance from their own Pausanias? Clearly Cimon was a Spartan agent. Clearly he was in Sparta's pay. Clearly the People could and should not trust him. Baseless though they were, such arguments might have gained traction had it not been for Themistocles' own moral failings, since if anyone could rightly be accused of bribery, extortion or corruption it was he. 'A clever man but powerless over his light fingers', he was said to betray even friends for money, among them the poet, Timocreon, exiled for pro-Persian affiliations. In excoriating verses, Timocreon invoked the goddess Leto who

> hates Themistocles—
> liar, criminal, and traitor—who, though he was his friend,
> was coaxed by sleazy bribes not to restore Timocreon
> to his home city of Ialysus. Instead he pocketed

three silver talents, then sailed away—to hell!
Glutted with silver he brought back some men
who did not deserve it, but others he banished,
and others still he killed.[22]

Aristides had already tried to warn Themistocles. Discussing generalship, while Themistocles maintained that the most important quality of
all was the ability to anticipate enemy strategy, Aristides suggested in response that, while that was, indeed, crucial, 'the best thing and the real
sign of a good general is control over his own light fingers.'[23]

In fact, while Themistocles had famously anticipated—and, indeed,
manipulated—Xerxes' strategy at Salamis, it was his inability to see the
consequences of his own behaviour now that in part led to his downfall.
As accusation met counter-accusation in the struggle to control and
shape Athenian political identity, Themistocles could not resist re-
hearsing his achievements. Time and again he cited Salamis, and his
brilliant deception of the Great King, thanks to which, he said, the
Greeks defeated Persia. Yet as years rolled on and Salamis became a
memory, as tragedies were staged in which it was the People as a whole
and not their nameless generals who had driven out the enemy, indeed
as Cimon led them in a string of victories that (while they still remembered past success with pride) caused them to gaze towards the prospect of a glorious future, Themistocles' insistence on his role as Greece's
saviour irritated even his most fervent followers. Each time he bleated
with increasing tetchiness, accusing Athens of capriciousness, berating
his power base, the People, asking why they were now bored of him
though he always treated them so well, a little of his lustre faded and,
whereas previously his devotees had turned a blind eye to his self-
importance and rapacity, now they began to question it.

Now even his public works came in for scrutiny and disapproval:
although no-one could fault him for rebuilding an initiation hall belonging to his family at Phlya a few miles north-west of Athens, his construction of a temple near his town house in the urban district of Melite
was a different matter altogether. While there was nothing contentious
in his dedicating it to Artemis, goddess of Artemisium where the fleet
first proved its mettle, the specific form in which he chose to worship
her proved deeply controversial. He named her Artemis Aristoboule,
Artemis Who Gives the Best Advice and, while Themistocles could argue

that the temple was a pious offering of thanks, a recognition that he owed his strategy at Salamis to the goddess, many saw it as another instance of his self-aggrandizement—especially since it housed a statue bearing an uncanny likeness to Themistocles himself; especially, moreover, when they compared it to Cimon's Temple of Theseus. For, whereas this paid honour to a national hero, a god's son, a saviour king who prized democracy, Themistocles' building (like Pausanias' inscription on Delphi's Serpent Column) seemed to glorify not just a living man but one who clearly thought that he alone had won the Persian Wars, in gratitude for which the People should bow down and follow him. Taken in conjunction with the memory of his Olympic tent, a cousin of the Great King's tent taken at Plataea, such behaviour smacked of tyranny. It called for a vote of ostracism.[24]

So eight years after Salamis, a decade after he himself had used the vote to banish Aristides, Themistocles found himself with just two months to turn the growing tide. He must have known the challenge was nigh-on impossible. For five years he had relished these late winter weeks, goading the People's jealousy and animosity towards whichever member of the upper classes he had chosen as his victim for that year, unleashing them like a pack of baying hunting hounds chasing a tiring deer. Now he was the People's quarry. Now, despite all that he had done for them, his once-adoring followers had turned on him. No matter that he built the fleet, it was Cimon who was leading it to victory; no matter that his brilliance had won out at Salamis, it was Cimon who was triumphing against the Persians; no matter that he championed the city poor, it was Cimon who was fuelling their belief in a new golden age. As the first sherds clattered into voting urns, Themistocles must have known the game was up. Perhaps he recalled his father's warning as he pointed out the hulks of decommissioned warships left on the shore to rot; perhaps he wondered if he should not simply have taken his father's advice; or perhaps he was already looking to the future and his journey south to Argos, a city he had championed, where he knew he could expect a friendly welcome, hospitality for ten years of exile, after which he would return to Athens. Once more, however, the arch-strategist was wrong; for it would not be long before he found himself embroiled in scandal of such magnitude that not even his quick wits and calculation could survive.[25]

The scandal involved another great war hero, Pausanias, still in Asia Minor, still living an un-Spartan life of rakish hedonism, and still (it was alleged) exchanging billets-doux with Xerxes. The ephors had had enough. They recalled him to Sparta and imprisoned him. But without concrete evidence they could not detain him. Instead, compelled to set him free, they played a waiting game. Back in the shadow of Taygetus, forced to bolt down black broth, Pausanias, his mind turned by the flesh-pots of the Troad, was clearly far from happy. Moreover, his demeanour, haughty even for a Spartan, suggested an unnatural desire for power. Spartans, when they spoke at all, voiced fears that he was plotting with the helots to overthrow the government, but although they tortured sus-pect helots into giving evidence against him they still lacked solid proof. At last the breakthrough came. Pausanias asked one of his most loyal friends to smuggle out a letter to the Great King. But his friend was anxious. In the past he had seen others tasked with taking corre-spondence from Pausanias to Xerxes, but not one of them returned. So before setting out he broke the letter open, read it and discovered at the end the grim instruction: kill the man who brought this. But still the ephors needed further proof. So they told his friend to meet him at Tae-narum, at the tip of the long promontory where Mount Taygetus meets the sea, close to a cave were tunnels were reputed to lead down to the ghostly Underworld. Here at the Temple of Poseidon, faced with the let-ter's evidence, Pausanias professed his deep remorse. His actions, he agreed, were indefensible—not only since the two had once been lovers, but because his friend, who knew about his dealings with the king, had never once betrayed him. Now, though, there was no time to lose. His friend would not be harmed, he gave his word on that, but it was still imperative he take the letter with all haste to Persia.[26]

Unbeknownst to Pausanias a group of ephors had concealed them-selves in an adjoining room, and in Sparta they ordered his arrest. Pau-sanias would not surrender willingly. As they approached him, he sensed danger, and in an instant he had taken to his heels, racing through the lanes until he reached the low acropolis with its Temple of Athena Po-lias, known as the House of Bronze from intricately-wrought bronze plaques displaying scenes from myth that hung on its inner walls. Here he took refuge in a tiny room, but still he was not safe. Securing the doors and posting guards around the temple, the ephors cut an opening in the roof and watched him grow ever weaker without food or water until he was delirious. Perhaps in these last painful days Pausanias recalled his visit to Heracleia on the Black Sea's southern shores, where at the necromantic oracle he summoned up the ghost of Cleonice, the Byzantine girl whom he had ordered to attend his bed but killed when she toppled a lamp in the darkness. As her spirit materialized, cold and implacable, her beauty still preserved in death, Pausanias begged forgiveness for what had been, he swore, an accident. At the time Cleonice's answer seemed to offer hope: in an otherworldly voice she said that all his troubles would be ended when he returned to Sparta. It was only now that Pausanias appreciated her oracular ambiguity. His troubles would end only with his death. But he must not die in the temple. To do so would pollute the goddess. So with little time still left, the ephors (pious to a fault) unbarred the doors and dragged him out before he could expire on sacred ground. Then, his corpse still warm, they went through his belongings.[27]

They found a dossier of documents including (as might be expected from such an avid letter writer) a cache of correspondence with Themistocles. The two were old friends. It was only natural that they should write to one another. But the letters' contents were incendiary: they showed beyond doubt that the Athenian knew all about Pausanias' plots with Persia. Indeed, they made it clear that, immediately Themistocles was ostracized, Pausanias approached him with a proposition: join in his negotiations with the Great King; help him bring Greece under Persian control; support him in exacting retribution on the Greeks for showing Pausanias and Themistocles, their saviours, such scant gratitude. The ephors dispatched messengers to Athens, where leading families heard their evidence with glee: through ostracism they had neutralized Themistocles for ten years; now they could destroy him forever. So with Leobotes, son of Cimon's ally Alcmaeon, appointed as chief prosecutor, they announced his trial. In Argos, Themistocles received the news with consternation. Barred from returning home he could not defend himself in person. But he could still set out his case. Using the medium by which he stood accused, he could write a letter to be read out in court, an impassioned statement of his innocence. For, while he admitted that Pausanias invited him to join in the conspiracy, he, Themistocles, had been so horrified that he refused point blank to be involved. He would never betray Greece to Persia. Even his worst enemies must accept that. Had he not shown how much he hated autocrats? Had he not incited Greek spectators at Olympia to destroy a tyrant's tent and bar him from competing in the Games? Had he not more than anyone withstood the power of Xerxes? So why would he willingly submit to him now? And if he failed to report Pausanias to the authorities, it was because he thought that they would find out anyway, since he was certain that Pausanias would either see the error of his ways and abandon his ambitions or be so careless that he would give himself away. Themistocles' one crime (if crime it really were) lay in not betraying a friend, and such a virtue did not merit punishment.[28]

Yet, with Leobotes' accusations ringing in their ears, such arguments read out in court made little impact on the jurors. There was just one sentence they could pass. Themistocles must die. Now all they had to do was find him. But already, friends had boxed up his gold and sped in a swift ship to Argos, while others smuggled his wife and children out of Athens. It would not be long before some of those responsible were executed, others exiled, all outlawed or condemned on Cimon's instigation. But for now, when a delegation of Athenians and Spartans arrived in Argos with warrants for Themistocles' arrest, they found he had already fled, loath to involve his hosts in awkward politicking. For, while Argives were his friends and while it was chiefly through his efforts that they had ceased being international pariahs, to harbour a convicted Persian collaborator would do nothing for their reputation as good patriotic Greeks. Much safer he should go. In time they heard that he had reached Corcyra, the one western ally that had promised to send ships to Salamis (though in the end none came), an island with which Themistocles (who had once settled a dispute with Corinth in their favour) enjoyed warm relations. But by the time the Spartans and Athenians arrived, he was long gone—across the straits, deep into Epirus and the jagged mountain kingdom of Molossia. And then he vanished.[29]

In Athens Themistocles' conviction left his supporters stunned. Frightened of being thought guilty by association, radical democrats—men such as Pericles—now easy targets for abuse, steered clear of trouble, lying low, while patrician rivals paraded their determination to humiliate the Persians. Although most of the Aegean had been persuaded or coerced to swear oaths of loyalty to Athens, much of its eastern shores remained in Persian hands; not only were important shipping lanes still vulnerable to attack, it was entirely possible that the Great King might be tempted to launch more attacks on mainland Greece. Indeed, there was already worrying intelligence from Rhodes of Persian troop deployments and the preparation of a fleet suggesting fresh invasion plans timed (as before) to coincide with the Olympic Games. With no guarantee that mainland states would rally behind Athens or advance beyond the Isthmus, it was vital that the enemy was stopped before they sailed, but to contain them would mean meeting them in Asia, which in turn meant opening a new front in the war. So, while previous strategy (essentially accomplished) involved reclaiming and protecting lost Greek lands, the theatre of war would now switch to those non-Greek Persian territories on the west and southern coasts of Asia Minor. There would be a major new offensive. And Cimon would command it, the League's most successful general, so popular his troops would follow anywhere he led. But, as the fleet was mustering, news came that threatened not just the viability of the campaign but the stability of Athens. One of her most important allies had revolted. Naxos was in meltdown.[30]

9

'I AM EURYMEDON'

All these are Persian possessions,
but the Persians themselves have long ago departed.

Phrynichus, *Phoenician Women*, fr. 8 (*TrGF* 1.3)

NAXOS, 468 B.C.

In recent years, Naxos' fortunes had fluctuated wildly. The largest and most fertile island in the Cyclades, its quarries an abundant source of emery and high-grade marble, it had once been spectacularly rich, the centre of a nexus of dependencies, a vibrant trading hub, whose sun-drenched hills and sandy coasts were home to wealthy sanctuaries and temples that proclaimed close bonds with the divine: with Zeus, worshipped deep in a cave near the summit of the highest mountain; with Demeter, whose temple built entirely out of marble nestled in a fecund valley; with Dionysus, honoured on an islet near the busy port, where once the god was said to have discovered sleeping Ariadne, the Cretan princess thanks to whose aid Theseus had slain the Minotaur and liberated Athens. Elsewhere, too, monuments funded, made and dedicated by Naxians proclaimed the island's wealth and piety: on Delos an impressive colonnade of marble lionesses that crouched like sentinels above Apollo's sacred lake; a cool, echoing hall adorned with a fine marble porch; a towering marble statue of the god, thirty feet tall, standing proud before his temple; while at Apollo's Delphic sanctuary an eight-foot marble sphinx perched high atop a thirty-foot-tall column, her lioness body echoing the bodies of the lionesses of Delos, huge wings curving from her feathered shoulders, her woman's features frozen in an enigmatic smile as elaborately plaited hair caressed her hybrid back.

An early colonizer, Naxos seeded cities on Amorgos to the east (a useful stepping stone to rich Ionian markets) and prosperous Sicily, where the first Greek outpost bore the island's name. But rival families came to blows, and in the turmoil of civil conflict one of their most powerful leaders, Lygdamis, installed himself as tyrannus. He had an influential ally in Peisistratus of Athens and, although he was subsequently overthrown, Athenians preserved close ties with Naxos. Both formed proto-democracies. Both did all they could to fend off Persian attack, but while Naxos withstood the four-month siege, brainchild of Ionian Aristagoras, it stood no chance when Datis unleashed Persian vengeance on his way to Marathon. Ransacked, fire-blackened, most of its people slaughtered or enslaved, the heady days of Naxos' prosperity were over and, although ten years later they had recovered sufficiently to send four ships to fight for Greece at Salamis, the islanders were more than ready to bow to Athens' leadership and join the Allied League. Now, though, with the prospect of fresh Persian wars darkening the eastern horizon, they were less confident. Sailing for mainland Greece, a fresh Persian fleet inevitably would pass by Naxos; the island had already felt the force of Persian wrath; it was only now recovering; it did not want to suffer once again, especially as this time surely Persia would win. Better to withdraw from Athens' League while the going was good. Better cleverly to claim that, now that Greeks so clearly ruled the sea, there was no more need for the alliance or for the hefty taxes paid into its coffers. Better to be relatively safe than ruinously sorry. So they announced their decision: they would exit the alliance.[1]

The revolt—for such it was (the mutual oaths of alliance had been sworn 'forever')—was for Athens worrying in the extreme, not merely for its own sake but for the impact it could have on any other allies considering their own commitment to the League: while the Persian threat was distant, their annual contributions seemed inordinately high; now that a fresh invasion appeared imminent, the price the Persians might make them pay for allying with Athens could prove considerably higher. And who could tell that Naxos' rebellion was not part of some well-orchestrated Persian plot, coordinated from the court at Susa with fifth columnists on the island? Who could tell whether other allied states were not rife with collaborators plotting other insurrections of their own?

Who could tell whether the whole Allied League and the fragile peace that it had won were not on the verge of implosion? It was essential to bring Naxos back into line—urgently, unequivocally, at almost any cost. But equally, the Naxian rebellion must not be allowed to draw focus from the looming danger posed by Persia's fleet and army gathering in south-west Asia Minor with apparently one purpose: a fresh invasion of Greece.

So, resources must be split, and while Cimon, commanding the crucial Persian expedition, prepared to set out east, a relatively small detachment of the fleet risked the still choppy waters of an early spring and sped off to blockade Naxos. In preceding months Piraeus had been witness to a frenzy of activity. Knowing that he was likely to be faced with fighting on both land and sea, Cimon had been turning his attention to increasing his triremes' capabilities, refitting them to double as troop carriers, with the result that—while previously a narrow walkway ran down the middle from prow to stern—widened, the entire hull was decked across, allowing each ship to transport several dozen hoplites. The drawback was that conditions for the oarsmen, most of them confined to their dark, airless, noisome rowing benches, were even more unpleasant than before. Yet the stakes were so high and the determination to prevent Persian ships from reaching Greece so great that, come the appointed day, the quayside at Piraeus was packed once more with men eager to report for duty. As they embarked, the captain of each trireme led hymns and prayers and offered a libation to Poseidon, the sea god, pouring wine from sacred vessels into harbour waters. And then a trumpet blared from Cimon's flagship, the signal for departure, and one by one the warships put to sea, their helmsmen leaning on the steering oars to turn them east along the coast past Sunium and out into the broad Aegean.[2]

Their course took them past Naxos in a show of strength that did much to contribute to the islanders' capitulation, and where, if Cimon asked for a debriefing from the general in charge of the blockade, he might have heard how, when a sudden storm blew up, Athenians had seen a merchant ship, waves crashing white across its bows, lumbering through lashing rain towards the safety of the harbour until, quite suddenly, it turned and headed back into the heaving swell. But it was only later that they learned the reason for its captain's almost suicidal change of course: a passenger had bribed him handsomely, a passenger who would prefer to risk his life at sea than fall into the hands of the Athenians: the fugitive Themistocles en route from mainland Greece; the exile riding out the storm until he could make landfall on the Asia Minor coast, where with his faithful retinue he took the road inland to fertile Aegae, its hills loud with a symphony of goats' bells, before (disguised as a Persian woman, his face veiled, riding in a carriage) the architect of Salamis struck east for Susa and the court of Xerxes, where, learning the Persian language, he offered oaths of loyalty to his erstwhile enemy. Perhaps he claimed that he had been favouring the Great King all along, that his ruse at Salamis had been a genuine attempt to undermine the Greeks, that it was really he (as he once claimed) who had restrained the allies when they wanted to destroy the bridges over the Hellespont, that he really was his friend. Whether he believed him or was simply amused by his audacity, the Great King rewarded him with gifts of lands and cities—as Darius had rewarded Metiochus, Cimon's elder brother, years before.[3]

Now across much calmer seas Cimon too scudded east, his destination the long, slim, partly mountainous peninsula—the so-called Dorian Peninsula—that forms the far side of a yawning turquoise bay south of now friendly Halicarnassus. Having surrendered to the Persians under Harpagus two generations earlier, the peninsula's main city, Cnidus, with close ties to Megara and Sparta, now made it clear that it was keen to flaunt its Greek credentials and more than willing for its own and local harbours to be used as bases for the allied fleet—which was just as well, for when they converged on the peninsula (200 Athenian triremes, 100 allied ships) they found that no single port was large enough to take them. In newly friendly waters this presented few problems, and Cimon was aware that he should bide his time. Intelligence from the south coast suggested that the Persian troops were mustering in Pamphylia some 250 miles west by sea outside the city of Aspendus, with a fleet of ships from Phoenicia, Cilicia and Cyprus due to assemble by the mouth of the nearby River Eurymedon. Commanding them was one of Xerxes' sons, Tithraustes, and with him Pherendates, the Great King's nephew, their presence proof of Persia's seriousness of purpose. But they seemed to be in little hurry, and Cimon undoubtedly knew why. Once more the Persians had chosen an Olympic year, calculating that (as twelve years previously) pious Greeks would find their loyalties divided between observing an important festival and opposing the invaders. Moreover,

August, as Persians also knew, was the month of the Spartan Carneia, whose observation had prevented the Identicals from marching north to Marathon. It seemed likely, then, that the invasion had been planned for August, and that its main goal would be Athens. If so, success was predicated, too, on Persian sympathizers working within the League, men who would foment rebellion, depriving Athens of her allies, even as Naxos had rebelled already. But there was another crucial consideration. With Cimon and the bulk of the League's triremes based at Cnidus, Athens was exposed. A fleet-footed change of plans could see Tithraustes and his ships race west, with Cimon scrambling to catch them before they reached the city. Timing was crucial. Too soon, before they had all their pieces in place, and the Athenians could be outflanked. Too late, and they risked losing everything. The stakes could not be higher.[4]

As he waited for his triremes to assemble, Cimon was far from idle. The Dorian Peninsula could be relied on, but many mainland cities were still in Persian hands, while settlements that lay towards the Persian muster-station near the mouth of the Eurymedon beyond the pale blue mountain peaks of Lycia were a largely unknown quantity. Strategic considerations dictated that before he could attack the Persian fleet and army Cimon must secure his rear. So while incoming allied vessels were directed into port to undergo the refits that would bring them into line with Athens' ships, Cimon toured Caria, turning his easy charm on its Greek settlers as he coaxed them to renounce all vestiges of their allegiance with the Great King, while unleashing the full force of his destructive power on cities that housed hostile garrisons until, through a persuasive combination of force and charismatic wile, he had purged coastal Caria of Persian influence. Only then, already past midsummer, did he give the order to sail.

Keeping the imposing Taurus mountains to the port side, his fleet made its commanding progress east past Lycia, receiving delegations from a string of wealthy cities (including now-repopulated Xanthus), whose rulers had already been approached by Cimon's diplomats, and who now proclaimed their friendship and provided food and much-needed supplies. Past stretching sandy beaches and well-watered valleys, past rocky inlets and bustling seaside cities they sailed on, until, rounding the rocky Islands of the Swallows, the Chelidonian Isles, the coast turned north to where, at night, unworldly flames were seen to flicker eerily above a hilltop, the fiery breath (so legend told) of the

Chimaera, that part-lion, part-goat, part-snake monster of supernatural strength, defeated by the legendary Greek Bellerophon and penned forever in the Underworld. For many in the fleet it must have seemed an omen, for theirs too was a heroic quest: to seek out an enemy at least as dangerous as the Chimaera, a hybrid formed from all the peoples of the east, a behemoth that threatened their existence. And like Bellerophon they were committed to destroy it.[5]

Yet when they came to Phaselis, a city founded by Rhodians on a stubby promontory backed by furrowed mountains, the allies met a hostile welcome. As an important entrepôt protected by the Great King, Phaselis with several small harbours and a breezy climate had for years enjoyed prosperity, building profitable trading partnerships with not just local Greeks and Lycians but Persians themselves and their dependencies on Cyprus and Egypt, adopting Persian currency to tie itself still closer to the Persian economy. Now, within well-built walls, its citizens had little reason to accede to Cimon's threatening demands that they switch sides. Instead, like the Naxians, anticipating Athens' imminent destruction at the hands of Persia, it made more sense to sit it out, endure a siege and hope that events would intervene to end it. But for Cimon waiting was not an option. He led his hoplites in an orgy of destruction through the local countryside, destroying trees, uprooting vineyards, setting fire to homes and farmsteads, while from ships and shore his men did all they could to find a means of entry. With frustrations rising and the growing likelihood of wholesale slaughter should the city fall, crewmen and captains from Cimon's Chiote allies who had close friends in Phaselis did all they could to stay his hand. At the same time, they wrote letters, which they tied to arrows and shot over the walls, advising swift surrender. At last, worn down by hunger and Athenian determination, Phaselis capitulated, and in return for leniency agreed to join the League, pay 10 talents there and then (a hefty sum), add their fleet to that of the alliance and sail with it to the Eurymedon. For with the moon already waxing, they no longer had any time to lose. In days the Persian expedition would be underway. All that stood between it and Athens, protecting the city from flames and her citizens from slavery, were Cimon and his ships and men. The time had come to crush the Great King's Persian fleet and neutralize his army. Or to die in the attempt.[6]

A trumpet call at sunrise; triremes backing out to sea; sails hoisted and oars shipped, the slap of waves on prow; the scraping purr of timber; salt breeze on cheeks, in hair; mountains—majestic—gliding past the port bow, before the coastline dog-legged east once more and flat plains shelved towards the shore, and evening came; and bivouacs on the beach; and any sleep a man could get, because tomorrow he would fight the Persians. Next day, the trumpet call again; sunrise behind the mountains and the sea an azure blue; no sails; no masts; anything extraneous that might weigh down a trireme or become dislodged offloaded, left behind, as oarsmen took their places and hoplites, fully armoured now, the gold sun flashing off their shields and spear points, stood side by side with archers on the decks; and 300 ships, 300 bronze rams, 300 pairs of marble, staring eyes stole east along the shoreline; and more than 50,000 oars in rhythm feathered the morning sea.

And so they came to the Eurymedon with its wide mouth and green sluggish waters and the shoreline invisible behind the black ships anchored there. The Persians knew the Greeks were coming, and for now they were unwilling to engage—especially since they themselves awaited reinforcements: eighty Phoenician triremes on their way from Cyprus, the cream of Xerxes' fleet with whose help they would surely smash the allies' ships and win revenge for Salamis. But Cimon did not have the luxury of time. Fighting close to shore meant danger, but delay would be more dangerous still. So he commanded his most trusted captains to row towards the beach close to the river mouth, and as archers fired salvos and hoplites threw spears and Persians realized that they made easy pickings, Tithraustes bowed to the inevitable and gave the word to push off from the shore. Now Cimon's ships backed water—back into the open sea, their natural element, joining the rest of the League's fleet that even now was arced around the river mouth like a gigantic net. And as the Persian ships spilled out, first one and then another—no time, no space for any rational formation—the Greek ships pounced and Greek rams tore through Persian hulls. Some of Tithraustes' vessels tried to break through the blockade, but they were chased and holed, their crews killed as they tried to swim to safety. As for the rest, they soon lost heart; their helmsmen turned to shore where, beached, their crews leapt out and ran for friendly Persian lines, since now the army had been mobilized and was drawn up beyond the beach, helpless to influence the outcome of the naval battle, ready to cut down any Greek who might be forced to swim ashore.[7]

But Cimon and his men were far from finished. Triumphant, with adrenaline still pounding and convinced they were invincible, they hungered to engage the Persian land troops, too. The risks were high. Defeat could wipe out the advantage of their victory at sea, while victory on land would deal a crushing blow to Persian ambitions. There was only one man who could decide how to proceed—Cimon—and there was no time for reflection. So, seeing how eager his men were, and knowing from Marathon and other Greek encounters with the Persians how the unexpected could so often tip the balance in the allies' favour, he ordered his trumpeter to sound the attack. Now League triremes were shooting in to shore and now they, too, were beached; now hoplites leapt onto the sand, as archers clattered down behind them, the oarsmen pouring out from rowing benches, seizing anything that they could find that might serve as a weapon; and so with Cimon, sword drawn, at their head, they thundered up the foreshore, bawling their paean battle hymns and bellowing their war cries, as the Greek wall smashed against the Persians' wicker shields and the ritual of butchery began: swords flashing, bodies slashed, blood blossoming from torn necks, chests and arms; the wounded trampled; the dead half-buried in the oozing mud and mire; the green Eurymedon turned red; while all the time the sun beat down on aching arms and knees that shook with tiredness. As long as they had any hope of winning, the Persians held out, but then—as happens on the battlefield—the comprehension flooded over them that they could not prevail, their spirit left them, and they turned and ran. And the triumphant Greeks pursued them. Then, as those Persians fortunate or fast enough to get away streamed up into the low, tree-studded hills above Aspendus, and their less lucky comrades were corralled and led off under guard soon to be either sold as slaves or ransomed, the victorious allies poured through the gathering dusk back into the abandoned camp to loot and plunder.[8]

Yet still Cimon could not relax. The Phoenician fleet—eighty deadly triremes, stationed previously on Cyprus—was expected imminently. It was vital that they should not find the allies unprepared. Better to intercept them before they even reached the mouth of the Eurymedon. Better still, if they had yet to hear the news of Persia's defeat. So next day as dawn was breaking, Cimon manned the captured Persian ships with his own crews and put to sea once more, his helmsmen setting course south-east, hugging the flat shoreline, as golden sunlight danced and sparkled in the foam that ruffled far behind them. Their destination was Syedra, just forty miles away, an ancient naval base protected by a citadel perched on a wooded hill that towered 1,000 feet or more above it. Surprise was everything, and Cimon was prepared. Not only was he usi g Persian ships, he had kitted out his men in Persian costume looted from the camp, so, as they scudded into view, oars raised in friendly greeting, the Phoenicians, embarked and ready to be off, had no cause for suspicion—until, sails quickly furled, oars beating now in deadly rhythm, the first of Cimon's triremes crashed into their hulls, and easy relaxation turned to terror. The enemy had little chance. Caught unawares, most crews and captains panicked. Those who did not were easily cut down, their warships holed and foundering. Almost before it had begun, the battle was all over: more captives bound and shackled, more triremes taken, lashed and towed back to the allies at the Eurymedon, the last sad remnants of the Persian fleet. It was the coping stone of Cimon's glittering campaign, and though for now the jubilation gripping his triumphant troops must have been all-consuming, its impact would be felt for many years to come.[9]

First, though, to divide the spoils. Along with 340 captured ships there were vast quantities of booty from the enemy encampment, since the Persians had brought not only personal wealth (adornments such as jewellery and bracelets) but those necessities of court life (gold and silver goblets, tables, couches, carpets, tapestries) that none of the royal representatives could do without—not to mention heavy crates of coinage, cash to pay troops and bribe enemies. And then there were the captives, around 20,000 men, themselves a potentially rich source of revenue. For although Xerxes' nephew, Pherendates, was killed in battle, there were many high-born Persians among the prisoners of war, and as Cimon knew from long experience, their families would give almost anything to ransom them, while anyone whose relatives could not afford the cost would be auctioned for the best price in slave markets. So on the banks of the Eurymedon, what started as a military campaign turned into a hard-headed business venture with tents stripped, bodies plundered and booty heaped in piles, some to be shared among the victors (with a substantial portion going to Cimon, the victorious general), most to be shipped to Athens or the treasury on Delos. So when the fleet did sail away they left little in their wake save churned-up, blood-streaked sand and smouldering pyres where corpses of Athenian and allied dead had

burned, leaving only ashes to be packed in urns, in the case of the
Athenians one for each tribe, and taken home and laid to rest with eu-
logies and solemn ceremony in Athens' public cemetery on the road
towards the Grove of Academus.[10]

Throughout the Greek world news of the Battle of Eurymedon was
met with celebration. In Athens, where men started naming sons Eurymedon, one vase painter commemorated victory in style: on one side of a
wine flask he showed a Greek, nude save for a short cloak, advancing
purposefully, left arm outstretched, his right hand clutching his erect
(if diminutive) phallus; on the other he painted a Persian, immediately
recognizable by his headgear, spotted body-suit and trousers, his quiver
empty of all arrows, his hands thrown up beside his face in a gesture of
terror or surrender, his stooping body turned away, his bottom facing
the approaching Greek; and in between the two, the words: 'I am Eurymedon. I stand bent over'. For Athenians familiar (as many were) with
sodomy the message was riotously clear: the Persians were well and truly
buggered.[11]

As for the architect of victory, Cimon was fêted with almost universal
praise. 'Like a formidable athlete' on one day he had won a double
victory—on land and sea—a feat unparalleled in history or legend, and
so removed all threat not just of imminent invasion but (now that the
Naxian rebellion was crushed and the town's walls torn down) of revolt
within the League. Even disgruntled aristocrats, who previously thought
Athens' leadership and her democracy to be vainglorious and venal and
yearned for Persia to liberate them, knew the game was up. There was
no longer any doubt who ruled the waves—and the western coast of Asia
Minor, too: even if he had the ships, the Great King would not dare to
sail beyond the Islands of the Swallows into what were clearly now Athenian waters. So, those islands, little more than rocks cascading out to
sea from the south-west tip of Lycia, came to mark the boundaries of
Persian rule and Athenian control; and whether the arrangement was
ratified in an agreement or simply understood, for the first time in over
thirty years, Ionian and mainland Greeks could sleep safe at night, free
for now from the fear of Persian attack. The wars begun with Miltiades'
victory at Marathon had been ended (if not forever, then at least for the
foreseeable future) by the double triumph of his son, Cimon, at the
Eurymedon. So, lionized throughout Greece for fairness, bravery and
military expertise, Cimon was determined not just to mark his own suc-

Created in the aftermath of victory, the 'Eurymedon Vase' (460s B.C.) shows a triumphant if diminutive Greek approaching a submissive Persian and bears the inscription: 'I am Eurymedon. I stand bent over.'

cess in style but, seizing the moment, to honour his father's memory in every way he could—not least at Delphi.[12]

For generations Greeks had used Delphi as a stage on which to vaunt victory and flaunt wealth, but no city had exploited its potential more than Athens. From the Stoa erected after Xanthippus' victories at Mycale and the Hellespont to the Treasury rebuilt after Marathon and the Temple of Apollo itself, completed through Alcmaeonid largesse, a cluster of impressive structures boasted Athens' power. Now Cimon won the blessing of his fellow citizens and Delphic priests to dedicate a group of statues close to a huge bronze horse (said to represent the wooden horse of Troy, that potent symbol of an earlier conflict with the East) at the entrance to the sanctuary, the first thing anyone would see as they approached the temple. Commissioned from Pheidias, a rising young Athenian sculptor, the bronze group comprised sixteen individual statues. Ten represented Athens' tribal heroes, embodiments of Athens' citizens; beside them in another group stood Athens' last king, Codrus, and two men who had played a crucial role in Cimon's own experience: Philaeus, founding father of his family, the Philaids; and Theseus, whose bones Cimon repatriated, whose temple he built, and whom he championed as the incarnation of Athenian virtues. But it was the third group that spoke most clearly to Cimon's personal involvement with the monument: three figures—two deities, Apollo, presiding god of Delphi, and Athena, patron and protectress of Athens; and one mortal, Miltiades, Cimon's father, victor of Marathon, elevated now to take his place beside the gods and heroes of antiquity. Moreover, to remove all ambiguity, his name (like those of his fifteen companions) was carved into the plinth beneath him, while an inscription on the platform on which the statues stood proclaimed that the monument was funded from a tithe of booty won at Marathon. To include Miltiades in such company was not just bold but revolutionary, a visual statement so unconventional as to be almost blasphemous. Not only did it single out one individual for praise—not some anonymous 'Greek man from the Athenian army' as Aeschylus called Themistocles in *Persians*— here at Delphi's Panhellenic sanctuary, just over twenty years after his painful death in a sordid, squalid prison cell in Athens, Miltiades was being hailed as victor, saviour, equal to the gods. More startling still, by singling out Marathon the memorial prioritized it as the key battle of the Persian Wars. And why? Conveniently sidelining Plataea's contribution, it pronounced that Marathon was Athens' victory alone; and since Eurymedon belonged to Athens, too, the statues' viewers could draw only one conclusion: Athens, not Sparta, was responsible for Persia's defeat, Athens, the preeminent Greek state, the leader of free Greeks, the rightful head of empire, under first Miltiades, and now his son, Cimon.[13]

To mark Cimon's own victory at Eurymedon Athenians set up another glittering memorial, this time outside Delphi's Temple of Apollo: a tall bronze palm tree in whose branches sat a gold 'Palladium', a copy of Athens' ancient olive-wood statue of Athena to which Cimon had once dedicated his bridle. The palm tree was itself a copy—of the tree on Delos to which Leto clung as she gave birth to Apollo. It was, therefore, not simply a fitting gift to the archer god, it was a strong political statement: for aside from being Apollo's birthplace, Delos was the spiritual, financial and administrative heart of the League of Athens and her Allies, and it was that League—not the old confederacy led by Sparta— that at Eurymedon put paid to Persia's plans. The power balance had shifted, the palm tree proclaimed; the world belonged to Athens and her allies; and if such blatant propaganda made Cimon uneasy, yearning still for harmony between his city and the Spartans, he could perhaps console himself that even with friends it is better to negotiate from a position of strength.[14]

Near Delphi's palm tree, further artwork suggested the burgeoning self-confidence of Athens and the Ionians. Enriched by booty from Eurymedon and emboldened by their role in the campaign, the citizens of Cnidus paid for an elegant new building on the slope above the Altar of Apollo. Just over sixty feet long and thirty wide, the Cnidian Lesche (Dining Hall), like the Temple of Apollo sited on an east–west axis, contained two internal rows of wooden columns supporting a clerestory through which Delphi's pure light flooded to illuminate paintings by Polygnotus of Thasos, the greatest artist of his day, on both of its long walls, depicting two scenes from the myth of Troy: the city's capture and Odysseus' visit to the Underworld. While the latter showed a cornucopia of characters—Odysseus himself; ghosts of warriors; doomed singers such as Orpheus; evildoers undergoing horrendous punishments—it favoured specifically Athenian or Ionian protagonists: Phrontis, Menelaus' drowned helmsman, honoured with a hero shrine at Sunium; Phaedra, Theseus' doomed wife, and her sister, Ariadne; and Theseus himself enthroned (albeit against his will), one of the few seated characters in the whole composition. Polygnotus' painting of the sack of Troy particularly encapsulated the zeitgeist, for by now the notion that the Persian Wars were somehow a replaying of the Trojan War was almost universally accepted, though with a crucial difference. Whereas Athenians had played a minor role at Troy, subordinate to Argive Agamemnon and Spartan Menelaus, in the Persian Wars—as their own fast-evolving narrative (of which the Cnidian Lesche was part) proclaimed—they and the Ionians played so prominent a role that it might seem that victory belonged to them alone: (downplaying Plataea's role) it was Athenians who drove the Persian troops from Marathon; who (downplaying the role of Sparta's admiral and the rest of the Greek fleet) smashed the Great King's ships at Salamis; and who, under Cimon, brought the war to its triumphant end, annihilating Persia's fleet and army by the banks of the Eurymedon—with help, of course, from Cnidians, by whom the paintings were commissioned.[15]

In Athens, too, artworks linked victories over Troy and Persia, not least in a stylish new stoa on the north side of the Agora, a gift to fellow citizens from Cimon's wealthy brother-in-law, Peisianax. Over 100 feet long and 40 wide, its back wall and two slim sides built from well-dressed limestone, its simple Doric colonnade looked out across the Agora and up towards the cliffs of the Acropolis. But what made it remarkable and gave it its common name, the Stoa Poicile ('Painted Stoa'), were three immense panel-paintings hung on the back wall. By the leading artists Micon, Panaenus (Pheidias' brother), and Polygnotus (who refused to accept payment for this project), each showed scenes of fighting that taken as a whole proclaimed a powerful message. The panel on the left showed the Battle between Greeks and Amazons—or more accurately Athenians and Amazons—when those female warriors invaded Attica to reclaim their queen (abducted by Theseus while helping Heracles with one of his labours). Like Xerxes' Persians they poured in from the east, occupied the Areopagus and attacked the Acropolis until, defeated, they were driven out of Attica. While the painting itself does not survive, representations of the scene from just a few decades later, perhaps influenced by it, show the Amazons as trousered warriors on horseback, female cousins of the Persian cavalry with which Athens' hoplites were all-too familiar. While the second panel showed another popular scene, the Sack of Troy, the revolutionary third depicted not a mythical encounter but a recent one—the Battle of Marathon, in all its bloody detail.

> [On the left] the battle is evenly matched, but at the centre of the fighting the barbarians are in flight, shoving each other into the marshes, while at the right of the painting are Phoenician ships and Greeks slaughtering barbarians as they try to get aboard. Here, too, is the figure of Marathon, the hero from whom the plain is named, and Theseus rising from the earth, and Athena, too, and Heracles . . . The most conspicuous of all the fighting men shown in the painting are Callimachus . . . , Miltiades . . . and the local deity, Echetlus.[16]

Just as in the Marathon Memorial at Delphi, so here on the painting in the Stoa Poicile, Miltiades was singled out, his name emblazoned in a caption next to him, a reminder to all of what his city owed him. But what made this triptych so remarkable was its fusion of contemporary history with heroic past, presenting Marathon as part of a continuum, one of a string of conflicts with the East that had seen Athens and Athenians emerge victorious, with Marathon's triumphant general Miltiades worthy of a place beside not just the city's heroes, mortals such as Theseus, but her patron goddess, too. Taken together with the Marathon Monument and the Lesche of the Cnidians at Delphi, the paintings of the Stoa Poicile were part of a well-coordinated strategy to boost the reputation of both Athens and Miltiades, a strategy that bears the hallmarks of Cimon himself. It can be no coincidence that soon after the Stoa was constructed, Cimon named his next son for its sponsor, Peisianax.[17]

Despite the jingoistic patriotism of much contemporary art, as he 'embellished the city with liberal and refined leisure spaces', Cimon did not forget the Spartans, friendship with whom was so essential to his vision of a healthy and well-balanced Greece. Leading from the Agora behind the Stoa Poicile, through the Cerameicus and a mile out northwest of the city walls, he had a trench dug and pipes laid to irrigate a newly-landscaped lush oasis at the shrine of Academus, one of Theseus' contemporaries, a pro-Spartan Athenian, honoured in both cities for helping to avert a war. When Theseus abducted the young Spartan princess, Helen, he concealed her in Aphidnae (an Attic village south of Marathon). But during his protracted absence in the Underworld (when he tried to kidnap Persephone), Helen's brothers led an army against Athens, demanded to know where she was hidden and threatened destruction if they were not told. As Athenians weighed up their options, whether to betray their king or risk their city's safety, Academus, acting for the common good, revealed Helen's whereabouts, so earning the goodwill of her brothers and their people. For Cimon, bent on maintaining good relations with the Spartans, ever keen to forge close ties, never willing to offend without good reason, it was a salutary story, especially since he had built a lavish hero shrine for Theseus. How politic to honour Academus equally, to celebrate a local hero who was also championed by Sparta. So Cimon set his gardeners to work, breaking the cracked earth, irrigating it with freshly-channelled water, planting groves of olives and avenues of plane trees, smoothing the sandy soil between them to form speed tracks and arenas where, near the sacred precinct, its honeyed walls built by Hipparchus years before, youths could wrestle while old men chatted in the shade. It was the most enchanting area outside the city.[18]

From spoils of war Cimon transformed the very heart of Athens, too. For centuries the Agora had been the site of such diverse activities as markets and processions, equestrian displays, theatrical performances and ostracisms; but every building round it had been razed or vandalized by Xerxes' Persians. Now, while public offices along the western side beneath Colonus Hill, a Stoa to the south and two fountain houses, had been rebuilt, much of the remaining area was little but a broad, flat, dusty space, which at the height of summer simmered in the baking heat. For months on end it was beyond endurance. Temporary awnings might be rigged but they did little to reduce the temperature, and for the moment, with so much still to build, Athenians could not commission cooler but more costly marble stoas. But Cimon had the answer. Ironically he may have learned it from the Persians. Horticulturally ingenious, these lovers of the paradise garden were experts in planting shaded walkways with fragrant shrubs and overarching trees, and the tree that most delighted their Great King was the oriental plane. With wide-spreading branches, plane trees are both utilitarian and beautiful, their broad canopies of leaves providing deep shade in summer before turning a rich gold in autumn; and while their roots must be kept moist, the Agora enjoyed a good supply of water: the overflow from its two fountain houses. So, on Cimon's advice, Athenians dug trenches round the Agora's perimeter (as they had dug them out to the Academy), laid pipes, and planted avenues of plane trees, leafy boulevards alive with birdsong and the chirring of cicadas, where men could conduct business or converse at leisure shielded from the searing sun.[19]

At the same time, determined not to neglect the gods, Cimon proposed (and the Assembly agreed) a range of civic projects paid for from war booty. Above the Agora, on the north face of the Acropolis above Theseus' temple, high in the sheer wall, near where the Temple of Athena Polias once stood, the bastion was both strengthened and adorned with a row of column drums positioned on their sides, whose round profile stood out in contrast to the squared stone all around them. They had been salvaged from the temple started after Marathon but unfinished when the Persians took Athens, and their inclusion in the wall was far from accidental. Seen clearly from the Agora, they reminded citizens not just of Persian sacrilege, but of Athens' steadfast determination not to yield that had seen them sacrifice their city in their quest for victory. On the south side of the Acropolis plateau, too, by the site of the aborted Marathon temple, where the rock sloped gradually to cliffs, a tall retaining wall was now constructed, soil and rubble packed between it and the bedrock, and its top made level with the rest of the Acropolis, in preparation for the day when Athens could construct a new, and perhaps larger temple in this quadrant. And while Athenians for now had sworn not to rebuild ruined temples, they could still erect new statuary. Fresh from the Marathon Monument, Pheidias (the sculptor du jour) was commissioned to create a thirty-foot-tall bronze Athena Promachus, a statue of the goddess as warrior, facing west to Salamis, shield raised, helmet down, a spear held high in her right hand, its cruel tip like the helmet crest, seen glinting in the sun from ships 'as soon as they had rounded Sunium'. Once more it bore the iconography of triumph over barbarism: the shield showed images of Greeks subduing the unruly Centaurs, while verses cut into its plinth celebrated victory at Eurymedon:

> Ever since the sea split Asia from Europe
> and maddened Ares poured into the cities of mankind,
> nothing like this was ever won by men who live on earth:
> victory on a single day on land and sea.[20]

Meanwhile, yet another project was afoot. Whenever he returned to Athens from Piraeus along the narrow causeway road where the Ilissus and Cephisus rivers leached into the sea, attacked by insects and assailed by noxious odours, Cimon viewed the marshes with dismay. Not only was their air unhealthy, not only did they make for a humiliating introduction to a city that increasingly demanded high esteem, they were waste ground that could be utilized more profitably. With every journey, Cimon's commitment grew to drain the swamp; and while the People might not sanction opening their coffers for such an unglamorous project, his conquests had made him richer; he himself could well afford the cost. So, for months, long lines of labourers—free citizens and slaves—dumped wagonloads of heavy stones and rubble from the city and surrounding countryside, working outwards from the road, raising the ground level while channelling the rivers, until at last there was dry, solid land between the city and the sea. Within only a few years, Long Walls would be constructed on this new earth, linking Athens with Piraeus, ensuring safe passage to the fleet in times of siege and rendering the city almost impregnable. Whether this was part of Cimon's grand scheme or not, the work his men had just completed would prove crucial to the city's long-term strategy.[21]

Wearing her snake-fringed aegis and wielding her spear, Athena
Promachus advances as if to battle (Attic pseudo-Panathenaic
Amphora, 500–475 B.C.).

However, private interests called out to be cherished, too, not least the
fertile fields and orchards of Cimon's Laciadae estate, the haven where
Isodice was bringing up their family. While others might rely on revenue
from farms for livelihoods, the wealthy, canny Cimon turned produce
to more profitable use to marry public good with private benefit, or-
dering every fence and wall to be removed, letting it be known that any
citizen who happened to be passing, be they members of his local deme
or men from wider Attica, should take whatever foodstuffs they might
need. At the same time he regularly held dinners on his lands, inviting
fellow demesmen; he helped struggling families pay for funerals; and
in the Agora he could often be seen surrounded by a retinue of young
men, each wearing well-spun clothing, which they would offer to old or
needy citizens, accepting their soiled, threadbare tunics in exchange,
and pressing coins into the palms of the deserving poor, men whom they
deemed to be of noble character. So Cimon's reputation and support
base grew, until it could be said (as it still was a generation later) that
he made money simply to spend it in a way that brought him honour.[22]

Cimon was behaving as Athenian elites had always done, not least the tyrannus Peisistratus. And while he was enhancing the life of every citizen, in honouring Theseus and Academus, he was focussing attention on two blue-blooded heroes, aristocrats like him, charismatic leaders who through courage or conviction had saved Athens. Both were paradigms of benign patrician government: respecting the People and consulting them, they were free from the constant need to work, had time to see the bigger picture, and were trusted to act wisely of their own accord. Of course there needed to be checks and balances for politicians as there were for military commanders, who at their term's conclusion could face prosecution if they were suspected of abusing power, of corruption or of making bad decisions, as Miltiades had found when he returned from Paros. Nonetheless, it was because her citizen militia put its trust in skilled commanders, obeying orders, winning victories, that Athens had become so strong. And what worked on campaign would work equally at home, if men such as Cimon and Aristides were permitted to guide policy. And with Cimon bearing such a likeness to the tousle-headed Theseus, son of an Athenian general and foreign princess, liberator of Ionians from foreign tribute, what more evidence was needed that Athens was entering a new heroic, reassuringly aristocratic Golden Age.[23]

Not everyone was minded to agree. When Themistocles fled to Persia, ostracised by public vote, condemned by the elite court of the Areopagus, the populists had been seriously undermined, but while for now the unashamedly patrician Cimon was enjoying stratospheric military and political success, behaving in their eyes more like a tyrant than a democrat, privileged young progressives such as Pericles (now in his late twenties) still nursed ambitions of their own. Avidly they sought a charismatic leader who might stand up to Cimon and, by uniting the People once more in the cause of radical democracy, achieve for them the status that they felt had been denied them for too long. They found him in the chauvinistic Ephialtes, a man who like Pericles was prominent and rich enough to be appointed general, but who was more than ready to pander to the People in his desire for power. A year or so after Eurymedon, he led his ships beyond the Islands of the Swallows out into hostile waters, hoping beyond hope to meet a small detachment of the Great King's fleet, which he prayed he would defeat, thus letting him claim a victory to rival Cimon's. But when no Phoenician ships came, not even he could be presumptuous enough to claim it was because of him. The man the Persians feared was not Ephialtes, son of the otherwise unknown Sophonides, but Cimon.[24]

Yet, as Ephialtes and his zealots sat beneath the stars round campfires on campaign, or mingled with struggling voters as they streamed onto the Pnyx, or toured the wharves and quaysides of Piraeus and the smoky backstreets of the Cerameicus, there was cause enough for Cimon to fear them, for they were stoking up an atmosphere of simmering disquiet, where feelings could spill over into violence. Half a century before, as Athenians knew well, tensions had erupted from beneath the surface at the sacred Panathenaic Procession, when without warning Harmodius and Aristogeiton had attacked Hipparchus and knifed him to death. Now they feared that violence might erupt again, this time at another festival, the Great Dionysia, where citizens and foreign residents of Athens mingled with foreign Greek delegates in processions and three days of dramatic competition. Part of the Athenian state calendar for nigh on seventy years, drama could not help but be political, for politics was everywhere in this most radical of cities, and, since plots of tragedies invariably revolved round powerful rulers whose decisions had deep consequences for themselves, their families and their people, at their heart were questions of how best to act both as an individual and (by extension) as a state. Since Phrynichus' controversial *Capture of Miletus*, almost all playwrights had steered clear of setting dramas in the real contemporary world, preferring to locate them in the parallel yet safely distant realm of mythology, so they might claim, if challenged, that any similarities between characters such as Agamemnon or Orestes and modern politicians was coincidental. Of course, there were exceptions. Phrynichus and Aeschylus had dramatized the Persians' defeat, but both knew that while nothing in these scripts would offend, much would delight both audiences and judges. But now a new tragedian emerged, whose world-view was less cosily democratic than that of Aeschylus, against whom he would compete at this year's Dionysia, a young man who held Ephialtes and Pericles in some suspicion: Sophocles. The son of an arms manufacturer, Sophocles' love of Athens was unquestionable—it was he who as a youth had led the victory ode for Salamis—but, conservative to the core, he was suspicious of the new wave of People's politicians questioning the status quo, for whom the ends might seem to justify the means.[25]

With Ephialtes' partisans championing Aeschylus and Cimon's followers supporting Sophocles, with both factions at loggerheads, and with Dionysus, for whom the festival was held, being not just the god of wine and drama but the lord of misrule, the stage seemed potentially set for violence. Such desperate times required desperate remedies. Dispensing with the tradition by which judges were appointed by lot, the Archon, Apsephion, waited until preliminaries were over—the processions and the sacrifices, the libations of fine wine poured out in gratitude to Dionysus at his altar in the 'orkhestra' where choruses would dance and actors move their audience to tears—before making a startling announcement. Because the atmosphere in Athens was so strained, Cimon and the generals (who had offered the libations and still stood in full view of the audience) would serve as judges. The citizens in the audience accepted their decisions on the battlefield; now they must accept them in the theatre, too. So the festival went ahead; the dramas were performed; there was no violence. Yet, when Sophocles was announced victor there were those who grumbled—not least Aeschylus, his rival; and whether the judgement was reached on artistic or political grounds remained a matter for unresolved debate.[26]

As the Persian threat receded, Athens turned her gaze to northern Greece and the lands of Thrace that, dotted with trading posts, stretched west from the Chersonese to Eion and the mouth of the River Strymon. While Eion had not been occupied since its liberation, ambitious merchants were aware of the potential profits to be had if Athens controlled it and its hinterlands—not just fertile fields, lush vineyards and towering forests (from which triremes might be built) but strapping tribesmen who could fetch high prices at slave auction, marble quarries, and the gleaming goldmines of Pangaeum. Like the Persians before them they fantasized about the wealth that might be theirs, and plotted how to make their dreams reality. If Cimon was consulted when the People called for plans and strategies, if he was present at discussions in the generals' headquarters a stone's throw from the Agora, his loyalties cannot but have been conflicted. Half his family was Thracian; lands close to Eion had belonged to them for generations. Nonetheless, as an Athenian patriot he could not disagree that, if a colony were founded, the best site was the existing town of Ennea Hodoi (Nine Ways) named from the trackways that converged to cross the Strymon three miles upstream from Eion, where Persian Magi had once sacrificed white horses to appease the river before Xerxes' engineers embarked on bridging it, and the Great King himself (so it was darkly rumoured) buried nine girls and nine boys alive as sacrifices to a local earth god. Athenians were rightly famous for their 'can do' attitude, for the speed with which they put proposals into action, and with optimism running high after Eurymedon, it took just a little time before excited families from Attica and allied states were entering their names on lists, eager to start a new life up in Thrace, with its unlimited potential and myriad possibilities.[27]

On quaysides at Piraeus, in sun-drenched harbours on Aegean islands, in glittering Ionian seaports, tearful scenes of fond farewells played out as sons or brothers and their families climbed onto tarry transport ships clutching what possessions they could carry, some hoisting carefully-strapped chests or crates that squawked with cackling hens, still others trying to reassure their bawling children or cajoling frightened dogs, as men, expected and expecting to fight for their new territories, ensured that slaves were keeping watchful eyes on weapons, shields and armour. For their mission was not simply to set up home in Ennea Hodoi, but to cleanse the surrounding lands of Edoni, the Thracian tribesmen who had filtered back when Cimon drove the Persians from Eion ten years earlier. It would be no easy undertaking, which was why they had appointed Sophanes as one of their commanders, the bluff, blunt-speaking, strapping giant who once dispatched Aegina's general in single combat, who after Marathon refused Miltiades the victor's olive crown, who at Plataea sowed fear into Persians' hearts, wielding his shield emblazoned with an anchor, slicing at the enemy with its sharp edge. Like his colleague, Leagros, a close friend of Themistocles who escaped being tainted by his fall, Sophanes was a loud and proud opponent of Cimon, whom he scorned as a privileged aristocrat. How welcome, then, this chance not just to found a city, where democratic principals might truly hold sway, but to extend Athenian control, increase Athenian revenue, and win kudos that would force Athenians to consider him at least an equal of Cimon. Men such as he and Leagros, would surely make light work of Thracians. With them as their protectors the colonists of Ennea Hodoi would be secure.[28]

Even before the colonists set out for Eion, others in the region were feeling nervous. Parts of Thrace—parts of the Chersonese, indeed—still hosted Persian garrisons, relics of the glory days of Darius when Persian expansion seemed unstoppable. Now from towns and strongholds in the northern Chersonese, from mainland Doriscus and Sigeum in the Troad, frightened Persians were sending messengers to Thracian allies nurtured over thirty years, calling in favours, urging their assistance. Athenian ambitions shone out all too clearly. Having cleansed the east Aegean of Persian influence, those democrats were turning their attention to the north. Their plans for Ennea Hodoi were only the beginning. They would not be satisfied until the whole coast from the Islands of the Swallows round to Eion lay under their control. As the drums of war reverberated louder by the day, Cimon knew that Athens must act swiftly. The last thing she or her many thousand settlers needed now was a joint Persian-Thracian offensive. So with just four triremes he scudded north with all speed towards lands remembered from his childhood. Perhaps as he passed Imbros he recalled those other triremes—four then, too— in which he and his family had escaped the Persians thirty years before, while the enemy encircled his brother in the fifth. Perhaps when he saw the thirteen Persian ships as they materialized, spectral from the ghostly, glinting haze, he remembered the Phoenician galleys gaining on them, their silhouettes becoming ever sharper, like a shoal of hungry sharks. But this time Cimon would not turn and flee. This time he gave the order, and across the vastness of the sea the trumpet sounded the attack. Four ships against thirteen: it should have been no contest. But Athens' crews were tried and tested, battle-drilled and confident; they had tasted victory at the Eurymedon and Syedra and they longed to taste it once again. More inexperienced, the Persians and Thracians stood no chance and, in those so-familiar waters Cimon set his men to work. Even as his triremes were torpedoing towards them with such terrifying, unerring aim, the enemy surrendered.[29]

With news of captured vessels towed to hostile shores, and captives, some begging to be ransomed, others destined for the slave market, thrown in chains, morale among the Persians ebbed. As Cimon's troops poured onto beaches at Sigeum and across the northern Chersonese, and victory followed victory in hard-fought battle, the last remaining Persians quickly packed up their belongings and tried to make their perilous escape. Only Doriscus managed to hold out, its adamantine governor rallying his men, determined never to betray his fortress town—before parleying with Cimon, coming to a deal that would allow him to remain, the last Persian grandee on European soil, remembered by the Great King every year with gifts to both him and his family, but cut off now from Persia, the ruler of an ineffectual last outpost, a forlorn reminder of ambition thwarted.[30]

Yet it soon became apparent that it was not just an external enemy that Athens and her League must dread. As Athenian ambitions snapped into ever sharper focus, allies began to fear the worst. The revolt of Naxos had been stamped out with well-oiled efficiency, its city torn down, its contributions to League coffers reassessed, increased. What kind of an alliance treated member states with such high-handed disregard? Not one formed of equals. Instead it seemed increasingly that, rather than existing for the common good, the League enhanced the fortunes of one member above all, the member with the largest fleet, a fleet paid for from the taxes of the rest. And now Athens was positively undermining one of the League states. Like the Thracians, the islanders of Thasos, owning gold mines on the mainland, whose annual revenue was 80 talents, had grown rich from trading with the Edoni (many of whom owned houses on the island), and all were understandably concerned that an Athenian colony at Ennea Hodoi and a port at Eion would be bad for their economy. At meetings of moneyed businessmen, worry turned to anger at the presumptuousness of professed allies, who showed concern for no-one but themselves. What did the Assembly in distant Athens care if Thasos' economy was ruined, as long as the island paid its taxes? Incensed at the prospect of financial disaster, they talked openly of withdrawing from the League, ignoring any who appealed to history or reminded them how Naxos' rebellion had ended in defeat. They would not be cowed. They would stand up to Athenian aggression. They would not let Athens tell them what to do. Which left Athens, determined to maintain her empire, with no option. When the Assembly learned of the revolt, the People voted overwhelmingly to send the navy, under the command of their top general. Call-up lists posted in the Agora; oarsmen trooping to Piraeus; hoplites stowing arms on board; and with libations poured and trumpets blaring triremes put to sea. Cimon was sailing north.[31]

IV

PERIPATEIA

10

EARTHQUAKE

Poseidon, the great god, who shakes the earth and stirs
the barren sea,
lord of the ocean . . .
blessed one, be kind and help those voyaging in ships.

Homeric Hymn to Poseidon, 1–2, 7

THASOS, 465 B.C.

At first all went to plan. As Cimon's fleet swung east around the northern
tip of Thasos (a saw-toothed range of mountains on the starboard side)
and, on the gently folded promontory ahead, the town itself came into
view, a skein of triremes sped to meet them. By now the Athenians' response was second nature: sails lowered; masts removed; hoplites, fully
armoured, ranged along ships' decks; helmsmen marking targets;
oarsmen flexing fingers ready for their muscle-tearing spurts of speed;
while on the flagship, Cimon's trumpeter awaited the command, as
Cimon made sacrifice and offered prayers and poured libations of rich
wine that stained the glassy waters black as blood. And then, so well-
rehearsed, the order given; the clarion call heard; the rhythm of long
oars increasing speed; sleek ships hurtling towards targets; timber
creaking; bronze beaks crashing into groaning hulls; and then, as one,
the rowers backing water; helmsmen leaning hard on steering oars; the
whole procedure starting once again. The captains had received their
orders—to attempt the periplous, when ships would row at speed around
the enemy's two flanks before attacking from the rear, or the diekplous,

where triremes at the centre of the line smashed through the enemy's formation, fanned round and launched their deadly strikes before the opposition could recover from their disarray. For, while each ship's performance was important, it was but one piece in the larger battle game, whose rules Cimon and his Athenians had made their own, as that day in the bay outside their harbour Thasos' fleet learned to its dismay. From city walls, the townsfolk watched their warships, wallowing, disabled, make desperate attempts to row to safety, while shipwrecked sailors swam in terror from the hail of arrows smacking into waves around them, and keels that sliced the seas close to their heads. At last it was all over. Cimon had won the day. But to win the city and the island would not be so easy.[1]

For generations Thasians had been preparing for attack. In Cimon's childhood their city had been ringed with mighty bastions—made mightier still when Histiaeus, enjoying his short-lived command of mainland Myrcinus, blockaded them—but, his ships wrecked on Athos, and fearing that the Thasians (despite meekly surrendering) were plotting to rebel, Darius ordered them to hand over their fleet and pull down their walls. While Persia ruled the North Aegean, the mineral- and mine-rich islanders, valued members of the empire, thrived, and, though they resented the 400 silver talents spent on feeding Xerxes and his army on their way to the canal cut through Mount Athos, they paid up nonetheless. But once the Persian fleet withdrew, Thasos again felt dangerously exposed. Once more walls were a priority, and the islanders could afford the best: a well-dressed semicircle studded with eleven towers enclosing both town and acropolis, flanking the shoreline, linking military and commercial harbours, each of which was equally well fortified. All Cimon and his men could do was disembark, mount a blockade by land and sea, and wait. For with siege equipment in its infancy, even experienced generals relied for success on human failings: thirst, hunger and frustration which could only increase over time; a desire to do down rivals, which might cause a man to throw open a city gate even to an enemy with whose cause he did not agree; and greed. But the Thasians were wealthy. They had no need of Cimon's silver. Besides, being in close contact with their mainland Thracian allies, they knew he might be called away at any moment. For the Thracians, too, were plotting, since they, too, feared the threat of Ennea Hodoi.[2]

By now the settlement was taking shape. With memories of Cimon's capture of the burning port of Eion fresh, the colonists' landfall had met little opposition, and soon their ships were nosing up the River Strymon and on to where it looped between two low escarpments before the great plain opened out, and in the distance a broad lake stretched for miles towards a chain of rugged mountains that embraced the far horizon. Now they had reached the site of Xerxes' bridge, and on the starboard side the plateau where the Edoni had lived for centuries, the teeming hub of nine roads, their vibrant entrepôt, commanding a safe crossing of the river, controlling trade between the Thracian heartlands and the sea. While men—helmeted and armoured, clutching shields and spears and swords—scoured the abandoned town for trouble, settlers, stiff from their long voyage, clambered out onto the riverbank, unloaded their possessions and, when word reached them that all was safe, entered the stockade to climb the hill and claim the homes and homesteads of the Edoni. For weeks they worked on their new houses, erecting altars, making sacrifices, offering prayers for prosperity. An assembly was convened; a city council sat; men were appointed to administrate the marketplace; and land was parcelled out. And all the while, no sign of trouble from the Thracians—just rumours that the Edoni were grouping in the hills, that they were watching everything they did, that they were waiting, ready for the moment when, like hungry mountain lions, they would attack.[3]

But Sophanes and Leagros, Athens' generals, were not content to wait. They knew that to ensure their city's safety, they must subdue the neighbouring territory. So on a hot, oppressive morning they told 300 men of fighting age to don their armour and begin the process of securing local Thracian settlements. First on their list was Drabescus, ten miles to the north-east. So, north along the Strymon's banks they trooped towards the shimmering lake's shores, scouts on the lookout for the enemy reporting nothing untoward. Then as they trudged across hot, sloping fields, as if from out of nowhere, the Thracians attacked: foot soldiers with crescent shields and javelins, axes, slashing swords; archers with quivers full of deadly arrows; cavalrymen mounted on tough wiry ponies, long hair streaming down their backs; and all eyes on the Greeks, the hoplites falling into battle line, shields locked, long spears held firm, protruding like a hedgehog's spines, standing their ground to meet them. Many had fought the Persians—at Plataea or Mycale or the Eurymedon. Those who had not had heard old soldiers' tales of how barbarians would turn and flee in terror at the very sight of well-drilled phalanxes. Surely all that these Thracians were doing now was posturing. They seemed so ill-disciplined, breaking ranks and rushing forwards, throwing javelins, loosing off their arrows, before falling back once more, apparently in fear. But as the heat built and the thunder came, the Thracians' javelins found their mark; their arrows did, too. And now the cavalry was surging round them. Now, as lightning flashed and thunder boomed, Greek lines were giving way, Greek swords flailing, Greek friends falling to be trampled on the pale dun earth beneath a galloping of hooves. Now Sophanes was down; Leagros, too; and, with no-one to command them, no-one who could see how it was all unfolding amid the din of dying men, the battle cries, the cataracts of blood, the sheeting rain, the mud, the terror, the exhaustion, the finality, those Athenians still standing tried to hack a path out of the carnage. But the press of Thracians hemmed them in, and one by one they fell, knees buckling, shield arms limp, swords dropped from enervated hands as daylight tunnelled into darkness.[4]

Then, fresh from victory, the Thracians rallied, horsemen thundering across the plain, foot soldiers running through the lashing rain, their lust for blood unsated, a longing for destruction burning in their eyes until they came to Ennea Hodoi, so unprotected now, so unsuspecting. Up into the town they poured, along the newly-laid-out streets past newly-set-up houses, the scent of sawdust mingling already with the choking stench of smoke, the reek of blood, the brays of tethered donkeys and the frenzied bark of dogs, the reedy shouts of old men, screams of women for their butchered children silenced by a slicing blade. In those terrible last hours the Thracians vented all their pent-up anger on the Greeks who had presumed to take their homes, just as the Persians before them had presumed to settle in their lands, extracting their gold, growing rich on trade that once was theirs, an anger that each slight, each setback, each defeat served only to swell, until it could be glutted only with the burning of a city and the slaughter of 10,000 Greeks—men, women, children; free and slaves—for there were very few survivors left to steal back under truce into the town or to the battlefield, to heap up corpses, light the pyres, fill urns with cooling clinker, all that was left of those excited, vibrant settlers, who once looked forward to a new life in the north but were now 'exchanged for ashes', as Aeschylus would write, by the war god 'Ares, who barters lives for gold and holds the scales in battle at the clashing of the spears'. The ashes of the fighting men were taken home to Athens to be buried in a grave beside the road to the Academy. The ashes of their families stayed in Thrace.[5]

How Cimon's men on Thasos greeted the news of the massacre can only be imagined. Most if not all knew murdered settlers and soldiers, and, while many must have itched to cross the sea and take revenge on the triumphant Edoni, others must have thanked good fortune that a channel separated Thasos from the mainland. Meanwhile, morale among the islanders surged. On one rain-drenched afternoon, the myth peddled by a generation of Athenians—how their democratic constitution bestowed a mantle of invincibility—had been shattered. Perhaps the balance that had seen the city rise was already poised to tip. After all, as all Greeks knew, gods did not permit mankind unqualified success forever. Carved into Apollo's Delphic temple were the words, *Meden Agan* ('Nothing in Excess'), a warning not to strive for too much, not to overstretch, but to remember limits set for humankind by divine law, to cross which risked the anger of the gods. Was Persia's fate not evidence enough? The gods would not let the Persians expand their bloated empire further into Europe, nor countenance the arrogance of the Great King, who wanted to impose his will on Nature, bridging continents divided by the divine Hellespont, carving a canal through the peninsula of Athos. The storm off that very cape, the defeat of both attacks on mainland Greece, the fact that gods and demigods had been seen fighting side by side with Greeks—all this was evidence that Zeus and his Olympians were punishing the Persians for hubris, for forgetting they were only men. And Athenians were doing the same. Now they too were trying to build an empire, turning an alliance between equals into an autocracy, imposing taxes as the Persians had done, causing economic hardships, trampling on treaties, assaulting so-called allies when they tried to leave. Surely the gods were angry with them, too. Surely the lightning bolts exploding at Drabescus, the massacre and the destruction of Ennea Hodoi, were proof of divine punishment. And if the gods were now abandoning the overconfident Athenians, they would not let Thasos fall. So, confident that they would win, the Thasians, blockaded, tightened belts and waited for Cimon to sail away.[6]

Meanwhile, with his enemies seeking every opportunity to undermine him (at home, on Thasos, perhaps even in the ranks of his own army), Cimon's connections with the Thracians furnished welcome ammunition. He was, after all, the son of a Thracian princess and, while some Greeks believed that mothers were simply incubators for a father's seed, even if Cimon himself was an Athenian, half his family—the half that shaped him as a child and taught him those manners that his rivals still regarded as uncouth—were what Greeks now called 'barbarian', outré, beyond the pale, and consequently dangerously suspect. So, radical opponents such as Pericles and Ephialtes need not look far for ammunition with which to tarnish Cimon. But for the moment far more worrying—with the potential to threaten his immediate campaign and upset the delicate balance of interstate relationships at the heart of Cimon's vision for the wider Greek world—was that somehow someone had slipped from the beleaguered city past night patrols, down to the sea to make a desperate dash south for Sparta, where he urged the kings and ephors to support the Thasians by invading Attica, so forcing Cimon and his men to hasten home and thereby lift the siege.[7]

In recent years, Sparta had experienced a series of setbacks. The disgrace of King Leotychidas, exiled for taking bribes from the Thessalian Aleuadae, and of the treacherous Pausanias, regent for Leonidas' son, Pleistarchus, had revealed potential fault lines: the Spartan education system may have trained young men to endure austerity at home, but once abroad, exposed to life's luxuries, many Spartans (and not least their royals) seemed too easily seduced by wealth and pleasure. The felling of these powerful leaders, one from each of the two ruling families, might suggest that Sparta's constitution was being undermined by factionalism. Not that this would be surprising. Losing leadership of the Greek League had seriously dented Sparta's kudos, crucial to her standing among not only fellow Greeks but helots, too, the enslaved native population, constantly persecuted, constantly resentful, constantly looking out for any chink in Sparta's armour that would suggest even the faintest hope that one day they would be free. Recently there had been reason to clamp down on the helots even more heavily, when a group of them fled to Poseidon's temple at Taenarum. Reluctant to attack them in a sanctuary, the Spartans had coaxed them out with promise of safe passage, but then all pledges were forgotten; the slaves were slaughtered to a man; and so resentment grew.[8]

Menaced by helots and sold out by generals, the Spartans found themselves threatened, too, by a new alliance led by Argos, which, rehabilitated from her soi-disant 'neutrality' and excused her Persian sympa-

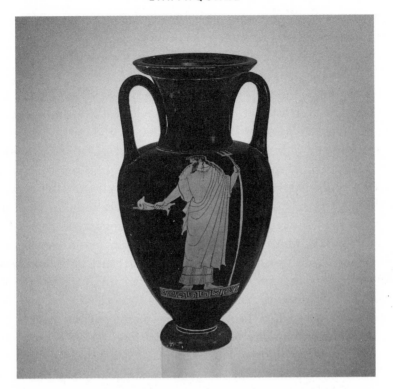

Poseidon the Earthshaker clutches his trident in his left hand
and a trireme-shaped dolphin in his right (Attic red-figure neck
amphora, c. 470–465 B.C.).

thies, had lost little time in wooing much of the northern Peloponnese
from Elis in the west to a network of Arcadian states including Mantinea.
Spears had been brandished and swords drawn, but a battle at Tegea
saw Sparta triumphant. Then gradually the tide had turned. In Argos
pro-Spartan aristocrats assumed control; sandwiched between Argos
and Sparta, Mantinea reconsidered her position and withdrew from the
alliance; and just that year—the same year that the messenger from
Thasos pled for help—a Spartan army triumphed at Dipaea in the
maquis of the mountains of Arcadia. At last Sparta had good reason to
be proud again; at last her men were winning back the prominence they
knew was rightly theirs; and now the time seemed ripe to reassert herself and challenge upstart Athens, especially since Athens was already
reeling from events at Ennea Hodoi. The Thasians' request for help

could not have come at a more perfect time and as their messenger set sail for home, confident that in a few short weeks the siege would be all over, Spartans were already making sacrifices as their rituals ordained to Apollo and the war god, Ares.

Instead, they should have made their offerings to Poseidon, the god Greeks called 'Earthshaker', the god who bellowed like a subterranean bull, whose power lay in the bucking of a stallion and the surging ocean swell—or in the rolling, heaving liquefaction of an earthquake—who gave mankind no warning, though in Sparta dogs' fur stood on end, and a hare raced in terror into a wrestling school's courtyard. The older youths ignored it, but the boys gave chase and pelted out into the road; and as they did, the ground began to slide; columns cracked; roof beams snapped, and the whole edifice imploded, burying their friends beneath the rubble. Across Sparta's villages and outlying districts, buildings were collapsing, houses crumbling, temples being torn apart, as roof tiles smashed into the streets, and bricks and stone slabs shattered, and a pall of choking dust engulfed the valley, while—most terrifying of all—above them the whole mountain seemed to be disintegrating as high peaks fractured and huge boulders rolled and ricocheted down gullies, scarring hillsides, ripping swathes through forests as they plummeted like missiles hurled by gods. It seemed to last forever, but as aftershocks convulsed Taygetus and the Eurotas valley, survivors raced for where their homes once stood, tearing through debris with bare, bleeding hands, shouting frantically to those they hoped were still alive, trapped beneath a chaos of smashed bricks and broken rafters.[9]

Only Archidamus understood the greater danger. He had assumed the throne a decade earlier when his grandfather, the disgraced Leotychidas, fled to Tegea in exile, but despite his relative youth he possessed clear vision. Within Sparta only five homes remained standing. That itself proclaimed the scale of the catastrophe. As for the dead, for now their numbers were incalculable. The youths crushed in their wrestling school were just a tiny fraction of the dead and injured. Who knew how many fighting men were lost? For a city at war such losses could be devastating—and Sparta *was* at war; not with her neighbours but with her helot slaves, a war that was renewed each year. Always alive to signs of insurrection, she was forever fearful of a change in circumstance that might herald a full-scale revolt. Now circumstance *had* changed. Drastically. With so many Identicals out of action, Sparta was vulnerable, and only Archidamus seemed to see the risk. He scoured the streets for his lieutenants, diverting them from rescue work, directing them to rally the Identicals, seize any weapons they could find and stand firm, ready to respond to any sign of trouble. As trumpet calls echoed through the eerily quiet valley, the Spartan war machine snapped into action—and not a moment too soon. In helot farms and settlements, proud men whose freedom had been crushed for generations were rallying, too. To them the earthquake proved Poseidon's anger with the Spartans who had coaxed his helot suppliants from his altar at Taenarum and killed them in cold blood. Such sacrilege must be punished, such wrongs reversed, and now with the help of the great Earthshaker the helots would shake off their slavery, destroy their persecutors and reclaim the country that was rightly theirs.[10]

Although not trained to the same standards as their masters, helots were not strangers to the arts of war. At Plataea 35,000 of them swelled Spartan ranks—seven times as many helots as Identicals—so, given their experience and numbers, it was entirely feasible that they might emerge victorious. Yet they lacked the ruthless self-control instilled in every Spartan, a discipline designed for just this situation. When amid the aftershocks they marched to Sparta, to find ranged against them depleted yet still-steely ranks of hoplites standing firm, emotionless, behind their shields, not even their superior numbers could persuade the slaves to fight, and they dispersed, cowed, for the safety of the mountains. Yet this was just the start. As the scale of the disaster became clearer (with 20,000—perhaps half the Spartan population—dead) the helots grew increasingly courageous, seizing outlying towns and villages, encouraging the Perioikoi, the free class of farmers, merchants, artisans and tradesfolk, to join their cause. In Messenia, the helots' ancestral heartlands, where two Perioikic towns did rally behind them, they grew so emboldened that near their ancient capital of Stenyclerus they engaged a Spartan army under Aeïmnestus, a hero of Plataea, whose boast was that he killed the Persian general, Mardonius—and slaughtered him together with 300 men, whom Sparta could ill afford to lose. Yet unwalled Stenyclerus was too vulnerable: better to take to the hills, to towering Mount Ithome, where on its high plateau an ancient sanctuary of Zeus commanded views across the plain. Here in their mountain fastness the helots hunkered down to wage a long guerrilla war that would in time (they hoped) defeat their Spartan overlords.[11]

Many hundred miles away on Thasos, Cimon, too, hunkered down. The earthquake had come at the right time: there would be no invasion now of Attica, no need for him to lift the siege and hurry south, no more distractions. So, as summer failed and autumn's seas turned choppy, as winter gales roared down from Thrace to lash the coast with driving snow, and then as spring returned and mountain slopes were flecked with flowers, Cimon stayed firm while Thasos slowly starved, waiting for the day when, their provisions gone, their spirit broken, the islanders would sue for terms. With wages to be paid, supplies to be shipped in, triremes to be beached and serviced, hulls scraped, planks replaced, and ropes and sails maintained in excellent condition, the siege was cripplingly expensive. But for Athens it was worth the cost: the mission must not fail. At stake was the League's future, for its strength lay in its integrity, a powerful network of poleis in the Aegean and beyond, where a strong united navy led by Athens guaranteed safe waters and unimpeded trade. Failure at Thasos would encourage other dissidents; the League would fall apart; the situation would revert to the pre-war status quo: a miscellany of independent rival poleis, each trying to do down its neighbour, wasting its men and its resources, powerless in the face of vigorous, dynamic enemies such as Persia or the Spartan League. Instead, member states should recognize that they had given up their sovereignty. Swearing their everlasting oath at Delos, the Ionians had requested that Athenians should lead them; and look where they *had* led them: to great victories against the Persians. They all knew Athens furnished the most ships. They all knew Athens held most power. Surely by now they knew, too, that, no matter what they had imagined at the start, the notion of a league of equals was a fiction; that the union they had embraced with such enthusiasm was transforming (organically, it seemed) into an empire—which was why Thasos must fall, regardless of the time the siege might take, regardless of the cost. For Cimon personally, too, remembering his father's fate, condemned for failing to take Paros, success was critical. He knew that he would have to face *euthyna* (accounting), the procedure whereby public officers must justify how they had spent their budgets and discharged their duties, and convince the People they had done what they were tasked to do. Haunted by the memory of his father's prison cell, Cimon was determined not to be found wanting, or let himself be punished by his enemies at home for failing to defeat their enemies abroad.

Another autumn passed, another winter, before at last the spring of 463 came and the result they had been waiting for: a gate opening the merest crack; an emaciated figure squeezing through, clutching a *kerukeion*, a bronze pole topped by intertwining snakes, the symbol of the messenger god, Hermes, protector of all heralds under international Greek law. Escorted to Cimon, the gaunt envoy made his proclamation: the city was ready to capitulate; the siege was over. For Cimon the challenge now was to preserve discipline. Thasos was an ally, a subject state of Athens, and there must be no looting. Instead, as his men marched through the empty streets past doorways where skeletal adults and emaciated children, hollow-eyed, exhausted and diminished by the horrors they had suffered, stared impassively, Cimon set out his terms. Thasos' walls must be demolished and its fleet surrendered; the islanders must pay a huge indemnity upfront (that would more than reimburse the costs of the two-year siege) and an annual tribute of 30 talents; and most crushingly of all they must cede their mainland interests to Athens, not least their mining rights, so lucrative, so coveted. Powerless, the islanders agreed and, with order restored, Cimon, once more triumphant, his flagship laden with gold bullion, set sail for Athens.[12]

By rights he should have had a hero's welcome for having brought the islanders to heel. Yet, no sooner was he home than the process of *euthyna* began, and Cimon found himself accused of failing to discharge his duties to the People's satisfaction. During his absence his rivals, Pericles and Ephialtes, had been leading military missions of their own, sailing south again beyond the Islands of the Swallows in the hope of seeing action, wooing the Assembly, working to undo the damage that Themistocles' disgrace dealt to the progressive democratic cause, encouraging the notion that Athenian hegemony was a god-given right, and stoking suspicions against such old-school patriarchs as Cimon with his blatant admiration of all things Spartan, suspicions fuelled by Sparta's willingness to help the Thasian rebels by invading Attica. And why, when he was so close to Drabescus and Ennea Hodoi, had Cimon done nothing to protect the settlers from being massacred by Thracians? Was it because of his own Thracian blood? Yet, this was not the basis of the prosecution before the Court of the Areopagus. Instead, Pericles demanded why, when he had the opportunity, when he was in theatre, Cimon did not punish Alexander, the slippery king of Macedon, who in the Persian Wars had vacillated between acting as a Persian envoy and seeming to support the allied cause. Surely it was because the Macedonian had bribed Cimon and bought him off.[13]

Even Pericles cannot really have believed such a hackneyed accusation, a variation on the charge made by Xanthippus, his father, against Miltiades, that he was bribed by Persia not to capture Paros. He must have known that Cimon's rules of engagement did not include attacking Alexander; that there was nothing to link Alexander with the Thasian revolt; and that, while he may have had designs on Ennea Hodoi himself, a territory he may once have owned, Alexander was not complicit in the settlers' massacre. Moreover, despite collaborating with the Persians, the Macedonian had done all he could to help the Greeks, and Athens in particular: his advice at Tempe and Plataea had been invaluable, and (as he took great pain to stress) he had withdrawn support from Xerxes as quickly as he could, harrying the Persian army as it retreated through his lands; since then Athens had appointed him her proxenus in Macedonia and (for providing timber for her fleet) awarded him the honorific title 'Euergetes' ('Benefactor'). Despite the charge being farcical, the trial went ahead—which played perfectly to Pericles' strategy. To prosecute Cimon, the establishment's darling, enhanced his kudos, not only mirroring Miltiades' trial (perhaps reminding the Athenians how Cimon's father had been tried, too, for acting like a tyrant) but giving Pericles and Ephialtes a golden opportunity to demonstrate that, even if the case could not be made to stick, Cimon, the victor of Eion, Eurymedon and Thasos, was still subject to the People's law.[14]

On the eve of the trial there came a quite extraordinary intervention: acting entirely independently, Elpinice, Cimon's sister, the wife of wealthy Callias, took it upon herself to visit Pericles' house, where she berated him for spearheading the prosecution and urged him to think again. For most high-born Athenian women, such action would have been unconscionable: unless they were priestesses they were expected to stay demurely at home, venturing out only to attend processions and state festivals, and their greatest aspiration was or should have been (in words attributed to Pericles himself) 'not to be spoken of for either good or ill'. Women who did attract attention, who let themselves become the subject of male gossip, must be prepared for calumny and insult, to be branded as a termagant or whore. Yet such proprieties meant little to Elpinice. Tough and intelligent, she was, after all, a part-Thracian princess, who had grown up far from Athens, and for whom the niceties of social convention meant little, while, since her husband was the richest man in Athens, she could afford (within reason) to be eccentric. Nonetheless, to visit Pericles at home took determination, and to lay out her case rationally before him required cool self-control. Yet the self-control she needed to endure his glacial response was greater still. Smugly, Pericles replied: 'You are an old woman, Elpinice, an old woman, and too old to be doing business like this.' The implication that she was somehow offering herself to Pericles, prostituting herself for her brother's sake, combined with the harsh reminder of her age (Elpinice was in her forties, Pericles was thirty-two) were as unkind and uncalled for as the rumour that Cimon and she had been incestuous lovers. Still, when the case did come to trial, Pericles' performance was noticeably limp. All that he did was stand, read out the charge and sit down quietly, while Cimon spoke passionately and at length. He had not, he thundered, been bought off by Alexander. He was not, like some in Athens, the hired lackey of Ionian tycoons or a lobbyist for foreign plutocrats such as Thessaly's Aleuadae. And if he were to champion the cause of any foreign state, it would be Sparta, for it was the Spartans' way of life, their moderation, their frugality that he admired the most. He had no wish for personal enrichment—but he would strive for the enrichment of his city and he was proud to have made Athens greater through his victories.[15]

Cimon's acquittal can have surprised no-one—least of all Pericles and Ephialtes. Yet, as his supporters celebrated victory, some must have questioned how advisable it was for him to place such emphasis on his close ties with Sparta. While the Assembly was used to hearing Cimon arguing that only a strong alliance between Athens and Sparta could ensure lasting stability, and his constant mantra, 'what would Sparta do?', had it not been for the earthquake, Sparta would have answered Thasos' request for help by invading Attica, and the two poleis would now be at war. For many, Cimon was a fantasist if he thought that Sparta would cooperate with Athens as an equal. Surely he must see the rivalries, the mutual suspicions, the old fault lines that ran through interstate relationships and meant that even temporary peace could be achieved only through war. Plainly he must realize that Sparta was the enemy, that, once recovered, she would do all in her power to hold back Athens' growth and undermine her empire. It was simply not in Athens' interests to view Sparta as a partner, but rather give thanks for the earthquake, and exploit the situation to her own advantage. Yet even as such arguments were being debated, an envoy came from Sparta, Pericleidas, wrapped in his red cloak, to sit as suppliant beside an altar in the Agora, where calling on the gods as witnesses he requested that Athenians, those proven experts in siege warfare, come to Messenia to help fight the helots who had occupied the heights of Mount Ithome.[16]

His arrival caused a stir; soon curious onlookers were gathering near the altar, keen to gawp at this unprecedented sight, a supplicating Spartan, an Identical, his hair and beard long, upper lip close-shaved, his icy gaze, his face betraying no feelings as the artisans and shop-keepers of Athens grinned at his discomfiture. That he had come, that Sparta's ephors had dispatched him to a city that a year before they had been ready to attack, that they were willing to admit their need for help showed the magnitude of the crisis facing them. It could, of course, have been much worse. A few years earlier, before oligarchs seized power in Argos and the Arcadian alliance fractured, Sparta's enemies might easily have seized the moment to sweep south, ally with helots, annihilate the Spartans (so desperately outnumbered) and put an end to their regime. Remembering the massacre at Sepeia and ambitious still to be preeminent within the Peloponnese, many Argives must still have advocated such a course of action; and there was no guarantee that their views would not prevail. Which was why, with much soul-searching, the Spartans had been forced to swallow their pride and appeal not just to Athens but to all those who had fought with them against the Persians in the name of freedom (by which, of course, they meant the freedom of free Greeks, not slaves or helots). To Argos pointedly, however, they sent no appeal: the city had not joined the anti-Persian alliance; for Sparta it remained beyond the pale; it was enough that it stayed neutral.[17]

In Athens, meanwhile, Pericleidas' petition was proving divisive, and as leaders of the two main factions stood before the crowds in the Assembly, the sheer scale of the schism became apparent. Of immediate concern was whether to send help or to abandon Sparta in her hour of need, yet the implications of each course of action were enormous. On one side of the political divide were Ephialtes, Pericles and the populists, for whom oligarchic Sparta was anathema, to whom the earthquake seemed not just fortuitous, but further proof of the extent to which gods favoured Athens. For Sparta was no friend. Her recent support of Thasos was evidence enough. And who could forget the Persian Wars, when Sparta had let Athens burn—twice—rather than march to help her? In fact, the only time that Sparta intervened on an Athenian's behalf was when she backed Isagoras against Cleisthenes and the early democrats. No, Sparta was a rival, not a friend, and Athens owed her nothing. In fact, Athens owed it to herself and Greece not only not to help the Spartans but to take this opportunity—god-given—to trample Sparta underfoot, to grind her under heel, to put an end to Spartan arrogance.[18]

Yet to Cimon this policy remained instinctively and dangerously wrong-headed. He still believed that Greek stability required Athenians and Spartans to be equal partners. After all, their interests lay in different spheres: preoccupied with maintaining her internal security and proud of her ancient role as leader of a Peloponnesian-based league, Sparta had no overseas ambitions. Her withdrawal from the Greek League was proof of this and, even recently, she had shown no real will to undermine Athenian ambitions. As for her helping Thasos by sending troops to Attica, no such invasion had transpired, and if the Spartans realized that Athens posed no existential threat there was no reason that the two most powerful states in Greece should not exist in harmony, Athens exercising leadership at sea, Sparta holding sway over her confederates on land. Besides, Sparta was still technically an ally, and under the conventions of international conduct allies should help one another. The earthquake—the catastrophe—had altered nothing. Rather, it offered Athens a fine diplomatic opportunity, since by helping stamp out the revolt she would be seen to occupy the moral high ground, put Sparta in her debt, and demonstrate not just to Sparta but all Greece the wisdom of Cimon's policy of partnership, the policy he summed up again in his impassioned peroration: 'Do not let Greece go lame! Do not rob Athens of her yoke-mate!'[19]

Few on Pnyx Hill can have been blind to the magnitude of the occasion. Without doubt their intervention, whether as friends or foes, would affect foreign policy for years to come. Given their background and history, many embraced Ephialtes' proposition, boldly cynical and blatantly opportunistic as it was—given their ambitions, too, since removing Sparta from the game would surely open up new possibilities for new alliances and perhaps fresh land-based conquests. Yet there were others ready to resist such tantalizing visions—not just conservative landowners, who (like Cimon) enjoyed friendships with individual Spartans and admired the Spartan way of life with its reassuring hierarchies and respect for class, but oarsmen whom Cimon had led to victory, farmers and artisans proud to have served in his campaigns, still basking in the glow of his charisma, urban and rural poor still grateful for his gifts of clothes and money and the shade of leafy plane trees in the Agora, Athenians who believed that it was Cimon's brilliance and energy that helped them rise again to greatness in the wake of Persian destruction, that it was Cimon's flair that helped them build their empire, that it was thanks to him that they could now stand tall. Yet the outcome of the vote was far from certain. The Assembly seemed almost equally divided; a forest of hands raised; officials trying to gauge the numbers; intense discussions; and only at last the result: Cimon's argument had won the day, albeit by a small majority. Sparta would receive their aid.[20]

All that remained to be decided were the size and nature of the task force. A mountain siege called for both hoplites and light-armed troops, and while they might be transported into theatre by sea it made more sense to send them overland. Sparta, after all, might baulk at seeing Athens' navy anchored off her shores, or entertaining (even for a short time) many thousand oarsmen on her coast. How many troops, therefore, to send? Too large an army, and those Spartans who had been reluctant to enlist Athenian help (and there were surely many who opposed requesting aid, just as in Athens many were reluctant to provide it) would suspect its true objectives, thinking it had come to overrun not liberate their lands; too small a force, however, could not achieve its goals. In the end Cimon—for command fell naturally to him—mustered 4,000 hoplites, perhaps a fifth of the total available, and together with a crowd of light troops and attendants, accompanied by Sparta's envoy Pericleidas, marched out through the Sacred Gate, past his orchards at Laciadae, past Eleusis, on past Megara, across the Isthmus past the ruins of the wall thrown up against the Persians, down through the fields and hills of Corinth and the mountain passes of Arcadia until he reached the broad Messenian plain and, to his left, the foothills of Ithome, where they found a sizeable encampment—Spartan Identicals and Spartan allies, too, summoned to lend help in Sparta's hour of need.[21]

From the start the atmosphere must have been awkward. What was the chain of command? Surely the Spartan king assigned to this campaign took ultimate control. But Athenians had not taken orders from a Spartan for over fifteen years, and even then—at Artemisium and Salamis, Plataea and Mycale, or in the brief months when Pausanias commanded the alliance at Byzantium—they had obeyed reluctantly and grudgingly. Now lords of their own empire, they were unaccustomed to playing a secondary role and disinclined to be dragooned by a tyrannical, despotic Spartan. Nor would it have been surprising if the mood among the other Greeks was less than welcoming. While none had actively opposed her siege of Thasos or her treatment of those other members of the League reluctant to remain, many regarded Athens with suspicion, some with barely repressed hostility. In such a climate of distrust, even Cimon's motivations appeared questionable, and, as he tirelessly directed the siege operations, sharing with Spartan colleagues and their allies his experiences of taking Eion, Phaselis and Thasos, some began to question the advisability of admitting such a man and such an army into Sparta's heartlands—especially since, disgruntled and disillusioned, not a few Athenian hoplites had been overheard expressing sympathy for the rebellious helots, who many will have realised for the first time were fellow Greeks, suggesting that in the helots' shoes they would have done the same, even hinting that it would be better if, instead of trying to defeat the helots, they did all they could to help them. Athenians were used to grumbling. They cherished their free speech that enabled them to sound off, construct castles in the sky, express extreme ideas that few would ever think of putting into action. But Spartans were not used to such behaviour, which to them revealed a lack of discipline, while such opinions seemed dangerous. Gradually, despite Cimon doing all he could to offer reassurances and smooth things over, relations soured until after many months of tension the Spartan king commanded Cimon to his tent. The Athenians, he told him, were dangerous subversives bent on revolution; they had clearly come to Mount Ithome not to help the Spartans but to undermine them; their sympathies lay with the helots; they were clearly following the strategy laid down by Ephialtes, and their aim was nothing less than Sparta's overthrow; but the Spartan king was no-one's fool; he had seen through them; and now he needed them to leave; he would be better off without them. Undoubtedly Cimon protested, but he could not change the Spartan's mind. Angry and humiliated, all he could do was order his men to strike camp, and endure the black looks and jeers of his beloved Spartans and their allies as, unbowed, his men filed out of camp and down the mountain for the long march home.[22]

With no time to put proper protocols in place and seek advance permission from those states en route to pass through sovereign territory, the Athenians stormed northwards, outrage and indignation growing with each mile they put between themselves and Mount Ithome. When they reached the Isthmus, with its wall a stark reminder of how Sparta had left Athens to the mercy of the Persians—the antithesis of Athens' policy of friendship and cooperation seen on this present mission—tempers were at breaking point, so when they found their way blockaded by Corinthian hoplites they were in no mood to compromise, especially when a horseman galloped up and scornfully addressed Cimon. Where were his manners?, the Corinthian, Lachartus, taunted him. Had he been invited? Did the half-Thracian not know that well-bred people waited at the door until the owner asked them in? If these words were provocative, they were meant to be, for a spirit of belligerence had taken hold in Corinth. Border squabbles with both Megara beyond the Isthmus and Cleonae to the south had seen her army on manoeuvres, while, her economy relying heavily on seagoing trade, she viewed the growth of Athens' power with anger and concern, and many like Lachartus would relish the chance to bloody an Athenian nose, especially when (as now) they had the moral high ground on their side. Many in Cimon's frustrated army would relish an encounter, too, and Cimon was in no mood to back down. 'From what we heard', he growled back threateningly, 'you Corinthians didn't even have the courtesy to knock on the doors of Cleonae or Megara—you simply broke in fully-armed.' Then he threw down the gauntlet. 'Your point was that all roads lie open to the stronger side.' Cimon's threat was clear: stand in our way and we shall fight you; fight and we shall win. With Corinth's hoplites before him and her city to his rear, it was a high-risk gamble. Yet to negotiate or (worse still) apologize would do great harm to Athens' reputation, especially after her humiliating treatment at Mount Ithome. So, with shields raised and javelins ready, Cimon and his men stared down the Corinthians. For a moment the situation might have gone either way; and then the Corinthian lines parted; the road was clear; and Cimon's hoplites, still in a heightened state of readiness, passed through, across the Isthmus and back onto the coast road into Attica.[23]

Once back in Athens Cimon could find no respite. In his absence his enemies had been untiring. The closeness of the vote to send troops to Ithome confirmed that the Assembly had undergone a seismic change and that, despite the setback at Drabescus, increasingly convinced by iterations of their glorious past in artworks and speeches foregrounding their role in standing up to Persia, Athenians were ready to embrace the narrative aired so repeatedly by Pericles and Ephialtes: that their destiny was to rule and to increase their empire, that the time had come for them to turn their backs on policies of privilege peddled by the likes of Cimon, whose behaviour at home seemed increasingly hidebound, patriarchal and patrician, and whose foreign policies (favouring Sparta, wanting the two states to be equals) were preventing them from seizing opportunities to spread their power more widely. And what of Cimon's scurrying to Mount Ithome, jumping when a Spartan snapped his fingers, forced to dance attendance on a Spartan king? What of the slight to Athens' reputation when the Spartans on a whim had sent them home? Even Cimon's hatred of the Persians was now being questioned—when a Persian aristocrat, Rhoesaces, had turned up recently in Athens ostensibly to seek political asylum, suspicious citizens placed him under surveillance and tailed him to Cimon's house, where he placed two bowls on the threshold, one filled with gold, the other with silver; admittedly, the spies found nothing wrong with Cimon's reaction when he discovered them: 'Does Rhoesaces want to be my friend or buy my service?', he demanded; 'To be your friend', came the reply; 'Then keep your money,' Cimon told him, 'Since we're friends, I'm sure you'll let me use it if I need it.'[24]

Yet, nonetheless, the sheer wrong-headedness of Cimon's standpoint was so clear for anyone to see—the sheer wrong-headedness of his patrician colleagues, too. The time had come to take a stand and show the world that power lay with the People; the time had come to scrap the last remaining bastion of privilege that blighted democratic politics; the time had come to end the power of the Council of the Areopagus, many of whose members were entitled and elite, a throwback to the days before democracy. Already Ephialtes had been working to subvert the Areopagus, picking off individual members, arraigning them for maladministration. But the Spartan debacle and Cimon's part in it were a gift they simply could not overlook—for it was the Areopagus that had acquitted Cimon on his return from Thasos, proof positive of how detached it was from the mood of the People, especially since it was thanks (in part) to his acquittal that Cimon marched down to Sparta and exposed his city to such gross humiliation.[25]

The Council of the Areopagus consisted solely of ex-Archons, originally elected from Athens' leading families, advisors to first kings then tyrants, drafting legislation to be rubber-stamped by a tame popular assembly, giving guidance on the arcane business of religion and the law, though two years after Plataea its membership had been thrown open to men chosen by lot from the top two property classes. Already the Areopagus had ceded many of its powers to the Boulé (People's Council), notably the choice and drafting of motions to be debated in the Assembly, but still in several important areas—religious and judicial—it remained supreme. Its members were the 'guardians of the law', the protectors of the constitution, responsible for scrutinizing magistrates, ensuring no abuse of power, the ultimate judicial court with the authority to fine or exile or pass sentence of death. Yet in a modern radical democracy the Areopagus seemed outdated—at least to Ephialtes and his followers, for whom it was the essence of everything they loathed, the symbol of entitlement, the preserve of the elite, men such as Cimon. And now that Cimon's star had been so palpably eclipsed with the debacle at Ithome, the time seemed right to strike a blow and curb the powers of the Areopagus—but not abolish it. Ephialtes let it keep a vestige of its former role. While justice would now pass to the People (juries normally of 501 but in principle of up to 6,000 citizens chosen by lot who could try, convict and sentence unsupervised by a presiding judge), the Areopagus could, he allowed, retain the right to sit in judgement over unintentional homicide, assault and arson; but that was all; from now on it would have no further powers. A bristling of hands, and his proposal passed.[26]

The vote was as important for its symbolism as for its constitutional impact. It marked a shift of power—from Cimon and his now beleaguered followers to the triumphant Ephialtes, a change of policy away from Cimon's world view (favouring a steady growth of power that focussed on containing Persia, removing Persian influence from areas where Athens had an interest, maintaining the growing number of protectorates, ensuring that Athenian ships could ply the waves unchecked, and all the while maintaining a cordial relationship with Sparta) to that of Ephialtes and his lieutenant, Pericles, politicians who (their enemies maintained) had built their power by pandering to the poor, radicals in a hurry whose policies could lead to instability, iconoclasts who threatened to turn Athens upside down. Now that these young thrusting men had elbowed their aggressive way into the limelight, their next move was inevitable. To prove their new authority they would stage an unambiguous show of power, remove their foremost rival, and do it in the most spectacular and public way the constitution would allow. It can have come as no surprise to anyone when, at a meeting on Pnyx Hill that winter, the motion was proposed and passed: in just ten weeks the citizens of Athens would conduct an ostracism; and top of the list of candidates was Cimon.

11

AFTERSHOCK

When I look on the stupidity and ruinous dissent
among the Greeks,
I'm struck with fear.

Theognis, 780–781

ATHENS, 461 B.C.

Public opinion, once it decides to shift, can swing rapidly, and in the weeks between the decision to hold the vote and the ostracism itself, Cimon's enemies did all they could to whip the People into a frenzy. As judgements were revised and opinions recast, as friends and rivals did all they could to distance themselves from Sparta, as one, Alcibiades the Elder, even went so far as to renounce his Spartan proxeny (though this did not save him from ostracism a few years later), opinions about Cimon, scourge of Persia, victor of Eurymedon and Eion, underwent a metamorphosis. Viewed now as a patrician patriarch whose loyalties were not to democratic Athens but to hostile Sparta, even his public works became suspect. Enlarging the Acropolis, building the Temple of Theseus, enhancing facilities at the Academy and Agora, draining the swamps: were these not the kind of grandiose projects in which the tyrants, Peisistratus and Hippias (and his reviled brother, Hipparchus), had once delighted? By pushing such programmes through and paying for many from his own resources, had Cimon not shown that he was cast from the same mould, that he saw himself as their successor? And no-one should forget that Cimon was a tyrant's son, that his father ruled the Chersonese as

his own fiefdom, or that his mother was a princess, a barbarian, a Thracian, like those Thracians who massacred Athenian troops in ambush
at Drabescus and settlers at Enna Hodoi. And look at Cimon's entourage, those young men trailing in his phosphorescent wake, with their
upper-class accents and their air of entitlement, condescendingly distrib-
uting largesse to the poor. Look at how Cimon proclaimed his own
ambitions by foregrounding his father in his Marathon memorial at
Delphi. Look at his sister, the debauched Elpinice, who (the scandalmon-
gers gloated), bored with her incestuous relationship with Cimon, was
conducting an adulterous affair with Polygnotus, the evidence for which
was plain to see, since in the Stoa Poicile his painting of the Sack of Troy
included a depiction of Laodice, most beautiful of all Trojan princesses,
which bore such likeness to Elpinice that she had clearly modelled for it
in a state of déshabillé, if not worse. Not for these gossips the sad truth
that she was now 'an old woman, too old to be doing business such as
this'. And then, what of her intervention—a woman's intervention!—in
her brother's trial, when she tried to influence his prosecutor, Pericles?
The opportunities afforded by the ostracism for the malicious, misogynistic masses to vent their spleen were simply too enticing to ignore. For
years, accusations fostered in those spiteful months would linger in the
public mind, with verses penned to keep their memory alive:

> He wasn't a bad man (or poor), but how he loved his liquor and siestas.
> From time to time he'd sleep away from home in Sparta
> even if it did mean having to leave Elpinice alone in bed without him.[1]

Now they were persuaded that Cimon was a threat, the People—freed
from the menace of Persian invasion thanks to his victories; growing
prosperous from trade routes secured by his campaigns; enjoying the
power and revenue of empire thanks to his diplomacy and military
prowess; but poisoned now by Ephialtes' posturing and the partisanship
of his coterie—voided their scorn on him. Astute, alert to public sentiment, Cimon must have predicted how the vote would go, and as dawn
broke over the Acropolis on the morning of the ostracism, and sunlight
glinted golden from Athena Promachus's spear-tip, he must already have
been making preparations for his exile. Then the crowds began to
gather, peasants pouring in from the surrounding countryside, seafarers
from Piraeus, artisans from narrow city lanes or soot-black foundries in
backstreets of the Cerameicus, many clutching potsherds on which they

had already written Cimon's name, others approaching Ephialtes' agents to collect the damning token, all congregating at the edges of the Agora beneath the budding plane trees, and filing through past voting urns, the clack of broken pottery drowned out by the excited hubbub. It need not have taken long: entering or leaving the Assembly on Pnyx Hill, finding seating in the theatre or identifying their proper place in tightly-organized processions for their gods, Athenians were aficionados of large crowds. Six thousand men and more filed through; 6,000 votes and more were cast; and when the voting urns were lugged onto the central platform and the potsherds shaken out and counted there could be no remaining doubt. Although a scattering of other names had garnered a few votes, by far the greatest number went to Cimon. One even bore the message: 'Cimon, son of Miltiades, go! And take Elpinice with you.'[2]

Of course, that would not happen. Callias' wife would stay in Attica. So would Cimon's three surviving sons, twins Oulius (lackadaisical and lacking in ambition) and Lacedaemonius (his very name now tainted by growing anti-Spartan prejudice) both adults, the youngest, Thettalus, still in his teens. There had been other sons—a Cimon, a Miltiades, a Peisianax—but all died young, and now their mother, Cimon's beloved Isodice, was dead, too. Her passing had broken Cimon's heart and, despite the sympathy of friends and elegiac poems composed to comfort him, he had been inconsolable. Like the union of Elpinice and Callias, theirs had been that rare thing in the Athens of their day, a loving and respectful marriage, their relationship more truly like the pairing of the two racehorses yoked beneath one chariot of which he dreamed than that of Sparta and his city would ever be. Now aged almost fifty, for ten years he was compelled to leave her grave and those of his dead sons, his town house in the hills of Athens, his farmhouse and the well-tilled fields and orchards at Laciadae; now he was compelled to take his leave of family, friends and well-wishers, all keen to embrace him one last time before he disappeared for exile, all promising to do everything they could to look after his interests in his absence. The ten-day interval between the vote and his departure must have passed quickly in a whirlwind of encounters and emotions—not least fear that the fate that befell Themistocles, the last man ostracised before Cimon, might befall him, too. For who could guarantee that, with the People prejudiced against him, the likes of Ephialtes would not indict him in his absence on a trumped-up accusation of conspiring with the Spartans, as they

A broken ostrakon (perhaps from the vote of 461 B.C.) bears the fateful name:
Cimon, son of Miltiades.

charged absent Themistocles with conspiring with Pausanias and Persia?
Then the tenth day came, and Cimon was gone, though where to is un-
recorded. Perhaps he sailed north to the Chersonese and to the sights
and cities of his childhood; perhaps he renewed ties with family in
Thrace; perhaps from time to time at Panhellenic festivals he managed
to catch up with friends and keep his finger on the pulse of politics, to
discover what was happening in Athens and abroad, how his careful policies were being unravelled, how mainland Greeks were threatening to
tear themselves apart.[3]

With Cimon neutralized, Ephialtes and his partisans lost no time in
making their mark on the fabric of the city. At the west side of the Agora,
in the heart of the administrative quarter, they constructed a round
building with a conical pitched roof, the embodiment of their egalitarian ambitions. Soon given the nickname 'Skias' ('Sunshade'), the
Tholos was built to be the residential headquarters of the revolving Pry-
taneis, fifty 'presidents' out of the 500 annually appointed representatives who, for thirty-six days, formed the executive committee of the
Boulé, the deliberative council, while their tribe held the presidency.

Here they ate at state expense; here, too, many slept, to ensure that even in the hours of darkness officials were at hand in case of an emergency; and here they guarded the official weights and measures against which all others in the city and the empire must be calibrated. Coinciding with power passing from the lofty Areopagus to the democratic Boulé, the timing of the Tholos' construction was not coincidental. Nor was its siting. There were still men in Athens, veterans of Marathon and the attack on Sardis, who recalled that here beneath the low hill of Colonus Agoraius once stood the palace of Peisistratus, from whose doors they forced Hippias to flee. How fitting, then, that democrats should sleep where once these tyrants took their rest, and eat where they had banqueted. What better way to prove how far the city had advanced in fifty years?[4]

If the Tholos was a sign of how democracy was flourishing, Ephialtes could take pleasure, too, in the People's passionate approval of his policies. Of course, Cimon still had supporters, not least his relative (perhaps his son-in-law) Melesias' son, Thucydides, an up-and-coming politician, now champion of the conservatives, opposing what he saw as dangerous populism. Yet it was almost impossible to make his voice heard. With Athenians resentful of their treatment at Ithome, it took Ephialtes little effort to whip up anti-Spartan prejudice or convince them to rescind arrangements still in place from the dark days of Xerxes' invasion, and sign treaties instead with Sparta's staunchest enemies, Thessaly and Argos, no matter that both states had either sided with the Persians or remained resolutely neutral in the months when Greece's fate hung in the balance. With Thessalians mistrusting Sparta since Leotychidas' attack sixteen years earlier, and the Argives (now flirting with democracy) again keen to challenge Sparta's role as leader of the Peloponnese, and with both peoples grateful for being readmitted to the Greek fold chiefly through the efforts of Ephialtes' mentor, Themistocles, it was enough that this new axis gave Athenians the opportunity to expand their influence on land to complement their dominance at sea. Thanks to the undermining of the Areopagus, the tearing up of Cimon's policies and possibilities afforded by this new alliance, Ephialtes' star was in the ascendant. He must have seemed unstoppable.[5]

Then one morning, as cocks crowed through the twilight of the dawn and dogs barked in awakening courtyards, a corpse was found sprawled in the street, a viscous mess of blood. Knife wounds showed the man had been the victim of a merciless attack, dumped here deliberately for anyone to see. But this was not some random act of violence or simple robbery gone wrong. It was a political assassination. For as more people came to gaze on it they all agreed they recognized the face; they all had seen those hands, now lifeless, slicing the air in emphasis; they all had heard the dead man's voice raised in heart-stopping peroration, fulminating against social injustice and the perfidy of the pro-Spartan landowning elite. They all knew that it was Ephialtes—so much was clear. Yet the identity of the murderer (or murderers) eluded them, as it eluded subsequent investigation. Some not unnaturally accused Ephialtes' many enemies, conservatives sympathetic to Cimon, furious at the speed and scope of domestic reform and the volte-face in foreign policy. Somehow Thucydides escaped the charge, but in time a suspect did emerge: Aristodicus, a Boeotian from Tanagra, twenty-five miles north of Athens near the Attic border and the sea, a city whose power had grown since the Persian Wars, that was vying with diminished Thebes to lead Boeotia, and that now was turning a rapacious eye on Attica. To destabilize Athens would suit Tanagra well. Others, however, pointed the finger of suspicion much closer to home—at one of Ephialtes' closest colleagues, the man who stood to benefit most from his death by stepping seamlessly into his shoes as figurehead and leader of the progressive faction: Pericles.[6]

Certainly he stepped up to the plate immediately, and that there was no more bloodshed or unrest was evidence both of his statesmanship and of the Athenians' political maturity. Indeed, they had much to distract them. Inspired by Athens' recent treaty with Thessaly and Argos, Megara, her western neighbour, weary of constant Corinthian incursions, announced her decision to leave the Spartan league and join the new confederacy instead. Undoubtedly the fruit of painstaking negotiation, the announcement was most welcome. Sited just north of the Isthmus, Megara (like Corinth) boasted ports on two seas: Nisaea on the Saronic Gulf across the straits from Salamis; and Pegae on the Corinthian Gulf, from which the way lay open to the west—not only to Corcyra and the Ionian Sea but further to South Italy and Sicily, home to so many thriving colonies. For Athenians to sail west from Pegae would not only cut crucial travel time, it would remove the need to sail around the Peloponnese, especially Cape Malea, so often plagued by high winds and high seas, the site of many shipwrecks. Megara's decision, then, to switch sides and enter an Athenian alliance marked a turning point, the start of a new chapter in Athens' economic and imperial ambitions.[7]

For those ambitions knew no bounds, as Athens' latest project showed. Almost certainly Thucydides approved—and Cimon, too, when he heard of it in exile—for again it involved liberating lands from Persia. This time, though, the land in question was not Greek; it did not even border the Aegean; it was an ancient empire, proud of its millennia-long history, but more importantly for Athens, fertile almost beyond imagination and burgeoning with rich resources: Egypt. Greeks had been trading goods and ideas with Egyptians since at least the Bronze Age, a relationship enhanced in the early sixth century through a charter to establish a permanent *emporion* (or entrepôt) in the Nile Delta at the aptly-named Naucratis ('Supremacy of Ships'). A thriving community, where Greeks, whose native cities often found themselves at war, lived side by side in seven-storey high-rise blocks, worshipped together, and worked cooperatively in docks and warehouses, Naucratis was a physical reminder of pharaohs' gratitude towards Greek mercenaries who helped them keep or gain the throne—Psammetichus I, restored by hoplites, shipwrecked 'men of bronze', after a revolution; Apries, leading 30,000 hired Ionians and Carians against his rebel general, Amasis; Amasis himself, who, defeating Apries, admired his Greeks so much that he engaged them as his bodyguard, instructed them to teach Egyptian boys their language, and formed an alliance with Polycrates, tyrant of Samos. Yet, while Amasis ruled with energy and vision, extending his kingdom west to Libya and north to Cyprus and beating off the Babylonians, within sixth months of his death the Persians had overrun his country and carted off his son, Psammetichus III, in chains to Susa, where he committed suicide. Under Persian suzerainty, Naucratis was allowed to flourish, untroubled by revolts in Asia Minor, invasions of Greece's mainland or insurrections within Egypt itself. Nor was it especially troubled now, when Libya's King Inaros, seized the moment, launched an attack on Persia's garrisons in Egypt and sent a messenger to Athens to request military aid.[8]

It happened that an Athenian League fleet of 200 triremes was already in the seas off Cyprus in the ongoing hope of prising control of the copper-rich island from the Great King, Artaxerxes I. Now in the fifth year of his reign, Artaxerxes (nicknamed 'Long-Hand', since his right hand was longer than his left) was elevated to the throne after a botched but bloody palace coup, when on a sultry August night, cicadas rasping in the trees outside, his father, Xerxes, then in his mid-fifties, was stabbed repeatedly in his own bedroom by his chief advisor's son. The assassin was clever. He had planned his next move well. With blood still sticky on his hands and clothing—the result, he claimed, of trying to staunch the dying king's wounds—he clattered to Artaxerxes' chambers, where with histrionics worthy of a tragic actor he poured out his fake news that the assassin was none other than Darius, Xerxes' eldest son. Distraught and bent on vengeance, Artaxerxes, his bodyguard beside him, swept through the corridors and on into Darius' room, where, unhesitatingly, he knifed his brother to death. By now, however, the assassin had himself arrived with other members of the royal household including his own sons, urging them to cut down Artaxerxes where he stood, red-handed by Darius' corpse, proof, he assured them, that he murdered Xerxes, too. But no-one could touch Artaxerxes. Valiantly he and his lone bodyguard fought off all comers, until the last of his attackers was lying dead. Then, after the usual rituals of mourning, in Pasargadae he was proclaimed Great King of Persia. Or so the story went, and somewhere it may hide a grain of truth. Certainly transitions from one ruler to the next are often fraught with peril, with new loyalties sought and old scores settled, but, if after four years the Great King Artaxerxes thought he had consigned all dangers to the past, he now discovered he was wrong.[9]

Diverted south to Egypt, the Greek ships dealt swiftly with a small Phoenician fleet they caught patrolling off the coast. Then, nosing up the Nile, they found two massive armies drawn up near the city of Papremis on the riverbank. On one side was Inaros, his Libyan troops, wearing stiffened leather armour, their javelins hardened in the fire, augmented by myriad Egyptians, including men from far-off Ethiopia, their bodies smeared half-red, half-white with vermilion and chalk, their shoulders trailing lion- and leopard skins, and clutching clubs or long bows in their hands; the Persians—perhaps as many as 300,000—in their trousers and scale mail led by the wily old Achaemenes, the Great King's uncle, a veteran of Salamis, who had long presided over Egypt as its satrap. As up to 40,000 Greeks poured out from their black ships to swell Inaros' ranks as hoplites or as slingers, captains patrolled the lines and barked out words of exhortation. And then the orders came, and arrows flew, and the light of the bright, baking sun became diminished as the two sides clashed and clouds of sand were kicked up by men's feet and horses' hooves that thundered round the flanks as spears and javelins found their marks and brains exploded beneath deadly clubs; and so the killing multiplied.[10]

Used to such battles with the Persians, the League's hoplites led the push that broke the enemy's formation. Now they were through; the Persians' morale was breaking; Achaemenes was down, dragged from his horse, his body brutalized; and Persians were running, racing for their lives, cascading in a screaming mass south for the safety of nearby Memphis, the victors on their heels, the corpses of the dead left on the battlefield. And now Inaros and his men had entered Memphis; now they had overrun and occupied two-thirds of Egypt's sprawling ancient capital with its temples and its nearby pyramids, its palaces adorned with lakes and lovely parklands. But one-third remained, and at its heart the seemingly impregnable White Castle, whose gleaming walls gave Memphis its Egyptian name, Inebu-hedj, where behind its gates the Persians regrouped and, confident that they could not be taken, settled down for a long siege, as Greeks and Libyans dug in outside and waited.[11]

That the Athenian League could readily commit so many troops and ships to a potentially long-term campaign so far from home spoke to its almost boundless confidence and rich resources. For in Greece its troops and navy were campaigning, too. To mark Athens' new alliance with Argos and advertise her rejection of Cimon's pro-Spartan policy— perhaps, too, wishing simply to be provocative—Pericles had persuaded the Assembly to send ships to Halieis at the south tip of the Argolid Peninsula, a strategic town controlled by Epidaurus, and annex it for Athens. The Epidaurians sought help from Corinth (still reeling from Megara's decision to ally with Athens) and soon a combined army had forced the aggressors back to the ships. At sea, though, Athens continued to fare better. In waters off Cecryphaleia, an island between Aegina and the mainland, she routed a fleet led by Corinth. Evidence of the truth that their supremacy lay on sea, not land, these two encounters should have caused Athenians to pause for thought. But already conflict was beginning to pick up an unstoppable momentum of its own.[12]

On Aegina, long Athens' enemy (no matter that the two had fought together side by side against the Persians at Salamis), merchants and strategists alike were growing nervous. From their northern coast they, too, could glimpse the pinprick flash of sunlight from the spear tip of the statue of Athena Promachus high on the Athenian Acropolis, and they saw it as a threat. For while Athens' grip on sea lanes menaced the island's economic capabilities, Athenian ambitions on the mainland might menace her very independence. Athens' attack on Halieis (and her recent takeover of Troezen) showed her interest in controlling the coastline of the Saronic Gulf, at whose heart Aegina lay. Surely it would not be long before she turned her gorgon's glare on Aegina as well. What better time to take on Athens' navy than now, when, with many of its ships in far-off Egypt, it was understrength? So, joined by Corinthian allies, Aegina put to sea in a show of strength that Athens could not ignore, and now League triremes, too, were shearing the dawn swell; but while the Aeginetans were fine sailors, and Corinthians were better, none were a match for the Athenians. As spume dripped from oars and rippling wakes criss-crossed the surface of the Gulf, once pristine but now scattered with ships' wreckage and the bobbing corpses of the dead, it was clear why Athens ruled the waves. Within hours Athenian troops were splashing onto Aegina and laying siege to the city.[13]

But the Corinthians would not renounce their ally. Reluctant to engage again at sea, they marched on Megara, intent on either prising back their neighbour from the hands of Athens or distracting overstretched Athenians from besieging Aegina. They achieved neither objective. With almost every man of fighting age already on campaign, Athens' general, Myronides, a veteran of Plataea, who before that battle had been part of Cimon's diplomatic mission to the Spartans, had no choice but to enlist the very young, youths on the cusp of adulthood still undergoing their training, and the old, those veterans over sixty who had fought with Cimon in his wars with Persia. Neither frailty nor inexperience would daunt them. Donning armour, dented or shining new, they confronted the Corinthians and crushed them. No wonder that they felt invincible. At no time before had Athens campaigned in so many theatres simultaneously. Casualty lists mixed grief with pride, one prefacing the names of its 107 dead: 'From the tribe Erechtheis these men fell in the same year fighting wars in Cyprus, Egypt, Phoenicia, Halieis, Aegina and Megara'. The city's energy was breathtaking, her military prowess stratospheric. Yet Athenians could not afford to be complacent. They knew that both Boeotia and Sparta had superior land armies, which was why they had begun to build two battlemented 'Long Walls' between the city and Piraeus, so that, in case of siege, the well-protected strip between them would give constant access to the sea, turning the city in effect into a landlocked island. As long as their navy reigned supreme, Athenians would never starve. With Megarians already following their example, digging foundations for their own long walls to Nisaea, Athens' rivals, desperate to intervene, urged Spartans to show leadership, but with the helot revolt still ongoing and their numbers diminished by the earthquake, they were reluctant to leave home.[14]

But they could not stay passive forever. The stimulus came unexpectedly: a Phocian attack on three towns in Doris, a tiny state nestled in a valley between Mount Oeta and Parnassus. To Sparta, this was not some trivial incursion into some remote, inconsequential canton, it was an assault on her very soul, for it was from Doris that the Dorian Spartans believed they had first come, the sons of Heracles, migrating south to stake their claim on lush Laconia—and Doris must be saved. A force of 1,500 Spartans and 10,000 allies lost little time in liberating Doris. But instead of then going home, it marched to Thebes. At Plataea twenty-two years earlier, Spartans and Thebans had fought against each other. Now, though, the kaleidoscope had shifted. Now Athens, Sparta's erstwhile ally, was Sparta's enemy, the bellicose democracy apparently hell-bent on expanding its already powerful empire. Even in Athens some were nervous—patricians who saw the Long Walls as yet another step towards the rise of the seafaring poor; grandees, fearful for the future, already in communication with the Spartans, making plans and trading confidences, declaring themselves ready to betray their city if Sparta guaranteed them power. Thebes, too, was seeking favours. Weakened since the Persian Wars, humiliated by the rise of rivals such as Tanagra, the city wanted to reclaim her status as Boeotia's hegemon, and with Sparta's help she knew that she could do it. For their part, too, the Spartans knew that to place Thebes in their debt would bring strategic benefits, short term as well as long, for with Boeotia tied to their alliance, with a Boeotian army marching by their side, with Athens not just overstretched but harbouring men keen to overthrow the constitution, they might well in this very fighting season crush the Athenians. With such a prize apparently within their grasp, Thebes and Sparta concluded an alliance and set off across the plain towards Tanagra and the trackways that would take them into Attica.[15]

The Athenians had no time to lose. Engaged in Egypt and on Aegina, their numbers were dangerously depleted, and while they had recently defeated the Corinthians in Megara, a combined force of Spartans and Boeotians was a different proposition. With 1,000 Argive allies, light-armed troops and hoplites from cities favourably disposed to them or hostile towards Sparta, and a squadron of Thessalian cavalry, they could field a force of over 14,000 men; and, while they would be outnumbered, they would be fighting for their homeland and their constitution, taking the battle to the enemy, not waiting passively to be attacked, or worrying lest traitors should throw open Athens' gates and let the Spartans in. North through the saddle between Parnes and Pentelicon they marched, while a fleet of fifty triremes nudged up the coast past Marathon a few miles to the east. Then veering round through baking fields and pastureland the army splashed across the slow Asopus, little but a trickle in the summer heat, and on into Boeotia and the low range of Teumessos, its hills cascading westwards towards Thebes. Here on the high eastern slopes Tanagra stood, its hilltop temples to Apollo, Hermes, Aphrodite, Themis, Dionysus, set discreetly in a sacred quarter beyond the secular city. And here beside vineyards thick with ripening grapes and thrumming to the sound of insects, the Spartans and Boeotians were drawn up between the river and the hills, while Athens' army took its place and waited.[16]

At first no movement, as both sides stared across the empty void of no-man's-land, trading insults, rattling spears on shields, reluctant to engage the enemy. Impasse. But then, far to their rear a sudden dust cloud and the sound of pounding hooves; a small bunched band of horsemen galloping at full tilt into the Athenian camp and making for the men of the Oeneid tribe, who leapt to arms and stood, suspicious, as the leading rider leapt down from his saddle, fully armoured before, bare handed, he removed his helmet, shook out his greying curls and wiped the dust-caked sweat from his face. To a man they recognized his easy smile: Cimon, come to stand beside them in their hour of need; Cimon, one-time champion of Sparta, here to prove his patriotism and expose the petty partisanship of political detractors by fighting in his country's ranks against the Spartans.

Yet, as friends were pressing round him, cheering, the news reached his rivals. Within the army were many members of the Boulé, and they hastily convened a meeting. It was unconstitutional, they argued, to let Cimon return. He had been ostracised and, although he was not technically on Attic soil and there was nothing in the regulations to prevent his free association with Athenians abroad, how could they know that they could trust him? Chief among the reasons they had exiled him had been suspicions that he favoured Sparta, so how could anyone be certain that his coming now was not a ruse? How could they know that, in the heat of battle, he would not switch sides and turn his followers against his people, lead his long-haired Spartan friends to Athens, be installed as tyrant? Burning with manufactured rage, the council members scuttled crabbily to find the generals. Citing the constitution, they readily persuaded them, and a pompous delegation bustled off to track down Cimon and officiously impart their news. There was nothing he could do. He must obey the People. Yet his friends—not least those youths who once had walked beside him, giving gifts of clothes and money to the poor—were loath to see him go, especially since they, too, were suspected of favouring the Spartans. So, urging them to fight with courage and give battle with such single-mindedness that no-one could accuse them of being traitors, Cimon unstrapped his armour; and on a hastily-built frame they fixed it like a trophy—the breastplate and shield, the spears, the sword and sword-belt, and above them all the burnished helmet with its nodding horsehair crest—before, falling into rank around it, they swore that they would never leave their post. Some final words of exhortation, a last farewell, and Cimon swung into the saddle, took up the reins, wheeled round and galloped out of camp.[17]

By now the pre-engagement sacrifices made, entrails examined, and assurances of victory conveyed to generals on both sides, trumpets blared, and all across the plain, men lowered helmets in a rippling of bronze, raised shields and hefted spears, chanting their paean hymns and battle songs before, with arrows flying and sharp slingshot screaming overhead, the Spartans and Boeotians began their terrifying advance to unleash years of pent-up anger on Athenians and Argives. The rituals of Ares, god of war, were underway. At stake was not just victory in this one battle but the honour of every man and every state that fought there—Thebans, Thessalians and Argives, tarred with the brush of cowardice and treachery for their collaboration in the Persian Wars, keen to wipe the slate clean with the blood of hostile Greeks; Spartans, resentful of their rival Athens' kudos won by ridding the Aegean of the Persians; Athenians, still smarting from their treatment at Ithome, convinced by democratic propaganda that destiny demanded they increase the scope of their command to take in the whole mainland—outrage and honour boiling in a frenzied orgy as one-time foes fought side by side against their recent allies.

Yet even now, no-one could know who was a friend and who an enemy. As they held back their stamping, nervous horses, waiting for the moment to engage, Thessalian cavalrymen watched waves of fighting to see how the battle was progressing, trying to second-guess the outcome, weighing the wider consequences of Athenian or Spartan victory. Yes, they had ties with Athens that stretched back to before Peisistratus had been restored to power by their great-grandfathers, and, yes, they owed much to Themistocles for rehabilitating them after the Persian War; but Boeotia and Doris were almost on their border; they had already been invaded once by Sparta; they did not wish to be attacked again, especially if Athens were to lose this battle at Tanagra, as in the dust and turmoil it appeared might be the case. And Thessalians thought nothing of being turncoats—they had switched sides when the Persians came, and a generation earlier they had abandoned Hippias—and their wealthy cavalry had little sympathy for democrats. Much better to throw in their lot with Thebes and Sparta. Much better to switch sides. So, as the afternoon wore on, Athenians and Argives, scarred, bleeding, blood-soaked, discovered themselves harrassed not just by Spartans and Boeotians but by swiftly-galloping Thessalians, their horses streaking by them in a blur of hooves and javelins.[18]

There was still more treachery to come. Lumbering across the mountain pass a baggage train was on its way from Athens, heavy with supplies to feed the army. For the Thessalians it made for pretty pickings and, having wolfed down a hasty supper, they cantered off into the falling night. Reaching the wagons they were hailed as friends—the guards and drivers had not learned of their betrayal, so death came unexpectedly: the dull thud of a javelin; the cold edge of a sword; screams echoing throughout the valley, rousing Athenian troops guarding the camp, who grabbed weapons and raced to their defence. Now archers were drawing bowstrings; hoplites were charging at a run against the horses; now the Thessalians were falling back; but now, too, Spartans, who had discovered what was happening, were marching in close order to their rescue, crossing the muddy Asopus, throwing themselves into the backs of the Athenians, who, swinging round, consumed by anger, matched blow for blow and death for death in vicious fighting. At last dusk fell and night engulfed the plain, and all who still could withdrew. As Athenians,

exhausted, picked their way across the battlefield, lit only by the guttering flames of smoky torches, they discovered Cimon's armour, still
intact, still where his friends had set it on its frame, a fixed point in a
sea of carnage, for every one of his companions was dead. Determined
to uphold his reputation, they had fought until the end, and now they
lay, a hundred corpses, limbs intertwined with those of Spartans they
had killed, their hero's panoply their proud memorial.[19]

Though Sparta and Boeotia claimed victory, the outcome was unclear.
All anyone could tell was that, once both sides had under truce reclaimed
and burned their dead, and the Athenians had collected their comrades'
charred bones and ashes in shared urns for transport home, the Spartans had no stomach left for fighting, turned back for Thebes, and hurried south—past Megara, where they vandalized fruit trees to make
themselves feel marginally better for failing to invade Attica. A flurry
then of diplomatic envoys, and the Athenians and Spartans signed a
treaty for four months until the end of the campaigning season. But this
did not mean that Athens was at peace. In Egypt and on Aegina sieges
were still underway, and after just two months the People sent an army
out to punish the Boeotians for daring to oppose them at Tanagra. Commanding was the leathery Myronides, who the previous year had
drummed out the Corinthians from Megara, and who saw no reason
(now Sparta had no interest in the game) not to trounce Boeotia. Not
everyone in Athens agreed. Many whose names appeared on call-up lists
failed to report for duty, while those who came, disheartened, demanded
that they wait for friends to bring their numbers up to strength. Myronides, irate, refused: that they had stayed away showed that the absen-
tees were cowards; he had no need of them.[20]

So, with a much depleted army, he marched for the Asopus, where at
Oenophyta on the farther bank, with Tanagra just a few miles to the
west, he met the massed troops of Boeotia and, heavily outnumbered,
defeated them. Elated, his triumphant men pursued the fleeing enemy
by country tracks and through the open gateway of Tanagra, where they
quickly took command, tore down the walls, and installed a garrison.
Then they marched on through Boeotia. Around the shores of shallow
Lake Copaïs, Haliartus fell; and Chaeroneia; and Orchomenus. Only
Thebes, recently refortified by Sparta, held out, an island in a sea of conquered cities. But Myronides had no time for a siege. With most of
Boeotia in his hands, he pressed on further. Soon Locris fell; soon

Phocis, too; and, at the head of a surly retinue of hostages, Myronides returned to Athens triumphant. In one short campaign he had established the beginnings of a mainland empire that stretched from Delphi in the west to Cape Sunium in the east and took in not just Attica but Megara, Boetoia, Phocis and Locris, a swathe of territory that already rivalled Sparta's land protectorates and that, added to her existing League, suggested Athens soon would dominate all Greece.[21]

The speed of these new developments was remarkable. A Corinthian enemy is said later to have summed up the energy of the Athenians grudgingly, admiringly:

> They're always doing something new; and they're so quick at coming up with new ideas and putting into action whatever they decide . . . When they defeat their enemies, they advance the farthest; when they're beaten, they retreat the least. They do not even consider their bodies as their own, but use them for their city. Their minds, too, they focus on their city's good; and if they do not act immediately on what they have decided, each thinks it his own personal loss, whereas when through action they achieve success, they think it insignificant compared to what they will do next. If they fail in anything, they do what must be done to remedy the situation and immediately come up with new ambitions. Thanks to the speed with which they follow thought with action, it can be said of the Athenians alone that they immediately possess whatever they desire. Throughout their lives they work hard and run risks, without stopping to enjoy what they do have—so constantly ambitious are they for more. Their idea of a holiday is working to achieve what must be done; leisure is more disagreeable than toil. In short, one might fairly say that it is not their nature to enjoy peace and quiet—and they can't let anybody else enjoy it either.[22]

When Myronides and his hoplites re-entered Athens fresh from victory, they found the two Long Walls that stretched down to the sea complete. Now, even if Spartans did invade (although, with neighbouring Megara and Boeotia in Athenian hands, it was unlikely that they could), they would find Athens not only impregnable but impossible to starve into submission. That Athens was in such a strong position was surely vindication of the aggressive and progressive policies of Pericles and his supporters. But Myronides' was not the only victory. During his absence, another enemy had fallen: Aegina. Once more a city's gates had opened and a herald stumbled out; once more emaciated residents watched listlessly as an Athenian army occupied the streets; once more a conquering general gave orders to his men to tear down city walls. For years in hectoring speeches, Pericles had called Aegina and its city, close to Attic shores, the 'eyesore of Piraeus', a blot on the horizon, since almost alone of islands it had resisted conquest. Now it, too, was in Athenian hands, its native population driven out—but resettled by Sparta.[23]

It was imperative to keep up the momentum. So next spring, rather than renew the truce with Sparta, Athens went on the offensive. Under Tolmides, a rising star, keen to prove his mettle, 50 triremes shot out of Piraeus. On board were 4,000 hoplites, 3,000 of whom volunteered to row as well as fight on land, all fired by the promise that for the first time in Greek history they would be taking the offensive onto Spartan soil, laying waste to Spartan villages and farmsteads as Spartans had once ravaged theirs, destroying military installations, undermining enemy morale. Rounding Malea, they sheared on west towards Messenia and the Peloponnese's westernmost peninsula, where just beyond the cape they beached their triremes on Methone's sandy beaches and poured onto the shore. As news of their landing spread, a blur of scarlet could be seen approaching from the east, a well-drilled army of Identicals intent on driving out these upstart Athenians, who (they were convinced) were there to support the rebel helots (still besieged on Mount Ithome), to finish what they had begun years earlier when they came with the well-meaning Cimon, before their treachery was uncovered, before they were expelled. Yet, instead of staying to fight, the Athenians embarked and put to sea. Their strategy was working perfectly: their goal was not Methone—their landing there was just a decoy. Instead the prize was Gytheum, the port of Sparta with its dockyards and ship sheds, the nerve centre of Spartan (albeit negligible) naval operations. Now with Sparta's army many miles off in Methone, Gytheum lay unprotected. A race south-east and round the Mani, cutwaters sheering the dark waves; a merciless swoop against an unsuspecting town; and now Gytheum was in flames: ships, boats, warehouses, workshops and homes; and blood was seeping into gutters and dripping black into the translucent waters. Then, as quickly as they came, Tolmides and his triremes put to sea, doubling back the way that they had come, not worrying this time about Methone—sailing instead straight for Zacynthus and Cephalonia near the entrance to the Gulf of Corinth, strategic prizes that they energetically subdued and claimed as part of the Athenian Empire. And, with this achieved, they sailed into the Gulf itself.[24]

Scouting the northern shore, triremes debouched men onto the beach. A skirmish, and the local Ozolian Locrians were taking to their heels, while through its gates Athenians poured to occupy the well-appointed town: Naupactus, whose name (auspiciously for seafarers) meant 'Boatyard'. To take Naupactus was a bold strategic coup. Sited a little east of Antirhium, where a promontory gives way to open sea, a fleet based in its harbour could monitor all traffic through the Gulf, ensuring safe passage for merchant ships along its northern shores between Megarian Pegae and the Ionian Sea islands of Zacynthus and Cephalonia, now also in Athenian hands. In time the whole Gulf might belong to Athens, too. Even now its peoples would do well to be on guard—as Tolmides took great delight in showing them with a lightning raid on Sicyon, the wealthy, cultured city on the south coast. As for Corinth a few miles east, Tolmides did not dare assault so strong a settlement, but as he sailed back through the Gulf, he did attack one of her allies, nestling beside the shore beneath two towering mountains just west of Naupactus. Even he was probably surprised when the town surrendered, offered terms, and swore allegiance to Athens. If these sorties were exploratory, their success gave cause for optimism. Come the new campaigning season, clear targets had already been identified for the next phase of the war.[25]

Then, as Tolmides and Pericles were basking in the adulation of their fellow citizens, the possibilities afforded by Naupactus became even greater. On Mount Ithome, perhaps stimulated by the raids on Gytheum and Methone, the stalemate siege of Sparta's rebel helots was drawing to a close, as both sides realized that realistically they had no hope of winning—the helots because they could not break out and defeat the Spartans and their allies, the Spartans because they could not force the helots to surrender. Instead, the Spartans offered terms. Leave Mount Ithome, renounce the cause of wider helot personal and political freedom, and given safe passage from Messenia the besieged could go wherever they wished. Perhaps the Spartans pictured them as homeless refugees, trailing their ragged way across harsh, unforgiving mountains, shut out from every scornful city to whose locked gates they came. What were helots, after all, but pitiful subhuman animals? How shocking then when Sparta heard what did become of them. The Athenians no sooner learned the siege was over than they offered new homes to the helots, a new life and freedom, but not in Athens—in Naupactus, from where they could look every day towards the land of their former enslavement, the massing mountains of the Peloponnese glowering like a threat beyond the sea. What better garrison for this new outpost than these emancipated helots, whose hatred for their former masters knew no bounds? What better signal to send Sparta that her entente cordiale with Athens had ended? What better way to show that the Athenians would no longer pander to those anti-democratic Spartan oligarchs, those friends of the disgraced Cimon, those so-called allies who stood by as Athens burned, those turncoats who had contemplated marching against Attica when Athens was legitimately bringing Thasos back in check, those shameless, arrogant, entitled Spartans who had dared seek Athenian assistance against rebel helots and then publicly humiliated her? Perhaps the Spartans had been right to fear that Athens might support the helots. Look where those helots were now: safe, well fed and standing guard for Athens at Naupactus.[26]

It was not just in Greece that the speed, scale and sheer audacity of Athens' operations, so seemingly unstoppable, were raising worried eyebrows. In the hushed halls of his Persian palace, where the melody of plucked harps mingled with the distant plash of fountains, the Great King Artaxerxes was briefed regularly about the doings of his bitter enemies. Did their ambitions know any limits? On mainland Greece, in the Aegean, at the fast-swirling Bosporus, in the Black Sea, and now, too, in the desert sands of Egypt their power and influence were spreading; and they must be stopped—even if it meant cementing strange alliances; even if it meant courting Sparta. Hence the Phoenician trireme tied up at the blackened quay at Gytheum, and the Persians riding with their Greek interpreters, and wagons laden heavily with treasure chests trundling towards the villages that formed the nucleus of Sparta. But while the ephors were delighted to accept the Great King's money, there was little they could do. Without Megara onside, it was impossible to invade Attica by land, and no-one was in any doubt that Athens ruled the sea. Perhaps in time a chance might come, and then they would be sure to take it, but for now it was impossible. Disappointed and disgruntled, their coffers noticeably lighter, the envoys and their entourage sailed home.[27]

The next year Tolmides was on campaign once more, this time to Boeotia, whose towns were trying to reassert their independence. It was a mundane mission, and easily achieved, and if it seemed odd that Tolmides, fresh from such dazzling success the year before, was chosen to command it, the reason was not hard to find: Pericles, the arch-political-manipulator, did not want anyone to steal his limelight. So it was he, who now with 50 triremes and 1,000 hoplites left a trail of blazing towns and villages behind him as he sailed first up the west coast of the Peloponnese, then on to Acarnania, where a persuasive mix of ruthless generalship and honeyed promises saw the entire region—from the Gulf of Calydon to the Ambracian Gulf and from the rugged coast of the Ionian Sea inland to a chain of snow-capped mountains towering in the haze—fall with elegant efficiency into his outstretched hands. Only Oeniadae, a city in the swampy south on the banks of the languid River Achelous, its torpid waters dancing with mosquitoes, stood firm. But the next year its luck ran out; and so did Athens'.[28]

The campaigning season had begun with such high hopes. Responding to a plea from Thessaly's exiled King Orestes to restore him to the throne and thereby gain a useful ally, the Athenians, ranks swollen by Phocians and Boeotians, whose men were trusted now that Tolmides had won their loyalty, dropped down from mountain passes to the plain at Pharsalus. As they torched undefended villages and farmsteads, and dragged knives over unprotected throats, the Phocians especially experienced a frisson of grim joy: Thessalians were their sworn enemies; it was Thessalians who had fired the Persians to commit such terrible atrocities, killing and raping and burning their way through the Cephisus Valley; and now the day of reckoning had come. Yet, on Pharsalus' deep-soiled plain beneath tall walls in the shadow of a steep acropolis, even the determined allies realized they were outmatched when the city gates swung open and well-drilled cavalry came thundering out; and when they kept on coming, day in, day out, always when least expected (a sudden swoop of battle cries and terror, a lightning hail of javelins), even King Orestes knew the game was up; so in the night as expeditiously as possible they melted back across the hills, their mission ignominiously aborted.[29]

Meanwhile in the Gulf of Corinth, Pericles had landed troops at Sicyon to work their way through orchards, fields and vineyards, burning crops and slashing branches, until the Sicyonians, unable any longer simply to stand behind their battlements and watch, filed out onto the plain and offered battle. They were no match for Pericles, and soon the men of Sicyon were turning tail, trying to outrun the racing Athenians who, as wives and children looked out, screaming, from the ramparts, cut down as many as they could, while the rest fled panting for the city. And then the siege. Yet Sicyon had allies: the Spartans would not let her down. They had no intention of forgoing the chance to face Athenians in battle for the first time since Tanagra. But Pericles had no stomach for engaging with the Spartans. He rushed his men back to their ships and cast off for Acarnania to quench his hoplites' thirst for blood in the marshy flatlands of Oeniadae, which done, he sailed back home to Athens, discontented and dissatisfied. But such frustrations soon seemed petty, for he disembarked into a nightmare.[30]

Unable to persuade the Spartans to invade Attica, Artaxerxes had taken war to the Athenians—in Egypt. Shadowed by 300 warships, tens of thousands of his troops led by Megabyzus, satrap of Syria, a hero of his father-in-law Xerxes' Greek invasion, and Artabazus, satrap of Hellespontine Phrygia, a cousin of Darius, had come to Memphis, whose garrison was holding out in the White Castle. Faced with such overwhelming numbers, the Athenians and Egyptian rebels fled back to the Delta and the island of Prosopitis, where their fleet was moored. But with the Persian army hot on their heels and Phoenician triremes blocking all approaches to the sea, they found themselves surrounded. The besiegers had become the besieged. Luckily they had water and supplies aplenty, and, with their ships forming a stout barricade and the Nile effectively a moat, there seemed no reason why they could not resist indefinitely—or at least until relief came from Athens. But as weeks turned into months, and boredom replaced battle-readiness, energy was enervated by the heat and still no help arrived. It took eighteen months before a fleet—and then just fifty allied ships—did sail. By then it was too late.[31]

Frustrated at the long delay, the satraps taxed their engineers with an ambitious project: to divert the River Nile. As pickaxes slammed into soil, and shovels heaped dark piles of earth onto the banks of freshly-dug canals, as sluice gates were thrown open and muddy water bubbled freely through a network of new channels, lookouts on Prosopitis' walls watched as the river level dropped, and ships that had been anchored in its current sank onto the silt, until all that remained of the encircling Nile were lazy streams that sparkled in the steaming, fetid ooze, before, the sun's rays baking down, broad causeways of dry land stretched over to the riverbanks. And then the Persians advanced, torching ships and firing fusillades of arrows to pepper down through choking smoke until their infantry poured up onto the island, stabbing spears and slashing scimitars, trampling the dead and dying, until Prosopitis fell. As their former comrades, the Egyptian rebels, were surrendering and desperately pleading for their lives, only a few Athenians escaped the massacre, slipping through Persian lines and stealing through Nilotic marshland west for Libya and the old Greek colony of Cyrene. Inaros, Egypt's captured rebel king, was not so lucky. Nails driven through his wrists, he was raised high on a cross, to die in fly-blown agony beneath the Egyptian sun. But still the Persians were not finished. Scudding south was the Athenian relief fleet, 50 triremes—nigh on 10,000 men. They knew nothing of the slaughter; they had no inkling that Phoenician ships were waiting; and when the trap was sprung, they scrambled in vain to furl their sails and assume their battle stations, as enemy rams smashed hulls and fellow oarsmen leapt into the muddy water knowing that death was waiting on the shore. It was the greatest loss of ships and men that Athens and her League had known, a squandering of six years, countless lives, so much materiel. For any other city it would constitute an almost fatal blow.

But not for Athens. Certainly it changed things; certainly it caused the People to rethink; but yet again they showed their mettle, and proved how accurate their reputation was: 'If they fail at anything, they do what must be done to remedy the situation and immediately come up with new ambitions.' So as well as grieving losses and consigning the debacle to the shadows of deliberate amnesia, they turned this staggering reversal to their own advantage, moving the League treasury from Delos (now potentially at risk from the Phoenician fleet) to Athens, while at the same time redefining their relationship with League members.[32]

For, following the Egyptian fiasco, Ionian states, whose citizens had served on the ill-fated campaign, announced that they no longer wanted to be a part of the alliance. Backing them was Persia, hungry to exploit her capital, now she had won a major victory, the first over the Greeks since Thermopylae. The wind was in their sails; the tide seemed to be turning. On Cyprus, Persian warhorses were disembarking, clomping down the ramps; platoons of infantry were pouring out of troop ships to tighten Persia's hold on subject cities, while Megabyzus and his colleague, Artabazus, keen to do the Great King's will, stroked well-oiled, well-curled beards and plotted their next move. Both could remember the Ionian Revolt, how easily the flames of revolution spread through Greek cities by the Asiatic sea as febrile citizens rose up against oppressors. Yet who were the oppressors now, and who might be the liberators? As winter passed and days began to lengthen as the equinox approached, on both sides of the Aegean there was much to play for. The kaleidoscope was shifting once again and strange new patterns falling into place. But even in the midst of such uncertainties, in Athens there was hope. For now, when they most needed him, a master strategist and arch-tactician, absent for ten years, had recently returned. His ostracism ended, Cimon had come home.[33]

12

AT THE RIGHT HAND
OF ZEUS

Of all the things I leave behind
the sun's light is the loveliest.
And after that: the shining stars; the moon's face;
plump cucumbers and apples; pears . . .

Praxilla, fr. 1

ATHENS, 451 B.C.

In the first weeks of Cimon's homecoming there was so much to do: catching up with estate business; reuniting with his sons and with Elpinice and Callias; attending banquets given in his honour by friends seen so infrequently in recent years, men such as Ion of Chios, the tragedian (who later recalled Cimon reminiscing how he ransomed Persian captives at Byzantium), and Archelaus, whose poetry had proved so consoling when Isodice died; being waylaid in the Agora beneath the shady plane trees (their trunks much thicker now, their branches noticeably wider) by crowds of well-wishers all keen to share with him their tales of hopes or woe; confirming details of political and military developments; and seeing for himself the changes wrought on his belovèd city in his absence. It was not just its fabric that had changed (the Long Walls; the People's Tholos; a new panel placed beside the triptych in the Painted Stoa showing victory not over barbarians, but Greeks: Athenians and Argives vanquishing a Spartan army), the very atmosphere seemed strangely foreign.[1]

With the acquisition of mainland territories, the realization that the League had turned into an empire, and the relocation of the treasury to Athens, a new chauvinism seized the city, a new pragmatism. Crushing insurgents in Ionia, Athens had imposed her own officials and established garrisons to ensure that henceforth cities toed the line, their presence a reminder of where true power lay while, to underline their dominance still further, Athenians were now requiring subject cities to send delegates to both the annual City Dionysia, where they paraded tribute through the streets into the theatre, and the Great Panathenaic Festival, where they must bring a heifer (symbolic of sustenance) and suit of armour (evidence of military support) to their mother city's goddess, Athena. At the same time, pandering to popular demand, Pericles had introduced new curbs on citizenship that required both parents (not just one as previously) to come from pure Athenian stock. Had this legislation been in place fifty years earlier, Cimon with his Thracian mother would not have qualified. Yet despite the bullishness, the loss endured in Egypt was weighing heavily. While time might dull the pain of grieving relatives, and official silence saw the episode deliberately wiped from public memory, Athens had lost her appetite for constant universal conflict. Now that Cimon had returned, it seemed as good a time as any to make peace—at least with Sparta.[2]

Ten years previously, to undermine him after Ithome, Pericles and his associates had done all they could to weaponize conservative Cimon's enthusiasm for the Spartans. Now the two factions found themselves in unexpected accord, both eager to return to the generally harmonious (if sometimes volatile) relationship with Sparta that existed in the decade following the founding of Athens' League. And who better to restore this spirit of cooperation or to conduct high-level talks than Cimon? Despite his willingness to fight for Athens at Tanagra, a brave display of patriotism that all Identicals would understand, he had undoubtedly kept up his links with Spartan friends during his exile, meeting them at festivals, staying with them in Laconia, nurturing relationships that no Greek would view as traitorous. So he knew that Archidamus, one of Sparta's kings shared his passion for close cooperation between Greece's two most powerful poleis—to such an extent that he had played no role in recent conflicts. Undoubtedly Cimon knew, too, that a majority of ephors would prove receptive to his overtures. But he knew certainly that, since the impetus for talks came from Athens, Sparta would drive a hard bargain. Even before he heard it, he probably already knew what such a bargain would entail: carving up mainland Greece. He cannot have been surprised, therefore, when the ephors laid out their terms. In exchange for recognizing Athens' hold on hard-won territories north of the Isthmus, Athens must let Sparta preside over the Peloponnese—which, of course, included Argos; as long as Sparta's old foe, Argos, was Athens' military ally, there could be no peace. The solution was simple. Athens must renounce her relationship with Argos, and Argos must instead make a treaty with Sparta—or, at the very least sign a non-aggression pact to last for thirty years. Meanwhile the Spartans would repudiate all interests they might have in Thebes. It made good sense. Sparta had no stomach for prolonged fighting far from home, and, although for Athenians to sacrifice their Argive allies meant a climbdown, it was by no means a humiliation. Instead, it was a price worth paying to ensure stability in Greece, while Athens campaigned overseas. It also underlined how parochial and insular the Spartans were. While Athenians set their sights on far horizons—Egypt, Asia Minor, the Black Sea—Spartans were entirely introspective, their ambition bounded by the shores of the encircling Peloponnese, and so long as they could exercise their leadership within the confines of these limited frontiers they would remain content. Presenting his deal to the Assembly, Cimon would be forgiven if he trotted out his well-worn image of the two yoked horses pulling Greece's chariot. The treaty Athens had just signed encapsulated everything that he had ever argued for.[3]

But Cimon's skills lay not just in diplomacy. Despite constitutional changes in the past decade and more, despite ten years of fulminating speeches from Pericles, despite the new role of the Areopagus even having been mythologized in Aeschylus' daring trilogy of 458, *Oresteia*, Athenians recalled how before his ostracism Cimon led them out to victory over Persia; now, defeated comprehensively in Egypt, with the Great King's army threatening Ionia and his triremes scoping the seas round Cyprus, they longed to follow him to victory once more. So they appointed him general, gave him a fleet of 200 ships and assigned his mission: to rid Cyprus of the Persians and avenge those who had fallen fighting by the Nile by launching an attack on Egypt to help the rebel rump still holding out there. It was nothing if not ambitious. It was also of strategic importance in terms of both overseas and more Hellenocentric foreign policy. With a hawkish can-do spirit once more gripping

Athens, if the newly-ratified settlement with Sparta were to last, aggression must be focussed back onto the Persians.[4]

But even more importantly, there were worrying indications that Artaxerxes was preparing a new military expedition of his own. Under Megabyzus' generalship Persian infantry were massing in Cilicia, while 300 Phoenician triremes commanded by Artabazus were stationed, poised for action, in Cypriot ports. What was their purpose? Surely not another expedition against Egypt: measures taken there following Inaros' defeat meant that (despite some pockets of resistance) the situation was mostly settled. What then? The north-west coast of Cyprus was dangerously close to lands and waters won by Cimon at Eurymedon. Did the Great King have his eye on Athens' subject allies in Asia Minor? Or were his ambitions more far-reaching still? Knowing (as he must) from agents and well-wishers not just of recent conflicts on the Greek mainland but of personal and factional resentments—in Boeotia (Athens' ancient enemy, now subject to Athenians), in Megara (Athens' ancient enemy, now allied with Athenians) and in Sparta (Athens' ancient enemy, now officially at peace with the Athenians), not to mention in those many subject states in Ionia and elsewhere that resented what they rightly saw as Athenian imperialism—had Artaxerxes calculated that the time was ripe for another swoop across the Aegean, an attack on Athens in the name of liberation that this time might earn not the hatred but the blessing of many Greeks? To wait and let the Persians sail, to see support from fellow mainland Greeks evaporate as the Phoenician fleet swept past Cape Sunium was not an option. Instead, it was critical for Athens to act, to launch raids on Cyprus, engineer diversions in Egypt, and take the war to Persia before Persia brought the war to them.

Loath to lose time and keen to campaign once more, Cimon, now in his late fifties, followed the road that he had taken almost thirty years before when he walked down to the sea from the Temple of Athena Polias, an encouragement to fellow citizens to trust their fleet, evacuate their city and choose a path of sacrifice that would bring victory. Now, as then, a great crowd followed him: oarsmen ready for the rowing benches; seasoned hoplites, servants freighted down with spears and shields and armour; families—parents, wives and children—come to wish them well and wave goodbye. Perhaps Pericles was standing on the quayside; Elpinice and Callias as well; and Cimon's sons. For no-one thought the expedition would be over soon or knew when they would next be reunited with their loved ones. Familiar routines of hugs and fond farewells, advice, instructions, tears suppressed, keepsakes passed surreptitiously into unsuspecting hands, solicitous reminders of devoted love; embarkation; sacrifices; hymns; the braying of trumpets; and the first ship—Cimon's flagship—eased out from harbour, its golden figurehead ablaze with sunlight, its long oars feathering the swell. A last look back—faces on the waterfront already indistinct; a warm glow radiating from the Long Walls and the far-off face of the Acropolis; and there, somewhere inland, Laciadae—the aulós player's rhythm (designed to keep oarsmen on stroke) already drowning out the faint cheers from the shoreline; and then the helmsman leaning on the steering oar, the flock of triremes wheeling east, sails hoisted, bellying; oars shipped; the only sounds now murmured conversations and the smacking of the sea, the slap of sails, the rap of ropes, as Athens dwindled in the haze, the sparks of sunlight coruscating from the spear tip of Athena Promachus' statue, the only marker now to show where Athens was—until they too disappeared from view.[5]

Past Sunium they sped; past Paros, Naxos and Amorgos; past the Dodecanese; past Rhodes, south-east to Cyprus and the flat dun coast of Marium, an ancient port, wharves bristling with merchant ships and bustling with stevedores weighed down with timber from the island's heartlands, heaving strongboxes of locally-mined gold and copper. With most of Persia's fleet far off in Citium in south-east Cyprus, it was the perfect target to begin a new campaign: an easy conquest rich with booty, a useful bonding exercise for newly-mustered troops, a victory to boost morale and reassure Athenians that their general knew how to win. Treated mercifully, Marium provided, too, a welcome respite from the voyage, a chance to stretch aching arms and legs, an opportunity perhaps for a brief visit to the springs a mere stone's throw away, where Aphrodite, goddess of desire, was said to bathe. For Cyprus was her island: off its south-west coast near Paphos, she had risen, dripping, golden, to her birth out of the waves; but if this were not sufficient to cause ardent, womanizing, passionate Cimon to feel affinity with Cyprus, in myth's shadow history a Philaid, a member of his family, Teucer, son of Telamon, brother of heroic Ajax, had founded what was now a thriving city on the Cypriot east coast, which still bore the name he gave it, the name of his birthplace, a name that would resonate through history forever: Salamis.

To liberate not only Cyprus but Salamis from Persia would bring Cimon joy indeed.[6]

He knew it would not be easy. His mission involved not only Cyprus but Egypt, too, where the self-proclaimed 'King of the Marshes', Amyrtaeus, was harrying the Persian occupation force; but obeying the People's orders meant dividing the fleet, just 200 triremes strong, and this could be dangerous. Learning that League warships were making for the Nile, the Persians might well sail out to intercept them, leaving the base at Citium exposed, but if a large Phoenician fleet joined battle with a small League squadron, the outcome could be disastrous. Timing was crucial. Before the Egyptian task force could set sail, it was essential for Cimon to be in place at Citium. So, assigning sixty vessels (roughly a third), he ordered their general to wait for a fixed time before sailing for the Delta. There he should do all he could to help Amyrtaeus spread revolution. In addition Cimon ordered him to send a delegation deep into the western desert to the shrine of Zeus Ammon at Siwah, where the oracle (as he had learned from Callias, whose grandfather was the first Athenian to question it) possessed uncanny powers. Now Cimon, too, desired its knowledge.[7]

So, as the trumpet sounded, as Cimon's flagship led his triremes out to sea, oars raised for a brief moment in a last salute, as tacking east his ships were swallowed in the haze, crews left at Marium counted the days. Then they, too, set sail around the north-west cape of Cyprus to race south across open seas until they reached the fertile Delta. But one ship did not remain there. Instead, it headed west, to hug the featureless flat sandy coast, its goal Amunia, where in a hot lagoon, it anchored, and in the baking fishing town the chosen delegates haggled for guides and camels, before lumbering south across the desert for Siwah, more than a hundred miles away. Sleeping by day in sweltering tents, they travelled over hills of shale that glimmered in the moonlight and tracts of long-ago deposited seashells that danced and sparkled like a star-speckled ocean, through eerie rock formations, across endless tracts of burning sand until at last—a seeming mirage—in a high-walled valley of lush palms they reached the first of the oases. But this was not their goal. Another night of travelling through suffocating canyons and scorching plains of sterile salt lakes, blinding sand, before once more: a fertile green oasis, trickling streams, lush fruit trees, palms alive with birds, and on a towering limestone cliff beside a sacred spring the temple of the oracle of Ammon, whom Greeks equated with their own god, Zeus, built by the first King Amasis and adorned with sculptures of Egyptian gods. It was here the delegates first met the priests; here, too, they witnessed the theatricalities that preceded every consultation—surrounded by a crowd of perfumed women singing hymns and bearing feathered fans, a dazzling jewelled statue of the god housed in a gilded model boat bedecked with silver bells was carried out into the courtyard on the shoulders of his sacred acolytes, whose apparently divinely-prompted movements would determine whether the consultation could take place. This time it could, and now Cimon's chief representative was ushered through into the inner sanctum, a cramped, airless chamber roofed with palm trunks, where left alone he put his question, and where, too, he heard the Voice of Zeus himself (or at the very least his priest) boom through the tiny slits in the far wall. The wording of the question was so secret that it remains unknown—but not the god's reaction. For the Voice proclaimed that Zeus had no more need to speak with Cimon through a mere mortal interpreter, since Cimon was himself already with him.[8]

Bewildered, the delegates were bundled out of Siwah; exhausted they retraced their long nocturnal trek, lurching on camelback until they reached the sea; anxious about how they might be greeted, bearers of such a strange oracular response, they sailed back to the Delta, where the scene that met them mystified them further. The entire League squadron was preparing to set sail—back to Cyprus, to Citium, where (as at east-coast Salamis) Cimon's men had been besieging Persian garrisons. But at Citium, too, they found the main fleet ready for the off. Denied a debriefing meeting with Cimon (he was, so they were told, too busy to see anyone; all reports must go through his staff), they were already so bewildered that they scarcely registered the officers' reaction to their message from the oracle. There was simply too much happening. The situation in the camp was desperate: for soon after Cimon and his troops arrived, men had begun to fall desperately ill. Soon pyres were burning on the outskirts of the camp, and bones and ashes were being packed in urns. At first Cimon had been everywhere, rallying, encouraging his men. But recently he had been so preoccupied with planning first the siege and then, when the full extent of what was now being treated as a plague became apparent, an orderly withdrawal, that no-one could recall when they last saw him. Yet still his orders came. And now they were to pack up camp, embark, sail round the coast to Salamis, evacuate the troops there, and withdraw to safety until the plague was past.

The Persians had other ideas. As the League fleet bore down on Salamis, 300 Phoenician triremes came into view. At the same time, the city gates swung open and a cloud of infantry poured out to challenge the Greek hoplites on the searing shore. At Marathon, Miltiades had seized the moment of evacuation to pounce when Persians were in disarray; now Persians had turned the tables; now they were striking when Athenians were at their weakest, their most vulnerable. There was only one response: engage and fight and win. From Cimon's flagship trumpet orders blared. Sails furled, masts were removed and stowed, while oarsmen (many weak from illness) focussed on captains' commands. All knew the drill, and all knew Cimon's expectations—and all had trust in him. Now was their chance to fight for him again. They would not let him down. So triremes lunged and parried, oars snapped, rams ripped hulls, men thrashed and floundered in the blood-streaked waves, and all the while the trumpet calls resounded and the Greek allies obeyed. On land, too, hoplites rapidly fell into rank to face the enemy. Here, too, the knowledge that they were fighting under Cimon raised their spirits, spurred them on, convinced them that they, too, would be victorious. So, as the sun wheeled round and heat blazed down, two battles unfolded, one out on the gently undulating sea, the other on the prickly shore amid sand dunes and scrub. And then the Persian fleet, already badly pummelled, panicked, ships peeling off and racing for the tip of the long Karpas Peninsula, from where they could see Asia and safety. Now flights of League triremes were scudding after them, holing some, and boarding others, while on shore the Persian army, too, was racing back inside the city walls. The Greeks had suffered heavy losses and many of their ships were gone, but the day belonged to them—and the 100 triremes they had captured more than made up for those that they had lost; and while they could not risk remaining, they knew that they had scored a major triumph: with more than a third of his fleet destroyed or captured, Artaxerxes would be loath to put to sea. The threat was over (at least for now); and if all Cyprus had not yet fallen, if Egypt's rebel king was not victorious, at least Athens had regained her pride and reconfirmed her power.[9]

But when the troops assembled for the last time before sailing back to Athens—perhaps at friendly Marium—to be addressed by their victorious general, they were greeted by not Cimon but one of his lieutenants, who at last could share his sorry news. Cimon would not be addressing them today or any other day. For the truth was that Cimon was dead. He had been dead for thirty days. He had contracted plague at Citium, and he had not survived it. But before he died, he issued orders to tell no-one until the expedition was successfully withdrawn, since he knew the news might undermine morale. He knew how much his men believed in him—as they had shown just now at Salamis, where against all odds, and thinking that he still commanded them, they had not just avoided defeat, but won a famous victory on land and sea, a victory to rival Eurymedon and confirm Athens as the ruler of the waves. It was their victory, but Cimon's too—albeit posthumous—for when they heard the trumpet calls, his men believed their orders came from him, when they crashed into the Persian hulls, they thought the tactics had been his, when they forced the enemy inside their city walls, they did so feeling Cimon's gaze was on them. Through his decision to conceal his death, Cimon had won his last great victory. When the delegates to Siwah counted back the days, they understood at last the oracle's response. There had been no need for Zeus to use them as his agents to communicate with Cimon, because Cimon was already dead and Zeus could speak to him directly—which meant, of course, that rather than descend to Hades (the fate of ordinary mortals) Cimon had been transported to the realm of the divine.[10]

In Athens, too, when reports of his death reached the city, stories quickly spread to show that Cimon had departed on his last campaign in the sure knowledge that he would not survive it. Men recalled how they had seen him on the eve of his departure, tall, mop-headed, his hair grey now, sacrificing near the theatre at the altar of Dionysus. The victim slaughtered, Cimon stood in rapt contemplation while the priest sliced open the carcass, prising it apart to examine the prophetic entrails for a sign; all the while, however, a regiment of ants, attracted by the clotting blood, began to carry it—not back to their colony but onto Cimon's foot, specifically his big toe, which soon was covered. As Cimon at last noticed, the priest approached him ashen-faced, the bloody liver in his outstretched hand. The caudate lobe, known to Greek seers as the 'head', was missing. Taken together with his blood-caked toe (the big toe, the leading toe), the meaning was all too clear: the army's leader was to die; its head would be removed. Cimon was not surprised. It was not the first such omen he had received. A night or two before, he had dreamt that a fierce dog, teeth bared, was barking at him, growling menacingly, when suddenly she started snarling in a human voice, 'Be on your way—you'll be a friend to me and to my puppies.' Like most of his contemporaries, Cimon believed that dreams were a conduit to another world by which gods and spirits communicated with mankind through words and images. Athens was home to a number of respected dream interpreters, experts in untangling (for a fee) the knotty nocturnal visions of their clients, and respected soothsayers accompanied the army on campaign and advised its generals. Among them was Cimon's trusted friend, Astyphilus, an émigré from Poseidonia in south-west Italy. His diagnosis was grim: the dream told of Cimon's death. A snarling dog, he said, is hostile to the man it barks at, and the best way to become an enemy's friend is to die; moreover, the combination of barking and human speech showed that the enemy in question were the Persians, since their army combined both Greeks (whose tongue was comprehensible) and barbarians (who, as the very word implied, sounded like animals). For Cimon, however, duty was everything. He knew that he must die some day, and death in the service of his country would be glorious.[11]

So Athens mourned her fallen general, and the Philaids their family head. His remains were laid to rest beside his ancestors outside Melite Gate near the road to his beloved Laciadae. His sons and brother-in-law, Callias, were no doubt present at the ceremony, his sister Elpinice tearing her cheeks in genuine lament for the man who had been a constant presence all her life, the man with whom she shared so much: their gilded childhood in the far-off Chersonese; time spent with Thracian grandparents, Olorus and his queen, and with their errant older brother, too—Metiochus, perhaps alive still somewhere in Persia, leading the life of an eastern grandee, his Greek rusty now, his loyalty to the Great King unquestioning; escaping with their parents from pursuing Phoenician warships; arrival here in Athens; their father's struggle for acceptance; the starburst of his victory at Marathon; the bitter sorrow of his death; marriage to Callias, one of Cimon's closest friends; the horrors of Persian invasion; evacuation; pride at the role Cimon was playing in that war; pride swelling as his energy and vision were recognized by fellow citizens, when he was elected general, when they placed him at the head of Athens' League, when he led his army out to victory after victory over Persia, when he used his power and kudos to restore their father's honour with the statue group at Delphi and the painting in the Stoa Poicile. Even during Cimon's exile Elpinice must have kept in touch with him, and when he came back for those glorious few months it must have seemed as if he had been resurrected from the dead. Now, though, he was gone for good. He would not return again. Nor would those he led to battle, their ashes laid to rest on the lovely road between the Cerameicus and the lush groves of the Academy, their glory praised in the annual sad ceremonial by one of their surviving generals, their reputation praised on a memorial erected in the Agora:

> Slaughtering so many Persians on Cyprus
> these men captured a hundred Phoenician warships out at sea
> together with their crews, and greatly did all Asia mourn them,
> struck down by hands and by the power of war.[12]

Their deaths were not in vain. When he heard of the loss of ships and lives in Cyprus and the return of an Athenian fleet to Egypt (albeit temporarily), Artaxerxes called a meeting of his counsellors. He had reached a pivotal decision. For nigh on fifty years the Persians had waged war with Greeks: the Ionian Revolt; Mardonius' attack on Greece's mainland thwarted by a storm off Athos; Darius' Marathon campaign repulsed; Xerxes' amphibious invasion cut to shreds at Salamis, Plataea and Mycale; new hopes dashed when fleet and army were destroyed at the Eurymedon before they even put to sea; the steady loss of hard-won territories in Ionia and Thrace; or Greek meddling in Cyprus and Egypt. 'Remember the Athenians', Artaxerxes' grandfather Darius was reminded every day. Now all that Artaxerxes wished was to forget them. It made no sense to keep on throwing men and money at a war that yielded such diminishing returns, especially when there was a massive empire to be run. Better to make safe existing frontiers; to secure the status quo; better, if the Great King could, to reach some kind of understanding with those troublesome Athenians, who kept on nipping at his flanks like tiresome gadflies; better to negotiate some form of peace. So ambassadors were sent and tentative negotiations started; and in the months after Cimon's death, his brother-in-law Callias was chosen by the People to lead the delegation that sailed eastwards to Ionia before trekking many weeks, a weary journey of 1,700 miles along the Royal Road to the heart of empire. Perhaps their visit was deliberately planned to coincide with the beginning of the Persian new year, when representatives from every nation ruled by the Great King gathered at Persepolis to file slowly up broad flights of steps (past friezes showing a similar procession of submissive subjects) to the sprawling Apadana, the royal reception hall (its seventy-two columns eighty feet high towering through incense to a ceiling crafted from fragrant cedar wood) to make symbolic offerings, prostrate themselves before the throne and renew oaths of fealty. This ceremony more than any other proclaimed Persia's power. As Callias and his triumphant colleagues watched the steady stream of sycophantic vassals, they could congratulate themselves that they had come not to fawn on the Great King but to negotiate, their city's glory not just undiminished but enhanced, for unlike these defeated nations they had withstood and, thanks to their bravery and to their gods, they had triumphed—they were free.[13]

If it made sense for Persia to make peace, it was in Athens' interests too. Although in the past decade she had somehow managed to field troops to fight in many theatres simultaneously, heavy losses on the Nile had led to real concern that, allied with Sparta, Artaxerxes might attempt to prise her empire from Athenian control and even annex Attica. The five-year treaty brokered by Cimon with Sparta had eased fears, but only the complete neutralization of the Persian threat would let Athens focus on her primary objectives: to ensure the stability of her empire (parts of which had recently shown evidence of a concerning lack of loyalty); to increase her power in mainland Greece; and to establish herself beyond all argument as Greece's foremost city, a city into which all things might flow be they necessities such as wheat from the Black Sea, slaves from Thrace and Asia Minor or papyrus from Egypt or luxury goods—African ivory, Carthaginian carpets, almonds from Paphlagonia, dried figs from Rhodes—or even new skills and ideas brought in by leading craftsmen and philosophers, poets and astronomers, artists and scientists from Ionia and Northern Greece and Sicily, all drawn by Athens' magnetism and the knowledge that the city was the most exciting and creative in the whole Greek-speaking world. And more. By concluding peace with Persia, Athens would announce the end of the long wars—one city acting for the whole of Greece, a clear sign to anyone, barbarian and Greek, of her supremacy.[14]

For it was Athens that had persevered from the beginning; Athens that had sent her men to Sardis at the start of the Ionian Revolt; Athens that had beaten off the Persians from Marathon. It was an Athenian whose cunning won the day at Salamis; and, in the face of Spartan disarray, it was Athenians who assumed the reins of leadership on behalf of all the Greeks, who drove out the Persians, who under Cimon's command at the Eurymedon and off Cyprus crushed and emasculated the barbarians until they begged for peace. It was Athenians, not Spartans who did all this, and when Callias returned from Persia to announce the terms agreed, he rightly met with approbation: in return for Athens staying out of Egypt, Cyprus, Libya and Persian Asia Minor, the Great King had agreed not just to recognize the freedom of Ionia but to keep his ships removed from the Aegean, and his army three days' distant from the coast. The terms were favourable to both sides, and both could rest assured that peace would last—at least as long as it was mutually beneficial.

Callias was not alone in feeling the warm glow of popular approval. Pericles, considerably more ambitious, significantly more astute, was quick to capitalize on Callias' diplomatic breakthrough. Almost at once the People passed his motion to send envoys to every Greek city 'large or small in Europe or in Asia' inviting delegates to come to Athens for a Panhellenic congress to discuss (now that the wars were won) 'Greek sanctuaries burned by the barbarians; and sacrifices promised to the gods for Greece during the war with the barbarians; and the sea, so that all might sail on it without fear and preserve the peace.' In truth, few can have been surprised when many cities—most significantly Sparta and her allies—refused to have anything to do with it, but Pericles had made his point: now that the Persian Wars were over and Athens held dominion at sea and over parts of mainland Greece, the centre of power had shifted; whereas previously Sparta would summon delegates to congress, Athens now claimed the right to do so; indeed, since it was she, not Sparta, who had carried through the war to victory, Athens (Pericles was none-too-subtly announcing) had surpassed her rival and was claiming the hegemony of the entire Greek-speaking world.[15]

If the Spartans thought that by boycotting the congress they would dampen Pericles' ambitions, they were wrong. Ruthlessly rational he might be, but he understood religion's power and how piety might be harnessed for propaganda. For years the desecrated sanctuaries had been a potent reminder of how Athenians had sacrificed their city for the common good, watching homes and temples burn as they waited in ships at Salamis, before wreaking retribution on the impious barbarians. Now though, Athens, that great phoenix, had risen from destruction's flames. Now it was time to sweep away the ruins of the past and build a brilliant future. Now it was time to proclaim in marble the pre-eminence of Athens and the land of Attica. So, using moneys not just laid up in Athens' treasuries from internal taxation as well as court fees and fines, but paid into the imperial treasury in annual taxation by the subject members of her empire, and with the People's backing, Pericles initiated a vastly ambitious construction programme. Harnessing the genius of the sculptor-designer Pheidias, whose vision of triumphant Athens already shone at Delphi in Cimon's Marathon Monument and in his statue of Athena Promachus on the Athenian Acropolis, and the leading architects Ictinus and Callicrates, Pericles presided over an extraordinary transformation, a network of new temples dedicated to the panoply of Athens' gods—Nemesis, the goddess of revenge, at Rhamnous north of Marathon; Poseidon and Athena at Sunium; Ares, god of war, at fire-ravaged Acharnae; and the gods of death and transformation, Demeter, Persephone and Dionysus, at Eleusis—while on Colonus Hill above the city's Agora a temple was erected to Hephaestus, god of craftsmen, ancestor (it was believed) of every Athenian.[16]

But the greatest glory was reserved for the Athenian Acropolis. Here the holiest of holies, the Temple of Athena Polias, where Cimon had once come to dedicate his bridle, was to be left in ruins, its foundations a reminder of all that Athens sacrificed to liberate her fellow Greeks. But, flanking it to north and south, would rise two very different and distinctive buildings. To the north, seen clearly from the Agora below as it rose above the column drums locked into the retaining wall in the years after the Persian invasion, a curiously composite temple would be dedicated to Athena Polias. Designed specifically to accommodate the uneven bedrock on which it was constructed, its main east-facing cella was to house the ancient wooden statue of the goddess saved during the evacuation of Athens. There would be several side chapels, too, one dedicated to the god Poseidon, another to the hero, Erechtheus, while to the west a garden would enclose the sacred olive tree, said to have been planted by Athena herself, that regenerated so miraculously after Xerxes torched it.[17]

If this was intended as the spiritual heart of Athens, the other new building to the south—called by contemporaries the Hecatompedos Naos, the 'Hundred-Foot Temple', would represent the heart of empire. The largest temple in mainland Greece, it would house a towering statue

The new Temple of Athena Polias (known today as the Erechtheum) rises behind the ruins of its predecessor, destroyed by the Persians in 480 B.C.

of Athena, the deliberate antithesis of both the small olive-wood effigy in the Temple of Athena Polias and the spear-wielding Athena Promachus that stood facing Salamis. Forty feet tall, its wooden frame faced with gold and ivory, it would show the unconquered, virgin goddess as a warrior at rest, her three-crested helmet on her head, her left hand resting on her shield, while in her outstretched right hand would be a fluttering winged Victory. And images of victory—the victory of civilized Greeks over barbarians—would permeate the building. Above the columns, metopés (self-contained panels) would show victorious Athenians fighting Amazons, or Centaurs, or Greeks fighting Trojans in the Trojan War (by now so widely recognized as the forerunner of the Persian Wars), while at the east end Greek gods would be defeating the unruly giants trying to topple them from Mount Olympus.[18]

This scene, the Gigantomachy, had featured large on the destroyed Temple of Athena Polias, where it had occupied a pediment, and it formed, too, the basis for the pattern on the robe presented every year to Athena's wooden statue at the climax of the Panathenaic Procession on the day of the goddess' birth. It was also painted on the inside of the new statue's shield (with the battles against Amazons and Centaurs shown elsewhere on this statue, too), while the presentation of Athena's robe would form the climax of the 524-foot-long frieze that ran round the whole Hecatompedos Naos, a frieze carved in the new style of super-realism that portrayed the human body heroically in a perfection of plasticity (the antithesis of the stiff orientalising art of pre-war temples), a frieze that would show Athens' citizens, their wives and daughters and the city's foreign residents joining in parade, some walking, others riding prancing horses, others leading sacrificial animals or carrying religious offerings and artefacts, until they came into the presence of not only Athena but the twelve Olympian gods. As viewers followed the procession, climbing the shallow incline from the west end of the temple (whose pediment would show the contest on the Acropolis itself between Poseidon and Athena to decide which of them should own Attica) to the east front (where the pediment would show Athena's birth in the celestial realm of gods), like their counterparts on the frieze, they would make a sacred journey taking them from their own world to the realm of the divine. For, unlike the sculptures at Persepolis, which showed subject peoples dutifully paying tribute to the Persian Great King, here on the Hecatompedos Naos the residents of Athens, by making willing sacrifice, would be admitted to the presence of the gods.[19]

Nor was this the only message Pericles and Pheidias intended to convey, for the arrangement of the gods as they received the city's sacrifice would be imbued with spiritual significance. They would be divided into two halves, each flanking a scene connected with the ceremony of Athena's robe. To the left (and to the left of Zeus and Hera, seated on their thrones) would be the gods of battle or the Underworld—Hermes, who guided dead souls, Dionysus and Demeter, gods of Eleusis, and Ares, god of war, all straining eagerly to welcome the procession—while to the right, gods of the city, crafts and generation (Athena and Hephaestus, Poseidon and Apollo, Artemis and Aphrodite) would be shown engaged in animated conversation. Reading from left to right, the message would be clear: while gods connected with the Underworld and death were accepting Athens' sacrifices, gods of prosperity and growth would already be planning future greatness. This vision of the city protected by her gods chimed closely with the ideas of its time. The olive shoot that sprouted on the eve of Salamis; the sea battle itself fought on the day of the initiations at Eleusis; the deities seen at that battle (and at Marathon) fighting on the side of Athens—all were proof that the gods had great plans for Athens' future. And while some might grumble that the frieze with its preponderance of horsemen seemed to spotlight the elite, the triumph of the common citizen at Salamis, the People's Battle, would be embedded at the heart of the Acropolis' new design: the Propylaea, the ceremonial gateway that led onto the rock would be realigned to face the island and the waters in which victory was won, and to underline both the importance of that battle and the role played by Eleusis and its gods in Athens' victory and transformation, Pheidias planned to incorporate bands of dark grey Eleusinian limestone into many of the temples and their sculptures: one in the gateway's inner walls; another in the bastions on either side; another on the outer wall around the Temple of Athena Polias, studded with the marble figures of the frieze; still other blocks built into statue bases—in the temples of Nemesis at Rhamnous, of Hephaestus in the Agora and the gold-and-ivory statue of Athena in the Hecatompedon Naos—all proclaiming the message of regrowth at the heart of the Eleusinian Mysteries.[20]

Always the Hecatompedos Naos (now called the 'Parthenon') was meant to be the centrepiece of this new vision of triumphant Athens. Constructed on an enlarged base on the site of the temple started after Marathon as a thank offering for victory but burned by Xerxes' occupying army, it was divided into two unequal parts: the east chamber, the cella, the sanctum housed the glittering statue, while the smaller western room would be Athens' treasury, guarding not just booty won in war but tribute from her subject states. For, if the Temple of Athena Polias represented Athens' soul, the Hecatompedos Naos was the embodiment of empire, proclaiming how willing sacrifices made by generations of Athenians ensured their city's triumph over the barbaric, temple-burning Persians and earned her citizens their rightful place as leaders of the Greeks. It was a heady vision, and one that Cimon, had he lived, would have embraced wholeheartedly. For, unlike in the Painted Stoa (where the addition of a panel showing Athenians and Argives fighting Spartans introduced a jarring note), here on the Hecatompedos Naos the enemy was the barbarian, the Other, never fellow Greeks.

If only base reality had reflected such high art. While Pericles' political opponents were voicing their hostility to Athenian jingoism and their disapproval of the building project—accusing Pericles of squandering resources (including tribute meant for strengthening the navy) on prettifying the city 'like some common prostitute'—tensions elsewhere in Greece were stretched to breaking point as Athenians and Spartans (despite their five-year truce) fought a proxy war over control of Delphi. Then trouble flared, too, in Boeotia, when enthusiastic oligarchs seized two towns and declared their independence. An Athenian task force sent to deal with them was initially successful, but, ambushed at Coronea, Tolmides, its general, and many of his men were killed. The rest were taken hostage—and when, to broker their return, the People pulled out of Boeotia, it was clear their dream of a land empire was in tatters. With Boeotia gone, Phocis and Locris must follow. Suddenly Athens was on the back foot, and her many enemies (including those in nominally allied cities) were keen to exploit her disarray.[21]

Within days Euboea had revolted. Strategically located on sea lanes from the Hellespont, its loss would spell disaster. With no time to lose, Pericles launched an attack, but no sooner had he crossed onto the island than he received dire news. The situation in Megara—Athens' western neighbour—was in meltdown, too. The Athenian garrison had been massacred. And worse. An invasion army led by Sparta's King Pleistoanax (with whom Cimon's five-year truce had just run out) was heading for Attica. Of course, thanks to her Long Walls, the city could withstand a lengthy siege, but such a situation could prove psychologically disastrous. Who knew how many other so-called allies would revolt once they saw Athens struggling? So Pericles rushed back to Attica, and on the ripening wheat fields near Eleusis his hoplites, drawn up in their ten tribes, the summer sunlight dancing on their polished bronze, prepared to meet the enemy. It was as if history had turned full circle. How many men remembered tales their fathers and grandfathers told them of how they too faced Spartans and Corinthians here on this very plain in the early days of their democracy? Then, too, Euboea was their enemy; Boeotia, too. Yet then against all odds their forefathers prevailed. No battle had been fought. The enemy had simply withdrawn. And now . . . ? As they stared hard at the enemy, their bristling spears, their sharp-edged shields, many in Athens' ranks must have experienced a sense of unreality. For once more: a miracle. From across the plain they heard the order barked, and relaxation rippling through the Spartan lines as first Pleistoanax and then his hoplites turned and marched

away, their scarlet war cloaks billowing, and after them their allies, too—
from Corinth and Sicyon, Megara and Epidaurus—filing back along
the coast road for the border.[22]

Perhaps Sparta and her allies simply lost their nerve; perhaps, as Pericles delighted in suggesting, the Spartan king had been bought off with
bribes; or perhaps Pleistoanax shared Cimon's vision of dual hegemony
and so an understanding had been reached, whereby the two commanders had agreed to return to the old status quo by which Athens
would command the sea, and Sparta the land. If so, Pleistoanax had
acted without proper authorization: the ephors forced him into exile.
Yet they sent no further armies. Confident he had secured his rear, Pericles returned to crush the revolution on Euboea, imposing harsh terms,
and establishing Athenian settlements both here and across the empire;
and that autumn, with stability restored at last, on behalf of Athens and
her allies, he and his fellow representatives put their name to a new treaty
with the Spartans, this time intended to last thirty years, whereby (with
the exception of the helot city of Naupactus) Athens renounced all ambition for a mainland empire in return for Sparta recognizing her hegemony at sea.[23]

At last Cimon's vision of the two cities as two horses racing side by side
to lead their chariot to victory had been made real, and for a decade it
seemed set to hold, as Pericles, elected general each year, tightened his
grip on both his city and her subjects. Recognized as their 'first citizen',
while escaping accusations that he harboured an ambition to be tyrant,
he wooed Athenians with honeyed words, enticed them with new opportunities, seduced them with luxuries imported from across the booming
empire, while at the same time crushing any who opposed him—from
individuals such as Thucydides, son of Melesias, ostracized in 443 ostensibly for opposition to the building programme, to entire peoples
such as the islanders of Samos, severely punished in 439 following a
botched rebellion. In sentencing them, Pericles followed the example
of his father, Xanthippus, when he punished Persia's governor at Sestus:
he crucified the ringleaders, removed them from their crosses while
they were still alive, clubbed them to death, and left their bodies lying,
unburied, rotting carrion. When he returned to Athens, swaggering,
triumphant, he delivered a bombastic eulogy at the annual ceremony
for the war dead but, as he stepped down from the rostrum by the road
to the Academy, garlanded with flowers 'like a victorious athlete', an

old woman came out of the crowd. 'What a marvel you are, Pericles,' she sneered, 'and how deserving of these garlands! You've sacrificed so many good men fighting not against the Persians or Phoenicians—as my brother, Cimon, did—but in grinding down a city of Greek allies.' All Pericles could do was fall back on his default position when challenged by this formidable lady. Quoting Archilochus, the Parian poet who lived a century or so earlier, he sneered: 'You are an old woman, and you'd not have doused yourself in perfume if it hadn't been for me.' It is the last we ever hear of Elpinice—spirited, intelligent, redoubtable, a fearless woman in a city dominated by paternalistic and at times misogynistic men, a doughty sister fighting for her brother's memory.[24]

As fight she must. In an age before written history, when knowledge of the city's past was shaped primarily through yearly speeches praising the war dead—speeches where mythology and fact were indiscriminately interlaced, where battles with Amazons were deemed to be as factual as Marathon, and where the speaker (ever partisan) strove to construct a chronicle that showed him and his soldiers' actions in the most heroic light—memories could fast be clouded. Yes, there were family traditions, but rival families keenly contradicted them; and there were archives of state documents as well, but only few might bother to consult them. With Pericles controlling the agenda for so long, it was unsurprising that the achievements of his rival, Cimon, should be at best overshadowed. Of course they could not be erased completely from Athenian memory. From herms commemorating Eion or the temple housing Theseus' remains or inscriptions honouring the victory at Eurymedon to the venerable plane trees in the Agora, the shaded running tracks at the Academy, the buttressed walls of the Acropolis on which the dazzling new temples stood—there was so much to remind his fellow citizens of Cimon every day; and if facts and details were forgotten, his reputation lived on—and not just in Athens (where, close to their father's sepulchre beside the resting place of Cimon Coálemos and his horses, Elpinice was laid to rest near Cimon's tomb). In Cyprus the citizens of Citium, where he contracted plague, built a cenotaph and consecrated it in Cimon's honour. Apollo himself, the god of healing, so they said, commanded them to do so for, when another epidemic gripped the city, they sent a delegation to consult his oracle and ask what they should do to end it. The reply was simple: remember Cimon; bring him offerings; revere him as a god.[25]

Yet in life none appeared more god-like than Pericles. Despite his peace treaty with Sparta and despite political opponents doing all they could to rein him, his boundless ambitions set Athens on a course for war. Perhaps Thucydides might have succeeded in opposing him, but by the time he returned from exile it was too late. He found Athens in a fervid state, for his arrival coincided with a visit from a group of delegates from Corcyra seeking Athens' backing in their ongoing struggle against Corinth. It was a complex situation. Corcyra had been founded by Corinthian settlers, but there was little love between them. Now political infighting in Corcyra's colony at Epidamnus had escalated into full-scale war as Corinth and Corcyra backed opposing sides. A naval battle saw Corcyra triumph, but Corinth was determined to prevail. For a year she had been building a new fleet, as recruiting officers toured harbours in the Peloponnese, cajoling sailors to enrol as oarsmen in return for handsome fees. They were clearly planning to attack Corcyra itself—which was why the islanders appealed to Athens. There was much to recommend supporting them: not only did they boast the third most powerful fleet in Greece (after Athens and Corinth themselves), they commanded crucial sea lanes west to Sicily and Italy, where Athenians had a decade earlier established a successful colony at Thurii. Moreover, Corinth was their economic rival; it would be good to clip her wings. There was, however, one important sticking point: Athens' treaty with Sparta applied to Sparta's allies, too, and chief among these was Corinth. To fight Corinth would therefore break the treaty's terms and risk total war and, although war seemed increasingly inevitable, they did not want it yet. So after two days of debate the Assembly, steered by the wily Pericles, reached an artful compromise. It would make only a defensive alliance with Corcyra and send only a token squadron of ten ships with strictly defined orders: under no circumstances must they engage the enemy at sea but, if any Corinthian should land on the island, their crews were at liberty to oppose them. Pericles must have known how difficult it would be to keep such tight rules of engagement—no commander would stand idly by and watch his allies being defeated when by intervening he could win the day—which was what made his choice of general so cynical: Lacedaemonius, Cimon's son, whose very name proclaimed his father's wish for closer ties with Sparta, dispatched now on a mission which, if bungled, could severely jeopardize the peace.[26]

The inevitable happened. In waters near the islands of Sybota between the mainland and the island's southern tip, Corinth's new fleet, supported by warships from Ambracia and Megara, clashed with the Corcyreans. At first Lacedaemonius' squadron managed to avoid being drawn into the fighting, but in the turmoil and confusion, as vessels tore across the rolling swell, as blood boiled and Corinthian triremes shot provocatively close in search of a Corcyrean hull, at first one then another of his ships was forced to take precautionary measures until of necessity their captains gave the order to engage. A sudden spurt of speed, the shock of impact rippling through the rowing benches, and the killing had begun.

From Corcyra hostilities spread through Greece. Reluctantly Sparta, whose assessment that Athens had broken the peace was supported by the oracle at Delphi, was sucked into conflict. At the head of a mighty army drawn from cities of her allied Peloponnesian League, her Identicals marched across the Isthmus into Attica to ravage orchards, fields and homesteads. Now at last the Long Walls played the role for which they were designed, as families poured in from the Attic countryside to cower behind battlements and watch farms and villages go up in flames, comforted at least that they would never starve as long as their fleet patrolled the seas. But ships brought more than sustenance. Within a year plague came to Athens, killing one in three of her inhabitants, including Pericles himself, though his death did nothing to assuage his city's warlust. If anything the politicians who succeeded him surpassed him in their radical enthusiasm to see the People triumph at almost any cost. Cimon and Miltiades would have despaired at how the city they had fought to save was now going cap in hand to Persia to seek the Great King's gold. Yet Darius II, who had occupied the throne since 424, chose to support the Spartans, his satraps seduced partly by the calculated blandishments of a renegade Athenian—Pericles' wayward ward, the complex Alcibiades, who had been forced to flee to exile in part for parodying the Mysteries of Eleusis. In the Assembly the man who brought the charge against him was Cimon's son, Thettalus. Perhaps behind his motivation was the ongoing family feud or a sense of public duty instilled in him by his late father. It is the last we hear of Cimon's sons, though Philaids still played a minor part in civic life for a century to come.[27]

The Great King's price for funding Sparta was Persian reoccupation of all Asia, which included, of course, Ionia. So, in their lust to conquer mainland Greeks, the Spartans willingly abandoned those Greek cities of Asia for whose freedom so much Greek blood was spilt at Sardis and Marathon, Thermopylae and Salamis, Plataea and Mycale, and in doing so ceded Persia access to the Aegean Sea, denied since the Battle of Eurymedon. Not that anyone was overly surprised: after the defeat of Xerxes' army at Mycale, the Spartans had suggested the evacuation of Ionia, whose peoples had much closer blood ties with Athens than they did with Sparta. Yet (possessed perhaps of greater vision) there were not a few—men such as the sophist, Gorgias, and the comic poet, Aristophanes—who were concerned that Sparta might be playing with fire: who was to tell that Persia was not just stringing them along, that the Great King's policy might be to wear down both sides with internecine fighting, so that once Greece was exhausted he might launch a new invasion of the mainland, which this time might be successful. Who was to say the Persian Wars were truly over? Certainly Persepolis would interfere with Greek affairs for many years to come. Thanks to the backing of Darius II and his son Artaxerxes II, the Spartans did at last crush Athens and her empire, impoverished by many years of fighting, but her triumph was short-lived. Once more the arrogance of her commanders alienated her potential allies. The Persians switched sides; now they were supporting Athens and her unlikely ally, Thebes; now they were brokering a peace.[28]

Yet what neither Greeks nor Persians foresaw was that in Macedon, for so long sidelined, a kingdom regarded by Athenians as at best semi-barbarian, a new dynamic dynasty would rise to shatter old complacencies. First their king, Philip, exploded into mainland Greece to vanquish an alliance of independent cities on the plain of Chaeroneia before removing their autonomy and ending the centuries-old network of self-governing poleis. Then his son, Alexander, in a bid not only to unite his new domain behind a common cause but to rival the great heroes of Homeric myth—Achilles, Ajax, the Aeacidae—of whom he was in awe, took his own army into Asia proclaiming his ambition to seek retribution from the Persians for their destruction of the temples on the Athenian Acropolis. Only when he had defeated them conclusively, when he had occupied their lands, when he had torched the Great King's palace at Persepolis would the Persian Wars be truly over. Within ten years he did what allied city-states had failed to do in centuries.

Yet as he swept like wildfire through the lands of Greece's ancient enemy, in Egypt he permitted himself pause. He had heard tell of the

A modern bust of Cimon supported by a soaring eagle stands
by the shore in Cyprus at Larnaca near Citium, where he died.

oracle of Zeus Ammon at Siwah and wished to learn from it. So with a handpicked band of close companions he set out across the endless desert, travelling by night beneath the stars until (past suffocating canyons and baking plains and sterile salt lakes, white with blinding sand) he reached the fertile green oasis with its towering limestone cliff where he was ushered through into the inner sanctum to hear the Voice of Zeus himself (or at the very least his priest). Perhaps he knew that once before, here in this very chapel, envoys from the great Athenian general had been assured that Cimon was already sitting at right hand of the god. Perhaps he hoped that he might follow in that hero's path, that he, too, might be chosen for divine beneficence. Yet nothing could prepare him for the answer he received when, reverberating through the tiny slits in the far wall, a disembodied voice proclaimed that Alexander was the son of Zeus himself, or that, in accepting this was true, the world would be transformed forever.[29]

While Alexander blazed his trail through Asia to shape what he hoped would be a new united Panhellenic future, he took with him his court historians to chronicle his victories, determined as he was that (unlike so much history, unlike the details of Cimon's campaigns) they should not be forgotten. He knew that memories could fade and splinter, though literature might help preserve them—not only history but poetry and drama, too—and among the dramatists still read in Alexander's age was Cratinus, a comic poet, born nine years before Cimon, who, living to the age of ninety-seven, nonetheless outlived him by a generation. In his otherwise lost play, *Archilochi,* written shortly after Athens' ships returned from Cyprus carrying their general's remains, one of his characters paid homage to the recently-dead Cimon in lines that, more than any others, convey through their simplicity the impact of his character and his charisma on his fellow citizens. Cimon could have no better epitaph:

> I, too, the secretary, Metrobius, hoped
> I might see out my last years feasting
> to glistening old age beside that godlike man,
> the most hospitable of all,
> by far the best of all the Panhellenic Greeks: Cimon.
> But he has left before me. He has gone.[30]

Timeline

Note: All dates are B.C.

632	Cylon's attempt at tyranny
622 / 1	Dracon's reforms
605–600	Peisistratus II son of Hippocrates born
600 / 599	Cyrus II of Persia born
595	Athens annexes Salamis Croesus becomes king of Lydia
594 / 3	Solon's reforms
pre-585	Miltiades III (the Elder) born
c. 585	Cimon I (Coálemos) born
575–570	Hippias son of Peisistratus II born
566	Greater Panathenaic Festival / Games inaugurated
561–556	Peisistratus' first tyranny
560	Croesus becomes king of Lydia
mid-550s	Stesagoras II born
555–?	Peisistratus' second tyranny
555	Miltiades the Elder becomes tyrant of Chersonese
late 550s	Miltiades IV born
550	Cyrus founds Persian Empire
548	Miltiades III Olympic chariot victory Fire destroys Temple of Apollo at Delphi
547	Cyrus defeats Croesus and gains Ionia
546	Peisistratus' third tyranny
539	Cyrus takes Babylon
536	Cimon I's first Olympic chariot victory (when in exile, because he is the figurehead of political constitutionality)

534	City of Dionysia inaugurated
532	Cimon I's second Olympic chariot victory
530	Cyrus dies
528	Cimon I's third consecutive Olympic chariot victory
527	Peisistratus dies; Hippias succeeds as tyrant (collective leadership with Hipparchus?)
	Cimon I murdered (Stesagoras II already in Chersonese)
?525	Miltiades III dies
525 / 4	Cleisthenes eponymous Archon
?524	Themistocles born
	Aeschylus born
524 / 3	Miltiades IV eponymous Archon
	?Miltiades IV marries Archedice
521	Darius I becomes Great King
519	Cleomenes I becomes Spartan king
516 / 5	Stesagoras II killed in war with Lampsacus
	Miltiades IV becomes tyrant of Chersonese
?515 / 4	Miltiades IV divorces Archedice
	Miltiades IV marries Hegesipyle
514	Hipparchus assassinated
513	Darius' Scythian expedition
512 / 1	Persians take Thrace
510	Hippias expelled from Athens
	Cimon born
508 / 7	Cleisthenic reforms
506	Sparta invades Attica
	Cleisthenes temporarily exiled
	Athens defeats attacks by Sparta, Corinth, Boeotia and Chalcis
	Athens offers Persia earth and water
499	Ionian Revolt begins
498	Sardis burned

c. 498	Miltiades IV takes Lemnos and Imbros
494	Battle of Ladé
	Miletus sacked
	Sparta defeats Argos at Sepeia
493	Miltiades IV flees to Athens
	Themistocles eponymous Archon
492	Cimon comes of age
	Miltiades IV's first trial
	Abortive Persian invasion of Greece under Mardonius
491	Athens and Sparta put Persian ambassadors to death
490	Battle of Marathon
	Death of Hippias
489	Miltiades IV to Paros
	Trial and death of Miltiades IV
	Death of Cleomenes
	Accession of Leonidas I
?488	Callias marries Elpinice
487	Hipparchus son of Charmus ostracized (relative of Peisistratus)
	Statues of tyrannicides by Antenor (post-488?) playing on anti-Alcmaeonid version of events
486	Megacles son of Hippocrates exiled (nephew of Cleisthenes)
485	Xerxes becomes Great King
	'The Medizer' ostracized
484	Xanthippus ostracized
483	Rich seam of silver discovered at Laurium
	Athens begins building trireme fleet
482	Aristides ostracized
480	Cimon dedicates horse bridle to Athena
	Evacuation of Athens
	Battle of Artemisium
	Battle of Thermopylae
	Battle of Salamis

479	Cimon on embassy to Sparta
	Battle of Plataea
	Battle of Mycale
	Sestus captured
479 / 8	Athens (re)builds her walls
478	Greek alliance engagements in Cyprus
	Liberation of Byzantium
	Regent Pausanias shamed
	Delian League formed
477	Phrynichus' *Phoenician Women* staged
477 / 6	Statue of tyrannicides by Critias and Nesiotes
476 / 5	Cimon captures Eion from the Persians
475	Cimon takes Scyros and discovers bones of 'Theseus'
472	Aeschylus' *Persians* staged
c. 471	Themistocles ostracized
468	Cimon involved in Sophocles' first victory?
467	Revolt of Naxos
466	Cimon's operations in Phaselis and coastal Lycia
	Battle of Eurymedon
465	Xerxes assassinated; accession of Artaxerxes I
	Revolt of Thasos
	Massacre of Athenians at Ennea Hodoi and Drabescus
464	Sparta earthquake and helot revolt
463	Cimon prosecuted by Pericles but acquitted
462	Cimon's expedition to Ithome
	Democratic reforms of Ephialtes, supported by Pericles
461	Cimon ostracized
	Assassination of Ephialtes
460	Alcibiades the Elder ostracized
460–458	Athenian operations in Saronic and Corinthian gulfs, Cyprus, Egypt and Phoenicia
458	Aeschylus' *Oresteia* performed

457	Battles of Tanagra and Oenophyta
	Menon son of Meneclides ostracized?
	Athenian Long Walls completed
454	Athenian defeat in Egypt
	Delian treasury transferred to Athens
451	Pericles' citizenship law
	Cimon returns to Athens
	Five-year truce between Athens and Sparta
450	Cimon dies on Cyprus
449	Peace of Callias?
433	Lacedaemonius serves as general at battle of Sybota
431	Outbreak of Peloponnesian War
415	Thettalos indicts Alcibiades III
404	Defeat of Athens by Sparta and her allies
387	The King's Peace or Peace of Antalcidas brokered between Athens, Sparta, Thebes, Corinth and Argos ensures Persian control of Asia Minor
338	Philip II of Macedon's victory at Chaeronea ends the Greek polis system
332	Alexander III of Macedon visits oracle at Siwah
330	Alexander III of Macedon burns Persepolis, marking Greece's ultimate victory over Persia

Glossary

acropolis: literally 'high city', a citadel usually containing temples, especially to Athena Polias

aegis: magic snake-fringed goatskin breastplate worn by Athena

agogē: Spartan educational system

Agora: a wide flat area in the city centre used for commercial and political purposes

Athena Polias: Athena Who Protects the City (i.e., the Polis)

aulós: musical wind instrument rather like the chanter of Scottish bagpipes or the Armedian duduk

barathrum: deep pit in Athens into which criminals were thrown and left to die

deme: originally a village or urban district, under Cleisthenes' reforms a *deme* became a local political grouping (or ward), part of a larger Athenian tribe

ephor: literally 'overseer', a Spartan annually elected official (one of an elected board of five)

Gerousia: Spartan 'senate'

helot: Spartan serf

hoplite: heavy infantryman armed with a large round shield

isonomia: parity (literally, strict mathematical equality) before the law, the ideal behind Athens' proto-democratic constitution

leitourgia **(liturgy)**: mechanism by which wealthy Athenians compulsorily funded an aspect of public military or religious life

ostracism: voting mechanism by which a leading citizen could be expelled from Athens for ten years without loss of prestige or property

parrhesia: freedom of speech

Perioikoi: 'those who live all around', Sparta's free farming, mercantile, and manufacturing population

Pnyx: literally 'crowded place', a hill in west-central Athens opposite the Acropolis on which meetings of the popular assembly were held

polis (pural, poleis): city-state, a town or city together with its surrounding countryside

Proskynesis: ritual of obeisance or prostration demonstrating allegiance to the Great King of Persia

proxenos: a citizen who is the official representative of a foreign polis

satrap: Persian regional governor or viceroy

trireme: warship propelled by three banks of oarsmen

xenia: a bond of loyalty and trust between specific leading individuals of two Greek city-states, or between a Greek and a non-Greek, which obliged them both to further each other's interests in times of peace and do no harm to one another's person or property in times of war

xenos **(plural, xenoi):** one who enjoys *xenia*

Notes

Introduction

1. A delegation of Athenians: Herodotus, 7.140.

2. Herodotus on Cimon: 6.136, 7.107. See, e.g., R. Thomas, *Oral Tradition and Written Record in Classical Athens* (Cambridge, 1989); D. C. Yates, *States of Memory: The Polis, Panhellenism and the Perisnan Wars* (Oxford, 2019).

3. Thucydides: '*Pentecontaetia*', 1.89–117. Thucydides' relationship with Cimon: Plutarch, *Life of Cimon*, 4; J. K. Davies, *Athenian Propertied Families, 600–300 B.C.* (Oxford, 1971), 233–236; A. Blamire, trans. and comm., *Plutarch's Life of Kimon* (London, 1988), 88.

4. 'Epitaphios logos': see, e.g., N. Loraux, *The Invention of Athens: The Funeral Oration in the Classical City*, trans. A. Sheridan (Brooklyn, NY, 2006). The authenticity of the so-called Themistocles Decree and Oath of Plataea continues to be hotly argued: see, e.g., P. Cartledge, *After Thermopylae: The Oath of Plataea and the End of the Greco-Persian Wars* (Oxford, 2013).

5. Ephorus, Theopompus and Callisthenes are all cited by Plutarch: Blamire, *Plutarch's Life of Kimon*, 8–9. 'Both were men of war': Plutarch, *Life of Cimon*, 3.

6. See, e.g., Blamire, *Plutarch's Life of Kimon*, 1. His introduction gives a good overview of Plutarch's sources.

7. Discussed in Chapter 9.

8. The best modern forensic approach is M. Zaccarini, *The Lame Hegemony: Cimon of Athens and the Failure of Panhellenism, ca. 478–450 B.C.* (Bologna, 2017).

1. Ancestors

1. The story of the escape is told by Herodotus, 6.41.1–3. For trireme speeds, see J. S. Morrison, J. F. Coates, and N. B. Rankov, *The Athenian Trireme: The History and Reconstruction of an Ancient Greek Warship*, 2nd ed. (Cambridge, 2000), 264; P. Lipke, *Olympias 1992 Trials Report*, in *Trireme Olympias: The Final Report*, ed. B. Rankov (Oxford, 2012), 14–15. The fate of young Ionian men and women captured by the Persians appears at Herodotus, 6.32.

2. The location of Cardia is currently unexcavated and possibly unknown. The *Oxford Classical Dictionary* places it near Cape Bakla at the north-west of the Gallipoli peninsula.

3. 'There is a wide cave deep in the deep sea halfway between Tenedos and rugged Imbros. Here Poseidon the Earthshaker reined in his horses, unyoked

them from his chariot, gave them godlike fodder to eat, and hobbled their hooves with golden straps.' Homer, *Iliad*, 13.32–37.

4. Seventeen-year-old Cimon: Cimon's date of birth is not known. I accept the arguments of J. K. Davies, *Athenian Propertied Families, 600–300 B.C.* (Oxford, 1971), 302: 'Now that the thirty-year rule of qualification for magistracies (Busolt-Swoboda, *Griescgische Staatskunde* II.1070) is attested in operation at Marathon in the 480s (*SEG* X.2 B, lines 25–26), one is on rather safer ground in inferring, from Kimon's service as ambassador and general in 479 / 8, that he was aged over 30 in the summer of 479. A birth-year for him in or very close to 510 appears to be probable.' However, Davies notes that 'at the time of his father's death, ca. 489, Cimon was a μειράκιον (Plu. *Cim.*, 4.4), i.e. not yet twenty years old, assuming that Plutarch employs the term consistently.' That Plutarch does anything consistently is, however, quite an assumption to make.

5. Laciadae's fenced fields and orchards: Plutarch, *Life of Cimon*, 4; A. Blamire, trans. and comm., *Plutarch's Life of Kimon* (London, 1988), 90. It was probably sited in the modern suburb of Aigalion, now engulfed by Athens' urban and commercial sprawl; see R. Talbert, ed., *Barrington Atlas of the Greek and Roman World* (Princeton, NJ, 2000), 59. Man's care: Hesiod, *Works and Days*, 306–309. Eurysaceion: Philochorus, *FGrH* 328 Fr 26; see also S. Esposito, *Odysseus at Troy* (Indianapolis, 2010), 208. The location of the town house at Melite is extrapolated from Plutarch, *Life of Solon*, 10, which describes Philaeus' descendants settling at Melite in Athens (as well as Brauron in east Attica); taking this in conjunction with the location of Cimon Coálemus' tomb near the Melite Gate, a district that attracted other rich, important politicians, it is not unlikely that Melite was the location of the family's town house, too. Melite was also the site of the tomb of a later Philaid, Thucydides Olorou, the historian (Marcellinus, *Life of Thucydides*, 17 and 55).

6. Ajax, single combat with Hector: Homer, *Iliad*, 7.249–372; battle at the ships: Homer, *Iliad*, 379–457. Ajax's rescue of Achilles' body is contained in fragments of the post-Homeric *Aethiopis* and *Little Iliad*. See D. Stuttard, *Looking at Ajax* (London, 2019), 1–4. 'A good and noble man': Sophocles, *Ajax*, 1416–1418.

7. 'The best of men in thoughts and deeds': Pindar, *Nemean Ode*, 8.8. Aeacus as judge in Underworld: Aristophanes, *Frogs*, 460 ff.; Plato, *Gorgias*, 524a; Isagoras, *Evagoras*, 5. Shrine of Aeacus: Pausanias, 2.29. Images of the Aeacidae: Herodotus, 5.80–81, 8.64; cf. 8.83. Being able to trace one's family back to good, just founders was of supreme importance to aristocratic Greek families. As Aristotle (*On Nobility*, fr. 94 Rose) observed: 'Not all families who have good ancestors are necessarily noble, but only those whose founding ancestors are good.'

8. The date of Athens' annexation of Salamis is debated. Plutarch (*Life of Solon*, 10) associates it with Solon around 595, but the presence in his account of a Spartan arbitrator, Cleomenes (the name of a Spartan king who ruled from *c.* 519 to *c.* 490), leads some scholars to place it in the late sixth century. Plutarch is our

source, too, for the tradition that Philaeus settled at Brauron, but see Davies, *Athenian Propertied Families, 600–300 B.C.,* 310.

9. The chronology of Miltiades III (the Elder) is fraught with problems. A brief but comprehensive discussion may be found at Davies, *Athenian Propertied Families, 600–300 B.C.,* 299. Peisistratus as 'sole ruler': [Aristotle], *Athenian Constitution,* 28.2.

10. Date of chariot victory: N. G. L. Hammond, 'The Philaids and the Chersonese', *Classical Quarterly,* n.s., 6 (1956), 113. Davies, *Athenian Propertied Families, 600–300 B.C.,* 300, places it in 548.

11. Herodotus, 6.35. Description of Thracians: M. A. Sears, *Athens, Thrace and the Shaping of Athenian Leadership* (Cambridge, 2013), 6; K. Vlassopoulos, *Greeks and Barbarians* (Cambridge, 2013), 178. The year 555 B.C. is also the year in which Peisistratus was ousted as *tyrannos* for the second time (his first tyranny had lasted but a year or so).

12. Extent of Thrace: Diodorus, 12.50. Divisions: Herodotus, 5.3, 'If only they could unite, they would be the most powerful nation in the world, and none could resist them'.

13. Croesus and Delphi: Herodotus, 1.46–52. For an excellent overview of Delphi, its history and its oracle, see M. Scott, *Delphi: A History of the Center of the Ancient World* (Princeton, NJ, 2014).

14. Plato, *Charmides,* 164e–165a; H. Bowden, *Classical Athens and the Delphic Oracle* (Cambridge, 2005), 70; Scott, *Delphi,* 138.

15. Herodotus, 6.35–36; Nepos, *Life of Miltiades,* 1.

16. Nepos, *Life of Miltiades,* 1, sees the expedition as an act of Athenian colonization (but the account is confused and unreliable). The Dolonci and Peisistratus: see L. Scott, *Historical Commentary on Herodotus, Book 6* (Leiden, 2005), 508. Philaid largesse: Cimon was famed for opening his estates to his fellow demesmen, Plutarch, *Life of Cimon,* 10.

17. Greek colonization: see, e.g., J. Boardman, *The Greeks Overseas: Their Early Colonies and Trade,* 4th ed. (London, 1999).

18. Herodotus, 6.36. Aristotle, humankind is 'the creature of the city-state': *Politics,* 1253a1–3.

19. Herodotus, 6.37. Sardis' gold refineries: see A. Ramage and P. Craddock, *King Croesus' Gold* (Cambridge, MA, 2000). Croesus and Solon: Herodotus, 1.30–33. Croesus and Alcmaeon: Herodotus, 6.125. Chronology makes the factual truth of both visits dubious to say the least.

20. Cimon Coálemos' victories: Herodotus, 6.103, where we learn that the only other three-time victor was Euagoras of Sparta. Coálemos: Blamire, *Plutarch's Life of Kimon,* 93, discussing the nickname, suggests that it may be 'a foreign word of unknown origin' and that 'Koalemos' may originally have been 'some kind of mindless creature or personification of stupidity, whose name could be applied

to people as an insulting epithet'. Blamire, *Plutarch's Life of Kimon*, 93. 'Me, I can think': Homer, *Odyssey*, 9.27–28.

21. A neat overview of Peisistratus' achievements is contained in S. B. Pomeroy, S. Burstein, W. Donlan and J. T. Roberts, *Ancient Greece: A Political, Social and Cultural History* (Oxford, 1998). Eleusis: G. Mylonas, *Eleusis and the Eleusinian Mysteries* (London, 1961), 77–106.

22. J. Boardman, I. E. S. Edwards, E. Sollberger, and N. G. L. Hammond, eds., *Cambridge Ancient History III²* (Cambridge, 1992), 402–403; J. Boardman, N. G. L. Hammond, D. M. Lewis, and M. Oswald, *Cambridge Ancient History IV* (Cambridge, 1998), 297. Family connections with Thessaly: Herodotus, 5.63.4, 94.1. Peisistratus named a son Thessalus: *ref.* Connections with Sparta: Herodotus, 5.63.2. Sigeum: Herodotus, 5.94; Aelian, *Varia Historia*, 12.13. Hegesistratus: Davies, *Athenian Propertied Families, 600–300 B.C.*, 449–450.

23. Moralizing inscriptions: [Plato], *Hipparchus*, 229a–b records two ('A reminder from Hipparchus: think good thoughts as you walk'; 'A reminder from Hipparchus: don't cheat your friend'). Building projects: see M. Dillon and L. Garland, eds., *Ancient Greece: Social and Historical Documents from Archaic Times to the Death of Socrates*, 3rd ed. (London, 2010), 109–110 with references. Anacreon to Athens: [Plato], *Hipparchus* 228c. 'Eros, the lust god': Anacreon, 358.

24. Cimon's murder: Herodotus, 6.103 states unequivocally that Hippias and Hipparchus were behind the murder, a verdict that scholars have accepted ever since. However, this is (in my view) unlikely, not least because of their treatment of Miltiades IV so shortly afterwards, or their assumption that both Stesagoras and Miltiades IV would serve them loyally in the Chersonese. It is far more likely that Herodotus is blithely going along with a subsequent democratic (or Alcmaeonid) tradition that blamed Peisistratus' sons for every conceivable crime committed during their reign.

25. Burial: Herodotus, 6.103. Statue of horses: Aelian, *Varia Historia*, 9.32; N. Nicholson, 'Aristocratic Victory Memorials and the Absent Charioteer', in *The Cultures within Ancient Greek Culture: Contact, Conflict, Collaboration*, ed. C. Dougherty and L. Kurke (Cambridge, 2003), 112.

26. Modest Archedice: Thucydides, 6.59. The identity of Miltiades' first wife is not recorded (see Marcellinus, *Life of Thucydides*, 11; Blamire, *Plutarch's Life of Kimon*, 87). The reason for this is more than likely political—after the expulsion of Hippias, it was not in the Philaeds' interest to associate themselves with the tyrant's family. Davies, *Athenian Propertied Families, 600–300 B.C.*, 302, argues for a marriage between Miltiades and an elder sister of Archedice. Some scholars, e.g., Scott, *Historical Commentary on Herodotus, Book 6*, 180, accept the idea while others, e.g., S. C. Humphreys, *Kinship in Ancient Athens: An Anthropological Analysis* (Oxford, 2018), 84 n.56, dismiss it. In the absence of further evidence the argument will remain open. My reasons for identifying the bride as Archedice are outlined in the text, namely, her subsequent value as a political tool to bind together three power bases:

(1) Athens, ruled by her father, Hippias; (2) the Chersonese, ruled by her former husband, Miltiades, and home to her son, Metiochus; and (3) Lamspacus, ruled by her second husband, Aeantides. The use of elite women in this way is common throughout the period.

27. Herodotus, 6.38.

28. Miltiades to the Chersonese: Herodotus, 6.39. Triremes at Battle of Pelusium off Nile Delta: Herodotus, 3.44.

29. Miltiades' policy on arriving in the Chersonese: Herodotus, 6.39.

30. For too long these new marriage unions have been misinterpreted as somehow showing a split between Hippias and Miltiades following Miltiades' suggestion of destroying Darius' bridge across the Danube, an episode whose historicity is highly dubious (see Chapter 2). The arguments are well summed up in Sears, *Athens, Thrace and the Shaping of Athenian Leadership*, 67: 'It has been argued that Hippias attempted to ingratiate himself with Darius and thus abandoned Miltiades and the territory on the European side of the Hellespont' (H. T. Wade-Gery, 'Miltiades', *Journal of Hellenic Studies* 71 [1951], 218–219). Other scholars have suggested that Hippias might also have been motivated by family pride to break ties with the Philaids after Miltiades took a Thracian wife (Davies, *Athenian Propertied Families, 600–300 B.C.*, 302; Scott, *Historical Commentary on Herodotus Book 6*, 180–181).

31. Olorus' kingdom: while noting that 'there is no direct evidence for where Olorus ruled', Scott, *Historical Commentary on Herodotus, Book 6*, 181 (rightly in my opinion) argues for his kingdom including the Pangaeum mines. Miltiades' marriage to Hegisipyle: Herodotus, 6.39. Mining concessions: see K. Vlassopoulos, *Greeks and Barbarians* (Cambridge, 2013), 123. Buying a Thracian bride: Herodotus, 5.6. Sexuality: Herodotus, 5.5. Tattoos: Herodotus, 5.6; see also M. M. Lee, *Body, Dress, and Identity in Ancient Greece* (Cambridge, 2015), 84. Royal Thracian banquets: Xenophon, *Anabasis*, 7.3; L. G. Mitchell, *Greeks Bearing Gifts* (Cambridge, 1997), 138; Sears, *Athens, Thrace and the Shaping of Athenian Leadership*, 146, 208–212. At least one Thracian girl was immortalized in poetry by Hipparchus' court poet, Anacreon (fr. 417): 'Thracian filly, why shoot such sidelong glances? Why shy away so heartlessly? Do you doubt my skill, my prowess, my technique? Listen! I could harness you good and proper. I could take the reins in both my hands and spur you over the finishing line. But all you want to do is wander in the meadows and frisk around and play—and all because you refuse to let a master ride you; and all because you refuse to let me mount you.'

32. Archedice's marriage and sons: Thucydides, 6.59, which records the epitaph on Archedice's tomb, 'Here lies Archedice, daughter to Hippias, the greatest Greek of his age. She was the daughter, sister, wife and mother of tyrants, but she was never vain.'

33. For the Panathenaic Festival see, e.g., H. W. Parke, *Festivals of the Athenians* (London, 1977), 33–52; J. Neils, *Goddess and Polis: The Panathenaic Festival in Ancient Athens* (Princeton, NJ, 1993).

34. The earliest and most reliable (albeit diverging) accounts of the assassination of Hipparchus are contained in Herodotus, 5.55–56; Thucydides, 6.54–59 (who correctly notes that Hipparchus was not the tyrant); [Aristotle], *Athenian Constitution*, 18.2–6. By the time of historians such as Diodorus (10.17), the episode has become hopelessly romanticized.

35. Gephyraei: see Davies, *Athenian Propertied Families, 600–300 B.C.*, 472–479. 'Boy with a maiden's looks': Anacreon, 360. The slight to Harmodius' sister: Aelian, *Varia Historia*, 11.8. Totalitarian nightmare: Thucydides, 6.53, 59; [Aristotle], *Athenian Constitution*, 19.1.

36. Cleisthenes as Chief Archon: see Davies, *Athenian Propertied Families, 600–300 B.C.*, 375. Historians would still accept Alcmaeonid propaganda, were it not for the discovery in the 1930s of an official inscribed record (dating to *c.* 425) containing a list of Chief (eponymous) Archons, including Cleisthenes. The Cylon Affair: Herodotus, 5.71; Thucydides, 1.126; Plutarch, *Life of Solon*, 12. In 2016, the discovery at Phalerum of a mass grave including the skeletons of around eighty shackled men aroused excited speculation that these were the remains of Cylon's co-conspirators (see, e.g., R. Waterfield, *Creators, Conquerors, and Citizens* [Oxford, 2018], 76; T. Ghose, 'Shackled Skeletons Could Be Ancient Greek Rebels', Live Science, April 15, 2016, www.livescience.com/54432-mass-grave-unearthed-in-greece .html). While pottery associated with the burial dates from the second half of the seventh century, there is no firm evidence to confirm the men's identity, but it is not unlikely that the mass execution would have taken place away from the city, perhaps out of sight of friends and relatives.) Perhaps it is not coincidental that it was at Phalerum that the annual ritual cleansing of Athena's the olive wood statue took place: see Noel Robertson, 'The Praxiergidae Decree (*IG* I³ 7) and the Dressing of Athena's Statue with the *Peplos*', *Greek, Roman, and Byzantine Studies* 44 (2004), 111–161, https://grbs.library.duke.edu/article/viewFile/91/91.

37. Temple of Apollo at Delphi: Scott, *Delphi*, 97–98. Alcmaeonids win contract to rebuild Temple of Apollo at Delphi: Herodotus, 5.62–63; corrupt the Pythian priestess: Herodotus, 5.90. There is no need to follow Herodotus, who implies that the Alcmaeonids bribed the priestess to urge the Spartans to free Athens, unless the bribe lay in their generous funding of the temple. The story is simply yet another example of how hostile Greeks sought to mire the Alcmaeonids in the charge of impiety.

38. Herodotus, 5.65.

39. Cleisthenes reforms: for good discussions of the reforms in their context, see P. Cartledge, *Democracy: A Life*, rev. ed. (Oxford, 2018); P. Rhodes, ed., *Athenian Democracy* (Edinburgh, 2004); D. Stockton, *The Classical Athenian Democracy* (Oxford, 1990). Statue-group of tyrannicides: Pausanias, 1.8.5; V. Azoulay, *The Tyrant Slayers of Ancient Athens* (New York, 2017).

40. On the status of Oeneus before Cleisthenes, see D. L. Kellogg, *Marathon Fighters and Men of Maple: Ancient Acharnai* (Oxford, 2013), 174.

41. Herodotus, 5.66–73; [Aristotle], *Athenian Constitution*, 20–22. For a good overview of the conflict between Isagoras and Cleisthenes, see J. Ober, 'The Athenian Revolution of 508 / 7 B.C.E: Violence, Authority, and the Origins of Democracy', in *Cultural Poetics in Archaic Greece: Cult, Performance, Politics*, ed. C. Dougherty and L. Kurke (Cambridge, 1993), 215–232.

42. Invasion of Attica by Sparta, Corinth, Boeotia and Chalcis: Herodotus, 5.74–78.

43. Herodotus, 5.74–75.

44. Herodotus, 5.77; Diodorus, 10.24. Herodotus (5.78) used the episode to laud the virtues of democracy: 'So the Athenians grew in strength, and demonstrated the excellence of equality (*isegoria*) not just in this specific case but generally. When they were ruled by tyrants the Athenians were no better fighters than any of their neighbours; once they had got rid of them they were the best of all. This demonstrates that while tyrannized they were cowardly—like men working for a harsh employer—but when they were free each man was keen to do the best he could for himself.'

45. Boeotian and Aeginetan alliance: Herodotus, 5.79–90. Hippias to Sardis: Herodotus, 5.96.

46. The rise of Persia is discussed in greater detail in Chapter 2.

47. Athenians offer Persia earth and water: Herodotus, 5.73; P. Green, *The Greco-Persian Wars* (Berkeley, CA, 1996), 19. While no source records the names of the Athenian delegates, it would not be unlikely if Cleisthenes was one of them. His name falls out of the records at precisely this time, so either he died or he was somehow disgraced. If he was indeed responsible for agreeing to make Athens part of the Persian Empire, his reputation would have suffered a severe blow—one that is likely to have been conveniently glossed over by enthusiastic democrats, who wished to remember him simply as the father of their constitution. The allegation that the Alcmaeonidae were somehow collaborating with Persia in 490 (Herodotus, 6.121) may well reflect their willingness to give earth and water to Darius just sixteen years previously.

2. When the Persians Came

1. Cyrus' rise and defeat of Astyages: Herodotus, 1.46, 1.127–130. Entertaining though it be, Herodotus' tale of Cyrus' childhood (1.108–127) is no more likely to be true than that offered in Xenophon's much longer and more baroque fiction *The Education of Cyrus*. 'He seized': Nabonidus Chronicle, ii; see also S. Smith, *Babylonian Historical Texts Relating to the Capture and Downfall of Babylon* (London, 1924), 115; J. B. Pritchard, *Ancient Near Eastern Texts Relating to the Old Testament* (Princeton, NJ, 1955), 305; A. R. Burn, *Persia and the Greeks: The Defense of the West 546–479 B.C.*, 2nd ed. (Stanford, CA, 1984), 38.

2. Oracle about the Halys: Herodotus, 1.53. From crossing the Halys to the flight to Sardis: Herodotus, 1.75–77.

3. Battle outside Sardis: Herodotus, 1.79–80; a longer (and more fanciful?) description (on which my description is partly based) appears at Xenophon, *Cyropaedia,* 7.1. Croesus' fate: Herodotus, 1.86–87, where Croesus is placed on a pyre by Cyrus (unlikely, given that the Persians worshipped the purity of fire), is contradicted by Bacchylides, *Epinikion,* 3.23–56, where Croesus appears to immolate himself willingly—though in both versions he is saved by a rainstorm (sent by Apollo according to Herodotus, or Zeus according to Bacchylides). 'Killed the king': Nabonidus Chronicle, see Burn, *Persia and the Greeks,* 43.

4. Herodotus, 1.152–153. Shopkeepers: this is an oddly ill-informed remark to make about the Spartans, which might help suggest that it is genuine. As Herodotus tells us elsewhere (1.138), the market place epitomized everything that Persians found immoral, not least lying and incurring debt.

5. Herodotus, 1.154, 157–161.

6. Harpagus' campaigns: Herodotus, 1.162, 164, 171, 174, 176. Xanthus: Herodotus, 1.176. Phocaea: Herodotus, 1.163–168. Thales of Miletus: Herodotus, 1.74. Miletus: see Burn, *Persia and the Greeks,* 43. Burn points out that in giving Miletus special status Cyrus astutely split Greek resistance. Thales allegedly predicted the solar eclipse of 28 May 585 B.C., which occurred during fighting between the Medes and Lydians. The battle was abandoned and peace terms made.

7. Cyrus' Babylonian campaign: Herodotus, 1.171–191. See Burn, *Persia and the Greeks,* 54–55. Babylon: see, e.g., I. L. Finkel and M. J. Seymour, eds., *Babylon* (Oxford, 2009). Herodotus (1.192) tells us that tribute from Babylon accounted for a third of Persia's annual income.

8. 'Stretching to infinity': Herodotus, 1.204. 'The most bloody': Herodotus, 1.214. Massagetai campaign: Herodotus, 1.201–214. Encased in wax: Herodotus, 1.140. Herodotus (1.214) records a grisly little tale of how Queen Tomyris found Cyrus' body, cut off his head and immersed it in a wineskin full of human blood, while gloating, 'Now you can take your fill of blood.' 'The universal king': Cyrus Cylinder, 21.

9. Life being very much the same: the Persians drew on the experience of both the Assyrian and Median empires, which were administered in much the same way as theirs. Some peoples actually benefitted from Cyrus' conquests, not least the Jews who had been shipped to Babylon in the early sixth century B.C. and were now permitted to return to Jerusalem. 'They learned useless luxury': Xenophanes, fr. 3. Herodotus has no time for Cambyses, painting him as a deranged sacrilegious megalomaniac deaf to the need for diplomatic niceties. The truth is undoubtedly more subtle. Polycrates: Herodotus, 3.44. Yet again, Herodotus (3.40–43) cannot resist a fabulous tale, this time of how Amasis advised the tyrant that if he wished to avoid the gods' jealousy he must get rid of his prized possession. So Polycrates took his most valuable ring out to sea and threw it into the waters. Later, however, a fisherman brought a massive fish to court, which was duly cooked, but when Polycrates opened it he discovered his ring in its belly, a reminder (should we need it) that we cannot escape fate.

10. The plot and Darius' assumption of the throne: Herodotus, 3.61–88; Ctesias at Photius, *Bibliotheca*, 72. See also, e.g., P. Briant, 'Gaumata', *Encyclopaedia Iranica* (New York, 2000), 10.3, 333–335. 'I prayed': Darius' Behistun Inscription, 1.10 ff.

11. Blasphemous: Herodotus (3.72) has Darius say, 'If a lie must be told, then let it be told'. Persian religion: see, e.g., L. Llewellyn-Jones, *King and Court in Ancient Persia 559 to 331 BCE* (Edinburgh, 2013), 20–25; Burn, *Persia and the Greeks*, 63–89.

12. Rebellion: Darius' Behistun Inscription, 2–3; Burn, *Persia and the Greeks*, 96–104. 'I sliced off his nose': Darius' Behistun Inscription, 2.12.

13. Oroetes and Polycrates: Herodotus, 3.120–128. 'Ahura Mazda': Darius' Behistun Inscription, 4.13.

14. Burn, *Persia and the Greeks*, 108–114. The economic problems caused by taxation involving transporting so much gold annually to the central treasury at what the Greeks called Persepolis are well set out in P. Green, *The Greco-Persian Wars* (Berkeley, CA, 1996), 14.

15. Darius' Scythian campaign: Herodotus, 4.99–144; Nepos, *Life of Miltiades*, 3. Herodotus (4.138) gives a list of Greek commanders. That Histiaeus led the Asiatic Greeks can be inferred from how Darius rewarded him at the conclusion of the expedition.

16. Mandrocles: Herodotus (4.88) records that Mandrocles subsequently commissioned a picture showing Darius on a throne inspecting his army crossing of the bridge, which he dedicated in the Temple of Hera on Samos, complete with the inscription: 'Goddess, receive Mandrocles' gift. He bridged the Bosporus' seas, so rich in fish. King Darius praised his work, which brought Samos honour and himself a crown'.

17. The Great King's presence: Athenaeus, 12.514c; Esther, 15.5–7. *Proskynesis*: Llewellyn-Jones, *King and Court in Ancient Persia 559 to 331 BCE*, 71–72.

18. Royal travelling arrangements: Xenophon, *Cyropaedia*, 8.5.2–14; Curtius Rufus, 3.8.2; Llewellyn-Jones, *King and Court in Ancient Persia 559 to 331 BCE*, 88. Greek colonies: the most exhaustive modern study is D. V. Grammenos and E. K. Petropoulos, eds., *Ancient Greek Colonies in the Black Sea* (Oxford, 2007).

19. Herodotus, 4.89, 97–98; Nepos, *Life of Miltiades*, 3.

20. Wagons and archery: Herodotus, 4.46. Skinning, scalping, drinking from skulls: Herodotus, 4.64–65. Royal burials: Herodotus, 4.71–72. Scythians: see, e.g., St. J. Simpson, *Scythians: Warriors of Ancient Siberia* (London, 2017); B. Cunliffe, *The Scythians* (London, 2019).

21. Feathers: Herodotus, 4.31. Griffins guarding gold: Herodotus, 4.27. Royal gold: Herodotus, 4.7. Bronze bowl: Herodotus, 4.78. K. Vlassopoulos, *Greeks and Barbarians* (Cambridge, 2013), 159, points out that 'there are no figures of Greek mythology in the Scythian tale' of the objects falling from the sky, so this is likely to be a genuine Scythian myth.

22. Scythians at bridge: Herodotus, 4.136. Herodotus (4.133) describes an earlier visit to the bridge, too.

23. Herodotus, 4.137; Nepos, *Life of Miltiades*, 3; Green, *The Greco-Persian Wars*, 22; Burn, *Persia and the Greeks*, 133. For Miltiades' use of the episode upon his return to Athens, see Chapter 3.

24. Ctesias, 17, claims that, because of Scythian attacks, the bridge had to be destroyed before all the army had crossed, but this is probably romantic fiction. See also Burn, *Persia and the Greeks*, 132 n.13.

25. Herodotus, 4.143–144. That Miltiades was required to feed Darius and his army is inferred from the expectation that, albeit thirty-three years later, Xerxes expected such hospitality from reluctant hosts on his journey into Greece (see Chapter 6).

26. Megabazus in Thrace: Herodotus, 5.1–2, 15–16. Persians to court of King Amyntas: Herodotus, 5.17. Alexander's stories: Herodotus (5.18–21) tells how Alexander and his comrades massacred the Persian delegates, when they began abusing Macedonian women at a banquet, but the story is almost certainly a fabrication later spun by Alexander, when as King Alexander I 'the Philhellene' he wanted to establish his credentials with the Greeks.

27. Histiaeus on Thasos: Herodotus, 6.46. Histiaeus' fate: Herodotus, 5.23–24. On Persians rewarding benefactors see, e.g., Vlassopoulos, *Greeks and Barbarians*, 48. Coastal campaigns: Herodotus, 5.26–27. Persian Peace: In an oblique and unsatisfying aside, Herodotus (6.40) records that at some time during this period or slightly later Miltiades was forced to quit the Chersonese because of Scythian incursions. However, his chronology is so confused that no-one has been able to pin down when this may have happened. Nepos (*Life of Miltiades*, 3) muddles his timeline and has Miltiades leaving the Chersonese immediately the Scythian campaign is over, fearing that Darius would punish him for his (supposed) advice to destroy the Danube bridge. N. G. L. Hammond, 'The Philaids and the Chersonese', *Classical Quarterly*, n.s., 6 (1956), 118–119, 129, follows Nepos and proposes that Miltiades subsequently endured a prolonged period of absence from the Chersonese (from *c.* 511 to 496), during which he returned to Athens and after which he was recalled by the Dolonci. Given accusations of barbarism thrown at his son, Cimon, this is unlikely: for Hammond's chronology to be correct, Cimon would have spent only three years of his childhood (496–493) in the Thracian Chersonese, with the rest of his upbringing and education taking place in Athens, hardly enough time for him to have 'gone native'. The chronological problems are set out well by M. I. Vasilev, *The Policy of Darius towards Thrace and Macedonia* (Leiden, 2015), 68–72. See also L. Scott, *Historical Commentary on Herodotus, Book 6* (Leiden, 2005), 181 and Appendix 10, 522–532, who argues against Miltiades' flight from the Chersonese, contending that, if there was any Scythian threat at the time, and Miltiades was not at his post, it was because he was in Thrace marrying Hypsipyle, an event he places after the Scythian campaign. He does, however, conclude (rightly in my opinion) that 'Miltiades was in the Chersonese essentially

from first arrival to final departure'. The episode, however, is so fraught with irresolvable problems and ultimately adds so little to the present narrative, that I have chosen to omit it.

28. Alexander's Olympic victory: Herodotus, 5.22. The truth of this story is contested. It may have been invented by Herodotus or his source. See, e.g., D. Fearn in E. Irwin and E. Greenwood, eds., *Reading Herodotus: A Study of the Logoi in Book 5 of Herodotus' Histories* (Cambridge, 2007), 116–118.

29. One intelligence-gathering expedition (which must be seen as standing for many similar such voyages) is recorded by Herodotus (3.134–139) as part of a lengthy (if unlikely) discursion about Darius' court physician, Democedes, who, longing to return to his native Croton in South Italy, came up with a ruse by which he urged a maritime invasion of Greece, and persuaded the Great King to furnish him with two Phoenician triremes and a supply ship with which to sail round the Greek mainland on a reconnaissance mission. He then carried on to Croton, where he jumped ship. Thanks to shipwreck and enslavement, few of his crewmates made it home. However, 'these Persians', writes Herodotus (who surely cannot really have believed it), 'were the first ever to come to Greece'.

30. Trouble on Naxos: Herodotus, 5.28, 30; Burn, *Persia and the Greeks*, 195.

31. Herodotus, 5.32.

32. Herodotus, 5.35.

33. Herodotus, 5.36–37. Never one to pass up an opportunity to tell a tall tale, Herodotus (5.35) brings Histiaeus in on the rebellion at its conception. According to him, Histiaeus, homesick in Susa, had been keen for Aristagoras to rebel for some time, since this was the only way that he could think of for him to get back to Miletus. So he sent a secret message by a cunning means: he had a slave's head shaved, had the message tattooed onto his scalp, waited until the slave's hair grew over it again, and sent him to Aristagoras with instructions to shave his head again and read the message. Its words chimed with Aristagoras' own intentions, and convinced him that he was doing the right thing. Herodotus' insistence on what he presents as the geographer-scientist Hecateus' pusillanimity in opposing it (5.36) can almost certainly be put down to professional jealousy.

34. Aristagoras in Sparta: Herodotus, 5.49–51. 'The deadliest fighting force'; 'every sea and river': Herodotus, 5.49. Herodotus' account of Aristagoras' speeches to Cleomenes and later to the Athenian assembly is probably pure fiction, but (like Thucydides) the arguments he puts in his mouth are undoubtedly the kind of thing that he is likely to have said in the circumstances.

35. Spartans on Samos: Herodotus, 3.39, 54–56. Herodotus (5.50–51) tells us that the mission was thwarted in part by Cleomenes' young daughter, Gorgo (later wife of King Leonidas I), who warned her father that Aristagoras would corrupt him if he did not immediately send him on his way.

36. Herodotus, 5.97.

37. Herodotus, 5.99. At 5.97, Herodotus (echoing Homer, *Iliad*, 5.62 and to an extent 11.604) remarks ominously that the Athenian and Eretrian ships 'were the start of the troubles between Greeks and barbarians.'

38. Herodotus, 5.100–102. The burning of the Temple of Cybele (or Cybebe in Herodotus) was a turning point in Greco-Persian relations. Herodotus claims that it furnished the pretext for the Persians subsequently to burn Greek temples, including those on the Athenian Acropolis (see Chapter 5); Diodorus (10.25) writes that 'the Persians learned temple-burning from the Greeks, committing the same atrocities against those who first outraged Justice.' A fine study of Sardis during this period is E. R. M. Dusinberre, *Aspects of Empire in Achaemenid Sardis* (Cambridge, 2003).

39. Herodotus, 5.102–103.

40. Miltiades, Lemnos and the legends: Herodotus, 6.137–140. Diodorus (who is generally unreliable about the facts of the period and the motivation of the players) has a different version of the episode. According to him (10.19), fearing the Persians' approach the Lemnians under their leader Hermon evacuated the island and (albeit still influenced by oracles) willingly gave it to Miltiades. Nepos, *Life of Miltiades* (1–2) unconvincingly makes Miltiades try to capture it on his way to take up his position as tyrant of the Chersonese (516 / 5 B.C., at which time he learns the wording of the oracle), returning later (but still *before* the Scythian campaign) to take the island. In truth the timings are problematic. Hammond, 'The Philaids and the Chersonese', 122–127, follows Nepos.

41. Aristagoras to Myrcinus: Herodotus, 5.124–126. Aristagoras was subsequently killed by Thracians, whose town he was besieging. 'You made the shoe': Herodotus, 6.1. Histiaeus in Ionia and Bosporus: Herodotus, 6.2–5.

42. Battle and sack of Miletus: Herodotus, 6.14–20.

43. Herodotus, 6.41; Nepos, *Life of Miltiades*, 3.

44. 'It caused them to remember': Herodotus, 6.21. For a consideration of the impact of Phrynichus' play on Athens, see Green, *The Greco-Persian Wars*, 27. The date of the play's production is usually said to be 493 (as here), though, given the relatively short time between the capture of Miletus and the Dionysia festival, it is possible that it was a year later.

45. Darius swears revenge: Herodotus, 5.105.

3. Trials of Strength

1. Change in dress at the turn of the century: L. Llewellyn-Jones, *Aphrodite's Tortoise* (Swansea, Wales, 2003), 138. The drinking songs are numbers 893, 895 and 896 PMG, i.e., as catalogued in D. Page, *Poetae Melici Graeci* (Oxford, 1962).

2. Miltiades' first trial: Herodotus, 6.104 (a very fleeting reference, without which we might not even know it happened). The minumum age for entering the Agora was eighteen.

3. L. Scott, *Historical Commentary on Herodotus, Book 6* (Leiden, 2005), 181–182, suggests that most of Herodotus' knowledge about Miltiades' time in the Chersonese comes from speeches made at this trial, though, since no lawcourt speeches were published before the 420s, it is difficult to know how Herodotus discovered them. Miltiades elected general: Herodotus, 6.104.

4. Cimon's appearance: Plutarch, *Life of Cimon*, 5. 'Uncouth, poorly read', etc: Plutarch, *Life of Cimon*, 4. L. H. Jeffery, *Archaic Greece* (London, 1976), 42, believes that Cimon inherited his size and curls from his Thracian mother, being 'unusually large, shaggy, and simple by Athenian standards' (see A. Blamire, trans. and comm., *Plutarch's Life of Kimon* [London, 1988], 101). M. Zaccarini, *The Lame Hegemony: Cimon of Athens and the Failure of Panhellenism, ca. 478–450 B.C.* (Bologna, 2017), 28–30, considers that descriptions of both Cimon's appearance and character belong to a literary or biographical trope rather than necessarily to reflect reality. Singing voice: Plutarch, *Life of Cimon*, 9 (he sang 'most sweetly').

5. Cynosarges: a white dog (from which the building took its name) was said to have once interrupted a sacrifice, prompting an oracle which demanded that a temple should be built to Heracles: Suda κ2721; ε3160. Boys of mixed parentage: Plutarch, *Life of Themistocles*, 1. Themistocles' appearance: we are fortunate to possess a marble Roman copy of a bronze portrait bust which was arguably made in Themistocles' lifetime and now housed in the Archaeological Museum at Ostia. For arguments about its authenticity, see P. Green, *The Greco-Persian Wars* (Berkeley, CA, 1996), 294 n.1. Chief Archon: Dionysius of Halicarnassus, *Roman Antiquities*, 6.34.1; Thucydides, 1.93.

6. Themistocles' early life: Plutarch, *Life of Themistocles*, 2. 'In power': Plutarch, *Life of Aristides*, 2. Celebrity musician: Plutarch, *Life of Themistocles*, 5. For Themistocles and his family, see J. K. Davies, *Athenian Propertied Families, 600–300 B.C.* (Oxford, 1971), 211–220.

7. Thucydides, 1.93.

8. Themistocles' policies: Thucydides, 1.93. Persian control of eastern grain supply: Green, *The Greco-Persian Wars*, 25.

9. Mardonius' expedition: 492 B.C. Its goal: Herodotus, 6.43. There is, in fact, no evidence that this was the goal of Mardonius' expedition (which seems more like a consolidation exercise aimed at reclaiming and shoring up territories that had already been taken by Megabazus twenty years before), but Herodotus' statement (based on eyewitness interviews) is no doubt a reflection of the fact that this is how it was perceived in Athens.

10. Herodotus, 6.45. Green, *The Greco-Persian Wars*, 28–29.

11. Mardonius' campaign: Herodotus, 6.44–45. The storm off Athos: Herodotus, 6.44.

12. Treatment of Persian ambassadors: Herodotus, 7.133. Miltiades as instigator: Pausanias, 3.12. According to Pausanias, because of this, Miltiades' family was

haunted by the curse of Talthybius, Agamemnon's herald in the Trojan War and subsequently the patron of heralds.

13. Herodotus, 6.49–50.

14. Demaratus' chariot victory (504 or 500 B.C.): Herodotus, 6.70. He was the only Spartan king to achieve this success.

15. Seniority: Herodotus, 6.51. Relationship between kings and ephors: P. Cartledge, *The Spartans: An Epic History* (London, 2013), 64. Demaratus' pro-Persian sympathies might be inferred from his subsequent flight to Persia. Demaratus' paternity: Herodotus, 6.63 and 6.69. Cleomenes bribes the Delphic priestess: Herodotus, 6.66. Leotychidas' enmity to Demaratus: Herodotus, 6.65.

Herodotus' account of Demaratus and his parentage involves two haunting stories. The first concerns his mother (6.61). She had been such an ugly baby that her parents ordered her nurse to carry her every morning across the River Eurotas to Therapne where she must make offerings at the Shrine of Helen. One morning as she was leaving the shrine, she met a strange woman, who asked to see what she was carrying. The nurse told her that it was a baby, but initially, despite the woman's repeated requests, followed the parents' instructions and refused to show it to her. But the woman would not take 'no' for an answer, and, when at last she held the child, she stroked its head and said that it would grow to be the most beautiful woman in Sparta. So it turned out. Indeed, it was only by guile that King Ariston had married her, challenging her then husband to prove his friendship by exchanging whatever gift each man might ask for. The second story concerns the nature of Demaratus' conception. Herodotus (6.69) records how Demaratus' (sadly anonymous) mother told him that she believed she had been visited by her husband, who had slept with her, given her a garland and departed, but when Ariston appeared shortly afterwards he denied that he had come to her room previously. When the couple made enquiries and asked Sparta's seers, they discovered that the garland actually came from the shrine of the local hero Astrabacus, and that it was he not Ariston who had fathered their son Demaratus. This story of double parentage, divine and human, is tantalizingly similar to that of Heracles, son both of the mortal father Amphitryon and of Zeus. See D. Stuttard, *A Traveller's Guide to Greek Mythology from Mount Olympus to Troy* (London, 2016), 114.

16. Battle of Sepeia (494 B.C.) and its aftermath: Herodotus, 6.76–83; A. R. Burn, *Persia and the Greeks* (London, 1984), 227–232.

17. Herodotus, 6.27. See also Green, *The Greco-Persian Wars,* 30 (including the relevant endnote).

18. Herodotus, 6.26; Green, *The Greco-Persian Wars,* 237.

19. Herodotus, 6.27.

20. A weight of 300 talents is equivalent to 7,800 kilograms, 8.6 US tons or 7.6 UK tons. Darius and the sacred gardeners: R. Meiggs and D. Lewis, *A Selection of Greek Historical Inscriptions* (Oxford, 1969; new ed. 1988), 12. See also R. Stoneman, *Xerxes, a Persian Life* (New Haven, CT, 2015), 80–81. Earthquake and oracle:

Herodotus, 6.98. Herodotus, of course, interprets the earthquake differently. For him it was a divine signal to the Greeks of the troubles ahead.

21. Herodotus, 6.99; Burn, *Persia and the Greeks*, 238.

22. Herodotus, 6.100. On the defeat of Chalcis, see Chapter 1.

23. Herodotus, 6.101.

24. 'Having taken Eretria': Herodotus, 6.102. Peisistratus' third attempt at tyranny: [Aristotle], *Athenian Constitution*, 15; see, e.g., D. A. Stuttard. *A History of Ancient Greece in Fifty Lives* (London, 2014), 29.

25. Plataea: Herodotus, 6.108.

26. Pheidippides (or Philippides): Herodotus, 6.105. 'The runner, Pheidippides, left Athens while it was still dark, and reached Sparta by the following evening, having covered something like 140 miles over bad roads' (Green, *The Greco-Persian Wars*, 31).

27. Vow to Artemis: Xenophon, *Anabasis*, 3.2.12; see also P. J. Rhodes, *A Commentary on the Aristotelian Athenaion Politeia* (Oxford, 1981), 650; H. W. Parke, *Festivals of the Athenians* (Ithaca, NY, 1977), 55.

28. On hoplites and hoplite warfare, see H. van Wees, *Greek Warfare: Myth and Realities* (London, 2004); C. Matthew, *A Storm of Spears: Understanding the Greek Hoplite at War* (Barnsley, UK, 2012); D. Kagan and G. F. Viggiano, eds., *Men of Bronze: Hoplite Warfare in Ancient Greece* (Princeton, NJ, 2013); and V. D. Hanson, *A War Like No Other* (London, 2005), 136–146. Armour: Van Wees, *Greek Warfare*, 167–168; Hanson, *A War Like No Other*, 136–142. Pre-battle sacrifice: Van Wees, *Greek Warfare*, 120–121. No surviving source suggests that Cimon fought at Marathon, but (given his age) it is not unlikely that he did, the fact being overshadowed both by his father Miltiades' outstanding part in the victory and by his own subsequent war record.

29. Herodotus, 6.108. Cretan bull: see D. A. Stuttard, *A Traveller's Guide to Greek Mythology from Mount Olympus to Troy* (London, 2016), 128, 178.

30. Opinion among Athens' generals was split: Herodotus, 6.109.

31. Diodorus Siculus, *Library of History*, 10.27 (a feisty episode that should, perhaps, be taken with a pinch of salt, though there are several other instances of mythology being cited to justify the making or breaking of alliances during the Persian Wars).

32. Pheidippides: Herodotus, 6.106; Green, *The Greco-Persian Wars*, 31.

33. Despite its being one of the most famous battles in world history, our knowledge of what actually happened at Marathon is sketchy to say the least. My account, like all others, tries to make sense of what little we know. Herodotus, 6.102–120; Nepos, *Life of Miltiades*, 4–5; Pausanias, 1.15.3, 1.32.3–7; R. A. Billows, *Marathon: The Battle That Changed Western Civilization* (New York, 2010); Burn, *Persia and the Greeks*, 238–257; C. J. Butera and M. A. Sears, *Battles and Battlefields of Ancient Greece* (Barnsley, UK, 2019), 3–17; Green, *The Greco-Persian Wars*, 31–38; N. G. L.

Hammond, 'The Campaign and Battle of Marathon', *Journal of Hellenic Studies* 88 (1968), 13–57; G. Shrimpton, 'The Persian Cavalry at Marathon', *Phoenix* 34 (1980), 20–37.

34. Epizelus: Herodotus, 6.117. Hunting dog: Aelian, *On the Nature of Animals*, 7.38. Callias: Plutarch, *Life of Aristides*, 5. Theseus: Plutarch, *Life of Theseus*, 35. Heracles and Athena: Pausanias, 1.15. Echetlus (or Echetlaeus): Pausanias, 32; see also M. H. Jameson, 'The Hero Echetlaeus', *Transactions and Proceedings of the American Philological Association* 82 (1951), 49–61.

35. 'One, a young man, Cynegeirus': Herodotus, 6.114; P. Green, *The Greco-Persian Wars*, 37–38.

36. Herodotus, 6.116, 121–124.

37. Herodotus, 6.120. In time a hero cult grew up around the Soros at which local villagers made offerings to the Athenian dead, and every night, so it was said, the sound of fighting could be heard, and horses neighing (Pausanias, 1.32.3). 'At Marathon': Simonides, 21 (Page), quoted (150 years later) in Lycurgus, *Against Leocrates*, 109. See also J. H. Molyneaux, *Simonides: A Historical Study* (Wauconda, IL, 1992), 150.

38. Marathon monuments: Pausanias, 1.32. Sophanes in the Assembly: Plutarch, *Life of Cimon*, 8; A. Blamire, trans. and comm., *Plutarch's Life of Kimon* (London, 1988), 114; see also M. R. Christ, *The Bad Citizen in Ancient Athens* (Cambridge, 2008), 114. Aeschines (3.186) anachronistically suggests that Miltiades' request was for his name to appear on the Marathon painting in the Stoa Poikile. Dedications to Pan: J. Camp, *The Archaeology of Athens* (New Haven, CT, 2001), 50–51. 'Miltiades set up': Simonides, 5 (Page). See also Molyneaux, *Simonides*, 151. It is, perhaps, telling that Miltiades (or one of his successors, perhaps Cimon) chose to dedicate the helmet not to Athena Polias on the Athenian Acropolis but to Panhellenic Zeus in Peloponnesian Olympia, where it might serve as a reminder of the part that he and Athens played in ensuring Greece's freedom. 'Callimachus of Aphidnae': *Inscriptiones Graeci* (Berlin, 1873), 1^2, 609. See also C. M. Keesling, 'The Callimachus Monument on the Athenian Acropolis (CEG 256) and Athenian Commemoration of the Persian Wars', in *Archaic and Classical Greek Epigram*, ed. M. Baumbach, A. Petrovic and I. Petrovic (Cambridge, 2010), 100–130. The reconstructed monument can be seen in Athens' Acropolis Museum.

39. Athenian Treasury at Delphi: see M. C. Scott, *Delphi* (Princeton, NJ, 2014), 112–113; R. T. Neer, 'The Athenian Treasury at Delphi and the Material of Politics', *Classical Antiquity* 23, no. 1 (April 2004), 63–94.

40. 'This land': Herodotus, 6.107.

41. Our knowledge of the Parian campaign and Miltiades' subsequent trial is sparse and relies on unreliable sources. Herodotus (6.132–136) shows signs of being influenced by a hostile Alcmaeonid tradition. Nepos' account (*Life of Miltiades*, 7–8), while owing much to the now-lost history of Ephorus, is unusually detailed, but still leaves much unanswered. See P. J. Bicknell, 'The Date of Miltiades'

Parian Expedition', *Antiquité Classique* 41 (1972), 225–227; R. Develin, 'Miltiades and the Parian Campaign', *L'Antiquité Classique* 46 (1977), 46–52, 571–577. Death penalty: Demosthenes, 20.100, 135.

42. Bribed by the Great King: Nepos, *Life of Miltiades*, 7. The sum of 100 talents was a large and probably impossible amount even for marble-rich Paros to have been able to pay at the time.

43. Nepos calls Teisagoras Miltiades' brother (*Life of Miltiades*, 7), but see Davies, *Athenian Propertied Families, 600–300 B.C.*, 300–301. It is not unreasonable to assume that many of the anecdotes regarding Miltiades' early life have been culled from this defence speech (see Scott, *Historical Commentary on Herodotus, Book 6*, 181–182).

44. Plato (*Gorgias*, 516d–e) suggests that the death sentence was passed, but the relevant magistrate refused to confirm the sentence: see R. J. Bonner and G. Smith, *The Administration of Justice from Homer to Aristotle* (Cambridge, 1930–38), i.197, 207–209, 299; M. H. Hansen, *Eisangelia* (Odense, Denmark, 1975), 69; D. M. MacDowell, *The Law in Classical Athens* (London, 1978), 179–180. Nepos (*Life of Miltiades*, 7) says that the fine was equal to the cost of the campaign. Given a daily wage for oarsmen and crew of 2 obols, 50 talents would pay 14,000 men for approximately 60 days. Herodotus (6.135) tells us that the siege of Andros lasted 26 days. We do not know how long Miltiades took to sail to the island (it may be that he did indeed subjugate other islands on the way), but 60 days would not seem unreasonable for the entire duration. By another calculation, 50 talents represents more than 230 times the oarsman's potential annual wage, roughly six times as much as he could hope to earn in a lifetime, to the man in the Agora an astronomical amount of money. Zaccarini, *The Lame Hegemony*, 31, questions the size of the fine, noting that 'this astonishing sum corresponds to other more or less fabled amounts'.

4. Between Two Wars

1. Xanthippus' intention to 'divert hostility from his wife's kin': S. C. Humphreys, *Kinship in Ancient Athens* (Oxford, 2018), 464. Cimon in jail: Diodorus Siculus, 10.30, 10.32 (part of a very confused narrative); Nepos, *Life of Cimon*, 1. It is not impossible that Cimon was jailed until he could pay the fine in full. All that Herodotus (6.136) tells us is that he paid the fine. Imprisonment in Classical Athens was not a sentence in itself, rather a halfway house, a waiting room where some convicts (such as Miltiades, and possibly—after his death—Cimon) remained until fines could be paid, whereas others (such as Socrates), condemned on a capital charge, anticipated execution in their cell. A. Blamire, trans. and comm., *Plutarch's Life of Kimon* (London, 1988), 92, notes that a contemporary of Plutarch's, Aelius Aristides (ii.203, Dindorf), comments that Cimon's guardians did not allow him to manage his property because of his 'wild behaviour and heavy drinking'; however, Aristides is not an especially reliable source.

2. Liturgies (*leitourgia:* literally 'a work' *ergon* 'for the People' *leos*): see J. Davies, *Wealth and the Power of Wealth in Classical Athens* (New York, 1981); M. Munn, *The School of History* (Berkeley, CA, 2000), 57–58, 61–62; L. G. Mitchell, *Greeks Bearing Gifts* (Cambridge, 1997), 45.

3. Plutarch, *Life of Cimon*, 5; *An Seni Respublica Gerenda Sit*, 790f–791a, 795c; Blamire, *Plutarch's Life of Kimon*, 105. Aristides is generally believed to have been born around 520 B.C.: J. K. Davies, *Athenian Propertied Families, 600–300 B.C.* (Oxford, 1971), 48–49. Chief Archon (Archon Eponymous): Plutarch, *Life of Aristides*, 5; Davies, *Athenian Propertied Families, 600–300 B.C.*, 48. His character and political leanings: Plutarch, *Life of Aristides*, 2. Mentoring Cimon: Plutarch, *Life of Aristides*, 23.

4. Callias and his family: Davies, *Athenian Propertied Families, 600–300 B.C.*, 254–270. Olympic victories 564 B.C.: Herodotus, 6.122 (a passage whose authenticity is contested). Buying Peisistratus' property: Herodotus, 6.121. Estates at Alopece: Davies, *Athenian Propertied Families, 600–300 B.C.*, 256. Income from Laurium: Nepos, *Life of Cimon*, 1.3.

5. Consults oracle at Siwah: Davies, *Athenian Propertied Families, 600–300 B.C.*, 257. Lets daughters choose husbands: Herodotus, 6.122 (see also Davies, *Athenian Propertied Families, 600–300 B.C.*, 256). Aristides: Davies, *Athenian Propertied Families, 600–300 B.C.*, 48–49, 257.

6. Humphreys, *Kinship in Ancient Athens*, 125; Humphreys (452) places Callias' marriage to Elpinice slightly later, 'probably in the late 480s', adding that it was now that Callias cleared 'any outstanding debt'—which, of course, presupposes that there was an 'outstanding debt' to clear. 'So did Elpinice': Plutarch, *Life of Cimon*, 4 remarks 'Elpinice accepted'. As Blamire, *Plutarch's Life of Kimon*, 98, observes (a *kyrios*, literally 'lord and master', is a woman's closest male relative who serves as a guardian): 'Athenian marriages were normally arranged by the bride's *kyrios*, and it was most unusual for her to be given any say in the matter.'

7. Elpinice's beauty can be inferred from the otherwise baseless rumour that she posed for the portrait of Laodice (Plutarch, *Life of Cimon*, 4), since Laodice was agreed to be the most beautiful of all Trojan princesses (Homer, *Iliad*, 3.123, 6.252). Age at marriage: Athenian brides traditionally married at (or just before) puberty. Incest: Andocides, 4.33; Plutarch, *Life of Cimon*, 4; Nepos, *Life of Cimon*, 1 (where Cimon reacts scornfully to Callias' offer to 'buy' her, but Elpinice magnanimously accepts in order to free Cimon from prison); Diodorus Siculus, 10.31, a very confused passage, which is so muddled that, in addition to recording that Cimon and Elpinice were married, claims that Callias was Cimon's son, and which contains what for us should be a useful warning that 'the sheer number of people who have written about this is huge, including *comic poets* [my italics] and orators'. See Blamire, *Plutarch's Life of Kimon*, 95; Humphreys, *Kinship in Ancient Athens*, 107. M. Zaccarini, *The Lame Hegemony: Cimon of Athens and the Failure of Panhellenism, ca. 478–450 B.C.* (Bologna, 2017), 35–36, furnishes a useful warning that anecdotes about Elpinice's 'questionable sexual behaviour', political interference and half-Thracian blood brings her 'very close to some of the comic stereotypes of

"bad" women', concluding that 'we may suspect that Stesimbrotus and Attic comedy played a substantial role in defining and settling Elpinice's fame'.

8. Insider trading: Plutarch, *Life of Solon*, 15 (a story discounted by most—see Davies, *Athenian Propertied Families, 600–300 B.C.*, 255). Callias at Marathon: Plutarch, *Life of Aristides*, 5; Blamire, *Plutarch's Life of Kimon*, 98. The entire anecdote is a smear from Callias' 'kingly' appearance (i.e., he is no democrat) to his keeping state booty and butchering the prisoner. Callias' wealth: Lysias, 19.48; Nepos, *Life of Cimon*, 1; Xenophon, *Ways and Means*, 4.15.

9. Athenian weddings: J. H. Oakley and R. H. Sinos *The Wedding in Ancient Athens* (Madison, WI, 1993); M. Dillon, *Girls and Women in Classical Greek Religion* (London, 2002), 211; P. Brulé, *Women of Ancient Greece* (Edinburgh, 2003), 142–150; L. Llewellyn-Jones, *Aphrodite's Tortoise: The Veiled Women of Ancient Greece* (Swansea, Wales, 2003), 230–240; Humphreys, *Kinship in Ancient Athens*, 307–310.

10. Dowries: Brulé, *Women of Ancient Greece*, 122–126; see also S. Pomeroy, *Goddesses, Whores, Wives and Slaves: Women in Classical Antiquity* (New York, 2011 [London, 1975]). Cimon's two younger sisters: Davies, *Athenian Propertied Families, 600–300 B.C.*, 303–304, 232, 234. Melesias: Pindar, *Olympian*, 8.54–59; Davies, *Athenian Propertied Families, 600–300 B.C.*, 231. Miltiades' fine in the context of Callias' wealth: Blamire, *Plutarch's Life of Kimon*, 91; Zaccarini, *The Lame Hegemony*, 31–32, where Zaccarini also questions the truth of the tradition that Callias paid off the fine (n. 27: 'the tradition on [*sic*] Callias providing the means to pay Miltiades' fine is suspect enough, given its contamination with other stories, the incredibly high sum, and the financial disgrace of Miltiades' family'), noting alternative versions such as that of Ephorus, where 'Cimon paid Miltiades' debt by his own marriage with a "wealthy woman"' (F 64 *ap. school. ad* Aristid. 46.515.22 D. γυναῖκα πλουσίαν), and Diodorus (10.32), where, Themistocles (of all people) advises a 'wealthy man' to marry his daughter to Cimon.

11. Easy grace and humour: Cimon's character can be inferred from, e.g., Plutarch, *Life of Cimon*, 3, 10; Nepos, *Life of Cimon*, 2. Womanizing and debauchery: Plutarch, *Comparison of Lucullus and Cimon*, 1. 'Cavalier patrician playboy': Zaccarini, *The Lame Hegemony*, 27–30, correctly reminds readers both that it is in Plutarch's interests to present the young Cimon as possessing 'questionable features— especially his passion for wine—at the beginning of the biography' as one of his themes is his 'development from vice to virtue' and that elsewhere (*Moralia*, 782 f.) Plutarch states 'openly that the accusation of alcoholic excess was a διαβολή [slander] on Cimon'. Ill-educated: an aristocratic young Athenian's education would include athletics, singing, learning a musical instrument, reading, writing and arithmetic: Blamire, *Plutarch's Life of Kimon*, 92, follows the arguments of J. Wells, *Studies in Herodotus* (Oxford, 1923), 126–127, in asserting his belief that 'Kimon spent his boyhood and youth at the Thracian court of his grandfather, Olorus'.

12. Plutarch, *Life of Cimon*, 4, links Cimon to two women in particular: Mnestra (of whom nothing else is known) and Asteria ('Starry') 'from a Salaminian family'.

That an Asteria was the daughter of the mythological Teucer (one of the Philaid ancestors), fathered at the town of Salamis on Cyprus (the place of Cimon's death), might make the modern commentator wary of taking this particular detail at face value, though Plutarch cites as his source the poet Melanthius (420s B.C.), who was close enough in time to Cimon as to know the truth of the matter. Much of Plutarch's information about Cimon's behaviour in early life comes (he tells us) from the (lost) historian, Stesimbrotus of Thasos, whose work seems to have been characterized by a love of the salacious, and from Ion of Chios, a playwright. See Davies, *Athenian Propertied Families, 600–300 B.C.*, 304–305; Blamire, *Plutarch's Life of Kimon*, 6, 98; and Zaccarini, *The Lame Hegemony*, 32. Isodice: see Davies, *Athenian Propertied Families, 600–300 B.C.*, 376–377. Timing of the marriage: Davies, *Athenian Propertied Families, 600–300 B.C.*, 305 places the marriage 'in the years just preceding or just following 480'; Blamire, *Plutarch's Life of Kimon*, 99, suggests (without fully explaining his reasoning) that 'if Isodike *was* the mother of Kimon's son, Lakedaimonios, who was born *c.* 476 . . . , her marriage to Kimon should date *c.* 478', though he goes on to write, 'there can be no objection to the assumption that the marriages were contracted in the 480's, when the disgrace of Miltiades was still recent. In this case . . . the union between Kimon and Isodike should be interpreted less as a dynastic alliance than the best accommodation which two aristocratic families in temporary political isolation could arrange' (though this last argument stretches a point); the marriage age for men is generally supposed to be thirty, but this may be convenient shorthand: by this age (their fathers being old and frail), many would be about to assume the role of head of household, for which a wife was essential. Cimon, however, had already assumed this role in 489. It is unlikely, therefore, that (especially in the absence of Elpinice, unless his mother was alive and acted as chatelaine) he could afford to remain single for long.

13. Centre of a nexus of important ties: Davies, *Athenian Propertied Families, 600–300 B.C.*, 305; Zaccarini, *The Lame Hegemony*, 31. Archons: [Aristotle], *Athenian Constitution*, 26.2; R. J. Buck, 'The Reforms of 487 B.C. in the Selection of Archons', *Classical Philology* 60, no. 2 (April 1965), 96–101. Comedy introduced in 486 B.C.: Z. P. Biles, 'The Rivals of Aristophanes and Menander', in *The Cambridge Companion to Greek Comedy*, ed. M. Revermann (Cambridge, 2014), 44. Parrhesia: R. W. Wallace, 'The Power to Speak—and Not to Listen—in Ancient Athens', in *Free Speech in Classical Antiquity*, ed. I. Sluiter, and R. M. Rosen (Leiden, 2002), 222–223.

14. Ostracism: [Aristotle], *Athenian Constitution*, 22; Diodorus Siculus, 11.55; Plutarch, *Life of Aristides*, 7; Julius Pollux, *Onomasticon to the Ten Attic Orators*, 8.19; P. Cartledge, *Democracy: A Life*, rev.ed. (Oxford, 2018), 70–72; Humphreys, *Kinship in Ancient Athens*, 490.

15. Hipparchus: Androtion, fr. 6 (*Fragmente der Griechischen Historiker* 324 F6); Davies, *Athenian Propertied Families, 600–300 B.C.*, 451. Themistocles utilizing ostracism as a political weapon: P. Green, *The Greco-Persian Wars* (London, 1998), 59.

16. S. Forsdyke, *Ostracism, Exile and Democracy: The Politics of Expulsion in Ancient Greece* (Princeton, NJ, 2010), 175–177, 281–284. 'The Medizer' may be Callias son

of Cratinus (another Callias, not Elpinice's husband), a close associate of the Alcmaeonids. 'Comments scratched on *ostraka*': Humphreys, *Kinship in Ancient Athens*, 491.

17. Whether Cimon's name does appear on *ostraka* of this period is debated, and depends on the dating of a cache of potsherds discovered in Athens' Cerameicus, three of which (bearing the names of Megacles, Themistocles and Cimon, respectively) are fragments of the same pot. Blamire, *Plutarch's Life of Kimon*, 92, following G. M. E. Williams, 'The Kerameikos Ostraka', *Zeitschrift für Papyrologie und Epigraphik* 31 (1978), 103–113, believes that Megacles featured in only one ostracism, the one that saw him 'win' in 461. It is possible, however (if Megacles was a candidate for ostracism a second time—i.e., after his return from his first post-ostracism exile) that the sherds date from the 470s: see G. R. Stanton, *Athenian Politics C800–500 B.C.: A Sourcebook* (London, 1990), 112–113; Zaccarini, *The Lame Hegemony*, 48. However, Cimon's election as General in 479–478 and easy assumption of wider command thereafter is clear evidence that by then he was not only well known both as head of the Philaid family and in his own right but an experienced leader and politician. Indeed, Nepos, *Life of Cimon*, 2, tells of Cimon's rapid rise to great eminence thanks to both his military expertise and his skill in the law courts, but Nepos is likely to have been influenced by his own experience of the *cursus honorum*, the established route by which an ambitious young Roman progressed through a range of calibrated public offices as he strove for ever greater promotion (which is not to say, of course, that he is wrong).

18. The anecdote about Aristides, contained in Plutarch, *Life of Aristides*, 7, and Nepos, *Life of Aristides*, 1, is sadly anachronistic, since Aristides did not earn his soubriquet 'the Just' until the early 470s. Plutarch, *Life of Themistocles*, 5, suggests that ostracizing Aristides was the greatest triumph of Themistocles and his supporters.

19. Laurium mining dating from 3,200 B.C.: E. Choros, 'Newly Discovered Greek Silver Mine Rewrites History', Greekreporter.com, February 17, 2016. Peisistratus and Laurium: Green, *The Greco-Persian Wars*, 54. Coins in Athens from *c.* 530 B.C.: J. H. Croll and N. M. Waggoner, 'Dating the Earliest Coins of Athens, Corinth and Aegina', *American Journal of Archaeology* 88, no. 3 (1984), 339. Hippias and coinage: J. T. Roberts, *The Plague of War: Athens, Sparta and the Struggle for Ancient Greece* (Oxford, 2017), 16.

20. Herodotus, 7.144. Plutarch, *Life of Themistocles*, 4, which suggests, too, that before the new discovery, profits from Laurium were habitually divided among the People.

21. Relations with Aegina: Herodotus, 6.87–93. Aegina taking trade from Athens: Green, *The Greco-Persian Wars*, 49. With the benefit of hindsight (and perhaps influenced by Themistocles' own subsequent boasts), historians and biographers such as Plutarch (*Life of Themistocles*, 4) argue with one voice that, while Themistocles claimed that the fleet was intended to curb the power of Aegina, the real

enemy he had in mind was Persia. There is, of course, no way of proving or disproving this.

22. 'War is man's business': Homer, *Iliad*, 6.492. Plutarch, *Life of Themistocles*, 4 suggests that Miltiades opposed Themistocles' policy of enlarging the navy, but (if he is thinking of this episode, which is not absolutely certain) he must mean Cimon. Themistocles' reaction to Miltiades and Aristides: Plutarch, *Life of Themistocles*, 3.

23. 'Aristides—brother of Datis', quoted in Cartledge, *Democracy*, 71. Landowners' concerns: Green, *The Greco-Persian Wars*, 55.

24. Triremes: good descriptions and evaluations in J. S. Morrison, J. Coates and N. B. Rankov, *The Athenian Trireme* (Cambridge, 2000); J. R. Hale, *Lords of the Sea: The Epic Story of the Athenian Navy and the Birth of Democracy* (New York, 2009), 20–28.

25. Six to eight triremes: Green, *The Greco-Persian Wars*, 57. Triremes given female names: Humphreys, *Kinship in Ancient Athens*, 273.

26. Herodotus, 6.67–68, 6.70. Gymnopaediae: P. Cartledge, *The Spartans: An Epic History* (London, 2013), 56. A century later, Demaratus' descendants still ruled the roost in Persian-controlled north-west Anatolia (Xenophon, *Anabasis*, 2.1.3, 7.8.17; *Hellenica*, 3.1.6).

27. Herodotus, 6.74.

28. Herodotus, 6.75. Historians seem to accept Herodotus' bizarre account of Cleomenes' suicide. The story contains interesting echoes of the suicide of Ajax, who, deprived of what he considered his rightful honour, went mad, tried to kill his colleagues, the Greek generals at Troy, and, when unsuccessful, turned his blade upon himself.

29. Spartans' fear of helots (annual declaration of war): Aristotle, *Politics*, 1269b36–39. Sanctuary to Phobus: Plutarch, *Life of Cleomenes*, 9.

30. For the best general introductions to Sparta, see Cartledge, *The Spartans*, and P. Cartledge, *Spartan Reflections* (London, 2001).

31. Education: see Cartledge, *Spartan Reflections*, 79–90; P. A. Rahe, *The Grand Strategy of Classical Sparta: The Persian Challenge* (New Haven, CT, 2015), 7. 'Animal in nature': Aristotle, *Politics*, 1338b. *Crypteia*: Cartledge, *Spartan Reflections*, 88. Treatment of helots: Plutarch, *Life of Lycurgus*, 28; Athenaeus, 657D; see, e.g., Cartledge, *The Spartans*, 66.

32. Black broth: Plutarch, *Life of Lycurgus*, 12. 'Identicals or Peers': often translated 'Equals', or (more recently) 'Similars', ὅμοιος (homoios) suggests a very close equivalence, with οἱ ὅμοιοι (hoi homoioi) glossed in H. G. Liddell, R. Scott and H. S. Jones, *Greek Lexicon* (Oxford, 1968), 1224 as 'in aristocratic states, *peers, all citizens who had equal rights to hold state offices* esp. at Sparta'; my opinion is that in Sparta the term emphasizes the suppression of individualism in service of the state, where Spartiates operate like ants or bees for the good of the community as a whole, a concept expressed better by 'Identicals' or 'Peers' than by 'Similars' or 'Equals'.

'Scarlet and bronze': Xenophon, *Spartan Constitution*, 11.3. Spartan women: Cartledge, *Spartan Reflections*, 106–126.Voting by shouting: Thucydides, 1.87. This was also the method used to elect the twenty-eight non-royal members of the Gerousia (the Council of over-sixties Elders).

33. Equal 'vote': of course, voices differed in strength.

34. Spartan constitutional excellence: Herodotus, 1.65; Thucydides, 1.18. See also Rahe, *The Grand Strategy of Classical Sparta*, 1. For excellent discussions of Athens' perspective on Sparta in the fifth and fourth centuries B.C., see P. Cartledge and A. Powell, eds., *The Greek Superpower: Sparta in the Self-Definitions of the Athenians* (Swansea, Wales, 2018).

35. Meeting of Greek states: Herodotus, 7.145.

36. Herodotus, 7.1. Had this invasion of 485 come off, of course, it would have occurred two years before the discovery of the new vein of silver at Laurium and the consequent building of Athens' fleet. As a result, its outcome might have been very different from that of the 480 invasion. Increasing taxation: Green, *The Greco-Persian Wars*, 49.

37. Herodotus, 7.1. Egyptian revolt: Green, *The Greco-Persian Wars*, 49. Greek doctors: Stoneman, *Xerxes*, 63–66. Inscription: Naqš-e Rustam inscription DNb 37–60.

38. Succession: possibly for propagandist reasons, Herodotus (7.2–3) records that Darius was swithering between choosing as his successor his eldest son Artabarzanes or Xerxes, son of Atossa, and so Cyrus' grandson, suggesting that he reached his decision thanks only to the intervention of his wife Atossa—and Demaratus, the Spartan royal renegade; see also Stoneman, *Xerxes*, 23. The appearance of Darius' favourite: Herodotus, 7.187. 'Greatest, second': Persepolis, 'Harem Inscription' (XPf), 32–33.

39. 'One king over many kings': Persepolis, 'Apadana Inscription' (XPb), 8–10. Xerxes' investiture: Plutarch, *Life of Artaxerxes*, 3; L. Llewellyn-Jones, *King and Court in Ancient Persia 559 to 331 BCE*, 14–15, 146; Stoneman, *Xerxes*, 30–34. 'When Darius, my father, died': Persepolis, 'Harem Inscription' (XPf), 33–55.

40. Description of troops: Herodotus, 7.61–88. The number of troops is passionately debated. A good summary of the problems (including the 'attractive theory that Herodotus may have confused the Persian terms for chiliarch and myriarch . . . , thus automatically multiplying all his figures by ten') is contained in Green, *The Greco-Persian Wars*, 58–60. See also Stoneman, *Xerxes*, 121–122.

41. Spies and Xerxes' response: Herodotus, 7.146–147. Green, *The Greco-Persian Wars*, 61, suggests that the spies were sent home 'furnished, no doubt, with musterrolls, naval lists, and other hand-outs from the Quartermaster General's staff'. Xerxes' fleet: Herodotus, 7.89–99. Callias as Spartan *proxenos:* Xenophon, *Hellenica*, 3.6. Cimon is first recorded as going to Sparta on a diplomatic mission in 479 (Plutarch, *Life of Aristides*, 10; see also Green, *The Greco-Persian Wars*, 229), but he

is unlikely to have been chosen for this role at this critical time if he had not already made good friends and contacts there.

5. Dedication

1. Food dumps: Herodotus, 7.25. Road through Thrace: Herodotus, 7.115. Bridges over Strymon: Herodotus, 7.114.

2. Uniting in a common cause: Herodotus, 7.145; P. A. Brunt, 'The Hellenic League against Persia', in *Studies in Greek History and Thought* (Oxford, 1993), 47–83. That the missions included delegates from the three leading states may be inferred.

3. Herodotus, 7.148–152.

4. Crete: Herodotus, 7.169. Minos' death: see D. Stuttard, *Greek Mythology: A Traveller's Guide from Mount Olympus to Troy* (London, 2016), 189.

5. Gelon: Herodotus, 7.153–156; D. Stuttard, *A History of Ancient Greece in Fifty Lives* (London, 2014), 84–87. Carthaginian invasion: Herodotus, 7.165–167. Herodotus is surely correct to suggest (as he seems to here) that even without the threat of invasion, Gelon would not have helped the Greeks.

6. The account of the visit of the Greek envoys to Gelon and their speeches: Herodotus, 7.157–162. See also J. Grethlein, *The Greeks and Their Past: Poetry, Oratory and History in the Fifth Century BCE* (Cambridge, 2010), 158–173, which compares the Spartan speech at Syracuse with Nestor's speech in Homer, *Iliad*, 7.124–128, and his recollection of an embassy of his own at Homer, *Iliad*, 7.765–790.

7. Herodotus, 7.163.

8. Demands for earth and water: Herodotus, 7.32. 'Most had no belly': Herodotus, 7.138.

9. Xerxes' canal: Herodotus, 7.22–24. Canal's design: Herodotus, 7.23. Somewhat unconvincingly, Herodotus claims that the design was the brainchild of the Phoenician contingent of labourers: every other nation in the Persian Empire had cut down vertically from ground level, with the result that the walls kept collapsing in on themselves—an unlikely tale given that Persian engineers knew all about canal building, not least from working on Darius' canal in Egypt. Darius' canal: Herodotus, 2.158; P. Green, *The Greco-Persian Wars* (London, 1998), 13. Aristotle (*Meteorology*, 1.15) suggests that, unwilling to allow saltwater to flow into the Nile, Darius suspended work on the canal and never completed it. 'Shock and awe': Diodorus Siculus, 11.2.

10. Bridges: Herodotus, 7.33–36. Construction and distances: Green, *The Greco-Persian Wars*, 75–77.

11. 'Stop digging': Herodotus, 1.174. Treatment of Hellespont and engineers: Herodotus, 7.35–36.

12. Plane tree: Herodotus, 7.31. Pythias' plane tree and offer to fund expedition: 7.27–28. Pythias' request and Xerxes' treatment of his son: Herodotus, 7.38–39. Solar eclipse: Herodotus, 7.37. Xerxes at Troy: Herodotus, 7.42.

13. Description of the march: Herodotus, 7.40–41. Camp followers: Herodotus, 7.187.

14. Doriscus: Herodotus (7.44) sites Xerxes' review of his troops at Abydus, but, as Green points out (*The Greco-Persian Wars*, 78), this is impossible, if only due to lack of water.

15. Aleuadae support Xerxes: Herodotus, 7.6. Thessalians address the League: Herodotus, 7.172–173.

16. Herodotus, 7.173.

17. Delphi's opening season and consultation days: M. Scott, *Delphi: A History of the Center of the Ancient World* (Princeton, NJ, 2014), 13.

18. Consulting the oracle: although we have no firm evidence for the procedure, much can be tentatively reconstructed. See Scott, *Delphi*, 13–24.

19. 'Time-wasters': Herodotus, 7.140.

20. Herodotus, 7.141. Cithaeron is a mountain in Boeotia near Plataea and Thebes.

21. Herodotus, 7. 142–143.

22. Plutarch, *Life of Cimon*, 5; A. Blamire, trans. and comm., *Plutarch's Life of Kimon* (London, 1988), 100.

23. Blamire, *Plutarch's Life of Kimon*, 101, points out that one of Athena's epithets was 'Chalinitis', Athena of the Bridle. C. W. Fornara, 'The Hoplite Achievement at Psyttaleia', *Journal of Hellenic Studies* 86 (1966), 51–54, wrongly dismisses the episode as 'a myth of the purest transparency'.

24. R. Garland, *Athens Burning: The Persian Invasion of Greece and the Evacuation of Attica* (Baltimore, 2017), 46–50, contains an excellent survey of this first evacuation, though I disagree with some of the chronology.

25. Olympic Festival: D. A. Stuttard, *Power Games: Ritual and Rivalry at the Greek Olympics* (London, 2012). Full moon on 19 August 480 B.C.: Green, *The Greco-Persian Wars*, 137.

26. The oracle: 'O you, who dwell on Sparta's broad plain, / either your great shining city must be laid waste / by Persians, or, if not, the boundaries of Laconia / must mourn a dead king, Heracles' descendant' (Herodotus, 7.220). 'Marry a good man': Plutarch, *Sayings of Spartans*, 225B.

27. Herodotus, 7.179–182. Battle of Artemisium: Herodotus, 7.175–195, 8.1–23; Diodorus, 11.12–13; Plutarch, *Life of Themistocles*, 7–9. A good account, including geographical details, is found in C. J. Butera and M. A. Sears, *Battles and Battlefields of Ancient Greece* (Barnsley, UK, 2019), 67–81, esp. 74–81. For an excellent discussion of Artemisium and Thermopylae, see Green, *The Greco-Persian Wars*, 109–145.

28. Meltemi: information useful to both historians and mariners alike can be found at www.sailingissues.com/meltemi. 'Like a boiling cauldron': Herodotus,

7.188. Prayers to Boreas: Herodotus, 7.189. Athenians had a special relationship with Boreas, for mythology told how the god had married an Athenian princess.

29. Herodotus, 7.188–191. Magi: Herodotus, 7.191. Numbers of Persian casualties: Green, *The Greco-Persian Wars*, 124, 128. Offerings to Poseidon: Herodotus, 7.192 (which improbably has the Greeks make the offerings on the second day of the storm, when it is unlikely, to say the least, that they would have received reports of the destruction of the Persian ships).

30. Scyllias: Herodotus, 8.8. Persians round Euboea: Herodotus, 8.7. 'Not even a fire-signaller': Herodotus, 8.6. Herodotus, who is keen to expose arguments between Greek poleis, records that at Thermopylae, too, the Greeks were divided over whether to stay and fight or retreat to the safety of the Isthmus (7.207). Both episodes might be true, but equally they may simply be instances of Herodotus' love of the dramatic.

31. Storm: Herodotus, 8.12. 'The god's intervention': Herodotus, 8.13. Greeks receive news of Persian fleet's fate: Herodotus, 8.14.

32. The story of Thermopylae is contained in Herodotus, 7.201–238, and Diodorus, 11.4–11. P. Cartledge, *Thermopylae: The Battle That Changed the World* (London, 2006); Butera and Sears, *Battles and Battlefields of Ancient Greece*, 49–63; J. P. Stonk, 'Thermopylae 480 B.C.: Ancient Accounts of a Battle', *Talanta: Proceedings of the Dutch Archaeological and Historical Society* 46–47 (2014–2015), 165–236. Thermopylae became more significant in retrospect as a romantic paradigm—the tale of a handful of doomed Greek heroes standing up against the might of a 'barbarian horde' to defend their way of life—than it was in reality (an operation intended to halt the Persian advance for considerably longer than the three days it took Xerxes to defeat it). As Herodotus (7.206) confesses, 'no-one expected Thermopylae to be over so quickly'. Tactically it was disastrous: Leonidas clearly knew about the path over the mountains, but failed to assign any of his Spartans to bolster Phocian resolve. G. Cawkwell, *The Greek Wars: The Failure of Persia* (Oxford, 2005), Appendix 5; B. Strauss, 'Thermopylae: Death of a King, Birth of a Legend', *Military History Quarterly* (Fall 2004), 17–25. Carneia and Olympics: Herodotus, 7.206. Herodotus makes much of the synchronism of Thermopylae and the Olympic Games: when one of the Persian high command hears that the only prize in the Olympics is an olive crown, Herodotus has him exclaim: 'Phew! What kind of men have you brought us here to fight against, Mardonius? They don't fight for money but glory!' (Herodotus, 8.26).

33. Campfires: Herodotus, 8.19.

6. Firestorm

1. Crowded Salamis: R. Garland, *Athens Burning: The Persian Invasion of Greece and the Evacuation of Attica* (Baltimore, 2017), 52–53. Leonidas' head impaled: Herodotus, 7.238. Persians in Phocis: Herodotus, 8.32–33.

2. Persians on Euboea: Herodotus, 8.23. Messages to Ionians: Herodotus, 8.22; Plutarch, *Life of Themistocles*, 9.

3. Fear of blockade: Herodotus, 8.70. Fortifying Isthmus and destroying road: Herodotus, 8.71.

4. Many of these arguments are contained in Herodotus, 8.60.

5. Herodotus, 8.64; P. Green, *The Greco-Persian Wars* (London, 1998), 171.

6. Herodotus, 8.51–54; Garland, *Athens Burning*, 66–68.

7. Herodotus, 8.55.

8. Xerxes' causeway and bridge: Herodotus, 8.97; Plutarch, *Life of Themistocles*, 16; Green, *The Greco-Persian Wars*, 172–174. In fact, as Xerxes no doubt realised, to build a bridge to Salamis would be extremely difficult if not impossible, but the psychological effect of even threatening to do so was immensely powerful. The Greek war council on Salamis: Plutarch, *Life of Themistocles*, 11; Herodotus, 8.62.

9. Plutarch, *Life of Themistocles*, 12; Herodotus, 8.75–76; Aeschylus, *Persians*, 355–379. Troubles in the Persian Empire: Green, *The Greco-Persian Wars*, 178.

10. Full moon: 20 September 480 B.C. 'Golden canopy': Plutarch, *Life of Themistocles*, 16. 'Alive with doves': Aeschylus, *Persians*, 310.

11. Barnstorming speech: Herodotus, 8.83. 'Forward, Greeks!': Aeschylus, *Persians*, 402–405, which places the words in the mouths of the Greeks as a body, but Green, *The Greco-Persian Wars*, 196, argues convincingly that the sentiments echo the peroration of Themistocles' speech remembered by Aeschylus (who was present when it was made and who may have served as a marine on his brother Ameinias' trireme). Links with Eleusinian Mysteries: Herodotus, 8.65; Plutarch, *Life of Themistocles*, 15—Herodotus places this episode some days before Salamis, Plutarch at some point during the battle. It is Green, *The Greco-Persian Wars*, 176, who ingeniously links the sighting with Persian manoeuvres, though he places the march slightly earlier.

12. Plutarch, *Life of Themistocles*, 13, records the unlikely story (which he attributes to the fourth-century B.C. philosopher, Phanias of Lesbos) that among the offerings made before the battle were three human sacrifices (Xerxes' captured nephews) to Dionysus Flesh-Eater. Order of battle: Herodotus, 8.85. Ameinias: Herodotus, 8.84. Phoenician stern: Aeschylus, *Persians*, 410. Ameinias and the admiral: Plutarch, *Life of Themistocles*, 14. Nine in the morning: Green, *The Greco-Persian Wars*, 193.

13. Winds: Plutarch, *Life of Themistocles*, 14. Artemisia: Herodotus, 8.87–88. Ameinas and Artemisia: Herodotus, 8.93. 'Jabbing them': Aeschylus, *Persians*, 424–428. Aristides on Psyttaleia: Herodotus, 8.95. Cimon's bravery: Plutarch, *Life of Cimon*, 5. Curiously (and without evidence), A. Blamire, trans. and comm., *Plutarch's Life of Kimon* (London, 1988), 102, suggests that 'Kimon perhaps commanded a ship at Salamis'.

14. Herodotus, 8.86. Looting: Plutarch, *Life of Themistocles*, 18.

15. Refusal to destroy bridges: Herodotus, 8.108 (where it is Eurybiadas who refuses to accept Themistocles' proposal), and Plutarch, *Life of Themistocles*, 16 (where it

is Aristides). Herodotus (8.109–110) maintains that Themistocles then succeeded in hastening Xerxes' departure from Attica by sending a messenger (the same slave he had sent to him before Salamis) with the news that the Greeks were indeed intending to destroy the bridges and that if the Persians wanted to escape they should do so at once. It is unlikely, however, that Xerxes would trust the slave a second time, and the story is likely to be a tall tale, perhaps invented by the vaunting Themistocles himself. Xerxes retreats: Herodotus, 8.113.

16. Statues of the tyrant-slayers removed: see discussion in V. Azoulay, *The Tyrant-Slayers of Ancient Athens*, trans. J. Lloyd (Oxford, 2017), 32–34.

17. Garland, *Athens Burning*, 89–90. Structurally sound houses: since it was undoubtedly the Persians' intention not only to return the following year but to establish Athens as a Persian-ruled city, they are unlikely to have wished to destroy it utterly at this stage: it was only the next year, when their ambitions seemed impossible to achieve, that they would have unleashed their anger and frustration fully on the city.

18. Herodotus, 8.123–124; B. Jordan, 'The Honors for Themistocles after Salamis', *American Journal of Philology* 109, no. 4 (Winter 1988), 547–571.

19. Herodotus, 8.121–122.

20. Persian retreat: Herodotus, 8.113–120. Strymon: Aeschylus, *Persians*, 495–510.

21. Up to 100,000 men: C. J. Butera and M. A. Sears, *Battles and Battlefields of Ancient Greece* (Barnsley, UK, 2019), 86. 'Fighting in defence of Greece': Herodotus, 8.114.

22. Spartans honour Themistocles: Herodotus, 8.124; Plutarch, *Life of Themistocles*, 17. 'Without Themistocles': Plutarch, *Life of Themistocles*, 18. Spartan policy regarding Attica: Green, *The Greco-Persian Wars*, 211–212.

23. Herodotus, 8.136, 8.140.

24. Herodotus, 8.140–144. To many of Herodotus' audience and readers in the 420s B.C., embroiled as they were in the Peloponnesian War and longing for Persian assistance, Xerxes' proposition must have seemed increasingly attractive.

25. Lycidas and his family: Herodotus, 9.5.

26. Late June: Green, *The Greco-Persian Wars*, 229.

27. Argive promise to Mardonius: Herodotus, 9.12.

28. Plutarch, *Life of Aristides*, 10; Blamire, *Plutarch's Life of Kimon*, 104. I disagree with Green (*The Greco-Persian Wars*, 230), who describes the mission as 'a masterpiece of mistiming', but I follow him in accepting that there were two missions, since as it stands Herodotus (9.7–8) makes little sense. For an alternative view, see C. Hignett, *Xerxes' Invasion of Greece* (Oxford, 1963), 342–343. The archon shared the name Xanthippus with Miltiades' bête noire, who was even now sailing east; the general, Myronides, would play a crucial role at Plataea a few months later. Herodotus, 9.7; Plutarch, *Life of Aristides*, 10; Diodorus, 11.28. The need for top se-

crecy explains why accounts in Herodotus et al. make such little sense. Throne at Amyclae: Pausanias, 3.18–19. The Amykles Research Project has revealed its foundations: http://www.amyklaion.gr/?page_id=1299; https://warwick.ac.uk/fac/arts /classics/students/modules/greekreligion/database/template-copy14/. Hyacinthia: Athenaeus, 4.139–140; Strabo, 6.278; Xenophon, *Agesilaus*, 2.17; *Hellenica*, 4.5. 'Full of festival': Herodotus, 9.7.

29. Herodotus, 9.11.

30. Herodotus, 9.13–14.

31. Largest Greek army: Butera and Sears, *Battles and Battlefields of Ancient Greece*, 85. On the (hotly contested) text of the Oath of Plataea, see P. Cartledge, *After Thermopylae* (Oxford, 2013), 17–18. Cartledge discounts the oath in the forms we now have it, but accepts that *an* oath was taken.

32. Herodotus, 9.22–24. The Battle of Plataea: Herodotus, 9.1–18; Diodorus, 11.28–32; Plutarch, *Life of Aristides*, 11–19; Green, *The Greco-Persian Wars*, 239–271.

33. Herodotus, 9.39, 9.44–45.

34. Herodotus, 9.46–58.

35. Herodotus, 9.59.

36. Herodotus, 9.61–62. 'Each man': Tyrtaeus, fr. 11 (West), 21–34.

37. Herodotus, 9.63. Herodotus (9.64) remarks 'in such a way did Mardonius give satisfaction to the Spartans for the killing of Leonidas'.

38. Herodotus, 9.68–70.

39. Looting: Herodotus, 9.80. Gifts to the gods: Herodotus, 9.81.

40. Herodotus, 9.85–87.

41. Xanthippus overwintering at Sestus: Thucydides, 1.89; Diodorus, 11.37.

7. Hegemon

1. Delegation to Cimon: Plutarch, *Life of Aristides*, 23, and *Life of Cimon*, 6. Pausanias' behaviour: Plutarch, *Life of Aristides*, 23.

2. Pausanias at Plataea: Herodotus, 9.82. Pausanias' behaviour at Byzantium: Thucydides, 1.130; Diodorus, 11.44. Pausanias and Xerxes: Thucydides, 1.128; Diodorus, 11.44; C. W. Fornara, 'Some Aspects of the Career of Pausanias of Sparta', *Historia* 15 (1966), 257–271; A. Blamire, 'Pausanias and Persia', *Greek, Roman and Byzantine Studies* 11 (1970), 295–305.

3. Thucydides, 1.95; Plutarch, *Life of Aristides*, 23. A. Blamire, trans. and comm., *Plutarch's Life of Kimon* (London, 1988), 108 (citing Herodotus, 8.3; [Aristotle], *Athenian Constitution*, 23.4; Diodorus, 11.44.6), suggests that Artistides himself 'may have played a much more active role than Thucydides will admit' in Pausanias' deposition.

4. Plutarch, *Life of Aristides*, 20.

5. Offerings including serpent statue: Herodotus, 9.81. Serpent Column: Paul Stephenson, *The Serpent Column: A Cultural History* (Oxford, 2016). 'After defeating the Persians': Thucydides, 1.132. Athenian stoa and inscription: see G. Umholz, 'Architraval Arrogance? Dedicatory Inscriptions in Greek Architecture of the Classical Period', *Hesperia* 71 (2002), 261–293. 'Greece's liberators': Diodorus Siculus, 11.33.

6. 'If the greatest': Simonides, 8 (Page), in D. L. Page, *Further Greek Epigrams: Epigrams before A.D. 50 from the Greek Anthology and Other Sources, not included in Hellenistic Epigrams or The Garland of Philip* (Cambridge, 1981).

7. 'These men': Simonides, 9 (Page).

8. 'We are lying here': Simonides, 12 (Page).

9. 'Here—against three million—': Simonides, 22a (Page).

10. 'Stranger, report': Simonides, 22b (Page).

11. 'Naked, oiled': Anon, *Life of Sophocles*, 3. On Simonides' ode, see L. M. Kowerski, *Simonides on the Persian Wars: A Study of the Elegiac Verses of the 'New Simonides'* (London, 2012).

12. Funeral Games to honour the war dead: possibly referred to on inscriptions found on a bronze cauldron (*Inscriptiones Graeci* [*IG*] 1³ 523) from near Marathon, a cauldron (*IG* 1³ 524) and a water jar (*IG* 1³ 525). Themistocles and the walls of Athens: Thucydides, 1.90–93; Diodorus, 11.39–40; Plutarch, *Life of Themistocles,* 19.

13. Piraeus: Diodorus, 11.41–43 (where Themistocles again outwits the Spartans, using the same scheme as before—a dubious repetition).

14. Spartan plans for population exchange: Herodotus, 9.106; Diodorus, 11.37. Xanthippus to Sestus: Herodotus, 9.114.

15. Cimon's generalship: Plutarch, *Life of Cimon,* 6; *Life of Aristides,* 23. Note that the original editors of the Athenian Tribute Lists—the record of the quota dedicated from 454 B.C. on to Athena on the Acropolis from the money tribute paid by Athens' allies (B. D. Meritt, H. T. Wade-Gery and M. F. McGregor, *The Athenian Tribute Lists,* 4 vols. [Cambridge, MA, 1939–1953])—give the date of Cimon's first generalship as 477 / 6. However, Blamire, *Plutarch's Life of Kimon,* 107, comments, 'There can surely be no objection to the assumption that the Athenians appointed two members of the board of ten *strategoi* to accompany the Athenian contingent, and nominated Aristides as its commander, as the League system required'.

16. Lacedaemonius and Oulius: Plutarch, *Life of Cimon,* 16. J. K. Davies, *Athenian Propertied Families, 600–300 B.C.* (Oxford, 1971), 306–307. It has been suggested that Cimon named one son Lacedaemonius to mark the fact that he had been honoured by the Spartans with the position of their official representative (*proxenos*) in Athens: Blamire, *Plutarch's Life of Kimon,* 162–165; P. J. Bicknell, *Studies in Athenian Politics and Genealogy* (Wiesbaden, 1972), 91–92. Generalship: M. Zaccarini, *The Lame Hegemony: Cimon of Athens and the Failure of Panhellenism, ca. 478–450 B.C.* (Bologna, 2017), 49–51. Plutarch records a tradition that the mother of Lacedae-

monius and Oulius was 'a woman from Cleitor', a town in Arcadia, but as Blamire remarks, 'This tradition has suspicious features, in particular the absence of the lady's name and the sexual pun, Kleitor—clitoris, which can be read into her supposed place of origin' (163).

17. The relationship between Aristides and Cimon is implied by Plutarch, *Life of Aristides*, 23. Aristides as senior commander: [Aristotle], *Athenian Constitution*, 23.3–4; Diodorus, 11.44.2. Twenty new triremes: Diodorus, 11.43. Themistocles' plot: Plutarch, *Life of Aristides*, 22.

18. Aristides' advice: Plutarch, *Life of Aristides*, 23. Thirty triremes: Thucydides, 1.94; Diodorus, 11.44. Cyprus: Zaccarini, *The Lame Hegemony*, 51. Treatment of Persian garrison and governor: Herodotus, 9.118–121.

19. Plutarch, *Life of Cimon*, 9; Polyaenus, *Stratagems*, 1.34. Blamire, *Plutarch's Life of Kimon*, 126–127, thinks it likely that only those prisoners captured at Byzantium (i.e., not at Sestus) were treated in this way. He notes, too, that 'some scholars have suspected that Ion's recollections' (on which Plutarch's account is based) . . . 'may have been clouded by the amount of wine he had taken'.

20. Thucydides, 1.95. Cleonice: Plutarch, *Life of Cimon*, 6; Pausanias, 3.17. As A. Powell points out in 'One Little *Skytale*,' in *Xenophon and Sparta*, ed. A. Powell and N. Richer (Swansea, Wales, 2020), 10, 'Sexual predation of citizens . . . was seen as characteristic of tyranny'. Samian and Chiote generals: Plutarch, *Life of Aristides*, 23, where Aristides demands that the Ionians give proof of their good faith through 'some action which would commit them irrevocably to the Athenian side'; see also Blamire, *Plutarch's Life of Kimon*, 108. Blamire goes on to suggest that 'for Aristeides and Kimon to have communicated directly with the ephors in Sparta seems unlikely', but they had done so before and would do so again.

21. Plutarch, *Life of Cimon*, 6; Thucydides, 1.95–96, 1.130; Diodorus, 11.46; Blamire, *Plutarch's Life of Kimon*, 109. Pausanias' movements after his first recall to Sparta, together with the role of Sparta in Byzantium and the Hellespont, are contested. My reconstruction of events follows Thucydides' clear statement (1.131) that after he then left Sparta without official leave (foreign travel being strictly controlled by the Spartans) he sailed to Byzantium from Hermione (a port in the north-east Peloponnese, i.e., not the Spartan port of Gytheum, further suggesting that this was no official expedition). Thucydides says that at Byzantium he was subsequently 'besieged by force by the Athenians', which I interpret here as house arrest. To assume a mini war between Athens and Sparta over Byzantium is (I think) unjustified, and would make no strategic or political sense at this time. Given the current political situation, with Athens now de facto head of the alliance and so effectively in control of operations in Byzantium and the east, I can see no circumstances in which Pausanias (especially given his track record in the city) could have held an official position at Byzantium. However, the sources are confused, the chronology is difficult, and it is impossible to be certain either way. For other interpretations, see, e.g., Zaccarini, *The Lame Hegemony*, 94–98; Fornara, 'Some Aspects of the Career of Pausanias of Sparta', 257–271; G. E. M. de Ste.

Croix, *Origins of the Peloponnesian War* (London, 1972); M. L. Lang, 'Scapegoat Pausanias', *Classical Journal* 63 (1976), 79–85; W. T. Loomis, 'Pausanias, Byzantion and the Formation of the Delian League: A Chronological Note', *Historia* 39, no. 4 (1990), 487–492; T. J. Russell, *Byzantium and the Bosporus: A Historical Study from the Seventh Century B.C. until the Foundation of Constantinople* (Oxford, 2017), 57–58.

22. Purpose of alliance: Thucydides, 1.96. Aristides and the League: Plutarch, *Life of Aristides*, 24; Diodorus, 11.47.

23. Name of alliance: see, e.g., P. J. Rhodes, *A History of the Classical World, 487–323 BCE* (Hoboken, NJ, 2005), 18. 'Ionians in long flowing robes': *Homeric Hymn to Apollo*, 147–155.

24. Oath and ceremony: Plutarch, *Life of Aristides*, 25; [Aristotle], *Athenian Constitution*, 23; A. H. Sommerstein and A. J. Bayliss, *Oath and State in Ancient Greece* (Berlin, 2012), 205–208; Blamire, *Plutarch's Life of Kimon*, 108.

25. Diodorus, 11.50. See Ste. Croix, *Origins of the Peloponnesian War*, 170–171.

26. Diodorus, 11.50. Diodorus places this event in 475 (during the archonship in Athens of Dromocleides), but his chronology for this period is suspect: he wrote annalistically, and had nothing else to record for that year in Greece. Zaccarini, *The Lame Hegemony*, 55.

27. Cimon and Sparta: Plutarch, *Life of Cimon*, 16. Agent on a secret mission: Zaccarini, *The Lame Hegemony*, 96, quotes the example of Spartan Polycratidas in similar circumstances allegedly stating that 'we are here in an official capacity if we are successful, but in a private capacity if we fail' (Plutarch, *Life of Lycurgus*, 25).

28. Lemnos: Zaccarini, *The Lame Hegemony*, 48.

29. Herodotus, 7.107; Thucydides, 1.98; Plutarch, *Life of Cimon*, 7; Nepos, *Life of Cimon*, 2.

30. Menon of Pharsalus: Demosthenes (23.199) tells us that in thanks for his aid he was granted Athenian citizenship. Raids on the Thracians: Plutarch, *Life of Cimon*, 7; Nepos, *Life of Cimon*, 2.

31. Plutarch, *Life of Cimon*, 7. Herodotus (7.107) claims that Boges threw the gold and silver into the Strymon before killing himself, but it is difficult to see how he could achieve this; consigning it to the flames would surely have been more effective anyway. Equally improbable is Pausanias' claim (8.8.9) that to capture Eion, Cimon diverted the River Strymon.

32. Eion as a joint Thasian and Parian settlement: Zaccarini, *The Lame Hegemony*, 157. Blamire, *Plutarch's Life of Kimon*, 113–114, suggests that he believes Plutarch to imply that at this time 'the Athenians established two settlements on the Strymon, one on the coast at Eion and the other upriver on the future site of Amphipolis'; while he is wrong in reading this into Plutarch's account at this stage, his discussion of chronology is useful.

33. Statues of tyrannicides: V. Azoulay, *The Tyrant-Slayers of Ancient Athens: A Tale of Two Statues* (New York, 2017). Azoulay remarks, 'The group produced by Critius

and Nesiotes is generally recognized as marking the advent of the Classical style of art' (3). See also B. S. Ridgway, *The Severe Style in Greek Sculpture* (Princeton, NJ, 1970), 12; A. Stewart, *Arts, Desire, and the Body in Ancient Greece* (Cambridge, 1997), 245; C. Rolley, *La sculpture greque: Des origines au milieu du Ve siècle*, vol 1. (Paris, 1994), 329; R. T. Neer *The Emergence of the Classical Style in Greek Sculpture* (Chicago, 2010), 78.

34. Plutarch, *Life of Cimon*, 7; Aeschines, 3.183–185. Blamire, *Plutarch's Life of Kimon*, 112–114, gives a good discussion of the Eion Herms and their accompanying verses; cf. R. Osborne, 'The Erection and Mutilation of the Hermai', *Cambridge Classical Journal* 31 (1985), 47–73. While Zaccarini, *The Lame Hegemony*, 66–67, counsels against seeing the herms as 'an early example of Cimon's "propaganda"', Cimon cannot have been unaware of the power that messages such as these could convey. For a discussion of the verses themselves, see F. Jacoby, 'Some Athenian Epigrams from the Persian Wars', *Hesperia* 14 (1945), 157–211; H. T. Wade-Gery, 'Classical Epigrams and Epitaphs', *Journal of Hellenic Studies* 53 (1933), 71–82.

8. Securing Athens

1. Plutarch, *Life of Cimon*, 8, and *Life of Theseus*, 36; Pausanias, 3.3.7. Theseus as a national hero: C. Sourvinou- Inwood, 'Theseus Lifting the Rock and a Cup near the Pithos Painter', *Journal of Hellenic Studies* 91 (1971), 94–109; T. B. L. Webster, *Potter and Patron in Classical Athens* (London, 1972), 74–75, 82–85.

2. See, e.g., E. Hall, *Inventing the Barbarian: Greek Self-Definition through Tragedy* (Oxford, 1989).

3. Plutarch, *Life of Theseus*, 35; Pausanias, 1.17.5–6; Apollodorus, 1.24. World's first thalassocracy: Thucydides, 1.4.

4. Lichas dissimulating: for a good discussion, see A. Powell, 'One Little Skytale', in *Xenophon and Sparta*, ed. A. Powell and N. Richer (Swansea, Wales, 2020), 24. Herodotus, 1.66–68. P. Cartledge, *The Spartans: An Epic History* (New York, 2003), 74, almost certainly correctly observes, 'in point of sober scientific fact, the preternaturally large bones uncovered were most likely those of a prehistoric dinosaur', which at first sight makes the existence of a coffin all the odder. Perhaps an earlier Tegean had already found, misidentified and buried them. Tisamenus: Pausanias, 7.1.7. See L. E. Paterson, *Kinship Myth in Ancient Greece* (Austin, TX, 2010), 41–42.

5. Plutarch, *Life of Cimon*, 8. A. Blamire, trans. and comm., *Plutarch's Life of Kimon* (London, 1988), 117–118, contains a good discussion of the Amphictyonic League (called in my text the international court at Delphi).

6. Herodotus, 6.72; Pausanias, 3.5, 3.7, 3.79.

7. Plutarch, *Life of Cimon*, 8, and *Life of Theseus*, 36; Thucydides, 1.98; Blamire, *Plutarch's Life of Kimon*, 116.

8. Thetttalus: J. K. Davies, *Athenian Propertied Families, 600–300 B.C.* (Oxford, 1971), 307.

9. Plutarch, *Life of Theseus,* 36; Blamire, *Plutarch's Life of Kimon,* 121. That this was the site of Theseus' grave is speculated by N. McGilchrist, *Greece, the Aegean Islands* (Taunton, UK, 2010), 593–594.

10. The bare bones of Theseus' return are contained in Plutarch, *Life of Theseus,* 36. Early autumn: see, e.g., S. C. Humphreys, *Kinship in Ancient Athens: An Anthropological Analysis* (Oxford, 2018), 585.

11. B. Strauss, *Fathers and Sons in Athens: Ideology and Society in the Era of the Peloponnesian War* (London, 2011), 107.

12. 'In the heart of the lower city': Plutarch, *Life of Theseus,* 36, describes it as lying ἐν μέσηι τῆι πόλει (*en mesei tei polei*). Blamire, *Plutarch's Life of Kimon,* 121. The temple of Hephaestus sited on the lower hill of Agoraios Kolonos overlooking the Agora used to be mistakenly identified (and still is by some) as the Theseum. Indeed, the nearby Metro stop is still called Theseio. Description of Theseum: Pausanias, 1.17. 'Dolphins of the salt sea': Bacchylides, *Odes,* 17, 97–119. On allusions to Cimon and his family in the praise-poet Bacchylides (esp. 18.46–60), a relative of Simonides, see J. P. Barron, 'Bakchylides, Theseus and a Woolly Cloak', *Bulletin of the Institute of Classical Studies* 27 (1980), 1–8.

13. Humphreys, *Kinship in Ancient Athens,* 584–585.

14. 'The ship': Bacchylides, *Odes,* 17, 1–7. See also W. R. Connor, 'Theseus in Classical Athens', in *The Quest for Theseus,* ed. A. G. Ward (London, 1970), 143–174.

15. Theseus' ship: J. R. Hale, *Lords of the Sea: The Epic Story of the Athenian Navy and the Birth of Democracy* (New York, 2009), 88–90. 'More than any other': Plutarch, *Life of Cimon,* 8.

16. Phrynichus' *Phoenician Women:* see M. Wright, *The Lost Plays of Greek Tragedy* (London, 2016), 23–25, 209. Considered as a pair: while each play was part of its own trilogy, separated in time from one another by some fifteen years, we know from deliberate parallels and contrasts in the handling of the Electra story over some forty years by Aeschylus, Sophocles and Euripides, as well as from references in the comedies of Aristophanes that Athenian audiences were adept at finding echoes and drawing comparisons between contemporary and earlier dramas. Odysseus weeping: Homer, *Odyssey,* 8.522–531—'Tears fell from Odysseus' eyes and wet his cheeks. As a woman wails and hugs her darling husband who has fallen in full view of his city and his people, trying to protect his city and his children from the day when there will be no pity; as she seen him dying, gasping for his breath, she clings to him and screams her piercing screams, while soldiers strike her on her back and shoulders with their spears and drag her off to slavery, to hard work and misery, and her cheeks are shrivelled in her pitiful distress.'

17. Ameinias as Aeschylus' brother: Diodorus, 11.27—though perhaps Diodorus is mistaken; he calls him Ameinias of Pallene, whereas Aeschylus' family came from Eleusis. 'Whose eyes': Aeschylus, *Persians,* 81–82. 'In marriage beds': Aeschylus, *Persians,* 133–139. 'Payment for his hubris': Aeschylus, *Persians,* 808. 'Smashing wooden statues': Aeschylus, *Persians,* 809–810. 'Binding the current':

Aeschylus, *Persians*, 745–746. 'Never to march against': Aeschylus, *Persians*, 790–791. 'Oozing mess of blood': Aeschylus, *Persians*, 816. 'Mortals must not think': Aeschylus, *Persians*, 820. 'The very land': Aeschylus, *Persians*, 792. 'The gods protect': Aeschylus, *Persians*, 347. 'As long as she has men': Aeschylus, *Persians*, 349. 'Flowing stream': Aeschylus, *Persians*, 238. 'Stand tall, fighting': Aeschylus, *Persians*, 240. 'Who herds them . . . vassals': Aeschylus, *Persians*, 241–242.

18. 'A Greek man': Aeschylus, *Persians*, 355. Aeschylus' omission of Themistocles' name may be a result of tragic convention, though given that *Persians* is our only extant 'historical' tragedy it is difficult to be certain.

19. Tent: Plutarch, *Life of Themistocles*, 5. Speech against Hieron: Plutarch, *Life of Themistocles*, 25. Victories of Hieron and Theron: *Oxyrhynchus Papyrus*, 222. Andocides (4.33) suggests that Cimon himself may have won an Olympic chariot race, but it is just as likely that his is a confused memory of Cimon Coálemos.

20. Plutarch, *Life of Themistocles*, 20.

21. Herodotus, 8.112; Thucydides, 1.98. M. Zaccarini, *The Lame Hegemony: Cimon of Athens and the Failure of Panhellenism, ca. 478–450 B.C.* (Bologna, 2017), 79–85. Bronze bull: Pausanias, 10.16.

22. Attacking Themistocles: Plutarch, *Life of Aristides*, 24. Alcmaeon: Davies, *Athenian Propertied Families, 600–300 B.C.*, 382, 599, but see Blamire, *Plutarch's Life of Kimon*, 105. 'A clever man': Plutarch, *Life of Aristides*, 4. Plutarch, *Life of Themistocles*, 21. Themistocles' political decline: see, e.g., W. G. Forrest, 'Themistocles and Argos', *Classical Quarterly*, n.s., 10 (1960), 221–241; G. Cawkwell, 'The Fall of Themistocles', *Auckland Classical Essays Presented to E. M. Blaiklock* (Auckland, 1970), 39–58; G. E. M. de Ste. Croix, *The Origins of the Peloponnesian War* (London, 1972), 173–178.

23. 'The best thing': Plutarch, *Life of Aristides*, 24.

24. Plutarch, *Life of Themistocles*, 22.

25. Plutarch, *Life of Themistocles*, 22. The date of the ostracism is probably 472 or 471 B.C.

26. Thucydides, 1.132–134; Nepos, *Life of Pausanias*, 4–5.

27. Thucydides, 1.132–134. Plutarch, *Life of Cimon*, 6, and *De Sera Numinis Vindicta*, *Moralia*, 555C. Necromantic oracle (at Heracleia on the Black Sea): Pomponius Mela, 1.103. According to the traveller Pausanias (3.17.7–9), the Spartan general Pausanias consulted the oracle of the dead not at Heracleia but at Phigalia in Arcadia.

28. Thucydides, 1.135. Plutarch, *Life of Themistocles*, 23. Inciting spectators at Olympia to destroy a tyrant's tent: Plutarch, *Life of Themistocles*, 25.

29. Thucydides, 1.135–137. Plutarch, *Life of Themistocles*, 23–24. Prosecutions of Themistocles' friends: Plutarch, *Life of Themistocles*, 24; Demosthenes, 9.41–44, 19.271–272; Aeschines, 3.258. See also M. H. Hansen, *Eisangelia* (Odense, 1975), 70; D. M. MacDowell, *The Law in Classical Athens* (London, 1978), 176–177; F. J. Frost, *Plutarch's Themistocles: A Historical Commentary* (Princeton, NJ, 1980), 196–199.

30. Thucydides, 1.137. Plutarch, *Life of Themistocles*, 25. Persian preparations: R. Stoneman, *Xerxes: A Persian Life* (New Haven, CT, 2015), 200–201. R. Meiggs, *The Athenian Empire* (Oxford, 1972), 80–82, sees the Persian preparations as aimed not at the Greek mainland but Caria and Lycia. Chronology: Zaccarini, *The Lame Hegemony*, 103–110.

9. 'I Am Eurymedon'

1. The chronology is uncertain. However, given the Persians' experience of Greek behaviour, it is likely that they would have chosen an Olympic year, which would place both the revolt of Naxos and the Battle of Eurymedon in 468 B.C. Others place the events in 466: Diodorus (11.60–62) has Eion and Eurymedon happening in the same year (470 / 69), whereas several modern scholars such as R. Meiggs, *The Athenian Empire* (Oxford, 1972), 80–82, and E. Bayer and J. Heideking, *Die Chronologie des perikleischen Zeitalters* (Darmstadt, 1975), 119, date Eurymedon to 466.

2. Structural modifications to triremes: Plutarch, *Life of Cimon*, 12; J. R. Hale, *Lords of the Sea: The Epic Story of the Athenian Navy and the Birth of Democracy* (New York, 2009), 92; A. Blamire, trans. and comm., *Plutarch's Life of Kimon* (London, 1988), 139–140.

3. Plutarch, *Life of Themistocles*, 25–29. Goats' bells: Aegae (derived from the Greek, *aix, aiges*) means 'goats', and a goat was the city's symbol. The story of Themistocles' flight and its timing has excited much scholarly debate, while the idea of his dressing as a woman to escape from Aegae has been dismissed as a slur. However, there is nothing intrinsically unbelievable about it.

4. Plutarch, *Life of Cimon*, 12. Two hundred Athenian triremes, 100 allied ships: Diodorus, 11.60 (though Blamire, *Plutarch's Life of Kimon*, 139, declares that 'a combined Athenian and allied fleet of 300 ships is possible in theory, but . . . unlikely in practice. 200 ships is the maximum figure reported by Thucydides for a League fleet during Kimon's lifetime' (Thucydides, 1.104, 1.112). However, Thucydides (1.100) does not tell us the size of this particular fleet and, if it was indeed to prevent an invasion of Attica, it would have been as large as could be mustered. Cnidus campaign: M. Zaccarini, *The Lame Hegemony: Cimon of Athens and the Failure of Panhellenism, ca. 478–450 B.C.* (Bologna, 2017), 111–114. For the site of classical Cnidus, see Blamire, *Plutarch's Life of Kimon*, 138–139.

5. Chimaera's location: Pliny the Elder, *Natural History*, 2.105, 5.43; Strabo, *Geography*, 14.3.5. Bellerophon and Chimaera: D. Stuttard, *Greek Mythology: A Traveller's Guide from Mount Olympus to Troy* (London, 2016), 153. The Islands of the Swallows (the Chelidonian Islands lay about 6 stades, just over half a mile, off Cape Hieron (Strabo, *Geography*, 666): Blamire, *Plutarch's Life of Kimon*, 147.

6. Plutarch, *Life of Cimon*, 12. Phaselis: Strabo, *Geography*, 666. Moon waxing: the Olympic Games coincided with the full moon, the second after the summer

solstice: D. A. Stuttard, *Power Games: Ritual and Rivalry at the Greek Olympics* (London, 2012), 103.

7. Plutarch, *Life of Cimon*, 12; Diodorus, 11.61; Thucydides, 1.100. The accounts of classical historians are confused and contradictory. I try to steer a course between them. Blamire, *Plutarch's Life of Kimon*, 141–142. Zaccarini, *The Lame Hegemony*, 122–124.

8. Plutarch, *Life of Cimon*, 13.

9. Plutarch, *Life of Cimon*, 13; Diodorus, 11.61. Blamire, *Plutarch's Life of Kimon*, 143, calls this story 'absurd'.

10. Pherendates: Diodorus, 11.61. Public cemetery: Pausanias, 1.29; Zaccarini, *The Lame Hegemony*, 169.

11. Men named their sons: see, e.g., J. K. Davies, *Athenian Propertied Families, 600–300 B.C.* (Oxford, 1971), 334, 571, for how the name continued to be used down the generations. Eurymedon oinochoe: Circle of Triptolemos Painter (Hamburg, Museum für Kunst und Gewerbe 1981.173); for a full discussion and alternative interpretation, see M. C. Miller, 'I Am Eurymedon: Tensions and Ambiguities in Athenian War Imagery', in *War, Democracy and Culture in Classical Athens*, ed. D. M. Pritchard (Cambridge, 2010), 304–338.

12. 'Like a formidable athlete' and the extent of Athenian power: Plutarch, *Life of Cimon*, 13. Blamire, *Plutarch's Life of Kimon*, 147. Lionized: Diodorus, 11.62.

13. Pausanias, 10.10. Blamire, *Plutarch's Life of Kimon*, 103. For discussions of the Marathon Monument, see C. C. Mattusch, *Classical Bronzes: The Art and Craft of Greek and Roman Statuary* (Ithaca, NY, 1996), 44–47; P. Vidal-Naquet, 'Une Énigme à Delphes: À propos de la base de Marathon (Pausanias X,10,1–2)', *Revue Historique* 238 (1967), 281–302; J. P. Barron, 'Religious Propaganda of the Delian League', *Journal of Hellenic Studies* 84 (1964), 46–47, dates the Marathon Monument to the 460s.

14. Palm tree: Plutarch, *Life of Nicias*, 13; Pausanias, 10.15; M. C. Scott, *Delphi: A History of the Center of the Ancient World* (Princeton, NJ, 2014), 128.

15. Pausanias, 10.25–31; R. B. Kebric, *The Paintings in the Cnidian Lesche at Delphi and Their Historical Context* (Leiden, 1983), 24–25; M. Robertson, *History of Greek Art* (Cambridge, 1976), 242; Zaccarini, *The Lame Hegemony*, 111–114, 298–300. Polygnotus' painting also included the earliest recorded depiction of Charon ferrying the dead across the River Acheron in Hades.

16. Peisianax (senior): Davies, *Athenian Propertied Families, 600–300 B.C.*, 377–378. Stoa Poicile: Nepos, *Life of Miltiades*, 6; Pausanias, 1.15; J. M. Camp, *The Athenian Agora: Excavations in the Heart of Classical Athens* (London, 1986), 68–72; R. E. Wycherley, 'The Painted Stoa', *Phoenix* 7 (1953), 20–35; E. B. Harrison, 'The South Frieze of the Nike Temple and the Marathon Painting in the Painted Stoa', *American Journal of Archaeology* 76 (1972), 353–378. I am of the opinion that the painting of the Battle of Oinoe, which Pausanias saw hanging in the Stoa Poicile, was added

later in the fifth century B.C. and does not belong to the original concept. Blamire, *Plutarch's Life of Kimon*, 96, notes that Polygnotus' 'reward for this work, executed at his own expense, was to be made an Athenian citizen: cf. Harpokr. *s.v.* Πολύγνωτος'. '[On the left] the battle': Pausanias, 1.15.

17. Peisianax (junior): Davies, *Athenian Propertied Families, 600–300 B.C.*, 305. The chronology of Peisianax' birth is unknown, but it would make sense to imagine that he was named in thanks for his supporting Cimon by paying for the construction of the stoa. For a discussion of Miltiades' appearance in the painting and of Cimon's role in its commissioning, see Blamire, *Plutarch's Life of Kimon*, 103.

18. 'Embellished the city': Plutarch, *Life of Cimon*, 13; Blamire, *Plutarch's Life of Kimon*, 153. Hipparchus builds the precinct walls: Suidas, *s.v.* τὸ Ἱππάρχου τειχίον. Most enchanting area outside the city: Thucydides, 2.34.

19. Cimon's wealth: [Aristotle], *Athenian Constitution*, 27.3. Plane trees: Plutarch, *Life of Cimon*, 13; Diogenes Laertius, 3.7; Pliny, *Natural History*, 12.9. Blamire, *Plutarch's Life of Kimon*, 153, points out that 'Kimon's initiative is the earliest recorded example of the introduction of trees into the civic centre of a Greek town, but it is impossible to say whether the idea was original to Kimon or whether he was following a preedent established elsewhere.'

20. Plutarch, *Life of Cimon*, 13; Nepos, *Life of Cimon*, 2; Pausanias, 1.28. Blamire, *Plutarch's Life of Kimon*, 151. For a discussion of the Promachus statue, including its controversial dating, see 'Athena "Promachos"', *Bulletin of the Institute of Classical Studies* (Wiley Online Library) 56 (2013), 277–296. Discussing the argument in E. B. Harrison, 'The South Frieze of the Nike Temple and the Marathon Painting in the Painted Stoa', *American Journal of Archaeology* 76 (1972), 353–378, that the statue is later, Blamire, *Plutarch's Life of Kimon*, 104, concludes: 'The case for associating Kimon with the commissioning of the Athena Promachos remains strong.' 'Ever since the sea': Diodorus, 11.62.

21. Plutarch, *Life of Cimon*, 13; Blamire, *Plutarch's Life of Kimon*, 152. Plutarch suggests that the Long Walls were part of Cimon's original plan. Despite many scholarly articles having been written, there is no way now of confirming or refuting this.

22. Laciadae: Plutarch, *Life of Cimon*, 10; [Aristotle], *Athenian Constitution*, 27. Behaviour in Agora, etc: Plutarch, *Life of Cimon*, 10; [Aristotle], *Athenian Constitution*, 27.3; Nepos, *Life of Cimon*, 4; Theopompus fr. 89 (*FGrH* 115, in Athenaeus 12.533a–c); D. Shaps, *The Invention of Coinage and the Monetization of Ancient Greece* (Ann Arbor, MI, 2015), 132–133. Cimon's liberality is discussed by Blamire in *Plutarch's Life of Kimon*, 129–131.

23. Behaving as Athenian elites had always done: see, e.g., Blamire, *Plutarch's Life of Kimon*, 135; J. S. Boersma, *Athenian Building Policy from 561/0 to 405/4 B.C.* (Groningen, 1970), 58–64; L. Mitchell, *The Heroic Rulers of Archaic and Classical Greece* (London, 2013), 46.

24. Plutarch, *Life of Cimon*, 13. Blamire, *Plutarch's Life of Kimon*, 148. Chauvinistic: Ephialtes' subsequent policy towards Sparta shows that his aim was to 'put Athens first' in opposition to Cimon's more internationalist policies.

25. Plutarch, *Life of Cimon*, 8.

26. Plutarch, *Life of Cimon*, 8; Blamire, *Plutarch's Life of Kimon*, 122–124. The story is controversial and more than probably an invention. See, e.g., A. A. Mosshammer, *The Chronicle of Eusebius and Greek Chronographic Tradition* (Lewisburg, PA, 1979), 305–319.

27. Wealth of Thrace: Zaccarini, *The Lame Hegemony*, 156. Xerxes' bridges and sacrifices: Herodotus, 7.113–114; see D. Braund, *Greek Religion and Cults in the Black Sea Region: Goddesses in the Bosporan Kingdom from the Archaic Period to the Byzantine Era* (Cambridge, 2018), 77.

28. Sophanes: Herodotus, 9.73–75. Leagros: [Themistocles], *Letter*, 8; Davies, *Athenian Propertied Families, 600–300 B.C.*, 90.

29. Plutarch, *Life of Cimon*, 14. Persian garrisons: Plutarch is our only literary source for Athenian operations in the Chersonese at this time, but he is backed up by a fragmentary casualty list (*Inscriptiones Graeci* i² 928). Blamire, *Plutarch's Life of Kimon*, 154; Zaccarini, *The Lame Hegemony*, 149–153. The fact that Cimon captured and towed off all thirteen triremes suggests that none was holed.

30. Doriscus and its governor: Herodotus, 7.106.

31. Plutarch, *Life of Cimon*, 14; Thucydides, 1.100. Thasian gold mines at Scapte Hyle ('Mine Forest'): A. Boeckh, *The Public Economy of Athens* (London, 1842), 311; Blamire, *Plutarch's Life of Kimon*, 155; E. M. A. Bissa, *Governmental Intervention in Foreign Trade in Archaic and Classical Greece* (Leiden, 2009), 35.

10. Earthquake

1. Thucydides, 1.100; Plutarch, *Life of Cimon*, 14.

2. Darius and Thasos: Herodotus, 6.46. Xerxes and Thasos: Herodotus, 7.118; M. Zaccarini, *The Lame Hegemony: Cimon of Athens and the Failure of Panhellenism, ca. 478–450 B.C.* (Bologna, 2017), 157–158. Zaccarini (158) believes that Thucydides' statement (1.100) that Cimon disembarked ἐς τὴν γῆν suggests that Cimon conducted the blockade from the mainland, which seems to me unlikely.

3. Thucydides, 1.100; Diodorus Siculus, 11.70.

4. Thunderbolts: Pausanias, 1.29.

5. Ashes: Pausanias, 1.29; Aeschylus, *Agamemnon*, 437–438; J. V. A. Fine, *The Ancient Greeks* (Cambridge, MA, 1983), 345–346.

6. Plutarch, *Life of Cimon*, 11, credits Cimon himself with engineering the circumstances—mentioned already by Thucydides—by which the League transformed naturally into an Athenian Empire, 'accepting cash and empty ships from

those who had no wish to campaign, letting [League members] focus on domestic politics, seduced by the lures of an easy life—no longer fighing men but farmers and tradesmen, their military mettle sacrificed to self-indulgence and short-sightedness'.

7. Mother as seed bed / incubator: Aeschylus, *Eumenides,* 657–661; Thucydides, 1.101.

8. Helots at Poseidon's temple: Thucydides, 1.128.

9. Hare: Plutarch, *Life of Cimon,* 16. A. Blamire, trans. and comm., *Plutarch's Life of Kimon* (London, 1988), 169, calls this 'surely a guidebook story'. Earthquake: Plutarch, *Life of Cimon,* 16; Diodorus Siculus, 11.63, 15.66; Strabo, *Geography,* 8.5; Pausanias, 4.24; Aelian, *Varia Historia,* 6.7. But the chronology is confused: A. W. Gomme, *A Historical Commentary on Thucydides* (Oxford, 1945–1981), i.401–408; R. A. McNeal, 'Historical Methods and Thucydides', *Historia* 19 (1970), 306–335; D. W. Reece, 'The Date of the Fall of Ithome', *Journal of Hellenic Studies* 82 (1962), 111–120; P. Deane, *Thucydides' Dates 465–431 B.C.* (Don Mills, ON, 1972), 15–30; N. G. L. Hammond, 'Studies in Greek Chronology of the Sixth and Fifth Centuries B.C.', *Historia* 4 (1955), 371–381; P. Cartledge, *The Spartans* (New York, 2003), 137–138.

10. Anger of Poseidon: Thucydides, 1.128; Pausanias, 4.24; Aelian, *Varia Historia,* 6.7.

11. P. Cartledge, *Sparta and Lakonia: A Regional History* (London, 1979), 219. Half the Spartan population: J. Ducat, 'Le tremblement de terre de 464 et l'histoire de Sparte', in *Colloque: Tremblements de terre, histoire et archéologie* (Antibes, 1983), 73–85; see also D. Kagan, *The Peloponnesian War* (London, 2003), 14. Perioikoi: Thucydides, 1.101; Plutarch, *Life of Cimon,* 16. Stenyclerus: Herodotus, 9.64.

12. Thucydides, 1.101; Plutarch, *Life of Cimon,* 14; Blamire, *Plutarch's Life of Kimon,* 155. Cimon's *euthyna:* E. M. Carawan, '*Eisangelia* and *Euthyna:* The Trials of Themistocles, Miltiades and Cimon', *Greek, Roman and Byzantine Studies* 28 (1987), 202–205.

13. Pericles sails past the Islands of the Swallows: Plutarch, *Life of Cimon,* 13. Cimon brought to trial: Plutarch, *Life of Cimon,* 14; *Life of Pericles,* 10; [Aristotle], *Athenian Constitution,* 27.1. Blamire, *Plutarch's Life of Kimon,* 150, 156 (where the location of the trial is discussed). Pericles' role in the trial: R. J. Bonner and G. Smith, *The Administration of Justice from Homer to Aristotle* (Chicago, 1930–38), ii. 26–27; J. T. Roberts, *Accountability in Athenian Government* (Madison, WI, 1982), 55–59.

14. Alexander as proxenus: Herodotus, 8.140–143. D. Kagan, *The Outbreak of the Peloponnesian War* (Ithaca, NY, 1969) 63, observes: 'If family rivalries meant anything at all, then Pericles was the obvious choice to oppose Cimon ... Pericles appears not to have forgotten the old rivalry.'

15. Plutarch, *Life of Cimon,* 14. Blamire, *Plutarch's Life of Kimon,* 156–157. 'Not to be spoken of': Thucydides, 2.46. The implication that Elpinice was offering Pericles sexual favours probably comes from the salacious Stesimbrotus (107 F 5), but

recurs later in Cimon's career when (according to Plutarch, *Life of Pericles*, 10) she tried to persuade Pericles to recall her brother from exile (cf. Athenaeus, 13.589e).

16. Acquittal: Plutarch, *Life of Cimon*, 15. But Demosthenes (23.205) appears to suggest that Cimon was found guilty, with a fine being imposed instead of execution: see A. E. Raubitschek, 'Theophrastos on Ostracism', *Ciassica et Mediaevalia* 19 (1958), 91 n. 7. Plea from Sparta: Plutarch, *Life of Cimon*, 16. Proven experts in siege warfare: Thucydides, 1.102. There is a suggestion based partially on the appearance of the word αὖθις, 'again' in Plutarch, *Life of Cimon*, 18—see, e.g., V. Gouščhin, 'Plutarch on Cimon, Athenian Expeditions and Ephialtes' Reforms (Plu. *Cim*, 14–17)', *Greek, Roman and Byzantine Studies* 59, no. 1 (2019), 51—that immediately in the wake of his acquittal Cimon led a campaign to Cyprus (during which Ephialtes carried out his reforms), but the evidence for this is so slim and so contested that I have omitted it from my text. Pericleidas: That Sparta chose him as envoy was not accidental. In private correspondence Paul Cartledge observes that his name, Pericl-eidas, makes him the Spartan counterpart of the Athenian Pericles, writing that 'Leotychidas and Xanthippus had probably concluded a personal xenia-relationship in 479, hence the *xenia* between Archidamus II and Pericles in 432 / 1. Pericleidas I suggest was a Spartan from a family with Athenian *xenia* connections. Blamire's suggestion that he was an Athenian proxenus in Sparta is plausible—if so, he would likely have been appointed such by Archidamus.' See Blamire, *Plutarch's Life of Kimon*, 170.

17. Onlookers: the sight of Pericleidas at the altar was still fresh forty years later in Aristophanes, *Lysistrata*, 1137–1142.

18. Plutarch, *Life of Cimon*, 16. Blamire, *Plutarch's Life of Kimon*, 166, suggests that 'Sparta's secret promise of assistance to Thasos cannot have been known to the Athenians when they agreed to her request for assistance'. I do not agree. There was enough still binding the two states to encourage support, especially if Cimon's powers of oratory were sufficiently robust. Intriguingly, however, Deane, *Thucydides' Dates 465–431 B.C.*, 21, suggests that the Athenian hoplites found out about Sparta's aborted plans only after they reached Ithome, which could explain why relations soured.

19. Plutarch, *Life of Cimon*, 16. Blamire, *Plutarch's Life of Kimon*, 170–171, notes that 'Kimon perhaps derived this "lame hegemony" metaphor from conversation with Spartan friends, since it appears in the debate at Sparta recorded by Diodorus Siculus 11.50 under the year 475 / 4 in the form of an ancient oracle warning the Spartans to 'take care not to allow their hegemony to go lame.' The oracle was later resuscitated by Spartans opposed to having Agesilaus II as their king (Plutarch, *Life of Agesilaus*, 3).

20. No source records the size of the majority in favour of Cimon's proposal, but subsequent events show (admittedly with hindsight) that there was considerable opposition to his strategy of helping Sparta. Thucydides, 1.102; Aristophanes, *Lysistrata*, 1137–1146.

21.   Four thousand hoplites: Aristophanes, *Lysistrata*, 1143–1144. Plutarch, *Life of Cimon*, 17, appears to suggest *two* successive expeditions to Messene (the only source to do so). See Blamire, *Plutarch's Life of Kimon*, 171–172. Gouschin, 'Plutarch on Cimon, Athenian Expeditions and Ephialtes' Reforms', 38–56, makes a case for accepting Plutarch's version, suggesting a first expedition led by Cimon in 464 and a second in 462 / 1, the two straddling the siege of Thasos; but, if Athens had already helped Sparta in 464, and so shown her good faith, it is unlikely that Sparta would then agree to aid the Thasians by invading Attica just a year or so later (even if the Ephialtes' democratic reforms had by then been carried out). It is equally unlikely that the Spartans would have countenanced invading Attica if the helot revolt was already underway. I am unconvinced, as are R. Cole, 'Cimon's Dismissal, Ephialtes' Revolution and the Peloponnesian Wars', *Greek, Roman and Byzantine Studies* 15 (1974), 375–376; and P. J. Rhodes, 'The Athenian Revolution', in *Cambridge Ancient History*, vol. 5, 2nd ed. (Cambridge, 1992), 69. The perceived problem arising from the Aristophanes *Lysistrata* reference, in which it is suggested that the expedition 'saved Sparta', arises from a misunderstanding of the dramatic context: the whole point of this remark (in the 'Reconciliation Scene') is that both the Spartan and the Athenian diplomats are content to revise history in order to achieve their desired outcome. While S. Hornblower, *A Commentary on Thucydides*, vol. 1 (Oxford, 1991; rev. 1997), 164, suggests that Cimon sailed to Messenia, it is generally accepted that he marched overland.

22.   Plutarch, *Life of Cimon*, 17; Pausanias, 4.24. Thucydides (1.102, where the cause of the expulsion is not mentioned) calls this the 'first public quarrel between the Spartans and Athenians'. Blamire, *Plutarch's Life of Kimon*, 172.

23.   Plutarch, *Life of Cimon*, 17. Once more the chronology is uncertain. A. W. Gomme, *A Historical Commentary on Thucydides*, vol. 1 (Oxford, 1945), 411 n.1, imagines the encounter with the Corinthians occurring when Cimon was on his way *to* Messenia. See also Blamire, *Plutarch's Life of Kimon*, 171, who notes that Ion of Chios (the source of Plutarch's anecdote) 'may have participated in the Ithome expedition'. Dispute with Megara: Thucydides, 1.103.

24.   Rhoesaces: Plutarch, *Life of Cimon*, 10.

25.   [Aristotle], *Athenian Constitution*, 25; Plutarch, *Life of Pericles*, 9; Plutarch, *Life of Cimon*, 15. The chronology is notoriously difficult. For a discussion, see Blamire, *Plutarch's Life of Kimon*, 158–159. Many scholars believe that the Areopagus reforms took place when Cimon was absent in Messenia: Rhodes, 'Athenian Revolution', 69; S. Hornblower, *The Greek World, 479–323 B.C.* (London, 2011), 23; Kagan, *The Outbreak of the Peloponnesian War*, 71. However, given the shame attached to Cimon's enforced withdrawal, there is no real reason to suppose that he was absent from Athens when the reforms went through, simply that his power had evaporated. Plutarch does not connect the two events. Blamire, *Plutarch's Life of Kimon*, 158, comments: 'If, as seems probable, the Areopagus was the court which had acquitted Kimon [on his return from Thasos], his trial may be identified as the final incident which convinced the radicals that the power of the Areopagos

must be broken at the earliest opportunity.' Rhoesaces: Plutarch, *Life of Cimon*, 10; Blamire, *Plutarch's Life of Kimon*, 136.

26. Top two property classes: [Aristotle], *Athenian Constitution*, 26.2. Reforms: Demosthenes, 23.22; [Aristotle], *Athenian Constitution*, 57.3; C. Hignett, *A History of the Athenian Constitution to the End of the Fifth Century B.C.* (Oxford, 1952), 193–213; P. J. Rhodes, *The Athenian Boule* (Oxford, 1972; rev. ed. 1985), 199–207; Rhodes, *A Commentary on the Aristotelian Athenaion Politeia* (Oxford, 1981), 311–319.

11. Aftershock

1. Plutarch, *Life of Cimon*, 4. Alcibiades the Elder: Thucydides, 5.43, 6.89; A. Blamire, trans. and comm., *Plutarch's Life of Kimon* (London, 1988), 161–162. Laodice was agreed to be the most beautiful of all Trojan princesses (Homer, *Iliad*, 3.123, 6.252). 'He wasn't a bad man': Plutarch, *Life of Cimon*, 15, quoting the comic poet Eupolis (fl. 429–411 B.C.). 'Bad man (or poor)': the Greek word κακός (kakos) can mean both.

2. 'Cimon, son of Miltiades': *Supplementum Epigraphicum Graecum* (Leiden, 1923–), 46.79; Kerameikos, O 6874; M. Zaccarini, *The Lame Hegemony: Cimon of Athens and the Failure of Panhellenism, ca. 478–450 B.C.* (Bologna, 2017), 203; Blamire, *Plutarch's Life of Kimon*, 173–174.

3. Sons: Scholiast on Aristides, 3.515; Blamire, *Plutarch's Life of Kimon*, 165–166; J. K. Davies, *Athenian Propertied Families, 600–300 B.C.* (Oxford, 1971), 304–307. Isodice: Plutarch, *Life of Cimon*, 4. As Blamire, *Plutarch's Life of Kimon*, 175, rightly observes, 'Kimon's movements between 461 and 457 are unknown'; but, as he assumes wrongly that Cimon was recalled from exile in 457, we can emend those dates to 461–451 (with the exception of Tanagra in 458 or 457).

4. Tholos as Peisistratid palace: J. M. Camp, *The Athenian Agora: Excavations in the Heart of Classical Athens* (London, 1986), 94–97.

5. Cimon's relationship with Thucydides: Thucydides son of Melesias is described as Cimon's κηδεστής (kēdestēs) 'close relative by marriage' and γαμβρός (gambros), an ambiguous word that can mean both son-in-law and brother-in-law. Unless further evidence emerges, we shall be forever ignorant about the precise relationship of the two men. Suffice it to say that it was close and personal. See Davies, *Athenian Propertied Families, 600–300 B.C.*, 231–234.

6. Antiphon, 5.68; [Aristotle], *Athenian Constitution*, 25.4; Plutarch, *Life of Pericles*, 10; R. W. Wallace, 'Ephialtes and the Areopagus', *Greek, Roman and Byzantine Studies* 15 (1974), 259–269; D. W. Roller, 'Who Murdered Ephialtes?', *Historia* 38, no. 3 (1989), 257–266.

7. Thucydides, 1.103.

8. Seven-storey dwellings: conversation with Ross Thomas of the British Museum's Naucratis Research Project, 19 November 2019. Psammetichus II and Amasis: Herodotus, 2.152–154. Psammetichus III: Herodotus, 3.14–15. Inaros:

Thucydides, 1.104. For conflicting views on the date of Inaros' request, see V. Goušchin, 'Plutarch on Cimon, Athenian Expeditions and Ephialtes' Reforms (Plu. *Cim*, 14–17)', *Greek, Roman and Byzantine Studies* 59, no. 1 (2019), 48–49; D. Kagan, *The Outbreak of the Peloponnesian War* (Ithaca, NY, 1969), 82; J. V. A. Fine, *The Ancient Greeks: A Critical History* (Cambridge, MA, 1983), 352.

9. Artaxerxes' hand: Plutarch, *Life of Artaxerxes*, 1. Succession: Ctesiphon in F. Jacoby, *Die Fragmente der griechischen Historiker* (Berlin, 1923–1958), 688 F 14 (34); Diodorus Siculus, 11.69; Justin, 3.1. R. Stoneman, *Xerxes: A Persian Life* (New Haven, CT, 2015), 202–205, observes, 'One has to feel sorry for Xerxes, hoping for a quiet life in his fifties with a pretty young girl as his bedfellow, and trying to forget about the wretched Greeks' (205).

10. Naval encounter: Photius, *Bibliotheca*, 40 (a somewhat confused and confusing account). Libyan armour: Herodotus, 7.71. Ethiopian armour: Herodotus, 7.69. Battle of Papremis: Herodotus, 3.12; Thucydides, 1.104; Diodorus Siculus, 11.74; Ctesias, *Persica*, 36. See also Kagan, *The Outbreak of the Peloponnesian War*, 82–83.

11. Memphis: C. Lalouette, trans., and P. Grimal, *Textes sacrés et textes profanes de l'ancienne Égypte*, vol. 2 (Paris, 1987), 175–177.

12. Thucydides, 1.105; Diodorus, 11.78, who has Athens victorious on both land and sea, but see Kagan, *The Outbreak of the Peloponnesian War*, 84.

13. Thucydides, 1.105; Diodorus, 11.78.

14. Thucydides, 1.105–107; Diodorus, 11.79. Erechtheid casualty list: F. H. von Gaertringen, ed., *Inscriptiones Graecae* (Berlin, 1924), I² 929; R. Stroud, *Supplementum Epigraphicum Graecum* (Amsterdam, 1958), 58–62. As usual for this period, the chronology is not entirely certain, but it is likely that the helot revolt had not yet ended.

15. Diodorus, 11.81; Justin, 3.6. Fifth-columnists in Athens: Thucydides, 1.107.

16. Battle of Tanagra: Thucydides, 1.107–108; R. Meiggs, *The Athenian Empire* (Oxford, 1972), 417–418.

17. Plutarch, *Life of Cimon*, 17, tells us that Cimon gave instructions especially to 'Euthippus of Anaphlystus and others suspected of harbouring pro-Spartan sympathies'. Plutarch, *Life of Pericles*, 10, writes that it was friends of Pericles who drove Cimon away. Blamire, *Plutarch's Life of Kimon*, 175, notes: 'The role assigned to the *Boule* is difficult to explain, since there was no time for the generals to have referred back to Athens for a decision on Kimon's request to participate.' My interpretation tries to solve this problem. See R. Connor, *The New Politicians of Fifth-Century Athens* (Princeton, NJ, 1971), 59 n. 43. Zaccarini, *The Lame Hegemony*, 220, pours cold water on the historicity of Cimon's involvement at Tanagra, stating that 'the figure of Cimon's hundred *hetairoi* should be interpreted as void of any claim of verisimilitude'.

18. Thessalians' treachery: Diodorus Siculus, 11.80. Cimon's companions: Plutarch, *Life of Cimon*, 17.

19. Diodorus Siculus, 11.80. Cimon's companions: Plutarch, *Life of Cimon*, 17. Blamire, *Plutarch's Life of Kimon*, 176, observes that 'Plutarch's statement that Kimon's *hetairoi* fought and died as a unit of 100 men contradicts his earlier implication that the Athenian army was drawn up in tribal regiments'—unless, of course, these hundred were members of his own tribe. Connor, *The New Politicians of Fifth-Century Athens*, 60 nn. 44–46, discusses the impact that the loss of so many of his partisans must have had on Cimon's support base in Athens.

20. Outcome: Spartan victory—Thucydides, 1.108; Plutarch, *Life of Cimon*, 17; inconclusive—Diodorus Siculus, 11.80.

21. Myronides' campaign: Thucydides, 1.108; Diodorus Siculus, 11.83; Kagan, *The Outbreak of the Peloponnesian War*, 94–95.

22. Thucydides, 1.70.

23. Thucydides, 1.108. 'Eyesore of Piraeus': Plutarch, *Life of Pericles*, 8.

24. Diodorus, 11.84; Thucydides, 1.108.

25. Diodorus, 11.84; Thucydides, 1.108.

26. Diodorus, 11.84.

27. Thucydides, 1.109.

28. Diodorus, 11.85, 11.88.

29. Thucydides, 1.111.

30. Diodorus, 11.88.

31. Thucydides, 1.110; Diodorus, 11.77.

32. Thucydides, 1.96; Plutarch, *Life of Pericles*, 12.

33. The timing of Cimon's return from ostracism is debated. Plutarch (*Life of Cimon*, 17), following Theopompus (115 F 88), suggests that he was recalled early—after the Battle of Tanagra, thanks to a decree passed by Pericles at the urging of Elpinice (Plutarch, *Life of Pericles*, 10). Nepos (*Life of Cimon*, 3), probably also following Theopompus, agrees, as does A. W. Gomme, *A Historical Commentary on Thucydides*, vol. 1 (Oxford, 1945–1981), 326–327; Blamire, *Plutarch's Life of Kimon*, 174, 177–178; and Zaccarini, *The Lame Hegemony*, 220–222. An early recall begs the (unanswerable) questions: Why was Cimon not elected general in the five years following Tanagra, and why was peace with Sparta (to seal which, Andocides, 3.3–4 imagines Cimon being recalled) not concluded until 451? Some, such as G. Busolt, *Griechische Geschichte bis zur Schlacht bei Chaeroneia*, 2nd ed., 3 vols. (Gotha, Germany, 1893–1904), 1:317–318; Kagan, *The Outbreak of the Peloponnesian War*, 90–96; and Meiggs, *The Athenian Empire*, 111, 422–223 (who tries to solve the problem by having Cimon recalled early in 454), wishing to reconcile the irreconcilable, have tied themselves in knots imagining that, having been recalled, Cimon then went back into self-imposed exile until 451. However, using the principle of Ockham's razor, it is far more likely that the early recall never happened.

12. At the Right Hand of Zeus

1.   Relationship with Ion of Chios: Plutarch, *Life of Cimon*, 5, 9, 16, and *Life of Pericles*, 5. Ion and Archelaus: A. Blamire, trans. and comm., *Plutarch's Life of Kimon* (London, 1988), 87.

2.   D. Kagan, *The Outbreak of the Peloponnesian War* (Ithaca, NY, 1969), 98–103.

3.   Plutarch, *Life of Pericles*, 10; Kagan, *The Outbreak of the Peloponnesian War*, 104–105.

4.   Policy: Plutarch, *Life of Cimon*, 18; Diodorus, 12.3. Two hundred ships: Blamire, *Plutarch's Life of Kimon*, 179; Kagan, *The Outbreak of the Peloponnesian War*, 105.

5.   Hard facts disappear from view at this point, too. Plutarch's account (*Life of Cimon*, 18–19) is woolly, Diodorus Siculus' (12.3) confused. R. Meiggs, *The Athenian Empire* (Oxford, 1972), 128.

6.   Diodorus, 12.3; G. Hill, *A History of Cyprus*, vol. 1 (Cambridge, 1940), 123.

7.   Plutarch, *Life of Cimon*, 18; Thucydides, 1.112.

8.   Plutarch, *Life of Cimon*, 18. The expedition to Siwah is problematic. Blamire, *Plutarch's Life of Kimon*, 182, notes that it 'may have derived from an excursus in Kallisthenes' *History of Alexander*, in which Cimon was depicted as Alexander's precursor; see W. Uxkull-Gyllenband, *Plutarch und die griechische Biographie* (Stuttgart, 1927), 68; J. H. Schreiner, "Anti-Thukydidean Studies in the Pentekontaetia", *Symbolae Osloenses* 52 (1977), 21–29.' Oracle of Zeus Ammon: H. W. Parke, *The Oracles of Zeus* (Oxford, 1967), 194–241; T. Curnow, *The Oracles of the Ancient World: A Comprehensive Guide* (London, 2004), 33–34; see also R. Stoneman, *The Ancient Oracles: Making the Gods Speak* (New Haven, CT, 2011). An excellent account of consulting the Oracle at Siwah is contained in R. Lane Fox, *Alexander the Great* (London, 1986), 205–210.

9.   Thucydides, 1.111. Blamire, *Plutarch's Life of Kimon*, 183, interprets the fact that battle was joined at Salamis as a sign that the Athenians disobeyed orders.

10.   Plutarch, *Life of Cimon*, 19; Thucydides, 1.112; Diodorus, 12.3–4; Kagan, *The Outbreak of the Peloponnesian War*, 105. Hill, *A History of Cyprus*, 1:124 n. 3, contains a brief but thorough discussion of the problems posed by our available evidence, reaching many of the same conclusions as the present author. Whereas Diodorus' confused account suggests that Cimon's Cypriote campaign straddled two years, my own assessment suggests a shorter time frame: unless the Phoenician fleet were pinned down and effectively put out of action, it is in my view inconceivable that the Persians would have allowed such protracted Greek sieges of both Citium and Salamis, especially when their 300 vessels outnumbered Cimon's 140 (60 Athenian ships being in Egypt). Indeed, the expected arrival of the Phoenician fleet may well have been one of the reasons behind the recall of the squadron from Egypt and the raising of both sieges. After the swift fall of Marium, Cimon may have been expecting the equally speedy capitulation of the other two cities, which might explain his splitting his troops between them; while he had conducted a

lengthy siege on Thasos, its ultimate success lay in Athenians' control of the sea (which meant that the city could be surrounded and starved out) as much as in their rudimentary skills in siege warfare.

11. Plutarch, *Life of Cimon*, 18. Caudate lobe: see W. Furley and V. Gysembergh, *Reading the Liver: Papyrological Texts on Ancient Greek Extispicy* (Tübingen, 2015), 49. Plutarch loves dreams, especially those that presage death: F. E. Brenk, 'The Dreams of Plutarch's *Lives*', *Latomus* 34 (1975), 336–349; Brenk, *In Mist Apparelled: Religious Themes in Plutarch's Moralia and Lives* (Leiden, 1977), 214–235. Blamire, *Plutarch's Life of Kimon*, 180, proposes that 'the close association between Astyphilos and Kimon suggests that he was Kimon's personal seer.' Ants: Aristotle, *Historia Animalium*, 488a8–13.

12. Puzzlingly, M. Zaccarini, *The Lame Hegemony: Cimon of Athens and the Failure of Panhellenism, ca. 478–450 B.C.* (Bologna, 2017), 224, suggests that Cimon's remains were found and repatriated 'at some time', rather than immediately. Cimon's remains laid to rest beside his ancestors: Plutarch, *Life of Cimon*, 19. Blamire, *Plutarch's Life of Kimon*, 185, notes that, contrary to Plutarch's claims, 'Kimon himself may have been interred in the Kerameikos along with the rest of the dead from the Cypriot war.' Their ashes laid to rest: Pausanias, 1.29. 'Slaughtering so many Persians': Simonides, fr. 103 (Diehl) at Diodorus, 11.62; for a good discussion of Diodorus' misappropriation of this inscription to the Eurymedon monument, see Hill, *A History of Cyprus*, 1:124 n.3.

13. Plutarch, *Life of Cimon*, 13; Diodorus, 12.4. Blamire, *Plutarch's Life of Kimon*, 144–145, notes that Plutarch seems to suggest that the peace was made immediately after Eurymedon; in fact, Plutarch is being characteristically vague with his chronology of cause and effect. While the very existence—and not just the nature of the agreement and its alleged terms—of the Peace of Callias has been questioned since the fourth century B.C., some have seen evidence for its authenticity in a reference in Herodotus (7.151) to a mission undertaken by Callias to the court of the Great King at Susa. Certainly something appears to have prompted significant changes to Athenian foreign and domestic policy at around this time, and other fourth-century authors such as Demosthenes (*De Falsa Legatione*, 273), Isocrates (4.118 ff.) and Plato (*Menexenus*, 241d f.) believed in its authenticity. See, for example, Meiggs, *The Athenian Empire*, 129–151; E. Badian, 'The Peace of Callias', *Journal of Hellenic Studies* 50 (1987), 1–39; E. F. Bloedow, 'The Peace of Callias', *Symbolae Osloenses* 67 (1992), 41–68; G. L. Cawkwell, 'The Peace between Athens and Persia', *Phoenix* 51 (1997), 115–130; L. J. Samons II, 'Kimon, Kallias and Peace with Persia', *Historia* (1998), 129–140.

14. African ivory, etc: Hermippus, fr. 63, found in Athenaeus, 1.27E–28A.

15. 'Large or small', etc: Plutarch, *Life of Pericles*, 17. Hegemony: Kagan, *The Outbreak of the Peloponnesian War*, 120.

16. Periclean building programme: Plutarch, *Life of Pericles*, 12–13; Pausanias, 1.22; D. Stuttard, *Parthenon: Power and Politics on the Acropolis* (London, 2013), 105–190.

17. J. Camp, *The Archaeology of Athens* (New Haven, CT, 2001), 93–100.

18. Stuttard, *Parthenon*, 115–121.

19. Stuttard, *Parthenon*, 157–171.

20. Eleusinian limestone: A. Kosmopoulou, *The Iconography of Sculptured Statue Bases in the Archaic and Classical Periods* (Madison, WI, 2002), 12–14, 126; Stuttard, *Parthenon*, 165–170.

21. 'Common prostitute': Plutarch, *Life of Pericles*, 12. War in Boeotia: Thucydides, 1.113.

22. Thucydides, 1.113–114; Diodorus, 12.5–6; Plutarch, *Life of Pericles*, 2–3, 22–23; Kagan, *The Outbreak of the Peloponnesian War*, 123–124.

23. Thucydides, 1.114–115.

24. 'Like a victorious athlete' and anecdote: Plutarch, *Life of Pericles*, 28.

25. Elpinice's tomb: Plutarch, *Life of Cimon*, 4. Blamire, *Plutarch's Life of Kimon*, 90, comments: 'That Elpinike, still alive in 439 (Plu. *Per.* 28.4–7) should have been buried in the Kimoneia, rather than with her husband, Kallias (4.8), is surprising, but need not imply that their marriage had ended in divorce'. 'Remember Cimon': Plutarch, *Life of Cimon*, 19; Zaccarini, *The Lame Hegemony*, 225.

26. Thucydides, 1.24–45; Kagan, *The Outbreak of the Peloponnesian War*, 222–245. Plutarch, *Life of Cimon*, 16, and *Life of Pericles*, 29, suggests that Pericles often taunted Lacedaemonius and Oulius because of their maternal descent, but whether this was his way of suggesting that they were born out of wedlock to a woman called Cleitor, or because their father was half-Thracian, or simply because that was the kind of person that Pericles was, we cannot know. See also Blamire, *Plutarch's Life of Kimon*, 163–164.

27. Plutarch, *Life of Alcibiades*, 19, 22. Alcibiades: see D. Stuttard, *Nemesis: Alcibiades and the Fall of Athens* (London, 2018). Thettalus and Philaids: J. K. Davies, *Athenian Propertied Families, 600–300 B.C.* (Oxford, 1971), 307–310.

28. Aristophanes' *Lysistrata* of 411 B.C. has at its heart the fear that Persia will exploit a divided Greece, as does Gorgias' Olympic Speech of 408 B.C. The peace is the King's Peace or Peace of Antalcidas of 387 B.C.

29. Plutarch, *Life of Alexander*, 27; Arrian, 3.3–4; Strabo, *Geography*, 17.1.43; Fox, *Alexander the Great*, 200–218, with copious notes (522–524).

30. Cratinus (519–422 B.C.), *Archilochi*, fr. 1, *Poetae Comici Graeci* (in Plutarch, *Life of Cimon*, 10). It is perhaps ironic that this shining 'epitaph' for Cimon should have been written by a comic poet, whose main role was usually to ridicule and satirize politicians, not to praise them. This has led some to question whether he is being sincere. See Blamire, *Plutarch's Life of Kimon*, 131; Zaccarini, *The Lame Hegemony*, 245; A. Banfi, *Il governo della città: Pericle nel pensiero antico* (Bologna, 2003), 18–23.

Acknowledgements

To write about the Persian Wars so close to the 2,500th anniversary of Xerxes' invasion of Greece has been an exhilarating experience, if at times a taxing one, especially when the latter stages of the process coincided with a global pandemic. My heartfelt thanks go to my agent, Bill Hamilton, and to all at A. M. Heath for championing my proposal for this book, and to Ian Malcolm, commissioning editor at Harvard University Press, for taking it on with such enthusiasm. It has been a pleasure to work with him again and with his colleagues at the Press, including, in the United States, senior editor Katherine Brick, editorial assistant Olivia Woods, design manager Lisa Roberts, and Stephanie Vyce, director of intellectual property; and in the United Kingdom, associate director of international publicity Rebekah White. My thanks and admiration go, too, to Jill Breitbarth, who designed the book's stunning cover; to Isabelle Lewis for drawing such accurate, clear maps; and to John Donohue, production editor at Westchester Publishing Services. I am also extremely grateful to the two academic readers, as well as to Paul Cartledge, all of whose comments and suggestions have greatly enhanced the text. Any inaccuracies that remain are due entirely to my stubbornness.

The process of research and composition inevitably impacts on friends and family, and I would like to recognize especially the input of the 'home team': the constant encouragement of my mother, Kate, and the stalwart support of my wife, Emily Jane, who is to me as Isodice was to Cimon, and without whom I would simply not be writing. Finally, I must acknowledge the role played by our two cats, Stanley and Oliver, who defend our territory as passionately as any Athenian but in their wisdom have no ambition to overextend it.

Map and Illustration Credits

All maps are © David Stuttard.

Page

16   Petar Milošević / Wikimedia Commons / CC BY-SA 4.0

32   The Museum of Fine Arts / Wikimedia Commons

45   Hara1603 / Wikimedia Commons

50   Jastrow / Wikimedia Commons

85   Oren Rozen / Wikimedia Commons / CC BY-SA 3.0

87   © David Stuttard

99   Louvre Museum / Wikimedia Commons

105   Marsyas / Wikimedia Commons / CC BY-SA 2.5

131   Bibi Saint-Pol / Wikimedia Commons

166   National Museums of Scotland / Wikimedia Commons

185   Fingalo / Wikimedia Commons / CC BY-SA 2.0

193   Photograph by Chuzeville. Courtesy of the Louvre.

203   British Museum / Wikimedia Commons

229   Museum für Kunst und Gewerbe, Hamburg / Wikimedia Commons / CC 0 1.0

236   Walters Art Museum / Wikimedia Commons / CC BY-SA 3.0

251   Rogers Fund, 1941, Metropolitan Museum of Art

269   Giovanni Dall'Orto / Wikimedia Commons

303   © David Stuttard

312   Markus Leupold-Löwenthal / Wikimedia Commons / CC BY-SA 3.0

Index

Abdera, 43

Abydus, 48, 125

Academus, 67, 233, 237

Academus, Grove of, 228, 233

Acanthus, 70

Acarnania, 285–286

Achaeans, 160, 162, 180

Achaemenes, 273–274

Acharnia, 136

Achilles, 17, 139, 311

Acropolis, Athens, 16, 20, 58, 64, 72, 144, 201, 203, 232, 267, 293; brushwood stockade, 1, 133; Cimon's bridle offering on, 2, 134–135; Cimon strengthens, 234–235, 266, 308; dedications on, 38, 86, 132, 197; Hecatompedos Naos, 302, 304–305; in mythology, 205, 232; olive wood statue of Athena (*see* Athena, olive wood statue of); Panathenaic Procession to, 31; Propylaea, 305; referenced by oracle, 131; sacrifices on, 79, 202; sanctuaries on, 85; statue of Athena Promachus, 235, 267, 275, 293, 302–303; temples on, 24, 104, 119, 149, 192; tyrants take refuge on, 34, 36; during Xerxes' invasion, 136, 148–149, 155, 158, 170, 311

Adeimantus, 140, 146, 149

Aeacidae, 147, 152, 311; statues of, 17, 38, 147, 152, 198

Aeacus, 17, 38, 147, 152, 156

Aeantides, 30

Aegae (Asia Minor), 222

Aegae (Macedonia), 70

Aegean coast, 19, 23, 29–30, 38, 53, 62, 189, 191

Aegean islands, 29, 54–55, 57, 240

Aegeus, 81, 197, 205

Aegina: in Greek alliance, 121, 135; hostility towards Athens, 38, 76, 86, 105, 109, 120,

240, 274–276, 280, 282; links with Philaids, 17, 147; receives Athenian refugees, 148; sides with Persia, 72–73, 135; wins prize after Salamis, 156

Aegospotami, 181

Aeolians, 77

Aeschylus, 207–209, 230, 238–239, 248, 291; *Oresteia*, 291; *Persians*, 207–209, 230, 238

agelai, 113

Agiads, 72

agogē, 112, 114

Agora (town), 22, 53

Agora, Athens, 2, 58, 68, 134–135, 206, 239, 260, 289, 302, 308; age limit on entering, 66; altar in, 258; call-up lists in, 242; Cimon Coálemos murdered in, 26; memorials in, 193–194, 299; ostracisms held in, 101–102, 268; Panathenaic Procession in, 31; Peisistratid enhancements of, 24; rebuilt after Xerxes' invasion, 192–193, 231–232, 233–234, 266, 269; Temple of Hephaestus in, 305; tyrannicides in, 33, 35; during Xerxes' invasions, 148, 155

Ahura Mazda, 45, 47, 49, 63, 75–76, 115–117, 128, 136, 191

Ajax, 16–17, 36, 156, 293, 311

Akkad, 44

Alcibiades, 310

Alcibiades the Elder, 266

Alcmaeon (colleague of Cimon), 212, 216

Alcmaeon (sixth-century-B.C. plutocrat), 23, 99

Alcmaeonids: accused of shield-flashing after Marathon, 84, 89; cursed, 33, 89, 107; finance Temple of Apollo at Delphi, 34, 87, 229; linked to Cimon through Isodice, 99, 134; opposition to Peisistratids, 24, 33–34, 36, 65; opposition to

Alcmaeonids (*continued*)
Themistocles, 69, 212; ostracisms of, 102–103; relationship with Croesus, 23; rivalry with Cimon, 93, 100, 209
Aleuadae, 110, 128, 129, 199–200, 250, 257
Alexander I of Macedon, 53–54, 70, 129, 158, 165, 255–257
Alexander III of Macedon, 311, 313
Alopece, 95, 98
Amasis, 272, 295
Amazons, 6, 148, 197, 203, 232, 303–304, 308
Ambracia, 310
Ambracian Gulf, 285
Ameinias, 152–153, 207
Amorgos, 220, 293
Amphitrite, 204
Amunia, 294
Amyclae, 112, 161
Amyntas, 53
Amyrtaeus, 294
Anacreon, 26, 32, 43, 134
Anatolia, 40
Andros, 56, 154, 201
Angra Mainyu, 45–46, 63, 116, 149
Anshan, 40–41, 44
Antenor, 34, 193
Antirhium, 283
Apadana, 300
Aphetae, 140
Aphidnae, 86, 233
Aphrodite, 204, 277, 293, 304
Apollo: birthday, 113, 130; brother of Artemis, 79; connections with, dedications and temple at Delos, 75–76, 185, 219, 229; dedications to, 156, 168, 175; festival at Delos, 186, 205; god of healing, 308; helps build Troy, 17; honoured at Spartan Carneia, 82, 138; honoured at Spartan Gymnopaediae, 109; honoured at Spartan Hyacinthia, 161; as 'Lyceius', 67; oracle at Delphi (*see* oracle: Delphi); oracle at Didyma, 62; as 'Oulius', 180; paean, 187; on Parthenon Frieze, 304; priestess, 34, 73, 130, 132; priests, 20–21, 34, 130–131, 156, 229; revered by Darius, 76, 186; sanctuary at Amyclae, 161;

temple at Delphi (*see* Delphi, Temple of Apollo); temple at Tanagra, 277; temple on Scyros, 201
Apollonia, 49
Apries, 272
Apsephion, 239
Apsinthians, 19, 22, 181
Arabian Gulf, 40
Arcadia, 79, 81, 110–112, 251, 258, 260
Archedice, 27, 29–30, 38
Archelaus, 289
Archidamus, 252–253, 290
Archilochus, 308
Ares, 1, 131, 166, 194, 235, 248, 252, 278, 302, 304
Argos (city): enmity with Sparta, 57, 73–74, 82, 111, 115, 121–122, 188, 250–251, 258; friendship with Peisistratus, 25, 78; neutrality during Persian Wars, 9, 74, 146; rebuffs allied ambassadors, 121–122, 124; relationship with Themistocles, 188, 214, 216; treaty with Athens, 270–271, 274, 291
Argos (hero), 74
Ariadne, 75, 219, 231
Aristagoras, 55–59, 61, 71, 220
Aristides, 3, 7; background, 95–96; friendship with Cimon, 95, 100, 103, 179, 210; friendship with Cleisthenes, 100; helps establish Delian League, 184, 187–188, 211; 'the Just', 9, 94; at Marathon, 84, 94, 97; ostracism, 103–104, 107, 135; at Plataea, 165, 168, 175; political stance, 82, 104, 157, 160, 177; relationship with Themistocles, 107, 180, 213–214; at Salamis, 147, 149, 151, 153; shares generalship with Cimon, 174–175, 180, 182–184, 237; at Sparta, 162, 178; stratagem before Plataea, 160, 162
Aristodicus, 271
Aristogeiton, 32, 34, 64–66, 155, 192, 202, 238
Ariston, 73
Aristonice, 130–131
Aristophanes, 311
Aristotle, 6, 22
Artabazus, 286, 288, 292

Artaphernes, 55, 59, 61, 74, 76, 80
Artaxerxes I, 272–273, 284, 286, 292, 296, 299–300
Artaxerxes II, 311
Artaÿctes, 179, 181
Artemis, 79, 86, 213, 304
Artemisia, 150, 153
Artemisium, 138–144, 147, 170, 189, 210–211, 213, 260
Aspendus, 222, 226
Astyages, 40–41
Astyphilus, 298
Athena: altar of, 65, 80; birthday, 31; dedications to, 3, 38, 170; at Marathon, 83; olive wood statue of, 2, 31, 134, 148, 302, 304; owl symbol, 24, 103; portrayed in Stoa Poicile, 232; protectress of Athens, 1–2, 132, 208, 230, 290; sacred olive tree, 149, 151, 302; as ships' figurehead, 109; thank offerings to, 86, 134
Athens: Agora (*see* Agora, Athens); Areopagus, 2, 66, 89, 134, 148, 232 (*see also* Council of the Areopagus); barathrum, 71; Boulé, 264, 269, 270, 277; Cerameicus, 31, 64, 68, 134, 170, 233, 238, 267, 299; Colonus Agoraius, 234, 270, 302; Eurysaceion, 16; Hecatompedos Naos (*see* Acropolis, Athens: Hecatompedos Naos); Hill of Ares (*see* Athens: Areopagus); Long Walls, 235, 275–276, 281, 289, 293, 306, 310; Melite, 16, 18, 24, 213; Melite Gate, 24, 298; Painted Stoa (*see* Athens: Stoa Poicile); Parthenon (*see* Acropolis, Athens: Hecatompedos Naos); Pnyx Hill (*see* Pnyx Hill); Propylaea, 305; Sacred Way, 15, 151; Sanctuary of Athena Sciras, 204; Stoa Poicile, 232–233, 267, 289, 299, 305; Temple of Athena Polias (*see* Temple of Athena Polias, Athens); Temple of Olympian Zeus, 26; Theseum, 203, 214, 233–234, 266, 308; Tholos, 269–270, 289; wooden wall, 1, 3, 132–133, 136
Atossa, 116, 208

Babylon, 38, 43–44, 46, 117
Bacchylides, 204–206
Bactria, 40, 46

Balkan Mountains, 19
Bardiya, 44–45
Battle of Eurymedon, 3, 6, 8, 225–228, 299; commemorated, 228, 230, 308; legacy, 230–231, 237, 240–241, 247, 256, 266, 292, 297, 301, 311
Battle of Himera, 155
Battle of Marathon, 2–3, 78–82, 84, 89, 107, 115, 163, 308; Aeschylus at, 207; Aristides at (*see* Aristides, at Marathon); Callias at (*see* Callias, at Marathon); commemorated in Stoa Poicile, 232; Cynegeirus at, 84, 152, 207; Datis at, 80–81, 122; hoplites' role at, 79, 82, 106, 118; legacy, 88, 90, 93, 98, 101–102, 106, 109, 194, 226, 230, 240, 299–300, 305, 311; memorials of, 7, 85–87, 104, 134, 155, 229–231, 234, 305; Miltiades at (*see* Miltiades, at Marathon); role of Plataea at, 78, 80, 82–84, 162, 230–231; Spartan absence from, 78–79, 82, 84, 115, 137, 223; Theseus at, 83, 87, 196, 202
Battle of Mycale, 169–170, 178, 194, 199; dedications after, 229–233
Battle of Plataea, 163–169; Aeïmnestus at, 253; in Aeschylus' *Persians*, 208; Alexander I at, 165, 256; Aristides at, 165, 168, 175; commemorations, 175–176; helots at, 253; legacy, 170, 174–175, 183, 187, 199, 207; Myronides at, 275; Sophanes at, 240
Battle of Salamis, 3, 9, 150–153, 273–274, 305, 311; in Aeschylus' *Persians*, 206–209; commemorated, 176; Corcyra promises to send ships to, 217; fought on same day as Battle of Himera, 155; legacy, 15, 160, 170, 189, 211, 225, 231, 299, 301; Naxos sends ships to, 220; prizes awarded for, 155–156; Sophocles leads celebrations for, 176, 238; Themistocles boasts about his role at, 157, 210, 213–214
Battle of Thermopylae, 142–143; legacy, 157, 167, 187, 288, 311; memorials to, 176; only defeat in Persian Wars, 194
Bellerophon, 224
Black Gulf, 13
Boges, 190–191
Boreas, 139–140

Bosporus, 48–49, 53, 61–62, 125, 184, 187, 208, 284
bouai, 113
Brauron, 18
bribery: alleged of and by Themistocles, 140–141, 160, 212, 221; alleged of Cimon by Alexander, 256; alleged of Leotychidas, 199, 221, 250; alleged of Miltiades by Darius, 89, 256; alleged of Pleistoanax by Athens, 307; attempted at Sparta by Aristagoras, 58; by Cleomenes of Delphic priestess, 73, 110
Bull of Marathon, 80, 197
Byzantium, 48, 54, 57, 173–174, 181–184, 187, 260, 289

Callias (brother-in-law of Cimon): Acharnian estates, 136; Eleusinian priest, 83, 95; family, 95–96; husband of Elpinice, 96–97, 256, 268, 289, 292, 298; makes peace with Persia, 299–301; at Marathon, 83, 95; Spartan *proxenus*, 118; wealth, 96–98, 103
Callias the Elder, 95–96
Callicrates, 302
Callimachus, 80, 83, 86, 132, 232
Callisthenes, 6
Cambyses, 44
Cape Malea, 55, 162, 271, 282
Cardia, 13, 22, 28, 30, 53, 62, 67, 175, 181
Carneia, 82, 137–138, 144, 223
Carthage, 122–124
Carystus, 76–77, 154, 211
Caspian Sea, 40, 43, 83
Castalian Spring, 21, 130
Cecryphaleia, 274
Centaurs, 197, 204, 235, 303–304
Ceos, 201
Cephalonia, 163, 283
Cercyra, 55
Ceryces, 95, 97, 100
Chaeroneia, 280, 311
Chalcedon, 48, 54, 57
Chalcidice, 70
Chalcis, 37–38, 77, 139–141, 163
Chelidonian Isles. *See* Islands of the Swallow
Chersonese. *See* Thracian Chersonese

Chimaera, 224
Chios, 42, 47–48, 62
Cilicia, 74, 129, 142, 222, 292
Cimon: appearance of, 67; at Battle of Eurymedon, 225–226; at Battle of Salamis, 151, 153; at Battle of Tanagra, 8, 277–278; builds Theseum, 202–204, 233; buttresses Acropolis, 234–235; at Byzantium, 173, 181–182; campaigns in Cyprus, 293–296; as cavalryman, 98; at Cnidus, 222–223; commissions Marathon Monument, 229–230; commissions statue of Athena Promachus, 235; death, 297; dedicates bridle, 2–3, 134–135; defeats Persian-held Chersonese, 241; drains marsh south of Athens, 235; at Eion, 8, 189–191; enhances Academy, 233; enhances Athens' Agora, 233–234; in exile, 269, 290; faces off Corinthians at Isthmus, 262; first appointed general, 170, 174, 179–180; heavy drinking, 67, 98, 179; helps Athenian poor, 236; helps Spartans against helots, 8, 260–261; inaugurates festival for Theseus, 204–205; as judge at Dionysia, 239; makes peace with Sparta, 290–291; at Marathon, 80; marriage to Isodice, 99–100; on mission to Sparta before Plataea, 161–162, 180; omens of death, 297–298; ostracism, 7, 265, 267–268; pays Miltiades' fine, 98; at Phaselis, 224; policy towards Sparta, 114, 118, 188–189, 212, 231, 257, 259; as prosecutor, 103, 179; refits triremes to transport hoplites, 221; removes fences on estate, 236; repatriates bones of Theseus, 8, 196, 198, 201–203, 206; ruse regarding prisoners at Byzantium, 181–182; at Syedra, 227; at Thasos, 8, 245–246, 249–250, 254–255; trial after Thasos, 255–257; womanizing, 67, 98, 179; worshipped as hero, 308
Cimon Coálemus, 23–24, 26–27, 61
Citium, 293–295, 297, 308
Cleisthenes, 33–37, 39, 65, 95, 99–100, 102–103, 135, 188, 196, 259
Cleomenes, 34, 36–37, 57, 72–74, 82, 110–111, 114, 138

Cleonae, 262

Cleonice, 182, 216

Cnidus, 126, 222–223, 231

Codrus, 229

Corfu. *See* Cercyra

Corinth: ally of Sparta, 37–38, 307; Cypselus, tyrant of, 18; Games at, 18; geographical situation, 271; hires ships to Athens 106; hostility to Athens, 37–38, 309–310; joins alliance against Persia, 121; power of, 211; relationship with neighbours, 262, 274; relationship with Themistocles, 217; Xerxes intends to capture, 146–147

Coronea, 306

Coronides, 182

Council of the Areopagus, 69, 90, 101, 237, 255, 263–264, 270, 291

Cratinus, 313

Crete, 80, 121–122, 127, 204–205

Critius, 193

Crius, 72–73

Croesus, 20, 23, 38, 41–43, 99, 117

Crypteia, 113

Ctesium, 199, 201

Cybele, 23, 59, 66, 69

Cyclades, 55–56, 75, 219

Cylon, 33, 36

Cynegeirus, 84, 152, 207

Cynosarges, 67, 84

Cypselus, 18

Cyrene, 22, 287

Cyrus, 40–47, 57, 116–117, 208

Cyzicus, 48

Darius I: in Aeschylus' *Persians*, 208; annexes north Greece, 53–54, 189; appearance, 49; becomes Great King, 44–47; bridges Bosporus, 48, 53, 208; bridges Danube, 49, 50, 52–53, 81, 125; consolidates power in Asia, 47; constructs canal in Egypt, 125; crushes Ionian Revolt, 62; death, 116–117; envoys to Aegina, 72; family and inner circle, 55, 128, 286, 299; first (failed) invasion of Greece, 70–71; given golden plane tree, 126; plans further invasion of Greece, 115, 117; prepares to invade Greece, 54–56;

remembers the Athenians, 63, 299; reverence for Apollo, 76; Scythian campaign, 48–53, 81; welcomes Metiochus to Persia, 63, 222, 246

Darius, eldest son of Xerxes, 273

Darius II, 310–311

Datis, 74, 76–77, 80–81, 107, 115, 122, 220

Decelea, 86, 162

Delos, 75–76, 185–187, 191, 196–197, 205–206, 219, 227, 230, 254, 287

Delphi: Athenian Stoa, 175; Athenian Treasury, 87–88, 175; bronze palm tree, 230–231; Cnidian Lesche, 231, 233; consulted by Athenians before Salamis, 130–132; consulted by Cretans, 122; consulted by Croesus, 41; consulted by Dolonci, 19–20; consulted by Lemnians, 60; consulted by Miltiades the Elder, 21; consulted by Spartans, 73; Games at, 18; Gelon ships valuables to, 124; international court at, 199; Marathon Monument, 229–230, 232–233, 267, 299, 302; oracle (*see* oracle: Delphi); Serpent Column and inscription, 9, 175–176, 214; setting, 20; Temple of Apollo, 20, 34, 86–87, 130, 132, 175, 229–230, 249; victory monuments at, 86, 156, 168, 175, 211; war over, 306

Delta (of Nile), 28, 125, 272, 286, 294–295

Demaratus, 37, 72–73, 82, 109–110, 114, 117, 137, 199

Demeter, 25, 89–90, 219, 302, 204

Didyma, 62

Diodorus Siculus, 6

Dionysus, 94, 204, 277, 297; discovers Ariadne, 219; god of drama, 36, 151, 239; god of Eleusinian Mysteries, 25, 204, 302; on Parthenon frieze, 304

Dipaea, 251

Dodecanese, 293

Dolonci, 19–22, 28–29, 54

Dolopia, 198

Dorian Peninsula, 222–223

Dorieus, 123

Doris, 276, 279

Doriscus, 128, 241

Drabescus, 247, 249, 255, 262, 267

Ecbatana, 38, 41–42, 46
Echetlus, 83, 232
Edoni, 191, 240, 242, 247, 249
Egypt: Alexander the Great in, 311, 313;
   Athenian imports from, 272, 300; Cimon's
   campaign to, 291–292, 294; disastrous
   Athenian campaign to, 272–276, 280,
   284, 286–287, 290; Greeks in, 272; oracle
   (see oracle, Siwah); Persian control of, 44,
   46, 81, 120, 125, 224, 301; rebellions in,
   116–117, 272–273
Eion, 192, 239, 240–242; Cimon's siege and
   victory at, 8, 189–191, 194, 206, 211, 240,
   246, 256, 261, 266; herms commemorating (see herms commemorating Eion)
Elaeus, 125, 181
Eleusinian Mysteries, 25, 83, 95, 151, 161,
   305, 310
Eleusis, 15, 151, 197, 260, 302, 304–305;
   abortive battles near, 37–38, 72, 161–162,
   199, 306; Mysteries (see Eleusinian Mysteries); site of Greeks' oath-taking, 163,
   169
Eleutherae, 163
Elpinice, 100, 135, 268, 289, 292, 298–299;
   accusations of immorality, 97, 267;
   character, 96; criticizes Pericles, 308;
   intervenes with Pericles, 256–257;
   marriage to Callias, 96–97, 268; tomb,
   308
Ennea Hodoi, 239–242, 246, 248–249, 251,
   255–256
Ephesus, 59, 62
Ephialtes, 3, 237–239, 261, 263–264,
   268–270; campaigns in east Aegean,
   237, 255; murder of, 271; opposes
   Cimon, 250, 256–259, 264, 267–268;
   reforms Areopagus, 263–264
ephors, 72–73, 79, 161, 187, 250, 258, 284,
   290–291, 307; role in Sparta's constitution, 114; role in subverting Pausanias,
   183, 215–216; role in subverting Themistocles, 216
Ephorus, 6
Epidamnus, 309
Epidaurus, 121, 163, 274, 307
Epirus, 217

Epizelus, 83
Eretria, 25, 58–59, 69, 77–79, 81, 119, 163
Erythrae, 163
Euboea, 25, 37–38, 58, 62, 82, 128, 138,
   140–142, 144, 201; Persians capture
   areas of, 76–78, 146; revolts from Athens,
   306–307; strategic benefit to Athenians,
   198; strategic benefit to Greeks, 137;
   strategic benefit to Persians, 56, 72;
   Themistocles campaigns in, 211–212
Eupatrids, 114
Euripus, 38, 77, 140, 144, 146
Eurybiades, 137, 140, 176
Eurymedon, Battle of. See Battle of
   Eurymedon
Eurymedon River. See River Eurymedon
Eurymedon Vase, 8, 228
Eurypontids, 72
Eurysaceion, 16
Eurysaces, 16–18
Euthymus, 210
euthyna, 254–255

France, 22, 123

Gargaphia Spring, 164–165
Gela, 122–123
Gelon, 121–124, 155, 210
Gephyraei, 32
Gerousia, 114, 118, 187–188
Gorgias, 311
Gorgo, 138
Great Bitter Lake, 125
Great Dionysia, 100, 238, 290
Great Panathenaic Festival, 24, 30, 32, 197,
   238, 290, 304
Gulf of Calydon, 285
Gulf of Corinth, 283, 286
Gulf of Malia, 130, 142
Gulf of Pagasae, 128–129, 142
Gymnopaediae, 109
Gytheum, 58, 161, 282–284

Haliartus, 280
Halicarnassus, 222
Halieis, 274–275
Halos, 129

Harmodius, 32–34, 64–66, 155, 192, 202, 283

Harpagus, 40, 43, 222

Hector, 17, 106

Hegesipyle, 29–30, 63

Hegesistratus, 25, 34

Helen, 197–198, 233

Helice, 198

Hellenotamiae, 185

Hellespont, 19, 28, 34, 53, 70, 75, 127, 154, 181, 306; Athenian interest in, 21–22, 25, 29, 184, 187, 212; Croesus' interest in, 23, 41; in Ionian Revolt, 57; Persian interest in, 42, 47–48, 62, 286; Trojan control of, 26; Xanthippus campaigns at, 170, 179, 229; Xerxes' bridges across, 125, 127–128, 149, 154, 156, 175, 208, 222, 249; Xerxes scourges, 126

helots: accused of plotting with Pausanias, 215; butt of Spartan humour, 115; campaign with Spartans, 74, 162, 166, 168–169, 174, 253; danger to Spartans, 57, 82, 111, 160, 183, 188, 250, 252; revolt, 8, 111, 253, 258, 261, 276, 282–283; sacrilegious execution at Taenarum, 250, 253; settled in Naupactus, 284, 307; Spartan contempt for, 184, 284; status within Sparta, 111–113

Hephaestia, 60

Hera, 47, 304

Heracleia, 216

Heracles, 67; ancestor of Alexander I, 54; ancestor of Hetoemaridas, 188; ancestor of Spartan kings, 72–73, 276; in Athenian art, 87, 232; connections to Marathon, 80; death near Thermopylae, 138; fights Amazons, 232; seen fighting at Marathon, 83; at Troy, 17

Hermes, 193, 255, 277, 304

Hermione, 121, 163

herms commemorating Eion, 193–194, 308

Herodotus, 4–5, 21, 52, 58, 71, 78, 124, 165

Hesiod, 15

Hetoemaridas, 188

Hieron, 210

Hill of Ares. See Athens: Areopagus

Himera, 123; Battle of (see Battle of Himera)

Hipparchus (brother of Hippias), 26–27, 31–35, 65, 192, 233, 238, 266

Hipparchus (ostracized politician), 101–102, 148

Hippias: collaborates with Persia, 39, 55, 63, 70, 74, 76, 81, 110, 123, 192; at Delos, 186; death, 88; exploits Laurium's silver, 103; grandfather of Metiochus, 27, 62; invited to Sparta, 38; at Marathon, 78; marriage ties, 27, 30; overthrown, 34, 52, 65–66, 68, 89, 270, 279; at Panathenaic Festival, 31; remaining family and supporters in Athens, 74, 88–89, 102; ruthlessness, 33; superstitious nature, 26, 76, 88; tyrant of Athens, 26–27, 36, 202, 266

Hippocleides, 24

Hippoclus, 30, 48

Hipponicus, 95–96

Histiaea, 146

Histiaeus, 48, 54–55, 61–62, 246

Homer, 14, 18, 24, 106, 121, 123, 127, 194, 207; Iliad, 17

Homoioi. See Identicals

hubris, 126, 207–208, 249

Hyacinthia, 112, 161

Hyacinthus, 161

Hysiae, 165

Ialysus, 212

Ictinus, 302

Identicals, 188, 198, 233, 252–253, 258, 260, 282, 290, 310; at Byzantium, 182; defeated at Tegea, 198; outnumbered by helots, 253; at Plataea, 162, 169; role in Spartan society, 113–114; as royal bodyguard, 138, 157

Imbros, 14–15, 54, 60, 62, 66, 81, 90, 241

Inaros, 272–274, 287, 292

incest, 97, 257, 267

Inebu-hedj. See Memphis

Ionian Revolt, 57–61, 66, 69–70, 75–76, 206, 288, 299–300

Ion of Chios, 289

Isagoras, 36–38, 259

Islands of the Swallows, 223, 228, 237, 241, 255

Isodice, 99, 179–180, 236, 269, 289

isonomia, 35–37, 65, 99, 104, 106

Isthmia, 121, 136, 175

Isthmus (of Corinth), 79, 140, 163, 260, 271, 291, 310; defensive wall at, 146, 177, 262; Greek celebrations at, 155; Greek offerings at, 156; Peloponnesians' preferred line of defence, 137, 144, 146–147, 158, 160, 169, 177, 211, 218; Persians appear to attack, 151, 153–154; Theban collaborators executed at, 169

Istria, 49

Italy, 22, 55, 111, 123, 271, 298, 309

Karpas Peninsula, 296

Lacedaemonius, 180, 188, 200, 268, 309–310

Lachartus, 262

Laciadae: burned by Persians, 170; Cimon removes fences at, 236; Philaid estates at, 15–16, 18, 20, 23–24, 63, 96, 135, 200, 260, 268, 293, 298; repaired after Persian Wars, 188

Laconia, 79, 111, 160–161, 173, 177, 276, 290

Ladé, 61–62

Lake Copais, 20, 169

Lake Gyges, 117

Lampsacus, 22–23, 25, 28–30, 48

Laodice, 267

Larissa, 110

Lasus of Hermione, 26

Laurium, 95, 97, 103

Leagros, 240, 247–248

Lemnos, 54, 60, 62, 66, 81, 90, 189

Leobotes, 216–217

Leonidas: fails to avenge Dorieus, 123; father of Pleistarchus, 162, 250; head impaled on stake, 145; succeeds Cleomenes, 111, 114; at Thermopylae, 137–138, 141, 144, 157, 164, 167, 187, 210

Leotychidas: attacks Thessaly, 199, 270; becomes Spartan king, 73, 114; enemy of Demaratus, 109–110; exiled from Sparta, 200, 250, 252; mission to Aegina, 73; proposes population exchange, 178–179; Spartan naval commander, 169

Lesbos, 25–26, 61–62

Leto, 212, 230

Libya, 44, 46, 272, 287, 301

Lichas, 198

Lie, the. *See* Angra Mainyu

liturgy, 94

Lucullus, 7

Lyceum, 67

Lycia, 43, 120, 223, 228

Lycidas, 159

Lycurgus, 114

Lydia, 38, 41, 43–44, 47, 59, 70, 81, 182

Lygdamis, 220

Lysimachus, 96

Macedonia, 53, 70–71, 120–121, 129, 137, 154, 156–157, 256

Magi, 44–45, 127, 139, 239

Magnesia, Greece, 138, 142

Magnesia on the Meander, 42

Mandrocles of Samos, 48

Mani, 282

Marathon, 102, 135, 144, 233, 277, 302; Battle of (*see* Battle of Marathon); Bull of (*see* Bull of Marathon); Peisistratid estates at, 18; Philaid estates near, 18; war graves at, 85

Mardonius, 70–71, 74, 157–162, 164–168, 174–175, 253, 299

Marium, 293–294, 296

Marseille, 43

Masistius, 164

Massagetae, 43

Medea, 81, 197

Media, 41, 43–44, 81

'Medizer', the, 103

Medus, 81

Megabates, 56

Megabazus, 53–54, 189, 191

Megabyzus, 286, 299, 292

Megacles (Cimon's father-in-law), 99

Megacles I, 33, 99

Megara, 147, 260, 277; alliance with Athens, 271, 274–275, 281, 284, 292; hostilities with Corinth, 262, 275, 277, 280; joins alliance against Persia, 121; links with Cnidus, 222; massacres Athenian garrison, 306; metropolis of

Lampsacus, 23; ravaged by Persia, 162; role at Plataea, 164; wars with Athens, 17–18, 306, 310

Melesias, 98, 270, 307

Melite, 16, 18, 27, 213, 298

Memphis, 274, 286

Menestheus, 194

Menon of Pharsalus, 191

Messenia, 111, 253, 258, 260, 282–283

Methone, 282–283

Metiochus, 13–15, 27, 30, 62–63, 222, 298

Metrobius, 313

Micon, 204, 232

Miletus: Aristagoras as tyrant, 55–56; attacked by Persia, 61; Histiaeus as tyrant, 48, 54; mythical status as Athenian colony, 58; retains independence under Persia, 43; revolts from Persia, 56, 58; sacked by Persia, 62–63, 69, 71, 79, 119

Miltiades III (the Elder), 18–27

Miltiades IV (the Younger): appointed Chief Archon, 27; appointed to rule Chersonese, 28; on Athens' Stoa Poicile, 232; becomes head of Philaids, 26; captures Lemnos and Imbros for Athens, 60–61; connections with Peisistratids, 15, 27; at Danube Bridge, 50–52; death in prison, 90; dedicates statue to Pan at Marathon, 85–86; on Delphi's Marathon Memorial, 232; elected general, 66, 88; entertains Darius, 53; expedition to Paros, 88–90; fined 50 talents, 90; first trial, 65–67; flees Thracian Chersonese, 13–15, 62; helmet dedicated at Olympia, 7, 86; at Marathon, 80, 82–84; marries Archidice, 27; marries Hegesipyle, 29–30; memorial at Marathon, 84; properties at Laciadae and Melite, 15–16; proposes throwing Persian ambassadors into barathrum, 71; ruse to control Chersonese, 28–29; second trial, 89–90; takes part in Darius' Scythian expedition, 48–52

Minos, 80, 122, 197, 204–205

Minotaur, 75, 80, 197, 202, 219

Molossia, 217

Mount Aegaleus, 15, 152, 169

Mount Athos: Persian fleet destroyed off, 70–71, 125, 157, 246, 299; Xerxes' canal through, 120, 125, 149, 246, 249

Mount Cithaeron, 132, 163, 165, 168

Mount Cynthus, 75

Mount Eira, 111

Mount Helicon, 163, 165

Mount Hymettus, 104

Mount Ithome, 253, 258, 260–264, 282–283

Mount Mycale, 42; Battle of (see Battle of Mycale)

Mount Oeta, 276

Mount Olympus, 86, 128, 132, 161, 303

Mount Ossa, 128

Mount Pangaeum, 21, 29, 53, 190–191, 239

Mount Parnassus, 20, 163, 276

Mount Parnes, 80, 162, 177

Mount Pelion, 139, 142

Mount Pentelicon, 35, 38, 78, 80, 85, 87, 277

Mount Taygetus, 111–112, 118, 167, 215, 252

Mount Tmolus, 23, 59, 117

Mycenae, 121, 137, 163

Myous, 56

Myrcinus, 54, 61, 246

Myrina, 60

Myronides, 275, 280–282

Mytilene, 25, 210

Naucratis, 272

Naupactus, 283–284, 307

Naxos, 121, 219, 293; ally of Peisistratus, 25, 78; besieged by Athens, 221; besieged by Persia, 55–56, 58; revolts from Athens, 218, 220–221, 223, 242; sacked by Persia, 75–76, 79, 81, 119

Nemea, 18

Nemesis, 126, 302, 305

Neocles, 68

Nepos, Cornelius, 6, 8

Nesiotes, 193

Nisaea, 271, 276

Nisaean Plain, 128

Odysseus, 207, 231

Oeneid Tribe, 36, 277

Oeniadae, 285–286

Oenophyta, 280

Oetaean Mountains, 130, 276

Olorus, 29–30, 53, 190, 298

Olympia, 7, 18, 24, 26, 86, 137, 156, 175, 210, 217

Olympic Games, 19, 24, 54, 136–137, 144, 210, 218

oracle, Delphi: regarding Athenian peace-breaking, 310; regarding canals, 126; regarding Echetlus, 83; regarding Lemnos, 60; regarding Miltiades III and Dolonci, 19–20, 28; regarding repatriating bones, 196, 198; regarding Sparta's 'lame' leadership, 187–188; relationship with Alcmaeonids, 34, 36; relationship with Cleomenes, 73–74, 110; relationship with Croesus, 20, 23, 41–42; before Salamis, 1, 122, 130–132

oracle, Heracleia, 216

oracle, Siwah, 96, 294–295, 313

Orchomenus, 280

Orestes (king of Thessaly), 285

Orestes (son of Agamemnon), 198, 238

Oroetes, 47

Orpheus, 231

ostracism, 101–102, 120, 234; of Aristides, 103, 107, 135, 159; of Cimon 3, 7, 9, 265–268, 277, 288, 291; of Hipparchus, 101, 148; of Themistocles, 214, 216, 237, 268; of Thucydides, 307; of Xanthippus, 135, 159

Oulius, 180, 188, 200, 268

Pactyes, 42

Painted Stoa. See Athens: Stoa Poicile

Pamphylia, 222

Pan, 81, 83, 85–86, 153

Panaenus, 232

Panathenaic Festival, 30, 32, 197, 238, 290, 304

Pandora, 36

Panhellenic Congress, 301

Panhellenic Games, 94, 206

Paphlagonia, 300

Paphos, 293

Papremis, 273

Paros, 56, 89–90, 154, 192, 237, 254, 256, 293

parrhesia, 100

Pars, 40

Parthenon. See Acropolis, Athens: Hecatompedos Naos

Pasargadae, 44, 116, 273

Patroclus, 164

Pausanias: awarded tithe after Plataea, 168; at Byzantium, 173–175, 182–183, 260; death, 215–216; dedication at Delphi, 175, 214; at Plataea, 162–163, 165–166, 174; plots with Themistocles, 216–217, 269; recalled to Sparta, 183; unacceptable behaviour, 174, 182, 188–189, 215–216, 250

Pegae, 271, 283

Peisianax (Cimon's brother-in-law), 232

Peisianax (Cimon's son), 233, 268

Peisistratids, 34–35, 78, 102, 107, 148–149

Peisistratus, 68, 195, 237; annexes Sigeum, 25–26; becomes tyrant, 18–19, 27, 29, 78, 199, 279; death and succession, 26; expulsion from Athens, 18, 38, 95; extols Theseus, 196; palace, 270; purifies Delos, 76, 186; reforms and buildings, 24–25, 31, 100, 155, 186, 237; relationship with Alcmaonidae, 33–34; relationship with Cimon I, 23–24, 61; relationship with Lygdamis, 220; relationship with Miltiades the Elder, 19–21

Peloponnese, 55, 86, 144, 282, 284–285, 309; Argos as second city in, 84; Athenian refugees in, 148; cities aid Peisistratus, 25; cities join alliance against Persia, 121; Peloponnesian determination to defend, 137; Sparta and Argos vie to lead, 73, 251, 258, 270, 291; threat from Persia, 122, 146, 160

Pericleidas, 258, 260

Pericles, 290–292; ally of Ephialtes, 237–238, 250, 255, 258, 263–264; attacks Peloponnese, 274, 282–283, 285–286; calls Aegina 'eyesore of Piraeus', 282; citizenship laws, 290; condescending to Elpinice, 256–257, 308; crucifies Samian rebels, 307; death, 310; masterminds building programme, 302, 304, 306; political persuasion, 209, 217; proposes Panhellenic Congress, 301;

prosecutes Cimon, 255–257; sees off attacks from Sparta and Euboea, 306–307; sends Lacedaemonius to Corcyra, 309; suspect in murder of Ephialtes, 271

Perioikoi, 112, 162, 253

Persephone, 25, 197, 233, 302

Persepolis, 116–117, 189, 300, 304, 311

Perseus, 122

Persian Gulf, 40, 62

Phaedra, 231

Phalerum, 70, 77–78, 89, 102, 127, 144; Aeginetans attack, 38; Athens' ancient port, 63, 69; construction at, 105, 107, 109; festival of Theseus at, 204–205; Persians anchor off, 84; Spartans attack, 34; Theseus' bones brought to, 201

Pharsalus, 285

Phaselis, 224, 261

Phasis, 22

Pheidias, 229, 232, 235, 302, 304–305

Pheidippides, 79, 81

Pherendates, 222, 227

Philaeus, 17–18, 230

Philaids, 28, 36, 99, 100, 298, 310; Ajax as ancestor of, 156; Callias allies with, 96–97; Cimon as head of, 94, 174, 179; fame of, 27; generosity of, 21; Hippocleides as head of, 24; Miltiades IV as head of, 65; Philaeus as ancestor of, 18, 230; relationship with Peisistratids, 27; Teucer as ancestor of, 293

Phlius, 163

Phlya, 213

Phobus, 111

Phocaea, 43, 48

Phocis, 137, 145, 147, 166, 281, 306

Phoenicia, 43, 123, 222, 275

Phrontis, 231

Phrygia, 47, 59, 182, 286

Phrynichus, 63, 134, 208, 238; *Capture of Miletus*, 63, 149, 206–207, 238; *Phoenician Women*, 206–207

plane trees, 126, 233–234, 260, 268, 289, 308

Plataea, 78, 162–163, 165; Battle of (*see* Battle of Plataea)

Pleistarchus, 162, 250

Pleistoanax, 306–307

Plutarch, 6–7; *Comparison of Cimon and Lucullus*, 7; *Life of Cimon*, 7–8, 206

Pnyx Hill: assemblies held on, 58, 101, 104, 118, 132, 177, 179, 209, 238, 259, 265, 268; Philaid house on, 16, 63–64, 66, 89, 96, 104

Polycrates of Samos, 26, 44–47, 57, 186, 272

Polygnotus, 231–232, 267

Poseidon: dedications to, 140, 156, 302; gifts bulls to Minos, 80; helps build walls of Troy, 17; god of earthquakes, 150, 252–253; on Parthenon, 304; relationship with Theseus, 196, 204–205; sanctuary at Taenarum, 250, 253; stables horses near Imbros, 14; trident of, 107

Poseidonia, 298

Priene, 42

Proconnesus, 48

Propontis, 19, 23, 48, 63, 62, 174, 181

proskynesis, 49

Prosopitis, 286–287

Psammetichus I, 272

Psammetichus III, 272

Psyttaleia, 150, 153

Pythias, 126–127

Red Sea, 125

Rhenea, 76, 186

Rhodes, 218, 293, 300

Rhoesaces, 263

River Achelous, 285

River Araxes, 43

River Asopus, 162, 164–165, 277, 279–280

River Cephisus (Attica), 235

River Cephisus (Boeotia), 145, 285

River Choaspes, 49

River Danube, 5, 8, 19, 49–50, 52, 54, 66, 81, 125

River Euphrates, 43

River Eurotas, 79, 110, 113, 115, 159, 187, 252

River Eurymedon, 222–225

River Halys, 23, 41–42

River Ilissus, 26, 67, 84, 235

River Meander, 42

River Nile, 272–273, 286–287, 291, 294, 300

River Pactolus, 23, 59

River Peneus, 128–129

River Strymon, 120, 156, 190–192, 194, 239, 247

River Styx, 110

River Tigris, 43, 62

Salamis (Cyprus), 141, 293–297

Salamis (Greece): Athenian Propylaea turned to face, 303; Athenians evacuated to, 135, 145, 147–148, 159; Battle of (*see* Battle of Salamis); Greek fleet at, 144–146, 148; Greek war council at, 149–150, 162; oracle regarding, 132; Philaeus cedes to Athens, 18; statue of Athena Promachus facing, 235; Telamon as ruler of, 17; Xerxes at, 151, 153; Xerxes' causeway to, 149

Samos, 47–48, 57, 75, 160, 178, 182–183, 186, 272, 307

Sardis, 44, 52; Athenian ambassadors go to, 39; Croesus' capital, 23, 38, 41; Cyrus captures, 41–42; Darius at, 53–54; Greeks attack, 59, 77, 81, 270, 300, 311; Hippias goes to, 39; Persian provincial capital, 55, 61; Temple of Cybele, 23, 59, 63, 69; Xerxes musters army at, 115, 117–118, 120, 124, 126

Saronic Gulf, 3, 17, 79, 105, 135, 155, 271, 275

Scamandrius of Mytilene, 210

Scopelus, 138

Scyllias, 140

Scyros, 62, 197–200, 202, 206, 212

Scythians, 8, 50–53, 83, 115

Sepeia, 73, 82, 121–122, 187

Sestus, 53, 125, 170, 179, 181, 187, 307

Sicily, 22, 136, 155, 220, 271, 300, 309; Carthaginian aggression, 122–123, 210; grain shipped from, 69; Greeks seek help from, 121–122

Sicyon, 163, 283, 286, 307

Sigeum, 25–26, 34, 38, 241

Simonides, 26, 175, 204

Siwah, 96, 294–295, 297, 313

Solon, 23, 35, 97

Sophanes, 86, 240, 247–248

Sophocles, 176, 238–239

Sophonides, 238

Soros, 85

Spain, 9, 22, 123

Sparta: agrees to campaign north of Isthmus, 160–162; aids Peisistratus, 25; aids Sicyon, 286; allies with Thebes against Athens, 275–280; Aristagoras' mission to, 57–58; attacked by Athenians, 282; boycotts Panhellenic congress, 301; Cimon's relationship with, 4, 8, 98, 114, 118, 180, 188–189, 212, 233, 255, 257, 259, 263–264, 266, 274, 277, 290; clashes with Athens at Plataea, 175; commands Greek campaign to Thessaly, 128–129; commands Greek fleet, 137, 149; considers aiding Thasos, 250, 257; constitution and lifestyle, 72, 111–114, 174, 250; crisis regarding Cleomenes, 110–111; crisis regarding Demaratus, 109–110; defeat of Athens, 5; demands compensation for Leonidas' death, 157; earthquake at, 252; fails to fight at Eleusis, 37–38, 306–307; fails to send army to Marathon, 78–79, 82, 84, 137; fights proxy war with Athens over Delphi, 306; fractious after conceding hegemony, 188; gains bones of Orestes, 198; helot revolt (*see* helots: revolt); helps drive out Cleisthenes, 36; helps topple Hippias, 36, 65; humour, 115; ignored by Aegina concerning Persia, 72; invades Thessaly, 199–200, 270; lionizes Themistocles, 157–158; loath to campaign north of Isthmus, 158, 169; loses League hegemony to Athens, 183–184, 187, 199; loses Megara as ally, 271; loses respect at Byzantium, 182–183; offers asylum to Athenian refugees, 158–159; peace brokered by Cimon, 290–292, 300; in Peloponnesian War, 310–311; at Plataea, 164–168; policy of punishing Persian collaborators, 211; proposes population exchange, 178; relationship with Argos, 73–74, 121–122, 147, 250–251, 258, 270, 291; relationship with Crete, 122; relationship with Gelon, 123; relationship with helots, 82, 111, 160, 250; resettles islanders of Aegina, 282; seeks help from Athens, 258, 260; sends diplomats to

Cyrus, 42; spurns Athenian aid at Ithome, 261, 263, 270; strongest city in Greece, 18, 114–115; at Thermopylae, 138, 144, 194; ties with Cnidus, 222; treaties with Athens, 280, 307, 309; treatment of Persian envoys, 71, 124; tries to reinstate Hippias, 38, 66; tries to stop Athenian wall-building, 177–178; victory at Dipaea, 251; victory at Tegea, 251; wooed by Persia, 284, 310

Stesagoras, 26–28

Sumer, 44

Sunium, 77–78, 84, 95, 102, 106, 141, 144, 146, 156, 201, 205, 221, 231, 235, 281, 292–293, 302

Susa, 49, 220; Aristagoras suggests Sparta attack, 57; Darius returns with Histiaeus after Scythian campaign, 54, 61; Milesian captives taken to, 62; Psammetichus III taken to, 272; setting for Aeschulus' *Persians*, 208; Themistocles goes to, 222; tyrannicide statues taken to, 155, 192

Sybota, 310

Syedra, 227, 241

Syracuse, 122, 155, 210

Taenarum, 215, 250, 253

Tanagra, 8, 32, 271, 276–277, 278–280, 286, 290

tattoos, 37, 48

Tauris, 49, 51

Taurus Mountains, 23, 223

Tegea, 121, 163, 198, 200, 251–252

Teisagoras, 90

Telamon, 17, 197, 293

Temple of Apollo, Delphi. *See* Delphi: Temple of Apollo

Temple of Athena Polias, Athens, 119, 234, 292; altar of, 79; Cimon's dedication in, 2, 10, 134, 302; rebuilt as Erechtheum, 302–303, 305; sculptures on, 31, 303; Xerxes' destruction of, 3, 148, 155

Temple of Cybele. *See* Sardis: Temple of Cybele

Tenedos, 62

Tenos, 76

Teos, 43, 150

Teumessos, 277

Thales, 43

Thasos: blockaded by Histiaeus, 54; Cimon's siege of, 8, 245–246, 249–251, 254–255, 261, 284; falls to Persia, 70; gold mines, 21; joins Delian League, 192; revolts from League, 242; seeks Spartan help, 250, 251, 257–259

Theagenes of Thasos, 210

Thebes, 9, 78, 145, 162, 169, 177, 211, 271, 276–277, 279–280, 291, 311

Thebes (Egyptian), 38

Themis, 277

Themistocles, 3, 7, 9; accused of conspiring with Pausanias, 216–217, 268–269; advocates abandoning Athens, 133; in Aeschylus' *Persians*, 208, 230; at Andros, 154; arrogance, 157, 159, 210, 213; awarded honours after Salamis, 156, 157; builds city walls, 177–178; builds Temple of Artemis Aristoboule, 213–214; campaigns at Carystus, 211; campaign to Thessaly, 129; commands Athenian navy, 137, 146; communicates with Xerxes, 9, 150; constitutional reform, 100; disgrace damages democratic cause, 255; early career, 68–69; falls out of favour, 209; flees death sentence, 217, 222; greed, 212–213; leaves message for Ionians, 146; mentor of Ephialtes, 270; mentor of Pericles, 209; naval policy, 69, 103–106, 180; at Olympia, 210–211; ostracized, 214; in Persia, 237; proposes burning allied ships, 180; radical politician, 69, 82, 95, 100, 206; recalls exiles, 135; rehabilitates Argos and Thessaly, 211–212, 279; at Salamis, 149–153, 176; sponsors Phrynichus' *Phoenician Women*, 207; weaponizes ostracism, 101–102, 107

Theopompus, 6

Thermopylae: Battle of (*see* Battle of Thermopylae); Pass of, 130, 137–138, 141, 145, 210

Theron of Acragas, 211

Theseus: abducts Helen, 233; bones of, 8, 196, 198, 200–201, 230; captures Bull of Marathon, 80; childhood at Troezen,

Theseus (*continued*)
135; commemorated in art, 87, 203–204, 231–232; connections with Delos, 205; 'democratic' king, 202; discards Ariadne, 75, 219; rituals in honour of, 204–205; seen at Marathon, 83; son of Aegeus, 81; story of, 197; used in propaganda, 196, 202, 206, 211

Thespiae, 137

Thessaly, 128–129, 154, 166; Greeks march to defend, 129, 133; helps Peisistratids, 25, 34, 78; pro-Persian, 110, 128–129, 145, 147; re-establishes relations with Greece, 211; relations with Athens, 199–200, 270–271, 285

Thetis, 139

Thettalus, 200, 268, 310

Thrace, 19, 29, 75, 120, 139, 154, 212, 239, 254, 299–300; Athenians hope to settle in, 240; Cimon campaigns in, 190–191; Cimon perhaps spends exile in, 269; Cimon raised in, 15; Olorus king of, 29, 53; Persian occupation of, 15, 70–71, 121, 191; weddings in, 29, 97; Xerxes in, 137

Thracian Chersonese, 34, 62, 191, 239; Cimon campaigns in, 241, 269; Darius entertained in, 53; Dolonci in, 19; Miltiades III, tyrant of, 21–23, 26–27; Miltiades IV, tyrant of, 5, 8, 13–15, 28–29, 48, 52, 60, 64–67, 81–82, 98; Persian occupation of, 15, 53, 70, 125, 128, 240–241; Stesagoras, tyrant of, 26, 28; strategically important for Athens, 21; Xanthippus in, 179

Thriasian Plain, 162

Thucydides (historian), 5

Thucydides (politican), 270–272, 307, 309

Thurii, 309

Timocreon, 212

Tiryns, 73, 163

Tisamenus, 198

Tithraustes, 222–223, 225

Tolmides, 282–283, 285, 306

Tomyris, 43

Troad, 25, 54, 183, 189, 215, 241

Troezen, 135, 197, 275

Trojan War, 181, 187, 194, 196–197, 207, 231, 303

Troy: Achilles enemy of, 139; Aeacus at, 17; Agamemnon at, 123; Ajax at, 17; Athenians at, 18, 124, 194; epic tales of, 121; Greeks at, 26; Minos helps Greeks at, 122; Patroclus' remains at, 164; Poseidon at, 14, 17; sack of, 231–232; Telamon at, 17; wooden horse of, 229; Xerxes at, 127

tyrannicides (statues of), 34–35, 101, 155, 192–194

Tyrtaeus, 167

Vale of Tempe, 128–129, 133, 256

White Castle, 274, 286

Xanthippus, 157; challenged by Callias, 96; liberates Xerxes' ropes, 175, 181; at Mycale, 169, 199, 229; opposes Cimon, 93–94; opposes Miltiades, 5, 89–90, 99, 209, 256; opposes Sparta's policy on Samos, 178–179; ostracized, 103, 135, 159–160; at Salamis, 149; at Sestus, 170, 179, 181, 307

Xanthus, 43, 223

Xenophanes, 44

Xerxes, 122, 177–178, 191, 199, 206, 211, 222, 225, 232, 234, 270, 299; in Aeschylus' *Persians*, 208; assassination of, 273; assembles troops at Eurymedon, 222, 225; becomes Great King, 117; bridges Hellespont, 125–127, 154; burns temples, 148, 192, 203, 302, 305; constructs canal through Mount Athos, 125; coordination with Carthaginians, 123; decision to fight at Salamis, 149–150; entrusts Eion to Boges, 190; executes Pythias' son, 126; invades Attica, 145–148; invades in Olympic year, 136–137; invasion preparations, 118, 122; love of plane trees, 126; in Northern Greece, 128–129, 240, 246; punishes Hellespont, 126; relationship with Alexander I, 256; relationship with Pausanias, 174, 215; relationship with Themistocles, 9, 150, 213, 217, 222; retreats from Greece,

154, 156–157; at Salamis, 151–153; size of army, 118, 124, 135; tent, 168, 174, 214; at Thermopylae, 142–144; at Troy, 127

Yauna, 70, 75

Zacynthus, 55, 283
Zagros Mountains, 41
Zea, 69
Zeus: defines Delphi as centre of earth, 86; equated with Ammon, 295; father of Aeacus,

17; given tithe after Plataea, 168; gives oracle about Cimon, 295, 297; gives oracle to Alexander the Great, 313; helps find Theseus' bones, 201; honoured at Olympia, 136, 144; not wanting Cnidus to be an island, 126; offers hope to Athenians, 132; on Parthenon frieze, 304; punishes Persians, 249; sacrificed to by Demaratus, 110; worshipped in Naxos, 219
Zeus Ammon, oracle of, 96, 294–295, 313
Zoroaster, 45